Reassembling the Collection

Publication of this book and the SAR seminar from which it resulted were made possible with the generous support of Eric and Barbara Dobkin through their commitment to scholarly enterprises that foster positive social change in our world.

School for Advanced Research
Advanced Seminar Series

James F. Brooks
General Editor

Reassembling the Collection

Contributors

Joshua A. Bell
Department of Anthropology, National Museum of Natural History, Smithsonian Institution

Tony Bennett
Institute for Culture and Society, University of Western Sydney

Sarah Byrne
UCL Centre for Museums, Heritage and Material Culture Studies,
Institute of Archaeology, University College London

Anne Clarke
Department of Archaeology, School of Philosophical and Historical Inquiry, University of Sydney

Rodney Harrison
UCL Centre for Museums, Heritage and Material Culture Studies,
Institute of Archaeology, University College London

Kelley Hays-Gilpin
Department of Anthropology, Northern Arizona University

Gwyneira Isaac
Department of Anthropology, National Museum of Natural History, Smithsonian Institution

Chantal Knowles
National Museums Scotland

Ramson Lomatewama
Board of Trustees, Museum of Northern Arizona

Evelyn Tetehu
Coordinator, Santa Isabel Cultural Heritage Programme

Robin Torrence
Australian Museum/Department of Archaeology, School of Philosophical and
Historical Inquiry, University of Sydney

Chris Wingfield
Pitt Rivers Museum, University of Oxford

Reassembling the Collection
Ethnographic Museums and Indigenous Agency

Edited by Rodney Harrison, Sarah Byrne, and Anne Clarke

SAR
PRESS

School for Advanced Research Press
Santa Fe

School for Advanced Research Press
Post Office Box 2188
Santa Fe, New Mexico 87504-2188
sarpress.sarweb.org

Managing Editor: Lisa Pacheco
Editorial Assistant: Ellen Goldberg
Designer and Production Manager: Cynthia Dyer
Manuscript Editor: Merryl Sloane
Proofreader: Kate Whelan
Indexer: Margaret Moore Booker

Library of Congress Cataloging-in-Publication Data

Reassembling the collection : ethnographic museums and indigenous agency /
Edited by Rodney Harrison, Sarah Byrne, and Anne Clarke.
    pages cm. — (Advanced seminar series)
 Includes bibliographical references and index.
 ISBN 978-1-934691-94-6 (alk. paper)
 1. Ethnological museums and collections. 2. Indigenous peoples—Public opinion.
 3. Museum exhibits—Moral and ethical aspects. 4. Museums—Collection management.
 5. Indigenous peoples in popular culture. I. Harrison, Rodney, 1974- editor of compilation.
 II. Byrne, Sarah, 1976- editor of compilation. III. Clarke, Anne, 1959-
 GN35.R43 2013
 305.80074—dc23
                        2012039099

*The School for Advanced Research (SAR) promotes the furthering of scholarship on—and public understanding of
—human culture, behavior, and evolution. SAR Press publishes cutting-edge scholarly and general-interest books that
encourage critical thinking and present new perspectives on topics of interest to all humans. Contributions by authors
reflect their own opinions and viewpoints and do not necessarily express the opinions of SAR Press.*

Contents

List of Figures and Tables   ix

Preface   xi

1. Reassembling Ethnographic Museum Collections   3
   Rodney Harrison

Part I. Museum Networks and the Distribution of Agency

2. The "Shuffle of Things" and the Distribution of Agency   39
   Tony Bennett

3. Reassembling the London Missionary Society Collection:
   Experimenting with Symmetrical Anthropology and the
   Archaeological Sensibility   61
   Chris Wingfield

4. Assembling and Governing Cultures "at Risk": Centers of
   Collection and Calculation, from the Museum to World
   Heritage   89
   Rodney Harrison

Part II. Indigenous Strategies and Museum Collections

5. The Sorcery of Sweetness: Intersecting Agencies and
   Materialities of the 1928 USDA Sugarcane Expedition
   to New Guinea   117
   Joshua A. Bell

6. We'wha Goes to Washington   143
   Gwyneira Isaac

7. Creative Colonialism: Locating Indigenous Strategies
   in Ethnographic Museum Collections   171
   Robin Torrence and Anne Clarke

Part III. Objects, Agency, and the Curatorial Responsibility

8. Exposing the Heart of the Museum: The Archaeological
   Sensibility in the Storeroom   199
      Sarah Byrne, with comment by Evelyn Tetehu

9. Artifacts in Waiting: Altered Agency of Museum Objects   229
      Chantal Knowles

10. Curating Communities at the Museum of Northern Arizona   259
      Kelley Hays-Gilpin and Ramson Lomatewama

    References   285

    Index   331

Figures and Tables

Figures

1.1   Optical illusion known as the Rubin vase   23
1.2   Piece of paper twisted to form a Möbius strip   25
1.3   Schematic diagram representing the field of relations
       surrounding the museum   26
3.1   Engraved ostrich eggshell   63
3.2   Rupert Brooke's tomb in Skyros, Greece   64
3.3   Sequence and relationships of labels and objects   70
3.4   Carved figure, originally from Aitutaki   74
3.5   Maps showing locations of collector Harry Beasley's material   78
3.6   A'a, a deity figure originally from Rurutu   86
5.1   Botanical specimens at Wageningen   122
5.2   Film still of the Papuan native constabulary   125
5.3   Four skins of female common spotted cuscus   126
5.4   Unpublished photograph by Brandes of Natives   127
5.5   Film stills from Kaundoma on Lake Murray   134
5.6   Film still of another scene of exchange at Kaundoma   135
5.7   Film still of arrows, fiber basket, and pipe   136
5.8   Film stills of Kaundoma man and objects of exchange   137
5.9   Unpublished photograph by Brandes of a supposed sorcerer   139
6.1   We'wha weaving on the National Mall   144
6.2   We'wha setting up a loom in the National Museum   145
6.3   We'wha with students of the Presbyterian school, Zuni Pueblo   147
6.4   Matilda Coxe Stevenson   150
6.5   We'wha demonstrating spinning   154
6.6   We'wha holding a pottery bowl with sacred cornmeal   157
6.7   "Belt-maker" in the exhibition hall   159
6.8   We'wha weaving a belt   159
6.9   "Belt-maker" mannequin   163
7.1   Map of Papua New Guinea   172
7.2   Fighting or mouth ornaments   178
7.3   Short-handled, decorated man-catcher   182
7.4   Large tobacco pipe   183

7.5   Crudely incised design on a tobacco pipe   185
7.6   Chronological distribution of tobacco pipes from Central
      Province   186
7.7   Boat model   189
7.8   Contents of "a friend's store box"   190
8.1   Michael Kwa'ioloa, Ben Burt, Evelyn Tetehu, Sarah Byrne,
      and Kenneth Roga examining drawers of ornaments   213
8.2   Lime flask and its contents of black seeds and white seeds   216
8.3   Article by Edge-Partington   217
8.4   Golden mother-of-pearl spoon   218
8.5   Peter Solo Kingap inspecting green stone adze   220
9.1   Waka A.UC.767 in September 2006   230
9.2   The hull stern interior, showing repairs   237
9.3   Charles Stable working on a new stern for the hull   243
9.4   George Nuku carving an acrylic stern post   244
9.5   George Nuku and Tahiarii Pariente binding side strakes   245
9.6   A virtual reconstruction of the canoe with additional pieces 251
9.7   Te Tūhono in the Pacific Gallery   255
10.1 *Pottery Mound: Germination* by Michael Kabotie and
      Delbridge Honanie   271

Table

7.1   Comparison of the Occurrence of All Central Province
      Valuables in the Australian Museum with the Private
      Collection of a Single Individual from Delana   191

Preface

This book is an outcome of the advanced seminar "Reassembling the Collection: Indigenous Agency and Ethnographic Collections," hosted by the School for Advanced Research (SAR) in Santa Fe, New Mexico, 26–30 September 2010, and co-organized by Sarah Byrne, Anne Clarke, Rodney Harrison, and Robin Torrence. They were joined in Santa Fe by Joshua Bell, Tony Bennett, Kelley Hays-Gilpin, Chantal Knowles, and Chris Wingfield. Unfortunately, due to assuming the position of director of regional museums at National Museums of Kenya, Hassan Arero was unable to attend the advanced seminar or to contribute to this collection, despite his strong wish to do so. However, we were fortunate to be joined by Gwyneira Isaac, who kindly stood in for Arero at the last minute and who developed her chapter in direct response to the discussions that took place during the meeting in Santa Fe. Also, as a result of various discussions during the advanced seminar and the desire to include the viewpoints of indigenous collaborators, Hays-Gilpin was subsequently joined by Ramson Lomatewama, and we are pleased to have had the benefit of his insights in relation to the themes of the volume. Byrne received helpful input from Evelyn Tetehu in the revision of her chapter for publication. In addition, Tetehu generously contributed a formal comment, which immediately follows Byrne's chapter in this book. *Reassembling the Collection* stands as a testament to the creative energy of this unique group of scholars. The editors thank and acknowledge these authors for the time they gave to writing their own chapters, to developing the series of concepts that are outlined in the introduction and which frame the book as a whole, and to commenting on and discussing the other chapters within it.

While the book is a direct outcome of the SAR advanced seminar, it is also indirectly the product of a much longer collaboration by the co-organizers on issues relating to indigenous agency and the formation of museum collections. A previous conference session, held at the Sixth World Archaeological Congress (WAC-6) in Dublin in 2008, was awarded the inaugural World Archaeological Congress SAR Anthropological Archaeology

Prize and resulted in the edited volume *Unpacking the Collection* (Byrne et al. 2011b). The WAC conference session and the process of editing the papers presented there into a book helped identify many of the issues we subsequently sought to address by bringing together the scholars represented in this volume for the SAR advanced seminar. There were a number of themes we were only able to hint at in *Unpacking the Collection* or to deal with in the most cursory of manners. That book discussed the usefulness of thinking about museum collections simultaneously as material and social assemblages, and here we have been able to develop this idea into a fully realized model that underpins the chapters throughout. Similarly, in pointing to the agency of indigenous people in influencing the shape of ethnographic museum collections, we raised a series of questions but were only able to treat them superficially; we have been more fully able to explore those topics in this book. By contrast, the issues that arise from the "weight" of objects and a sense of curatorial responsibility to them and their source communities are new to this volume, and the topics relating to the archaeological sensibility and thing-focused routes to understanding the network or meshwork of museum/people relations were developed collaboratively by participants during the advanced seminar itself. We thank the School for Advanced Research for granting us the prize that made it possible for us to hold the advanced seminar as a follow-up to the WAC-6 conference session and to develop this book as a carefully worked-through "sequel" to *Unpacking the Collection*.

Thanks are due to the staff of SAR, in particular, James F. Brooks, John Kantner, Nancy Owen Lewis, Lisa Pacheco, and Leslie Shipman, for their generosity and hospitality during our stay in Santa Fe and for their assistance in bringing this volume to fruition. We also thank the resident scholars, Native artists, and interns who were on-site during our stay in Santa Fe for their input and discussion of the advanced seminar theme during our colloquium and for their hospitality in including us in various social activities during our stay. The SAR advanced seminar program has a crucial role to play in enabling scholars to undertake sustained discussions of topics of key contemporary social, political, and intellectual concern, and we are very pleased to have had the opportunity to be a part of it.

Rodney Harrison, Sarah Byrne, and Anne Clarke

Reassembling the Collection

1

Reassembling Ethnographic Museum Collections

Rodney Harrison

This volume addresses fundamental questions about the nature, value, and efficacy of museum collections in a postcolonial world and the agency of indigenous people in their production. The book's primary focus lies with those objects that, by way of their specific histories, have been defined as "ethnographic"; however, the question of the contexts in which things are defined as "art" as opposed to "artifact" (e.g., Clifford 1988, 1997; Danto 1988; Putnam 1991; Marcus and Myers 1995; Gell 1998; Thomas 1999b; Myers 2001) also constitutes a key concern. The book is most appropriately situated within the context of various postcolonial critiques of the role of museums and museum collections in the politics of indigenous represen-tation (e.g., Clifford 1988, 1995; O'Hanlon 1993; Greenfield 1996; Lidchi 1997; Barringer and Flynn 1998; Russell 2001; Karp and Lavine 1991; Fforde, Hubert, and Turnbull 2002; Kramer 2006; Cuno 2008; Lonetree and Cobb 2008; Sleeper-Smith 2009) and as a reaction to the perception that indigenous people had little or no agency in the processes that were responsible for the genesis of ethnographic museum collections (largely a phenomenon of the exercising of asymmetrical colonial power relations in the late nineteenth and early twentieth centuries). Although we see this book as a product of that literature and its accompanying themes, what sets it apart from much of the current literature is that it makes a signifi-cant attempt to move beyond the concerns of the politics of representation, which have tended to dominate critical museum studies (Macdonald 2011), to consider the affective qualities of things alongside their representational role in the museum. Similarly, in considering the complex material and social interactions of things, people, and institutions that constitute ethnographic collections, we attempt to move beyond the observation that indigenous people and ethnographic objects had (and continue to have) agency, to consider how concepts of agency and indigeneity need to be reconfigured in the light of their study within the context of the museum. In doing so, the volume develops a series of new concepts and considers their application to historical and contemporary engagements between ethnographic museums and the various individuals and communities who were and are involved in their production. These themes have profound implications not only for understanding the ongoing processes that have formed museum collections in the past and present but also for developing new and innovative curatorial practices in the future. Key concepts include the idea of museums as meshworks and as material and social assemblages; the ways in which the application of an archaeological sensibility might inform approaches to understanding the past and present relationships between people, "things," and institutions in relation to museums; and the curatorial responsibility that arises from a reconsideration of the nature of museum "objects."

Although the book develops novel concepts and approaches, this is not entirely new ground. Several important books and journal articles have trod parts of this path before us (e.g., Stocking 1985; Thomas 1991, 1994; Phillips and Steiner 1999; Myers 2001; Gosden and Knowles 2001; Edwards, Gosden, and Phillips 2006; Gosden, Larson, and Petch 2007; Larson, Petch, and Zeitlyn 2007; Sleeper-Smith 2009; Byrne et al. 2011). Indeed, after years of neglect, objects in general and museum objects in particular have come to the foreground of anthropological, archaeological, and sociological analyses, as part of what some have termed a broad "material-cultural turn" in the social sciences and humanities (cf. Hicks 2010; Joyce and Bennett 2010; Olsen 2010). The title, *Reassembling the Collection*, not only suggests that we aim to consider ways in which museum collections might be reconceptualized and reworked in a postcolonial present and future but also invokes the title of Bruno Latour's influential *Reassembling the Social* (2005). Latour is perhaps the most well-known of a series of scholars involved in the development of actor-network theory (ANT), and science and technology studies more generally, who have done a great deal to foreground the network metaphor in the study of social relationships and to promote an interest in the involvement of nonhumans (or things) in social networks. This work has generated much comment across the social sciences and humanities, particularly with regard to the contention that objects might be said to have "agency" and to act in ways that could be considered to be broadly "person-like" (e.g., Hicks 2010; Olsen 2010). We note a parallel set of interests here in the revisionary attribution of agency both to indigenous *people* and to indigenous *objects* in museum collections. Although the chapters have been more or less influenced by debates that arise from these parallel areas of research, the intention of this book is to move this area of research forward by developing a more sophisticated approach to agency and the fields of material and social relations that constitute the contemporary museum and its histories. Much of the work on indigenous agency in colonial contexts has relied on the concept of the "contact zone" (after Pratt 1992; Clifford 1997) in exploring the interactions of indigenous people and others. A key aim of this book is to move beyond what could be interpreted as an asymmetrical and broadly neo-colonial engagement with this concept (Bennett 1998; Dibley 2005; Boast 2011) to develop new models for understanding the networks of social and material interactions that center on the space of the museum collection.

Perhaps equally important, the book is also a product of what we discuss as the "curatorial responsibility," which arises out of a nexus of interests. For researchers, this curatorial responsibility results from engagements with particular individuals and groups, most especially, indigenous people, around museum objects and collections. At a broader level, it also arises from the "weight" of things in museums. In making reference to the weight of things, we mean not only the physical bulk of collections, which occupy vast storage facilities behind the scenes of museums around the world, but also their political and affective weight. The "affective" weight of things in museums refers to the charismatic (Wingfield 2010) or enchanting (Gell 1998; Harrison 2006) qualities of objects, their ability to engage the senses (Edwards, Gosden, and Phillips 2006:12), and their ability to act in ways that are both integral to and generative of human behavior or even in ways that are person-like, in conjunction with or independently of people (e.g., Harvey 2005; Jones and Cloke 2008; Olsen 2010; Basu 2011). Things also have a political weight, in the sense that they come to symbolize or stand in for various imperial and colonial processes, which underlie their presence in museum collections. In addition to reminding us of imperial and colonial histories, things speak to the contemporary political and ethical issues of the ownership of culture and its products. It has perhaps become passé to speak of the enthusiasm for objects that has driven many to a career in museum curatorship, archaeology (e.g., Shanks 1992; Webmoor 2012), object-centered anthropology (e.g., Miller 2010), or sociology. However, the genuine ideology of care that often underlies the practice of curatorship shares many characteristics with indigenous notions of the custodial obligations that arise from and in relation to things (e.g., Haber 2009; Kreps 2003, 2011). This book aims to explore these synergies and their ability to generate new conceptions of care and curation as genuine forms of respect and concern in the contemporary museum and beyond.

INDIGENOUS AGENCY

In putting together the proposal for the advanced seminar, the co-chairs asked contributors specifically to consider the issue of indigenous agency in relation to the formation of museum collections. In reflecting on this aim for the seminar, it is important to explore why we saw indigenous agency as worthy of special consideration. I have already noted that this book is perhaps best situated as emerging from, and forming a partial response to, scholarship on the politics of indigenous representation within the museum (e.g., Karp and Lavine 1991; Simpson 1996), itself a product of an indigenous critique of the role of anthropological and archaeological forms of expertise and knowledge production in processes of colonial governmentality and the subjectification of indigenous people (e.g., Deloria 1969; Tuhiwai Smith 2006[1999]; Nakata 2007; Hoerig 2010). As seminar organizers, our interest in indigenous agency emerged from what we saw as a lack of recognition of the many ways in which indigenous people had been active in shaping museum collections in the past and their ongoing role in doing so in the present (Byrne et al. 2011, 2011a; see also Jacknis 2002; Hoerig 2010; McCarthy 2011). For many of the participants, this interest emerged as a result of direct involvement in developing collaborative research around museums and material culture with particular groups of indigenous people and from an emerging sense that a consideration of "museum as method" (cf. Thomas 2010; see also Moutu 2007) might reveal new ways of reading objects and collections "along [and perhaps even across] the archival grain" (after Stoler 2009; see also Bell 2010a). Although the authors in this volume are interested in indigenous agency in different ways, all attempt to show how indigenous agency is connected with other forms of agency, drawing on a definition of indigeneity that is performed and emergent. Thinking about indigenous agency in this way raises questions of how it is manifested by, interpreted by, mediated by, distributed by, and entangled with museum collections.

Two of the key questions this raises for the contributors—a mixed group of mostly non-indigenous scholars—are, "Who are we to speak of and for indigenous agency?" and "What can we contribute to this issue?"

I have already noted the ways in which postcolonial literatures raise questions of indigenous agency and, in particular, the ways in which forms of governmental practice grounded in archaeological and anthropological expertise have denied indigenous agency in the production of museum collections. Given that these are, broadly speaking, the disciplinary areas from which each of the authors writes, we believe that the questions that have been raised by the assertion of indigenous agency require us to look into the histories of our disciplines and examine these concerns and to bring from that process insights that can reformulate questions of indigenous agency in relation to our disciplinary practices and to curatorial practices within the museum (see Nakata 2007; Hoerig 2010; Kreps 2011). Clearly, in light of the historical roles that each of the disciplines represented by the contributors has played in attempts to subjugate indigenous people, there is a need not only to be humble and listen to the points of view of indigenous people themselves, but also to speak from within our disciplines and respond to issues raised by external political contexts, to bring them back to look at questions of indigenous agency, and, in the process, to reformulate the questions and nature of our disciplines and their relationship to governmental processes in the museum.

Many of the contributions to this volume bring what might be called an "archaeological sensibility" (see Shanks 1992) to a contemporary version of the "hidden from history" problematic (or "history from below"; e.g., Samuel 1996) in their attempts to explore how indigenous people have contributed to the shape of museum collections. This is one of the reasons that the authors insist on the need to uncouple intentionality from concepts of agency. Many of the forms of agency explored in these chapters reveal the ways in which indigenous agency in the past was not necessarily formulated or enacted with direct reference to the question of museum politics but nonetheless had an important impact on the formation of museum collections and on the representation, conceptualization, and governance of indigenous people. We do not want to downplay the difference between unintended influences and the points at which indigenous agency asserts itself explicitly as a political project in relation to the museum. Instead, we seek to raise this as an important historical question. At what point does indigenous agency become a matter of specific intentionality in relation to the museum? Under what circumstances can we speak of indigenous agency occurring, and in relation to what?

Clearly, when indigenous agency takes the form of an explicit intentionality with regard to the museum, this has implications in terms of how a whole range of other agencies begin to interact, and the issue of the histories of categories of indigeneity is invoked. Significant contemporary indigenous networks deal with the extension of indigeneity as a concept and with the championing of indigenous concerns, for example, through global indigenous peoples movements. Nonetheless, we need to be careful about romanticizing indigenous agency or reading contemporary forms of agency backward into the past. This would simply serve to undermine the importance of the political project of the contemporary indigenous critique of museums in the same way as denying forms of indigenous agency in relation to the formation of museum collections would.

The project of seeking indigenous agency clearly raises a series of other questions, which the chapters in the volume address in different ways. What are the obligations that arise from the politicization of the relationship between indigenous people and museums? How do different methodologies allow us to explore agency? Can "things" be "indigenous"? Key to understanding these questions in relation to museum collections are processes of categorization, classification, ordering, and governance of things and people. One of the most important of these relates to the categorization and definition of "indigeneity" itself.

INDIGENEITY

To speak of "indigenous agency" raises the question of the definition and history of the concept of indigeneity, which itself is closely bound up with the history of museum collections. The rise of ethnographic collecting in museums in Western Europe, Great Britain, North America, and their colonies was closely associated with the projects of colonialism (e.g., Thomas 1991; Griffiths 1996; McCarthy 2007; MacKenzie 2010), imperialism (e.g., Coombes 1994; Barringer and Flynn 1998; Henare 2005), and the development of the professional field of anthropology (e.g., Hinsley 1981a, 1981b; Stocking 1985, 1991; Jenkins 1994; Conn 1998; Wolfe 1999; Jacknis 2002; Sherman 2004, 2011; Kuklick 1991, 2011; Shelton 2000, 2011). Although, historically, objects collected from indigenous people by Western travelers were perhaps acquired merely as curios or as a way of marking the achievements of voyages to exotic locations (Thomas 1991:141; Abt 2011), during the nineteenth century, museums came to form the spaces in which subsequent understandings of indigeneity (by way of discourses of "primitiveness" and "savageness") were defined, drawing on ethnographic collections that were perceived as the materializations of Otherness (e.g., Fabian 1983; Stocking 1985; Ames 1992; Pearce 1995:308ff.; Russell 2001; Bennett 2004). These ethnographic collections were defined as such not by where and from whom they had been collected, but by the ways in which they were detached and exhibited as fragments of other cultures (Kirshenblatt-Gimblett 1991). In this way, both things and their modes of exhibition and display became central to the definition of indigenous people. This process had far-reaching implications for developing normative notions of culture that could be employed within regimes of social management (Bennett 1995, 2004, 2005). Museums thus had a function in providing an ordered model of culture that reinforced evolutionary notions of social and technological progress.

It is customary to speak today of the category of "indigenous people" in relation to ethnographic museums, but when we begin to explore it as a category for analysis, its shallow history becomes immediately apparent. Indeed, the term "indigenous" has come into common use only since the mid-1970s through the prominence of globalized indigenous rights movements and the work of the United Nations and associated groups that have championed the shared experiences of marginalized peoples (Sanders 1989; Kuper 2003; Kirsch 2001; Feldman 2002; Niezen 2003; Merlan 2008). Rowse (2008) has shown how the category of "indigenous people" was first used in the 1920 Covenant of the League of Nations and subsequently found definition through the work of the United Nations' International Labour Organization (ILO) in the 1930s in relation to the potential of "native" labor and the idea that responsibility for the welfare of Aboriginal peoples should be removed from the nation-state and entrusted to an international body. As such, the term "indigenous" became a synonym for a sort of problematized difference that required careful management through international intervention. With the emergence of international indigenous rights movements in the mid-1970s, Rowse (2008) argues, indigeneity in the major settler colonial nation-states (Australia, New Zealand, Canada, and the United States) has been defined through an ambivalence toward national labor markets, which has contributed to the ongoing maintenance of difference between indigenes and settlers and the emergence of what might be perceived as a new "indigenous modernity." Key to the definition of indigeneity has been the delineation of a series of threats and forms of vulnerability that are perceived to be a direct function of indigeneity with regard to the common good of post–World War II development, especially in relation to international organizations such as the World Bank. Ironically, given the emphasis on the local within discourses of indigeneity, "indigenousness" has largely come to be defined through the work of various international conventions, in particular, the ILO's Indigenous and Tribal Populations Convention (1957) and its revision, the Indigenous and Tribal Peoples Convention (1989).

Merlan (2008) notes two broad ways in which indigeneity is defined in contemporary use. The first is "relational," in which indigenous people are defined in opposition to another category, for example, "settler colonists" or "the state." The second she terms "criterial," citing Martinez Cobo (1986:5, par. 379) for the United Nations, who defines indigenous communities, peoples, and nations as "those which have a historical continuity with preinvasion and precolonial societies that developed on their territories, consider themselves as distinct from other sectors of societies now prevailing in those territories...and are determined to preserve and transmit to future generations their ancestral territories, and their ethnic identity, as the basis of their continued existence as peoples" (Merlan 2008:305). The globalization of the term has tended to obscure the local variability of the self-definitions of indigenous peoples and communities; indeed, Béteille (1998; see also Kuper 2003) notes the ways in which the term "indigenous" has come to stand in for old anthropological notions of "tribal" or "primitive" people. In this way, the term "indigenous" has inherited the discursive baggage associated with the categories of primitiveness and savagery by way of their development through specific modes of exhibition and display in ethnographic museum collections. Nonetheless, there are important differences between contemporary understandings of indigeneity, "complexly understood as subjectivities, knowledge and practices of the earliest human inhabitants of a particular place and including legal and racial identities" (Delugan 2010), and the older anthropological notions of "tribal" people, which were created in museums. An important subject for discussion is thus the ways in which and the extent to which the contemporary museum is involved in the production of these new notions of indigeneity.

Indigeneity, drawing on the discourses of ethnographic museums, is defined as having a specific relationship with time and place: indigenous people are perceived to be both spatially bounded and relegated to the past (Byrne 1996). And while we do not deny the importance of the ethical and political issues raised by indigenous rights movements, nor the real need to acknowledge the impact of colonialism on first peoples, we are cautious about the ways in which old stereotypes of indigenous peoples as primitive, marginalized Others continue to be employed within the space of the contemporary museum (Prasad 2003; Dias 2008). Clearly, indigeneity cannot be taken as a given, and it is important to explore how it is constructed as a subject and category within the museum. Similarly, diasporic forms of indigeneity need to be recognized and placed in relation to narratives of continuity, and the relationship of indigenous people to other minorities and majorities needs exploration in relation to processes of transnationalism and globalization. This raises questions about the circumstances under which indigeneity emerged as a category and its relationship to notions of time, situatedness, place, and the politics of representation. Indigeneity needs to be perceived as a status that is subject to various modes of adjudication and different forms of authority, as a discourse of rights, as well as values. In this sense, despite its emphasis on the connection between culture and race (Kuper 2003), indigeneity must be perceived as contextual. Chapters in this collection address this problematic implicitly or explicitly in a number of different ways.

In thinking about indigeneity in relation to museum collections, the contributors are influenced by Clifford's (2001, 2004; see also 1997) discussion of indigeneity as performed and emergent (see also Merlan 2008), drawing on Stuart Hall's (1986) articulation theory. This acknowledges both the important work done by indigenous activists and scholars to demonstrate their sustained experiences of cultural continuity, survival, and resistance (e.g., Deloria 1969; de la Cadena and Starn 2007; Hoerig 2010) and a definition of indigeneity that is innovative, emergent, and mobile. Putting aside an organismic model of culture for an articulated one, the arrival and departure of traditions and practices are perceived not as aspects of cultural decline, but as necessary moments of uncoupling and rearticulation. Articulation theory recognizes that cultures and cultural forms can and must be "made, unmade and remade" (Clifford 2001:479). Thus, the transformation of one aspect of culture, for example, language, does not cause the "death" of the "culture-as-organism" but instead is seen as a moment of reassembling or remaking. This means that the question of authenticity is removed and cultural "invention" is rearticulated as cultural persistence and continuity.

CATEGORIES OF VALUE, GOVERNANCE, AND THE CLASSIFICATION OF PEOPLE AND THINGS

Central to the museum are processes of assembling, categorizing, comparing, classifying, ordering, and reassembling (e.g., Stewart 1993; Baudrillard 1994; Elsner and Cardinal 1994; Pearce 1995; Bennett 1995, 2004; Byrne et al. 2011b), processes that relate to modern scientific practices more generally (e.g., Latour 1993; Law 1994; Bowker 2005; Hopwood, Schaffer, and Secord 2010; Schlanger 2010). All of these processes involve judgments of value and putting "things" in place. We might think here of Mary Douglas's (2010[1966]) work on dirt; dirt is taboo because it represents "matter out of place." In the same way, museum collections have implicit within them particular sets of values, which are reproduced through particular systems of authority and expertise that seek to purify ethnographic objects as things simultaneously "in" and "out of" place. These categories of value help create the institutional spaces into which things can be slotted in the museum.

Although debates between indigenous peoples (and their supporters) and museums have often been perceived to center on repatriation and issues of ownership, it is possible to argue that these debates have more often been about the need to fundamentally reform curatorial practice in relation to things held in museum collections (e.g., Isaac 2009; Hoerig 2010). A major part of the indigenous analysis of museum practice has involved a critique of the categorization, management, and storage of things in ways that are not only foreign to indigenous ontologies but also potentially offensive or even dangerous (e.g., Henry 2004; Lonetree 2006; Sully 2007). Recently, museums have begun to acknowledge indigenous categories and curatorial practices as forms of expertise equal to those of museum curators (e.g., Herle 2002; Peers and Brown 2003; Chaat Smith 2008; Chavez Lamar 2008; Singer 2008). This is part of a broader process of the reorganization of contemporary museums in relation to the goal of widening access and engagement (e.g., Macdonald and Silverstone 1990; Karp and Lavine 1991; Message 2006; Macdonald 2011), a process that has in turn occurred alongside the "postmodern restructuring" (cf. Prior 2011) of museums as part of the development of new entrepreneurial cityscapes (Hetherington 2008; Frey and Meier 2011). In many instances, indigenous viewpoints about objects have been given their own space in museum catalogs and databases (e.g., Sleeper-Smith 2009). However, although this is obviously an important step in acknowledging indigenous forms of knowledge practices and expertise and emphasizes the museum itself as a space for reconciliation and social change (e.g., Kelly and Gordon 2002; Mpumlwana et al. 2002; Allen and Hamby 2011), this does not necessarily reform the system. The original categories and underlying values on which they rest often remain in place. Consequently, it does not lead to a real sharing of authority (Hoerig 2010; Boast 2011), only to a reorganization of existing categories to accommodate differing perspectives. This process can in turn often be redeployed within the context of contemporary museums in the production of difference (Hetherington 2002; Bennett 2006, 2011a; Dias 1998, 2008; Sherman 2008).

The incorporation of indigenous categories within the museum has emerged as part of a project of reforming the categories on which it was established as an institution, but the authors in this volume argue that we need to go further in drawing attention to the very nature of the categories themselves and the forms of authority on which they draw (and which they subsequently reproduce). Part of this process involves acknowledgment that classification and ordering can only ever be partially realized (cf. Law 1994) and, indeed, that any attempt to categorize will always produce anomalies (Douglas 2010[1966]). Revealing the process of categorization to be partial and incomplete undermines the universalizing mission of the museum (Bennett 1995) and draws attention to the ways in which the categories it employs are not "natural," but actively formed out of particular systems of value. Such a project contains the potential for a radical reconceptualization of things in museum collections and their relationship with people. For example, what would happen if we were to consider things in museums as "kin" (see Hays-Gilpin and Lomatewama, chapter 10, this volume), who might be displaced or "in diaspora" (Basu 2011)? How would this transform curatorial practices and modes of ordering and classification within the museum and in heritage practice more generally (see also Harrison and Rose 2010; Harrison 2012)?

Indigenous people have been articulating this point of view for some time (e.g., Viveiros de Castro 2004; Rose 2004; Harvey 2005; Haber 2009), but the "ontological turn" (cf. Henare, Holbraad, and Wastell 2007; Alberti and Bray 2009) in the social sciences and humanities has begun to trouble the strict impermeability of the categories of persons and things and has helped make possible such a radical new way of conceiving of museum objects. Adopting a perspective that acknowledges a broad ontology of "connectivity" (Rose and Robin 2004; Barad 2007; Rose 2011) between humans, objects, plants, animals, and the world in which they reside has radical implications for museum and heritage practices (see Harrison 2012). Contributors to this volume remain open to the ways in which contemporary indigenous agency may provide the basis for revising the underlying philosophy of curatorial practice, which could bring about the reform of museum categories and museums as institutions. This observation brings us to the next point about the curatorial responsibilities that arise from the weight of things.

CURATORIAL RESPONSIBILITY

One of the important themes that links many of the chapters in this book is a transformed notion of curatorial responsibility to things in museum collections. We suggest that this curatorial responsibility arises from two different (but closely linked) sources. The first is the obligations that arise from collaborations between researchers and indigenous and other minority community groups. Museums have recently adopted a

broader sense of accountability and an expanded conception of their publics, and many of the contributors to this volume approach their work as
museum professionals, archaeologists, and anthropologists as collaborative,
community-based research. Indeed, since the 1990s, collaborations between
museums and "source communities" have taken an increasingly central place
in exhibition development. Such collaborations are transformative not only
in terms of the results of the outputs of collaboratively designed museum
displays but also in terms of the practices of individuals as academics and
museum professionals (e.g., Young and Goulet 1998). However, as Schultz
(2011) argues, in many cases, the public is not aware of or even misunder-
stands the nature of these collaborations. Nonetheless, this way of working
not only generates creative friction, which is potentially generative of new
forms of knowledge, but also has the potential to transform the values of
researchers and their attitudes toward the objects with which they work. One
way in which it does this is by introducing new ontological models for conceptualizing the relationship between persons and things, which require a
sharing of curatorial expertise and authority (Boast 2011:67, after Clifford
1997:210; see also Hoerig 2010; Colwell-Chanthaphonh 2010). Knowles
(chapter 9, this volume), for example, addresses this issue directly in relation to her collaborations on the reconstruction of Te Tūhono, the Māori
waka in the National Museum of Scotland.

The second source of transformation of the notion of curatorial responsibility is linked to the obligations that stem from the historical, physical,
and political "weight" of objects. The chapters in this volume arise from a
particular intellectual milieu in which it is increasingly accepted that things
are not inert but play an active role in social relations. If we accept a model
of objects as agents, having "charisma" (Wingfield 2010) or even potentially
being "kin," this implies certain responsibilities to the things themselves,
which may be separate from our obligations to the individuals and groups
(indigenous or otherwise) outside the museum who relate to these things
in some way (e.g., as descent communities). If objects can behave in ways
that are person-like, should they also be treated as persons? Although not
all chapters address this question directly, all are conscious of the sense in
which museum practice is being transformed by the project of looking for
indigenous agency in relation to ethnographic collections and by new ways
of conceptualizing museum collections. Over the course of the advanced
seminar, the contributors developed a series of ideas that are central to this
process of reconceptualizing museum collections in relation to indigenous
agency. In the remaining part of this chapter, I outline the theoretical basis

for this new model of museums as heterogeneous assemblages of persons and things.

SPEAKING OF "THINGS": OBJECTS AND THE DISTRIBUTED NATURE OF AGENCY

It is conventional in museum literatures to speak of "objects," with all of the connotations of inanimacy, inertness, and disengagement from social relations that are carried by the term. Here, we speak instead of "things,"[1] "actors," "nonhumans," even "kin." We do so purposefully, not only to connect our work with a broad body of literature in anthropology, sociology, philosophy, material culture studies, and religious studies that is rethinking the relationship between human and nonhuman worlds (e.g., Viveiros de Castro 2004; Latour 2004a; Harvey 2005; Serres 2008; see discussion in Olsen 2010) but also to draw attention to the ways in which speaking of objects invokes an underlying idealist philosophy that places emphasis on the separation of matter and mind. To such a way of thinking, objects are defined by the absence of mind or spirit and, by extension, by their inability to embody agency and to act as agents in social relations, interactions that are perceived to be solely the preserve of humans (see Harrison and Rose 2010; Rose 1996, 2004, 2008, 2011; Haber 2009; and Harrison 2012 regarding the indigenous ontological challenge to this position). While the editors and contributors to this volume do not hold a unified materialist position in this regard, all seek to trouble this notion in various ways and to emphasize the agency and affective qualities of things in museums and collections.

The idea that "things" have agency, although increasingly discussed across the social sciences and humanities, perhaps still carries with it a sense of surprise. What do we mean when we say that things can have agency? To answer this question requires a consideration of the nature of agency itself. It is now becoming customary to consider agency not as an individual act of will, but as something that is distributed across collectives. Importantly, these collectives (or "assemblages"; see further discussion below) are defined as composed of both humans and nonhumans and as such are seen to include plants, animals, the environment, and the material world. Although different disciplines and authors draw on different versions of this notion—the "distributed action and cognition" approach of Hutchins (1995); Gell's (1998) and Strathern's (1988) "distributed agency" in anthropological studies of art; the distributed agency that arises from the actor-network framework of ANT (e.g., Latour 2005); the assemblage theory of

Deleuze and Guattari, which sees social life as composed of "semiotic flows, material flows and social flows simultaneously" (2004[1987]:25)—all share a radically transformed notion of social collectives and the ways in which agency is manifested within them. Fundamental to this new notion of "the social" is the dissolution of familiar, modernist dualisms such as "nature" and "culture," "human" and "nonhuman," "social" and "natural" (Latour 1993, 2004a; Law 1994), which are based on an idealist separation of matter and mind. Agency is thus contingent upon and emergent within social collectives, involving both human and nonhuman actors and taking many different forms (see also Joyce and Bennett 2010:4).

Callon (2005:3–5) has provided a summary of these arguments insofar as they relate to the question of agency. He notes that action is a collective property that "naturally overflows" and that, to be recognized as such, agency has to be framed in particular ways. For this reason, agencies are "multiple and diverse" and, depending on how they are framed, can be perceived to be collective or individual, adaptive or reflexive, interested or disinterested. These agencies are distributed among collectives that include humans, their bodies, the technologies they employ, and the natural world that surrounds them. These collectives are arranged in specific ways, and agency is made or remade through the assembling or reassembling of these collectives. Despite employing a "flat" notion of the social (Latour 2005) in which all parts of the collective are potentially involved in the distribution and redistribution of agency, asymmetries between agencies may be considerable; certain arrangements of collectives may be capable of deploying particular forms of agency strategically, and others may have less capacity for free will. Importantly, this allows us to simultaneously level out the priority usually given to humans as actors so that we perceive things and other nonhuman actors as equal players with humans. It also acknowledges the significant inequalities in the implementation of power that usually accompanied the colonial and imperial contexts that were central to the historical development of museum collections (e.g., Bennett 1995, 2004, 2009, 2010; O'Hanlon and Welsch 2000; Thomas 1994; Griffiths 1996; Gosden and Knowles 2001; Coombes 2006; MacKenzie 2010). In relation to this point, it is perhaps helpful to think of "handicaps" to account for "relations of domination-exclusion between agencies, and to interpret behaviors of resistance or recalcitrance" (Callon 2005:4–5). In the same way that individuals can behave in ways that are not always strategic and that might betray mixed allegiances to different, even opposing, interests, so different agencies can be perceived to mix and merge with one another in ways that are not unidirectional or always adaptive. In this book, the authors often use the term "relations" in preference to "social relations" to emphasize these mixed social/material collectives and the ways in which agency is expressed and distributed across them.

One of the important implications of requalifying or rethinking agency in this way is that it allows the notion of agency to be differentiated from that of "intentionality." Agency shifts from being defined solely in terms of intended action to being seen more simply as *an ability to make a difference*, or to effect change, in a field of relations (Latour 2005:52–53). By privileging only politically intended action as agency, scholars have overlooked the significant role that indigenous people played in the past in determining the nature of ethnographic museum collections (Byrne et al. 2011a). It is possible to argue that at least some indigenous people in the late nineteenth and early twentieth centuries may have been employing politically intended action in the selection of particular items for trade and sale with what we as academic researchers would perceive to be a more contemporary sense of the issues surrounding the politics of representation in a global art-culture market (e.g., Harrison 2006). Redefining agency in this way, however, allows us to take account of the many forms of action and interaction that involved asymmetrical colonial power relationships but that nonetheless had an enormous impact on the shape of museum collections (e.g., Torrence 1993, 2000; Gosden and Knowles 2001; Torrence and Clarke 2011; Bell, chapter 5, Torrence and Clarke, chapter 7, and Wingfield, chapter 3, this volume). By stretching the notion of agency beyond that of an explicit political intentionality, we do not deny the importance of intentionality but seek to give dignity and significance to the ways in which indigenous people played active roles in the construction of contemporary museum collections, the traces of which can be read in the evidence of processes of gifting, withholding, buying, trading, and selling (Byrne et al. 2011a). We also see *unintended* consequences as being equally important as *intended* ones. Given that many contemporary museums contain the traces of hundreds of years of collecting, bargaining, trading, stealing, buying, assembling, exhibiting, and educating with ethnographic objects, we believe that the ways in which forms of action in the past have a recursive and at times unintentional influence in the present should also be an important subject of analysis in relation to museum collections. Indeed, the historical changes in emphasis on the volitional agency of indigenous actors are partly explained by the shift from earlier forms of colonial rule to the inclusion of indigenous people in liberal forms of rule, which must produce indigenous agency as a condition for their operation, a point made by Bennett in his contribution (chapter 2) to this volume.

RODNEY HARRISON

APPROACHES TO (RE)ASSEMBLING: THE
ARCHAEOLOGICAL SENSIBILITY

One of the features that links the chapters in this book is that they take a thing-focused approach to exploring the set of relations that surround museums and their collections. Despite the range of disciplinary perspectives in the volume, including sociology, anthropology, and archaeology, we identify this thing-focused approach as drawing on a broadly archaeological sensibility. This term is not used in opposition, for example, to an "anthropological sensibility," but to draw attention to the particular inflections of a thing-focused analytical approach to understanding the field of relations in which museums, things, people, and places are caught up and distributed, as well as the ways in which elements from within this field are deployed in practices of governance and the distribution of power. In doing so, we draw on a series of linked metaphors from archaeology, which help to draw attention to the methods involved in taking such an approach, as well as to the forms of information it could be used to illicit (see Shanks 1992, 2012; Shanks and Witmore 2010 for a discussion of the "archaeological imagination"). We propose that this archaeological sensibility leads to a taphonomic approach to the study of museums and archives, which involves the study of the museum as an archaeological site and an exploration of the processes that led to the formation of the museum collection as an archaeological assemblage (see also Ouzman 2006; Torrence and Clarke 2011). Although this version of an archaeological taphonomy is (explicitly) not primarily concerned with discourse, as a method or approach it shares similarities with Foucault's *The Archaeology of Knowledge* (2002[1972]) in the sense in which it allows us to focus on difference and what Deleuze calls "the theory-practice of multiplicities," (2006[1988]:14), a key concern of postcolonial studies in general and postcolonial museum studies in particular (e.g., Sherman 2008; McLean 2008; Lydon and Rizvi 2010). Central to understanding the concept of the archaeological sensibility is the notion of the "assemblage."

ASSEMBLAGES

The authors draw on two distinct notions of the term "assemblage" (see also Harrison 2011b). The first, an archaeological conception, refers to a group of artifacts found in association with one another. For example, in the popular archaeology textbook *The Human Past*, Chris Scarre (2005:721) defines the term "assemblage" as "a group of artifacts occurring together at a particular time and place, representing the sum of human activities in that respect." Implicit in an archaeological use of the term is the idea of the assemblage as a contemporary construction; that is, the assemblage is created as part of the engagement of an archaeologist's contemporary classificatory gaze with a series of material remains from the past. It arises out of the relationship between past and present and between a contemporary external observer and a set of activities carried out by particular people and particular things in the past (e.g., Shanks 1992; Shanks and McGuire 1996). The formation of an archaeological assemblage is perceived to be the result of both natural and cultural processes, and the study of these archaeological site formation processes is known as "taphonomy." Michael Schiffer (1972, 1976) described the taphonomic processes by which a group of things becomes an archaeological assemblage by way of cultural ("C-transforms") and natural ("N-transforms") transformations. He referred to this as the movement from the systemic context (the original set of relationships between human behaviors and material things) to the archaeological context (the archaeological assemblage studied by the archaeologist). C-transforms include a range of cultural processes such as intentional or nonintentional discard, recycling, or reuse, whereas N-transforms include processes such as biological and chemical weathering and decay. In this model, the rapid burial of artifacts and stable biological and physical processes create more favorable conditions for the reconstruction of past human behavior than do long periods of exposure to cultural and natural transformation processes. We suggest that thinking of the museum as an archaeological field site and considering the taphonomic processes by which the museum collection was assembled raise significant possibilities for new understandings of the processes involved in the formation and maintenance of museum collections.

Archaeologists have not tended to perceive museum collections as assemblages because the collections do not appear in conventional archaeological contexts (the classic context being a buried archaeological deposit) and represent a heterogeneous jumble of things that have come together in complicated ways that are difficult to understand. Indeed, museum collections are often perceived as the very antithesis of archaeological assemblages—out of context, shuffled together in convoluted and confusing ways, and with much accompanying dissolution of "authentic" contextual archaeological information. However, this does not mean that museum collections cannot be studied as field sites (cf. Ouzman 2006; Gosden, Larson, and Petch 2007; Allen and Hamby 2011) and archaeological assemblages in their own right. Indeed, by foregrounding the taphonomic processes that have led objects from their original context of production and use to their residence within museum collections and by thinking about the relationships between these heterogeneous things, important questions are raised about the nature of museums and their histories, as well as the diverse agencies embodied in their collections. Doing so immediately shifts our perception of what is often presented within the museum as an entirely "natural" coexistence of objects from different times and places to ask, "How did all of these things make their way into this place?" and "What does it mean for them to be assembled together in such a way?" These are important first steps in "unpacking" the museum collection (Byrne et al. 2011a) so that we can begin to think about it critically. Indeed, we would argue that to conceptualize *anything* as an assemblage poses questions regarding its composition, structure, and function. We might extend this metaphor of the assemblage to distinguish between the assemblages that reside in museum storerooms, which are like subsurface archaeological assemblages, and those on display, which we might usefully compare to "surface assemblages" (see also Harrison 2011b). Assemblages in museum storerooms have different forms of visibility; they are more or less accessible to museum staff, but access by the public is controlled and mediated by museum staff as the "experts" (see Byrne, chapter 8, this volume). But we need to be careful of extending this metaphor too far—objects on display are as much a product of historical site formation processes as they are of careful curation and exhibition by museum personnel. This way of approaching museum collections draws on an archaeological sensibility, which involves the literal or metaphorical disassembly (or excavation) of an archaeological site and then its subsequent reassembly (for example, in post-excavation analysis) to understand its structure. Another aspect of this archaeological sensibility involves an awareness of the way in which a number of different people with different skills work at trying to reassemble meaning at the post-excavation stage of an archaeological investigation. As well as drawing *objects* together, a process of assembling and reassembling can draw *people* together in novel ways.

The second notion of the assemblage relies on Manuel de Landa's (2006a; see also J. Bennett 2010) articulation of Deleuze and Guattari's assemblage theory. Deleuze and Guattari (e.g., 2004[1987]) used the term "assemblage" to refer to a series of heterogeneous groupings in which the grouping itself could be distinguished as a whole from the sum of its parts. Importantly, such groupings are mixed, and social or cultural groupings are not distinguished from natural ones (or vice versa). Assemblage theory exists as an alternative to the metaphor of society as a living organism, which dominated social theory throughout the twentieth century. In perceiving social structures as assemblages as opposed to organisms, De

Landa (2006a:11) indicates that the properties of such natural/cultural groupings are not the result of the functions of the components themselves but instead are the product of the exercising of their capacities: they are not an inevitable outcome of the function of their components (i.e., they are not logically necessary), but a product of their particular histories and their relationships with other parts of the assemblage (i.e., they are contingently obligatory). Unlike organisms, assemblages are not governed by a central "nervous system," or head. In this way, agency is distributed across and through the assemblage, as well as within it.

Far from simply being a semantic point, De Landa (2006a) shows how replacing the organismic metaphor with that of an assemblage has a series of implications for the way we study relationships in the past and present. In the first instance, thinking of assemblages as heterogeneous groupings of humans and nonhumans has the effect of flattening the hierarchy of relationships that exists within idealist philosophies, which separate matter and mind. This progresses an aim of the authors of this volume: to address the ways in which things and people are involved in complex, interconnected webs of relationships across time and space. Second, the notion of the assemblage connects with other key theoretical influences on this volume. In *Reassembling the Social*, Latour argues that "the social" should not be considered a separate domain, but "the product of a very peculiar movement of re-association and reassembling" (2005:7). In this way, focusing on the assemblage helps us to concentrate on the formation and reformation of social processes across time and space.

Jane Bennett's (2010) discussion of assemblage theory also draws out another key issue we pursue in this volume. In thinking of museums as heterogeneous sociotechnical and biopolitical assemblages, unlike the organismic metaphor, we are able to identify both relationships of functional flow and more volatile relationships of *friction* and *conflict* (Bennett 2010:23). Perceiving social groupings as organisms tends to emphasize the relationships that lead to the functioning of the whole. Such a model has the potential to produce narratives of indigenous/non-indigenous contact as inevitable, in which the catastrophic clashes that often arose as a result of radically asymmetrical structures of power and unequal forms of authority are muted. The notion of an assemblage allows for relationships that are not necessarily directed toward the functioning of the whole but that might indeed cause a network to stall or even cease functioning. We discuss this concept of friction and its importance in understanding indigenous agency in relation to the museum in more detail below. But for now, it is important to emphasize the ways in which agency is distributed throughout the assemblage, which functions as a "federation" of actants in which all material and nonmaterial things are participants (J. Bennett 2010). Indeed, Latour speaks of a "parliament of things" (1993:144–145) to describe such collectives.

Where archaeologists have tended to focus on material things to help understand the behavior of people in the past, by defining assemblages as federations or collectives of things *and* people, we suggest that the archaeological sensibility of disassembling and reassembling provides innovative ways of approaching the study of museum collections. Indeed, we suggest that archaeological approaches to the study of human behavior might be conceived as being somewhat like what one sees when looking at a picture of a Rubin vase (see figure 1.1). By focusing on the vase, one overlooks the faces in the background. But thinking of the image as an assemblage enables one to see both the vase and the faces, both the material and the behavioral, or, in our case, the whole federation of human and nonhuman actors. Disassembling and reassembling this collective involves the excavation and study of both the vase *and* the faces, both the object *and* the people. In this way, the thing-focused approach to the study of museum collections outlined by the contributors involves a particular, *archaeological* sensibility.

NETWORKS, MESHWORKS, AND SURFACES

In *Unpacking the Collection* (Byrne et al. 2011a; see also Gosden, Larson, and Petch 2007; Larson, Petch, and Zeitlyn 2007), it was suggested that museums need to be conceptualized simultaneously as *material* and *social* assemblages:

> By saying this, we mean that museums, the people who staff and run them, the objects and the various individuals and processes which led to them being there, those who visit them and those who encounter the objects within them in various media, are all part of complex networks of agency. This agency does not cease with the acquisition of objects from their creator communities, but is ongoing in the material processes of curation and display, and the social processes of visiting, researching, learning and "knowing" things (after Gosden, Larson, and Petch 2007; see also Bennett 2010) which arise from them. (Byrne et al. 2011a:4)

In the study of these heterogeneous groupings of people, institutions, and things, the "network" metaphor became a key concept for understanding the fields of relations in which museums are entangled, drawing on

FIGURE 1.1

The optical illusion known as the Rubin vase. Public domain image created by John Smithson at the Wikipedia project.

actor-network theory (see also Bennett 2009, 2010). I want to pause here to consider arguments put forth by Ingold in defense of a metaphor of "meshwork" (2007a, 2007b, 2008b) in preference to that of the network to describe the relationships between people and things. Ingold (2007a:80) notes that the network metaphor tends to be used to describe a complex of interconnected points rather than a set of interwoven lines. Instead of the lines in a network simply representing movements or entities that "connect the dots," Ingold urges us to consider meshworks as the "lines along which life is lived" and the entanglement of lines, rather than the connecting of points, as the phenomenon by which the mesh is constituted (Ingold 2007a:81). Thus, for Ingold, action (or change) is not the result of agency distributed within a network, but "emerges from the interplay of forces that are conducted along the lines of a meshwork" (2008b:212). This directs us to think about not only the connections between people, things, and institutions but also the medium by which agency is transmitted. In a provocative article in which he places this notion in opposition to actor-network theory, Ingold appears to suggest that in the interaction of biological organism and medium (he gives the example of a fish in water or a butterfly in air), the medium has no agency: "Air and water are not objects that act. They are material media in which living things are immersed, and are experienced by way of their currents, forces and pressure gradients.... For things to interact, they must be immersed in a kind of force-field set up by the currents of the media that surround them.... Our concept of agency must make allowance for the real complexity of living organisms as opposed to inert matter" (Ingold 2008b:212–213).

Ingold goes on to stress the importance of skilled practice in defining agency, along with a consideration of the qualities of materials themselves (Ingold 2007b; see also Knappett 2007). What is appealing about Ingold's model is the way it forces us to pay attention to the particular qualities of the media through which agency is transmitted—its emphasis on the *mediation* of agency and the particular qualities of material things. Less helpful for us is its apparent denial of the agency of nonbiological entities. However, he expands on this point to suggest that the animacy of things be understood not in terms of the classical definition that has dominated anthropology since Tylor (1920[1871]; see further discussion in Harvey 2005) as the inhabiting of inert matter by spirit, but in terms of the "generative fluxes of the world of materials in which they came into being and continue to subsist.... Things are in life rather than...life [existing]...in things. Things are alive and active not because they are possessed of spirit...but because the substances which they comprise continue to be swept up in circulations of surrounding media that alternatively portent their dissolution or—characteristically with animate beings—ensure their regeneration" (Ingold 2007b:12).

Although the authors in this volume do not share a single position on this issue, we note the usefulness of both the meshwork and network metaphors in directing our attention to the relationships between people, things, and institutions with reference to museum collections. In this introduction, I prefer the term "meshwork," primarily because it seems consistent with Deleuze and Guattari's typologies and De Landa's work (e.g., De Landa 1997, 1998, 2006b; note that these sources are not cited explicitly by Ingold in the works discussed above) and focuses our attention on the mediation of agency and the qualities of the media by which it is transmitted. But we do not wish to lose the radical symmetry of actor-network theory and the way it encourages us to consider the involvement of what might otherwise be defined as inert substances in the transmission of agency throughout the meshwork. Both network and meshwork are useful concepts in relation to the study of ethnographic collections, and contributors employ either or both concepts.

FIGURE 1.2
A piece of paper twisted to form a Möbius strip. Photograph by Rodney Harrison.

Indeed, over the course of the advanced seminar, while working through the ideas of networks and meshworks and other ways of conceptualizing the complex field of relations in which museums are bound up, we began to think of the Möbius strip as a metaphor for thinking about this field of relations in a constructive way (see figure 1.2). The Möbius strip is a surface with a single side and only one boundary—a shape that is not mathematically orientable but gives the illusion of containing two sides. We started to use the strip as a way of conceptualizing diagrammatically the entangled relationships of various categories that are constructed discursively as opposites within the context of the museum—"indigenous" and "non-indigenous," "people" and "things," "colony" and "metropole," "primitive" and "civilized"—and the ways in which they are actually integrally connected with one another. Although the Möbius strip gives the illusion of these categories as opposites, they are constructed and arise out of a single flat plane, which in our model we interpret as a single field of relations. While we might "see" a single plane, by moving the strip we are able to draw different aspects of the field of relations into view. As in the metaphor of assembling and reassembling, the Möbius strip provides a model in which

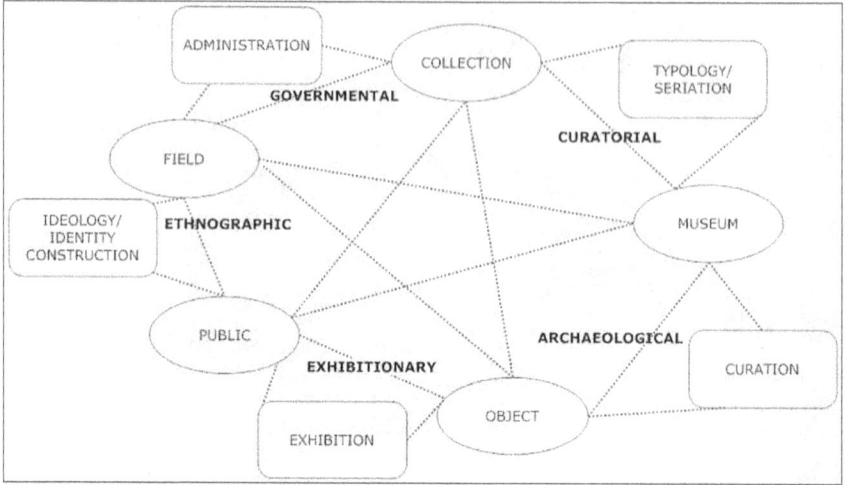

FIGURE 1.3

A schematic diagram representing the field of relations surrounding the museum, including sites of mediation (oval labels) *and various processes and relations that arise from them* (rectangular labels). *Different perspectives or disciplinary points of entry are shown as "cuts" across the mesh-work* (unbounded labels). *Drawing by Rodney Harrison.*

different aspects of the field of relations can be viewed in different ways by viewing the field from different angles and at different scales of analysis. One of the important aspects of this volume is that, unlike many anthro-pological studies of museum material culture, the authors do not seek to distinguish between indigenous producers and non-indigenous consumers but instead consider both as part of a meshwork, which in turn allows them to focus on the whole range of social and material relations that surround museum collections.

The field of relations can be further expressed as a series of points of analytical attention on a schematic circuit, which can be cut in differ-ent ways (figure 1.3). These "cuts" represent different points of entry into various sites of mediation of social and material relations. Several of the key nodes in the meshwork have been included in the diagram, delineat-ing field, museum, object, collection, and the public as important nodes and administration, typology/seriation, curation, exhibition, and ideology/ identity construction as important social processes that emerge from them. But returning to Ingold's point about meshworks forces us to consider the various ways in which these different relations are mediated and the quali-ties of the things that mediate them. The different qualities of these media in turn dictate different approaches to their study, or different disciplinary sensibilities, denoted in the diagram as governmental, curatorial, archaeological, exhibitionary, and ethnographic perspectives. These perspectives represent different ways of looking at, or cutting into, the meshwork to understand the processes at play within it. We have identified the archaeological sensibility as the key perspective for this book, which takes a thing-focused approach to understanding the field of relations surrounding the museum meshwork, but each of the chapters inflects the archaeological sensibility differently and each cuts into the network differently. The locations and fields of practice associated with the museum meshwork are characterized by different forms of relational dynamics and represent sites of mediation of different forms of agency. These locations and fields of practice have different relationships with one another, and all pose questions of indigenous agency in quite different ways.

FRICTION, FLOWS, AND MUSEUM ASSEMBLAGES

When considering the various points of entry into sites of mediation within the museum meshwork, it is important to reflect on governmental processes—listing, collecting, structuring, organizing—and the forms of authority associated with each. Similarly, it is important to consider the impact of these processes on practices and structures of indigenous governance. In this regard, museums and the museological disciplines (archaeology, anthropology, conservation sciences, and natural sciences) should, themselves, be seen as governmental assemblages and mechanisms for assembling and reassembling forms of power and authority (e.g., Bennett 2009, 2010; Ruppert 2009). Institutions are caught up in administrative processes and forms of assembling that are directed at controlling the conduct of people and things, directing our attention toward processes of management and organization. However, the authority that is attributed to museum collections, their modes of collection and presentation, and the forms of knowledge they are used to produce suggest that museums should also be considered governmental assemblages in the way in which they function toward the distribution and control of structures of authority and power. At any of the points in the meshwork, if we make reference to processes of assembling and reassembling, we also speak of forms of expertise and knowledge. Within the museum, as part of its exhibitionary complex (cf. Bennett 1995), these have traditionally been archaeological and anthropological forms of knowledge and expertise. So a key concern becomes exploring how different forms of knowledge and expertise have been involved in the process of assembling and how each has been employed in relation to processes of governance, particularly the governance of indigenous and local forms of knowledge (cf. Scott 1998).

It is also possible to apply the perspective of assemblage to the ways in which different governmental apparatuses *themselves* assemble—collections, things, people, ideas, techniques, technologies—in programs of governance that are aimed at regulating forms of behavior and conduct (cf. Foucault 2007, 2011; see also Rabinow 1989, 2003; Scott 1995; Pels 1997; Steinmetz 2007). They might address themselves, for example, by way of the exhibitionary complex (Bennett 1995), to the conduct of citizens or through the connection of museums and processes of colonial governance (Bennett 2009, 2010) with indigenous people (who may or may not be addressed as citizens, depending on the individuals, communities, time periods, and nation-states under consideration). Equally important, these governmental processes, by way of schema of classification and organization within the museum, address themselves to the governance of things, in terms of both their definition and the attribution of agency to them in relation to the possible relationships that might exist between them and humans.

I have already suggested that an important aim of this collection is to look critically at the notion of the "contact zone" in describing the field of relations surrounding museums and to consider whether it remains an appropriate metaphor for describing the relationships between indigenous and non-indigenous people in the light of the network or meshwork model of relations. Mary Louise Pratt (1992) introduced the notion of the contact zone to overcome the Euro American imperialist, expansionist perspective of the term "frontier zone." She used the term to describe

> the space of colonial encounters, the space in which peoples geographically and historically separate come into contact with each other and establish ongoing relations.... [The term] invoke[s] the spatial and temporal copresence of subjects previously separated by geographic and historical disjunctures, and whose trajectories now intersect. By using the term "contact" [she] aim[ed] to foreground the interactive, improvisational dimensions of colonial encounters...[to emphasize] copresence, interaction, interlocking understandings and practices, often within radically asymmetrical relations of power. (Pratt 1992:6)

The idea of museums as contact zones was popularized by Clifford (1997:188ff.), who used the term to emphasize the ways in which museums are best understood as locally *negotiated* responses to what are portrayed as dominant, universalizing, hierarchical notions of culture. He suggested that seeing them as such might have the effect of transforming and breaking down these dominant modes, which structure the governmental role of museums. While the authors in this book do not necessarily disagree with this point of view (but see responses by Bennett 1998; Dibley 2005; Boast 2011), this notion of the contact zone might appear to imply that the globalized, transnational flows of things, people, values, and information (cf. Appadurai 1996) are somehow frictionless. We know that the *contact* histories involved in the production and maintenance of such globalized flows have often involved violent *conflicts* and have occurred as the result of vastly unequal power relationships. In our accounts of the field of relations that surround the museum, we feel it is necessary to take note of not only globalized flows but also the sense in which moments of assembling and reassembling within the museum network also often produce friction and conflict (cf. Kratz and Karp 2006). We are mindful here of Anna Tsing's (2005) work on friction and the ethnography of global connection. Tsing argues that friction might be an outcome of the interactions of people and things in a globalized world but is also a creative force in the co-production of culture, which occurs across interactions of difference. The idea of friction acknowledges the fundamentally awkward, unequal, contingent nature of cross-cultural interactions and the relationships between the local and the global. She notes that all forces of globalization are driven by a modernist striving for universals, and it is in this way that her work connects directly with the idea of the museum, a universalizing, modernist institution par excellence (Bennett 1995; Harrison, chapter 4, this volume). The idea of the contact zone could be interpreted as a space in which contact and cross-cultural flow are unimpeded. Tsing (2005) shows how conflict and friction are not simply about slowing down social and material flows but are generative of new relations and are necessary to keeping both global and local flows in motion.

These ideas connect with the authors' shared conception of the museum meshwork in several productive ways. In the first place, the metaphor of friction seems to better describe the messy, sticky engagements that characterize the historical exercising of agency (indigenous and otherwise) and the contemporary processes of cross-cultural contact and collaboration within museum meshworks.

> It is important to learn about the collaborations through which knowledge is made and maintained.... Through the friction of such collaborations, global conservation projects—like other

> forms of travelling knowledge—gain their shape. [But] col-
> laboration is not a simple sharing of information. There is no
> reason to assume that collaborators share common goals....
> Overlapping but discrepant forms of cosmopolitanism may
> inform contributors, allowing them to converse—but across dif-
> ference.... Globally circulating knowledge creates new gaps even
> as it grows through the frictions of encounter. (Tsing 2005:13)

Second, the idea of friction emerges from a consideration of the properties of the parts of the meshwork by which agency is mediated. This assumes
that the rate and effect of the flow of information, material, and ideas will
not be equal but will depend on the media by which the flow is transmitted.
In turning our attention to the connections between people, things, corporations, places, institutions, and techniques of government, we also need to
be mindful of the qualities of the "stuff" that connects them and the ways
in which flow and friction themselves are creative and generative, leading
to processes of reassembling within the museum meshwork.

ORGANIZATION OF THE BOOK

While all of the contributions to this volume address a broad, overlapping set of themes relating to ethnographic museum collections and indigenous agency, the chapters have been organized into three parts to reflect
their emphases on one or more important sets of questions raised in this
introduction.

The chapters in part I, "Museum Networks and the Distribution of
Agency," are concerned primarily with the nature of museums and ethnographic collections as assemblages and the ways in which agency can be
traced in relation to the processes of their formation and ongoing maintenance. Tony Bennett (chapter 2) draws on Latour's discussion of museums
as centers of (and for) the collection and calculation of "immutable and
combinable mobiles" (1987:227) and, as Bennett puts it, "objects and texts
that, no matter how old they are or how far distant from the sites at which
they were collected, are 'conveniently at hand and combinable at will'"
and the ways in which the processes of assembling them within the late
nineteenth- and early twentieth-century museum led to the distribution of
"new forms of agency across the relations between museum and field, metropolis and colony, colonizer and colonized, scientist and subjects, and collector
and collected." This is a point also developed by Harrison (chapter 4) in his
comparison of late nineteenth- and early twentieth-century anthropological museum collections and late twentieth- and early twenty-first-century

lists of intangible heritage. Importantly, he discusses the ways in which both forms of collection are linked by the desire to assemble and govern cultures "at risk." A consideration of the processes involved in the assembling and reassembling of collections and the significance of the spaces "in between" the museum and the field informs Chris Wingfield's (chapter 3) reflection on the London Missionary Society "museum," a mobile collection that circulated in the mid- to late nineteenth and early twentieth centuries between London and various sites of missionary activity, with objects intended to serve both anthropological and proselytizing functions. Importantly, he highlights the process of dispersal and the movement of ethnographic objects between the field and multiple centers of missionary activity (themselves alternative sites of collection and calculation) as being as significant as field collecting itself, significantly deepening our understanding of the formation processes of museum collections.

Part II, "Indigenous Strategies and Museum Collections," focuses more specifically on the ways in which indigenous agency might be traced in relation to the formation of historic museum collections. Joshua A. Bell (chapter 5) explores the intersecting agencies of Papuans and field collectors during the 1928 US Department of Agriculture Sugarcane Expedition to New Guinea. In a sensitive and nuanced exploration of the various objects and records that were collected, he demonstrates how the expedition created distinct artifacts and networks, the narratives about which fed into and helped sustain colonial imaginaries of New Guinea as timeless and primitive, while simultaneously exploring the ways in which colonial science, exploration, and authority were made to articulate with indigenous New Guinean worldviews, interests, and cosmopolitics. Tracing the agency of an individual person through the contributions she made to a particular collection, Gwyneira Isaac (chapter 6) explores the objects and records relating to the Zuni *lhamana* We'wha' in the Smithsonian Institution in Washington, DC, produced during We'wha's six-month visit to DC in 1886 with the anthropological couple Colonel James and Matilda Coxe Stevenson. Isaac shows how the structure of museum catalogs serves to dissolve the identities of individual indigenous collaborators such as We'wha through its emphasis on the classification of artifacts by tribal and geographical grouping. Nonetheless, Isaac's chapter demonstrates how the identities of individuals and the details of the objects they produced might be retraced and the objects reunited with the identities of their makers. Robin Torrence and Anne Clarke (chapter 7) are similarly concerned with discovering traces of indigenous agency in museum collections, primarily in relation to processes of anthropological field collection, through a focus on the structure of museum collections themselves. Modeling their study on archaeological approaches to assemblage analysis and treating the museum explicitly as an archaeological field site, the authors attempt to identify strategies adopted by indigenous source communities to create, sustain, or avoid social interaction with European field collectors, and they consider how these strategies might have altered indigenous people's notions of themselves and others in a globalizing, colonial world.

The chapters in the third and final part of the book, "Objects, Agency, and the Curatorial Responsibility," focus principally on contemporary relationships between indigenous people and museums and the curatorial responsibilities that arise from a serious consideration of indigenous ontologies in relation to the agency of things. Sarah Byrne (chapter 8) recounts how new collaborative practices that emerged during the British Museum's Melanesia Project suggested new logics for the organization and storage of Melanesian artifacts within the museum, reflecting on the ways in which the application of an archaeological sensibility to the museum storeroom and a conceptualization of museum collections as assemblages could potentially open up new ways of thinking about the formation and location of ethnographic collections and the processes of collaboration they undergo. By drawing attention to the museum storeroom as the primary context in which ethnographic objects are found and by positing ways of exploring it as an archaeological site that has been created and structured in very particular ways, she suggests that curators have a responsibility to facilitate new collaborative strategies for working with source communities that acknowledge the agency of things. In a comment on Byrne's chapter, Evelyn Tetehu, one of the Solomon Islander women involved in the Melanesia Project at the British Museum, reiterates how an artifact's social function can significantly influence the ways in which it should be managed, and she discusses the ongoing social implications of engaging indigenous communities in such collaborations. This theme is discussed further by Chantal Knowles (chapter 9), who shows how ambiguous objects that are not able to be categorized using conventional museum categories can help trouble those categories. She draws attention to such categories as an invention of museum practice and also points out the ways in which museum objects are far more commonly the result of mixed agencies and makers than might generally be assumed. The collaborative reconstruction of the Māori waka taua in the National Museums Scotland draws into question a range of museological practices through the discussion of a shared practice, which drew on Māori approaches to conservation informed by a tradition of continual use, repair, and renewal. Finally, the implications of adopting Hopi ontologies for reshaping contemporary curatorial practices are explored by Kelley Hays-Gilpin and Ramson Lomatewama (chapter 10). In embracing a view of artifacts as animate and as having reciprocal relationships with humans (and one another) in terms of their life force, personhood, emotions, kin, life cycle, and function—which derives from Hopi cosmology but which can be seen as shared by other indigenous groups throughout the world—they suggest that museums might shift their emphasis to living people and the reciprocal relationships between museum staff and representatives from source communities, the relationships between artifacts and individuals, and the relations of artifacts with one another. This would have positive benefits not only for source communities but also for the recognition and re-ignition of the relationships that animate the things in museum collections.

CONCLUSION

I will conclude with some thoughts about how the ideas developed in this book might inform everyday museum practices. While it is well known that museums employ anthropologists, archaeologists, and non-indigenous curators alongside indigenous curators and consultants, in practice, a range of individuals work behind the scenes, such as exhibit designers, marketing managers, educational outreach staff, and cafeteria workers, who are perhaps far less likely to engage directly with the sorts of theoretical concepts developed in a book like this one. However, the themes developed here can and should articulate directly with the everyday practices of museum workers and goers and not just with those of museum curators or professorial staff, in that we call for a fundamental reorganization and sharing of authority between source communities, museum staff, and members of the museums' various publics, as well as museum objects and exhibits. It is not only the curator or consultant or source community member who interacts with the objects in collections and determines the ways in which they are managed and displayed, but a whole range of museum staff, visitors, and other agents within the museum meshwork. All might be encouraged to view their interactions with objects as more dialogical (cf. Harrison 2012), to consider objects as possible agents and interlocutors in their own right, and to establish practices that treat objects more democratically. Similarly, all museum staff and visitors might be encouraged to consider their own obligations, which arise as a result of an acknowledgment of this shift in modes of authority within the museum. As Schultz (2011) has argued, it is important to involve the public—as much as source communities—in collaborations if the new shared modes of authority within the museum are to be communicated.

In the introduction to the edited volume *Evocative Objects: Things We Think With*, Sherry Turkle (2007:4) urges us to reconsider Claude Lévi-Strauss's (1966) suggestion that we explore bricolage, the creative combination and recombination of a particular series of things, as a spur to new knowledge. The processes of reassembling the museum collection described by the authors in this volume owe much to the creative potential that Lévi-Strauss identified as a latent property of assemblages of people and things. These chapters go some way toward shifting the dominant orientation of critical museum studies away from issues of difference and representation and toward a more nuanced engagement with a broader range of concerns, including the exercising of authority and agency, the forms in which they manifest, and the materials and relations by which they are mediated within ethnographic museum collections, understood broadly as sociotechnical and biopolitical assemblages. Although the book focuses particularly on indigenous agency and the forms in which it has emerged in relation to the museum, its themes have broad relevance for museum and material culture studies more generally, drawing on an archaeological sensibility to argue the need for greater sensitivity to the affective qualities of things and the relationships in which humans and objects are bound up throughout the world. Similarly, the theoretical and methodological issues discussed here go beyond museums to raise questions relevant to the applied disciplines of archaeology, anthropology, and material culture studies more generally. Certainly, the fundamental implication of many of these chapters is that increased respect for material things follows from acknowledgment not only that the makers were "real people" but also that the objects themselves have been (and continue to be) involved in significant historical and contemporary relationships with a variety of other human and nonhuman actors. Museums are already adopting special practices for material thought to have important "sacred" or "spiritual" significance, and the chapters suggest that these practices, which acknowledge the dialogue between humans and things, might gainfully be extended to other museum objects more generally.

An important, growing literature parallel to the one explored here considers the relationship between science museums and climate change (e.g., Cameron 2010, 2011a, 2011b), for example, and is similarly beginning to emphasize the responsibilities and obligations that arise from a consideration of heritage as something produced in the dialogical relationships between human and nonhuman actors, who work together to curate the past in the present to collectively build a common world (Dibley 2011; see also Harrison and Rose 2010; Harrison 2012; and Meskell 2010:854 in relation to heritage more generally). Museum collections not only are spaces of display but also provide objects to think with, through, and in relation to—objects that continue to exercise their own forms of agency in a complex mesh of relations with those who have made, traded, received, collected, curated, worked with, and viewed them in the past and do so in the present. Recognizing these various forms of agency has profound implications for curatorial practices, implying not only an active engagement of people and things but also a curatorial responsibility that arises from the material, historical, and political weight of museum objects. Acknowledging this curatorial responsibility has the potential to transform our relationships with museums and their varied communities of interest in the twenty-first century.

Acknowledgments

This introduction summarizes the themes that arose from the advanced seminar "Reassembling the Collection: Indigenous Agency and Ethnographic Collections," hosted by the School for Advanced Research in Santa Fe. The advanced seminar ran 26–30 September 2010 and was co-organized by Sarah Byrne, Anne Clarke, Rodney Harrison, and Robin Torrence. In writing this introduction, I have drawn on the ideas and concepts that were collectively developed among the participants in the seminar, borrowing liberally from the discussions. For that reason, this introduction should be read as a direct product of the collaboration among advanced seminar participants, albeit one that has been filtered through a particular authorial lens. I thank all of the participants for sharing their ideas so freely and for allowing me to put them together in this way. In particular, I thank Tony Bennett, Sarah Byrne, Anne Clarke, Robin Torrence, and two anonymous reviewers for their specific comments on this introductory chapter, which were helpful in revising it for final publication.

Note

1. Gosden (2004) makes a similar distinction between "objects" and "things."

Part I
Museum Networks and the
Distribution of Agency

2

The "Shuffle of Things" and the Distribution of Agency

Tony Bennett

I take the first part of this chapter's title from Francis Bacon's reference to cabinets of curiosity as places where "whatsoever singularity and the shuffle of things hath produced...shall be sorted and included" (Henare 2005:60). I do so in order to establish a connection with Bruno Latour's discussion of the similarities between bureaus of statistics, the storerooms for the maps produced by La Pérouse's Pacific voyages, and the collections of natural history museums. These are all places whose occupants can "combine, shuffle around, superimpose and recalculate" the relations between the statistics, texts, and things they gather together to end up with, respectively, a "'gross national product'...'Sakhalin Island,' or 'the taxonomy of mammals'" (Latour 1987:227). Latour makes the point by way of stressing the importance for those engaged in scientific expeditions of producing "immutable and combinable mobiles": that is, objects and texts that, no matter how old they are or how far distant from the sites at which they were collected, are "conveniently at hand and combinable at will" (1987:227; see also Harrison, chapter 4, this volume). It is through their pliable "combinability" that such texts and objects can be assembled into new networks that, although produced at a distance—spatial and temporal—from their points of origin, may nonetheless make possible varied forms of action back on those points of origin, and elsewhere.

I will apply this perspective to the networks through which the materials that were assembled in museums during the early fieldwork phase of anthropology were brought together from varied sites of collection and mobilized as parts of both civic and biopolitical programs.[1] I do so in order to explore the new entanglements that these processes of collecting gave rise to and the new forms of combinability they permitted. These were, in the main, entanglements between materials coded as "ethnographic," museums and museum personnel, the institutions and practices of the public sphere, and the apparatuses of colonial administration. My concern will be with the distribution of new forms of agency across the relations between museum and field, metropolis and colony, colonizer and colonized, scientist and subjects, and collector and collected that these entanglements made possible.[2]

I shall, though, approach these questions via a detour suggested by the similarities Latour notes between nineteenth-century natural history museums and statistical bureaus as centers of calculation: that is, as places where objects and data collected from diverse sites are subjected to new forms of classification and ordering made possible by their being gathered together in one place.[3] Evelyn Ruppert draws on this perspective in her discussion of the 1911 Canadian Census, the first to attempt a "scientific" enumeration of the Aboriginal inhabitants of Canada's Far North. There are three aspects of Ruppert's discussion I want to highlight here. The first concerns her use of the concept of *agencement*, derived from Michel Callon (2005), to interpret census taking as a practice performed through the interactions between heterogeneous actors whose agency arises from, and is distributed across, the sociotechnical arrangements that bring them together. The particular value of this concept consists in the light it throws on the processes through which such actors come to be endowed with specific, and different, agential powers and capacities. The actors she identifies as components of the "census agencement" include "human actors (e.g., the mounted police, interpreters, the Aboriginal people), technological actors (e.g., 'special' population schedules, steamships, trading posts) and natural actants (e.g., ice, snow, seals)" (Ruppert 2009:13). Ruppert's reasons for including mounted police, trading posts, and seals, to come to my second point, concern their roles as occasions for bringing together the census enumerators and gatherings of Aboriginal people as the to-be-enumerated. Each of these, in constituting temporary gatherings of nomadic groups—around police patrols, visits to trading posts, and seasonal seal hunts—provided contact points for the practice of enumeration. Third, however, Ruppert notes the inability of the census agencement to transform Canada's Aboriginal inhabitants into "census subjects," that is, subjects able to place themselves, and able to be placed, within the census categories. Such identifications were not possible because the Aboriginal respondents could not be "fixed" into place in terms of either their age or place of abode. In view of this, she argues, "census taking could not produce or construct a population in the Far North but only a record of a census 'other'—an indeterminate multitude that could not identify and could not be identified as part of the population" (Ruppert 2009:14–15).

There was a census in Australia in 1911 too, and one again in 1921 when, although the 1901 Commonwealth Constitution had excluded Aborigines from being counted in the census (Povinelli 2002:22), Aborigines were included, although they were listed as a separate category, apart from the Australian population. Perhaps the most distinctive and consequential forms of collecting and enumerating in which Aborigines were gathered and collected during this period, however, were those associated with the new relations between anthropological fieldwork and museums. Although initiated in the 1890s (Morton and Mulvaney 1996), the involvement of museums in organizing anthropological fieldwork expeditions into the more geographically remote parts of Australia—Central Australia, the Northern Territory, Western Australia, northern Queensland—increased significantly in the early decades of the twentieth century.[4] This was also when Australia's major state museums installed their first permanent exhibitions of Aboriginal culture (Jones 2007:228). It is no accident that these were also the formative decades of Australian state formation with the development, after the Federation of 1901, of programs and agencies organizing what had hitherto been separate states into a national governmental domain (Rowse 1998). The new nexus of relationships between museums and anthropological fieldwork that was developed in this period was connected to new arrangements for the management of Aborigines within the emerging space of an Australian nation-state. As such, it was a nexus that enumerated and collected Aborigines as a race apart, as constitutively different—racially and culturally—from the Australian population and, therefore, as needing to be governed differently.

Although it is important to register these differences, the methodological perspective Ruppert outlines is helpful in considering the relationships between anthropology, fieldwork, and the practices of colonial governance that were developed in this period. Her concept of a census agencement finds a ready parallel in the concept of a "fieldwork agencement" made up of an equivalent range of different kinds of actors and the distribution across these of different agential powers and capacities. These included, in the Australian case, the role of the stations on the overland telegraph, newly opened between Adelaide and Darwin, and of railways and government ration depots in providing points where Aborigines periodically congregated and where, therefore, they might be brought into the orbit of fieldwork investigations (Jones 1987; Mulvaney, Morphy, and Petch 1997). These provided points of contact that situated field workers and their subjects in a new governmental domain—a regularized set of arrangements between government authorities and Aboriginal populations—which (partially) displaced the role that missionary stations had earlier played in this regard. There were the guides and, sometimes, Aboriginal trackers on whom the field workers relied to find their way around often hostile terrain and the horses and camels that were the main sources of transport for the anthropologists, their equipment, and the food supplies and gifts that proved crucial material mediators of the anthropological encounter. There were tents and camping equipment, which marked differential spatial relationships between anthropologists and their subjects: close to the field but not entirely immersed within it as the tents provided the anthropologists with places of retreat into their own culture and also with places for writing up their observations and with makeshift dark rooms for film development (Schumaker 1996).

Most important of all, perhaps, was the range of measuring and recording devices that mediated the relations between anthropologists and their subjects. These were of two distinct types. First, there were those related most closely to the developing field of social anthropology's concerns, which were focused on the customs, beliefs, and behaviors of indigenous populations. Film cameras and sound recording equipment were the two key new technological mediators here. Photography was important in this context too. However, the camera also remained caught up in another set of technological mediators, associated with the concerns of physical anthropology, which, although gradually ceding ground to social anthropology, remained important throughout the early decades of the twentieth century. Sliding calipers, radiometers, anthropometers, standard weighing machines, steel tapes—these are the items of equipment Roy Burston (1913) records using, at the request of Baldwin Spencer, for a series of measurements he took of 102 Aborigines from different parts of northern Australia. This was not a fieldwork study: Burston records his debt to the keeper of Darwin Gaol for being able to include its Aboriginal inmates in his study. However, it was indicative of the range of measuring devices that continued to inform Australian anthropological fieldwork into the 1930s. Indeed, there were often more: devices for assessing a range of sensory capacities, for measuring body pigmentation, for taking blood samples and fingerprints, and so on (Jones 1987). Spencer collected across the range: photographs, films, sound recordings, artifacts, anthropometric measurements, skin color tests (Batty, Allen, and Morton 2005; Spencer and Gillen 1899; Spencer 1921).

One merit of James Clifford's (1997) elaboration of the concept of the "contact zone" consists in the attention it has drawn to the different modes of indigenous agency that have been exercised in relation to the varied contexts in which Western knowledge practices and indigenous populations have become entangled with each other. This is true even where such encounters have been mediated by the most extreme forms of objectification. Jones (1987) records the responses of the Aborigines to the procedures they were subjected to in studies organized by the South Australian Board for Anthropological Research. These ranged from bemusement at the physical manipulations to which they were subjected, to tolerance of the procedures because it was believed they might bring benefits to instances of noncompliance: Linda Crombie's refusal to be photographed without her shirt on, for example.[5] The use of film also depended on collective indigenous agency through, first, the preparations required to stage rituals expressly for the purpose of being filmed and, second, the negotiations that were entered into as permission to film such ceremonies was discussed. There was also creative economic exploitation of the possibilities opened up by the new forms of collecting associated with the relations between museums and fieldwork: the "invention" of the toas—believed to be symbolically significant way-markers and location finders placed along Aboriginal routes—is a case in point.[6] Increasingly, too, anthropologists felt an obligation, in recognition of the principles of (uneven) reciprocity of the forms of exchange on which their work depended, to send or take back to their "subjects" the results of their work—sometimes in book form, sometimes in slide lantern presentations, sometimes in film showings.[7]

A significant limitation of the concept of the contact zone, however, is its tendency to focus on the forms of agency that are evident in more immediate and direct forms of encounter. This neglects the broader networks that, although not directly present or perceptible in such encounters, nonetheless significantly affect what takes place in them.[8] There are two such networks I focus on here. The first comprises the increasingly formalized international networks, which affected the forms of interaction that took place in fieldwork encounters. Burston, for instance, records that the measurements he took were those recommended by the British Association's Anthropometric Committee in 1909; Jones notes that the work of the South Australian Board for Anthropological Research was initially modeled on the 1912 Geneva international agreement for observations on living subjects. The second concerns the different networks through which the varied objects, texts, and images that were gathered from fieldwork sites of collection were circulated on the anthropologists' return to the centers of collection whence they came. These concerned, first, the networks of the public sphere; second, the increasingly close connections between museums and universities as, progressively, the balance of influence moved from the former to the latter;[9] and, third, increasingly formalized networks of colonial administration. These were closely overlapping networks. The circulation of anthropological fieldwork through the institutions of the public sphere played a considerable role in building up the cultural capital of the anthropologist as a new kind of scientific actor in the public field. The stronger connections between museums, anthropology, and universities lent a new quasi-scientific aspect to anthropology in its concern to model itself on the field practices of the natural sciences, particularly in mimicking the relations between fieldwork site and laboratory. The new forms of public and scientific prestige accruing to the figure of the anthropologist and the development of new, albeit often insecure and contested, connections between anthropology and the training of colonial administrators similarly helped to produce the anthropologist as a new kind of actor in both colonial and administrative fields. Taking account of these circuits and the forms of distributed agency they involve means taking an equivalently dispersed approach to questions of indigenous agency.

SPACES FOR AND FORMS OF AGENCY

The Māori population played a variety of active roles in the development of New Zealand's colonial museums: as visitors, as exhibitors, and as donors in a complex set of gift and symbolic exchanges enacted across the shifting boundaries of the colonial frontier. However, as Conal McCarthy (2007) shows, the forms this agency took oscillated in the context of changing relations between Māori and Pākehā (New Zealanders of European descent) just as it was affected by changing practices of collection and exhibition. In the mid- to late nineteenth century, Māori people were more actively engaged with commercial exhibitions and world's fairs than with New Zealand's emerging public museums. This was partly because the former presented a less restricted context for cross-cultural engagement and partly because of a greater elective affinity between their more spectacular exhibition practices and Māori conceptions of exhibition as a way of demonstrating power, or *mana*. By contrast, following the restrictions placed on the export of Māori cultural materials by the 1901 Māori Antiquities Act, the early decades of the twentieth century saw active Māori support for the inclusion of Māori material culture in the development of a national patrimony that was shaped by both Pākehā motivations to preserve Māori culture as part of a salvage operation and Māori aspirations to be included in a project of modern nation formation.

Peter Hoffenberg's (2001) discussion of Aboriginal participation in the colonial and international exhibitions that were held in Australia's state capitals in the 1880s and 1890s similarly testifies to a range of different types of indigenous engagement. On the one hand, many Aborigines from mission stations were keen to visit such exhibitions as an extension of the civilizing dynamic governing their daily lives on the stations. This was often combined with public performances that testified to the fruits of, and a capacity for, civilization via concerts, public readings, and the exhibition of craft products. However, this inclusion usually came at the price of also being called on to perform and exhibit savagery: through the exhibition of corroborees (ceremonial performances of the Dreamtime), mock reenactments of frontier combats, and the exhibition of traditional Aboriginal skills—boomerang-throwing displays, for example (Hoffenberg 2001:222–229). This tension was worked out, in the public culture of Melbourne, in the history of the Coranderrk Station, which was established in the 1860s. A good deal of Aboriginal cultural and intellectual leadership was invested in this station—originally led by Simon Wonga of the Wurundjeri people—as countering the widespread belief that the Aboriginal race was doomed to die out, by testifying to Aborigines' ability to become thoroughly self-civilizing in collaboration with sympathetic white management.[10] This involved careful and calculated strategies regarding the role that Coranderrk's inhabitants should play in the public performance of Aboriginality—via film and photography, participation in exhibitions, and their modes of self-presentation to weekend day-trippers from Melbourne. These strategies sought to negotiate the complex and fraught terrain between, on the one hand, Aboriginal aspirations to self-determination and, on the other, conformity to European conventions regarding the appropriate markers and signifiers of civilization. By the early decades of the twentieth century, waning government support for such civilizing strategies undermined the authority of Coranderrk's Aboriginal leadership. As a result, the station's main function became that of serving as a tourist destination where Aboriginal performances of similarity and difference, of domesticity (raffia making) and strangeness (boomerang throwing), provided "stereotypical souvenirs of Aboriginality that could be subsumed into larger narratives of nation and progress" (Lydon 2005:213).

The ways of exhibiting Aboriginal culture developed through the relations between museums and anthropological fieldwork over the course of the 1910s and 1920s rested on a different logic. These excluded Aborigines from post-Federation narratives of nation and progress by interpreting their "backwardness" as a consequence of the new evolutionary terms in which they were racialized as ineradicably and absolutely Other. Perhaps the chief defining characteristic of this disciplinary ensemble was its preoccupation with the (impossible) retrieval of precolonial Aboriginal forms of sociality and culture at the price of a more or less complete blindness to both the conditions of Aborigines living in or close to the white centers of population and the history of the interactions between colonizer and colonized. In common with the tendency that characterized the early phase of anthropological fieldwork internationally, the "authentic native" was to be found only in the remote parts of Australia—in the desert regions of South and Central Australia, in the Northern Territory, northern Queensland, and Western Australia. This entailed, Geoffrey Gray has argued, a focus on "a 'double' reconstruction—the 'pristine' (before contact) culture and the 'ideal frontier' (at the point of contact)"—through which the authentic Aborigine, the remnant of a lost past, constituted the "idealized space" of an "alternative now" (2007:24). It was this maneuver that supported the interpretation of Aborigines as, in Baldwin Spencer's terms, "the most backward race extant," revealing "the conditions under which the early ancestors of the present human races existed" (1914:33).

Spencer, together with his co-researcher, Frank Gillen, was the most influential representative of anthropological fieldwork in Australia and, indeed, a significant international innovator in this respect (Morphy 1996). His combined roles as museum administrator, university professor of biology, and pioneer ethnographer were significant aspects of the new relations within which the public representations of Aborigines and Aboriginal culture at the National Museum of Victoria (NMV) were set. At a time when, as in New Zealand, export restrictions were placed on Aboriginal cultural materials, Spencer contributed considerably to Australia's accumulating stock of such materials by donating to the NMV the artifacts, photographs, films, and sound recordings that resulted from his and Gillen's fieldwork trips to Central Australia.[11] As simultaneously the curator of the NMV's ethnological galleries, Spencer—combining the authority of direct witness, of "having been there" (Wolfe 1999), of the anthropological field worker with that of the natural scientist—mobilized the materials he brought back with him in a variety of contexts: the ethnological galleries of the NMV; the illustrated public lectures he gave on "the howling savages" of the Australian interior; his scientific publications; and presentations at scientific associations. Studies of Spencer's photographic practices have shown how much his work in the field depended on the active participation of his "subjects" and the enactment of reciprocal forms of obligation (Batty, Allen, and Morton 2005). But these forms of agency and reciprocity did not stretch from the field back to the colonial museum. What Spencer took back from the field were the objects, visual and sonic records, and anatomical measurements. None of the Aborigines themselves were ever "taken back" to Melbourne to be exhibited or to be consulted regarding the arrangement of their cultural materials in the ethnological galleries. Nor did they ever visit those galleries. Museum and field were, in this sense, radically distinct zones. In contrast to the situation McCarthy (2007) describes for New Zealand and to the calculated forms of engagement Coranderrk's inhabitants had shown in controlling the images of themselves that circulated in Melbourne's public sphere, this radical separation meant that the NMV's depictions of Aboriginal culture rested exclusively on the authority of science, uninterrupted by any input from or the live presence of the distant peoples they drew upon.

Views differ regarding Spencer's estimates of the "improvability" of Aborigines. In Henrika Kuklick's (2006:562–565) estimation, Spencer represented the liberal end of the spectrum of opinion in attributing to Aborigines a capacity for conscious innovation and gradual improvement, thus rebutting white settlers' views of Aborigines as a people without a history. While there is some truth in this, it fails to take account of Spencer's relations to the different wings of the divided legacy of liberalism he inherited.[12] If demonstrating a capacity for conscious innovation satisfied the requirement of will and volition that John Stuart Mill had judged necessary for the demonstration of progressive forms of human agency, the historicization of character developed across the human and natural sciences in the wake of Darwin's work made it possible to both recognize this and yet place Aborigines on the other side of a historical divide from the white settler.[13] In contemporary formulations produced in orbit around Edward Burnett Tylor's doctrine of survivals, formulations that found their echo in Spencer's work, the problem was not that the Aborigine was innately incapable of self-improvement or of being improved, but that he had *become* so.[14] Although the result of a particular set of circumstances (the absence of competition), this incapacity was nonetheless interpreted as racially constitutive, inscribed within a separate bloodline, which meant that the capacity for innovation and volition that Aborigines had once shown could not vouchsafe the race a future. Spencer's evolutionary museum displays, his public lectures (widely reported in the contemporary press), and scientific texts depicted Aborigines as radically Other—a remnant of prehistory within the present—and as an outsider to Australia's national and civilizing rhetorics. They stood only for a past that had to be left behind.

In his account of the relations between ethnography and the colonial state, George Steinmetz argues that the core business of the colonial state—understood, in Bourdieusian terms, as an autonomous state form that is relatively independent of its metropolitan overseer—is to identify, produce, and reinforce "the alterity that is required by the rule of hierarchical difference" (Steinmetz 2007:41). This entails the production of forms of Otherness that would put back into place the sense of an unbridgeable divide between colonizer and colonized to counter the effects of colonial mimicry. "Native policy," as Steinmetz puts it, "was an attempt to identify a uniform cultural essence beneath the shimmering surface of indigenous practice and to restrict the colonized to this unitary identity" (2007:43). The early twentieth-century development of permanent museum exhibitions of Aboriginal culture did precisely this by casting Aborigines in the role of a racially defined Other whose primitivism constituted the basis for their exclusion from the dynamics of Australian national development. This had profound consequences for the new systems of colonial administration that were developed in the second and third decades of the twentieth century.

CIVIC-PUBLIC AND BIOPOLITICAL ASSEMBLAGES

A key aspect of my argument so far, regarding the relationship between the "shuffle of things" and the distribution of agency, concerns the place that museums occupy as switch points in overlapping networks through which flows—of texts, objects, measurements, and people—are circulated. The NMV constituted just such a switch point. It was the place to which the artifacts, films, and sound recordings that Spencer and Gillen brought back from their fieldwork expeditions were sent to be classified, ordered, and exhibited. And it was the place from which exhibitions of and discourses about Aboriginal culture and Aboriginality were disseminated through the broader public spheres of Melbourne, the state of Victoria, and Australia more generally. It also provided a storehouse of material warrants for Spencer's and Gillen's scientific publications.[15] These were circulated via international scientific networks that were still dominated by Eurocentric forms of authority in which savants based in London and Paris—notably, James Frazer and Emile Durkheim—provided the key intellectual syntheses of the findings that were reported from diverse colonial points of collection.[16]

The organization of the flows and networks in which museums participate have definite consequences for the distribution of agency, determining the positions at which agency can be exercised and the distribution of different kinds of agents across those positions. The networks organizing the flows of people and things between the centers and sites of collection associated with the early phases of anthropological fieldwork in Australia afforded little opportunity for indigenous agency beyond the fieldwork site itself. There is no doubting the importance of these. Noting that the Arrernte (the Arunta in Spencer's orthography) had experienced contact with white settlers from the 1860s, Elizabeth Povinelli (2002:93) interprets the varied performances they staged for Spencer and Gillen as active attempts to communicate across semiotic and political boundaries at a time when they were "in the midst of being physically exterminated, having their ritual objects stolen, lost, or destroyed, and watching their lands be appropriated and, with them, their life-sustaining material and spiritual resources." Yet, the routes along which the measurements, artifacts, films, photographs, and recordings that were collected from the Arrernte traveled did not include the Arrernte themselves. Not even their names. Spencer's and Gillen's photographs and texts never specified identity beyond age, gender, and tribe—"elderly Warumungo woman," and so on.[17] This stood in contrast to and helped to undermine the forms of agency that had been developed by Aborigines living closer to Australia's main centers of population, who, aware of the significance that attached to the public circulation of images of Aboriginality, sought to limit and to direct the form that such images took. Indigenous agency (like any other) differed in its aims and effects depending on the points in different cross-cutting networks at which it was exercised.

The modes of collecting and interpreting the materials acquired from Spencer's and Gillen's fieldwork expeditions were also connected to the emerging forms of colonial administration in early Federation Australia. This was partly due to the positions that Spencer occupied in the administration of Aboriginal affairs;[18] it was also partly due to the authority that his racialized production of Aboriginality enjoyed in view of its validation by Europe's leading savants.[19] Before considering these matters, however, I want to look briefly at the different set of relations that was developed between museum, field, metropolitan public sphere, and colony during the formative years of the development of the Musée de l'Homme (MH) under Paul Rivet's direction (1928–1939).[20] This will prove helpful in identifying the terms of analysis I use when returning to Spencer. I shall limit myself to two aspects of these differences, considered in terms of their implications for the distribution of agency. The first concerns the role played by the MH in the development of the "anthropological humanism" that became the main signature of French anthropology during the interwar years. This was partly a matter of the progressive replacement of the earlier paradigms of physical anthropology with those of social anthropology, displacing the focus on collecting anatomical remains and measurements of the earlier tradition, represented by Paul Broca and Paul Topinard (Dias 2004), in favor of the collection of artifacts and texts as evidence of the distinctive ways of life of colonized populations. It also involved—as a major point of difference between Rivet and Spencer—a break with the principles of evolutionism in favor of diffusionist perspectives to account for the specificity of the practices congregated in distinct cultural areas. In truth neither of these shifts was ever carried through to the point of a complete break with earlier forms of racial science in Rivet's work or the practices of the MH more generally (Conklin 2008). There was, however, a significant shift in museum practice from the earlier exhibition, at the Musée d'Ethnographie du Trocadéro, of anatomically grounded racial hierarchies toward a concern with artifactual and textual markers of territorially distinctive ways of life.

I want, as my second point, to distinguish two ways in which this concern was manifested at the MH in view of its operations at the intersections of two different institutional networks. These can be usefully identified with respect to the MH's express conception as a vehicle for realizing the two-pronged program that Marcel Mauss had proposed for the development of French ethnology, which, through the Institut d'Ethnologie, established in 1925 as the intellectual hub of the ensemble of anthropological institutions that Rivet coordinated around the MH, recruited general support from within the discipline. The first prong of this program took its lead from Mauss's complaint that the "general public knows nothing of our research.... Scientists must do publicity, since a science can become popular only through vulgarisation" (qtd. in Fournier 2006:214). The MH was, in this regard, and quite unusually, established as a museum that was explicitly committed to a program of public pedagogy that aimed to transform public attitudes toward questions of race and the colonized. The second prong took its lead from Mauss's conception of the role that ethnology should play in support of a new phase of colonial policy governed by humanist conceptions: "Colonial policy may be the area in which the adage 'knowledge is power' is best confirmed. By respecting and using beliefs and customs, modifying the economic and technological system only with caution, not opposing anything directly, and using everything, [administrators] could arrive at humane, easy, and productive colonial practices" (qtd. in Fournier 2006:166).

These two different conceptions of the MH's function were performed through two different networks. They also entailed different mechanisms of effect. Michel Foucault's comments on the differences between governing strategies that operate through the mechanisms of the public and those of the milieu bear on the distinction I have in mind here (Foucault 2007:3, 19–21, 297). In the case of the former, governing relates to the population through people's beliefs, opinions, and customs, seeking to get a hold on these through public and educational programs and campaigns. Here, government relates to the members of a population as subjects of voluntary actions, whose conduct is to be changed by persuasive means oriented toward recruiting their assent to the aims and objectives of governing authorities. Where government relates to a population via the mechanism of the milieu, however, it applies specific forms of expertise to modifying the material conditions affecting that population—conceived not as subjects, but as an aggregate whose conduct is shaped by its relations to its milieu.

Shaped by international initiatives after the 1914–1918 war to develop museums as instruments of democratic education, and by the Greater France rhetorics and policies of the interwar years, the MH formed part of a network of public and civic institutions that sought to transform French attitudes toward the populations of France's colonies in West Africa and Indochina. This involved a revision of earlier hierarchically organized conceptions of racial divisions grounded in anatomical differences in favor of a humanistic conception of all races as being "equal but different," separated by different cultural histories and traditions overlaid on a shared substratum of a common humanity. It also involved a revision of attitudes toward the inhabitants of France's colonies as parts of the rich cultural diversity of Greater France, united with the French people as parts of a transnational family.[21] To France's colonial populations, although saluted as subjects of Greater France, this made little practical difference since this recognition of a certain kind of cultural kinship was not accompanied by any conferral of citizenship rights.

The MH participated in this new civic-public assemblage via its exhibition galleries. After an early period marked by distinctive aesthetic forms for valorizing Otherness, associated with the principles of "ethnographic surrealism," exhibitions were organized in accordance with the principles of the *museographie claire*. Developed by Georges Henri Rivière, these aimed to give material expression to the organizing principles of the new ethnography: the exhibition of the relations between the elements composing the distinctive fabric of different territorially defined cultures considered in their relations to their environments (Gorgus 2003:56–60). These exhibition galleries and the special exhibitions of the materials the MH collected through its fieldwork expeditions constituted, under Rivet's leadership, the most significant material culture contribution to the antiracist programs of the Popular Front. They were also significant points of engagement for the cultural project of negritude developed by French-trained African intellectual elites who traveled to Paris precisely in order to engage in a politics that was denied them in situ: a politics of culture and identity worked through via the mechanisms of the public and civic spheres.[22]

That this was so, Gary Wilder (2005) argues, was because of a contradiction at the heart of the governmental rationality of colonial humanism, a contradiction in which the MH participated in view of its contribution—particularly through its relations with the Institut d'Ethnologie—to the training of colonial administrators. Established with the support of and funding from France's key colonial and overseas ministries and committed from the start to providing the legislature with, as Mauss had proposed, "a systematic knowledge of the customs, beliefs, and techniques of the populations it is called upon to direct" (Rivière 1931), the connection between the differentiating particularism of post-Maussian ethnology and colonial humanism was a double-edged one. On the one hand, in the stress it placed on the distinctive qualities of different cultures, it served as a resource for antiracist programs of public education within France. As a scientific adjunct to the task of colonial administration, however, the MH conceived and addressed the inhabitants of France's West African colonies as the objects of a form of colonial rule that was brought to bear on them from without through the use of ethnology as a means for the scientific manipulation of the milieus governing the conditions of life of the colonized. This division of functions within the MH was expressed by the provision of a laboratory, set aside from the exhibition galleries, and reserved for the scientific study of the materials brought to the museum from its fieldwork exhibitions and for consultation, inter alia, by colonial officials and trainees.

Although not an exact parallel, it is worth recalling that, for Latour, the laboratory plays a significant role in the field sciences in the relations between sites of collection and centers of calculation by providing a context in which materials gathered from the former can be brought into new relations with one another. The relations between specimens collected from the field, he argues, can be reconfigured as "the researcher can shift the position of specimens and substitute one for another as if they are shuffling cards" (Latour 1999:38). Latour also stresses the ways in which such laboratory rearrangements provide templates that, once relayed back to the original site of fieldwork investigation, serve to organize various forms of scientific administrative action on that site. In this respect, the role of the MH in effecting a new shuffle of things that (partially) dismantled anatomically grounded racial hierarchies in favor of the differentiating particularism of colonial humanism also provided a template for new forms of action on the colonial social. These sought, as Wilder puts it, to combine a humanistic universalism with a respect for African cultural specificities and a residual but still potent evolutionism that would subject African societies to a program of guided social development to help overcome their backwardness. Here, the expert knowledge of indigenous customs, traditions, and economic and technological systems that Mauss called for provided the resources for programs of social development that failed to address indigenous populations as either subjects or citizens or to cultivate the institutions of colonial civil society needed for this purpose.

While providing a point of engagement for the cultural politics of deracinated colonial intellectuals in Paris, the MH was simultaneously an integral component of a scientific administrative complex that had significant consequences for the governance of colonial populations who had little, if any, inkling of its existence. The same was true of the relations between Baldwin Spencer's fieldwork, his museum practice, and the forms of Aboriginal administration that prevailed during the interwar years. I have already noted that Aborigines were not counted among the publics of Australia's museums. If their presence in museums was envisaged at all, it was as specimens rather than as a public. It was still possible as late as 1932 for the University of Adelaide's Board of Anthropological Research to apply (unsuccessfully) to the Anthropology Committee of the Australian National Research Council for funding to bring Aborigines from the River Murray area into the South Australia Museum, where, in return for a few shillings a week, they might be studied exhaustively (Gray 2007:55–61). Nonetheless, although not addressed via the NMV's public programs, Aborigines were significantly affected by the shuffle of things produced by Spencer's arrangement of the NMV's ethnological collections. These functioned as the material bank and guarantor for the representations of Aboriginality that were put into broader public and scientific circulation by Spencer and Gillen, and they played a part in furnishing new templates for the administration of Australia's indigenous inhabitants.

The logic of these arrangements, however, was quite different from the differentiating particularism of French colonial humanism. This is not to suggest that Spencer denied the existence of differences—in appearance, beliefs, and rituals—between different Aboriginal tribes. However, while recognizing these and as a counter to diffusionist accounts,[23] he interpreted them as the result of adaptations to varied environmental conditions encountered by the dispersion of a single racial group through the continent. Diversity was thus retrieved into an essential unity in that Spencer interpreted all Aboriginal customs, beliefs, artifacts, and so on, as the expressions of a primitive level of social development that was rooted ineradicably in a shared bloodline. This ruled out the prospect of any future development, whether from within, as a consequence of a built-in propensity for development, or from without, through religious or secular civilizing programs. The logical consequence of such conceptions consisted in the development of administrative arrangements, initiated in 1914 and lasting through the interwar years, that combined a program of passive genocide with one of civilization via the bloodline. This was to be achieved by separating "half-caste" Aborigines from their "full-blood" relatives and promoting intermarriage between them so that, via the dilution of their Aboriginal bloodline, they might, by becoming progressively whiter, acquire the ability to be civilized. Meanwhile, "full-blood" Aborigines were to be left to follow the road to extinction that the laws of competition prescribed.

It might be tempting to attribute the contrasting consequences of the differentiating particularism of French colonial ethnology and the racially homogenizing orientations of Australian anthropology to differences in the ethical personas of the key personnel involved—as a matter of Rivet's tolerant pluralism versus Spencer's evolutionism. Tempting but misleading. For these differences were, themselves, shaped by the different colonial logics bearing on the relations between fieldwork, anthropological practice, museums, and colonial administration according to whether these formed a part of settler colonialism (the Australian case) or were part of the administration of overseas colonies (the French case). Whereas the latter related to the colonized as an economic resource to be developed, the former related to them as rival occupants of the land and, as such, to be eliminated.

TIME AND THE RESHUFFLING OF THINGS

I will, in concluding, go back to my starting point by comparing the processes of collecting indigenous cultures that museums have been a party to with those statistical gatherings of indigenous populations effected by turn-of-the-century censuses in Canada and Australia. These, it will be recalled, failed to produce the indigenous in the form of what Ruppert calls "census subjects," registering them rather as "census 'others.'" While not dissenting from this assessment, Tim Rowse (2009:33) usefully highlights the use that indigenous Australians and Māori have made of census data in political processes of identity formation by translating their representations as census objects into "an ontological politics of 'closing the gaps.'" This politics consists of the use of census data that reveal the respects in which indigenous Australians fall short of average population norms (in terms of health, level of education, employment rates, etc.) to urge the need for policies to reduce or eliminate such gaps. This is, Rowse argues, a politics that also functions as a process of identity formation in lodging claims to distinctive forms of peoplehood.

The indigenous cultural materials that were collected in museums during the fieldwork phase of anthropology have subsequently played a similar role in political processes of identity formation. In a discussion of the distinctive role that museum collections play in the development of particular forms of sociality, Amiria Henare argues that the restricted mobility across space that results from the enclosure of objects in museums serves to enhance "*their ability to move through time*" (2005:9). They can thus, among other things, function as significant components in systems of distributed personhood that are spread across time, because museum collections have proved crucial to identity formation in view of their ability to enact what Henare calls "heritable communities of people and things" (2005:8).[24] While it goes beyond my concerns to engage with these matters in any detail here, the Aboriginal materials that were gathered in Australian museums in the early phase of anthropological fieldwork have since become profoundly politicized objects as museums and, more generally, Western exhibition forms have become sites of significant contention for indigenous Australians. The indigenous agencies that have been involved in these struggles have varied in form, in the political stances they have enunciated, and in the points at which they have been applied in the now more complex networks that mediate the relations between indigenous communities, collecting institutions, governmental bodies, schools, publics, tourists, and, post-Mabo (the judgment that overthrew the doctrine of *terra nullius* by recognizing traditional forms of land ownership), the legal system considered in its relations to the politics of land claims.[25]

Yet, as one aspect of these expanded networks for indigenous practice and intervention, there remains a legacy from the period I have discussed here. Povinelli (2002) identifies this in noting how, for Spencer and Gillen as, indeed, for earlier Australian anthropological traditions, the "real Aborigine" had always to be sought elsewhere, a constantly elusive object beyond the contaminations of white contact. This is now, she argues, coded into the complex relations between indigenous Australians, anthropologists, the collections of indigenous materials in museums, and the law in enacting the "heritable communities of people and things" that are the conditions for recognition upon which, post-Mabo, the confirmation of Aboriginal claims to land ownership depends. For this requires the demonstration of an effective continuity of tradition and practice that stretches back beyond the settler state, a capacity to somehow still be connected to and embody the lost ancient customs defining the position that indigenous Australians must be able to occupy within the time-space coordinates of the nation-state if they are to benefit from its new dispensations. To illustrate this point, Povinelli cites an exchange between a lawyer and an indigenous witness in the Kenbi land claim:

> *Lawyer.* What was it like before the white man?
>
> *Tom Barradjap.* I don't know mate I never been there. (2002:61)

The lawyer's question was, of course, Spencer's question also, and its continuing force shows how far the historically formative orchestration of the relations between the past, "Aboriginality,"[26] and the nation that his work established remain points to be negotiated in engagement with such relations today. Barradjap's response points to a politics that refuses these terms.

Notes

1. Marking a starting point for fieldwork in anthropology is notoriously difficult, partly because there is no clear dividing line between the forms of travel and reporting that such expeditions involved and earlier travel literatures (Debaene 2010; Defert 1982; Fabian 2000) and partly because wherever the line is drawn, earlier exceptions can be invoked. That said, anthropological fieldwork is conventionally described as beginning with the Torres Strait Islands expeditions led by Alfred Cort Haddon (1888, 1898), Baldwin Spencer's and Frank Gillen's fieldwork trips to Central Australia (beginning in 1896–1897), and Franz Boas's participation in the American Museum of Natural History's Jesup North Pacific Expedition (1897–1902). As Alison Petch (2007) and others have noted, *Notes and Queries*, which had played a key role in organizing earlier, more "amateur" forms of traveling among and collecting the Other, assumed, by the 1912 edition, anthropologically trained field workers as its primary addressees. Henrika Kuklick (2011) also advances a number of reasons for regarding this as a distinctive moment in the development of anthropological fieldwork practice in view of (1) its adoption of the scientific models for fieldwork developed in the natural sciences and (2) its dependence on the infrastructures of rail and telegraph and on the pacification of

colonial frontiers. However, I stretch this conventional definition to include the field-work expeditions organized by the Musée de l'Homme in the 1930s, the first effective period of fieldwork in French ethnology (Dias 1991; L'Estoile 2007).

2. I draw here and elsewhere on earlier engagements with these questions; see Bennett 2004, 2009, 2010.

3. Latour's assumption that centers of calculation were found only in European and North American metropolitan locations has been criticized for neglecting more localized centers of calculation operating in colonial contexts (Gascoigne 1996). My approach responds to these criticisms by considering the operations of museums as centers of calculation in both metropolitan (Paris) and colonial (Melbourne) settings.

4. The establishment of a chair in anthropology at the University of Sydney in 1925 and its central position in the organization of anthropological research funded by the Rockefeller Foundation marked a shift away from the strong links between museums and anthropology in Australia (Gray 2007:55–61).

5. The symbolic significance of such refusals, given the association of nakedness with savagery, is discussed by Jane Lydon (2005).

6. The more or less sudden appearance of toas in the early twentieth century suggests that they were produced in a calculated appeal to the interest in the exotic exhibited by the collectors of the South Australian Museum rather than being "genuinely" ethnographic (Jones 2007:ch. 6).

7. See Herle and Rouse 1998 and Mulvaney, Morphy, and Petch 1997 for accounts of this in relation to the Haddon and Spencer and Gillen fieldwork expeditions.

8. I have discussed this weakness of the concept elsewhere; see Bennett 1998:203–206, 210–213.

9. It is important to stress the museum-university interactions during this period to counter a tendency to read back into it the more radical separation between the two that is attributed to the phase of "fieldwork proper," conventionally marked by Malinowski's work in New Guinea. This is often connected to two other divisions: between the armchair phase of anthropology and the phase of the scientific investigator in the field and between the collection of artifacts and the collection of textual evidence relating to the social and cultural lifeways of the peoples under study. However, a strong connection between museums and fieldwork is evident in the Haddon, Jesup, Spencer and Gillen, and Musée de l'Homme expeditions. All of these retained a significant concern with the collection of objects, and strong connections between museums and universities were evident in all these cases.

10. The continuing significance of Coranderrk as a key site of Aboriginal intellectual and cultural leadership is shown by the prominence accorded it in the third

program—"Freedom for Our Lifetime"—in the television series *First Australians: The Untold Story of Australia*, first broadcast by SBS in 2008.

11. The NMV's ethnographic collections increased from twelve hundred to over thirty-six thousand items during Spencer's period as director; see Mulvaney and Calaby 1985:252.

12. John Mulvaney and Howard Morphy have tended to oscillate between praise for Spencer's (and Gillen's) liberal deeds and views on certain matters and condemnation of their subscription to manifestly racist conceptions of Aborigines as evolutionary throwbacks. Their equivocations fail to take adequate account of the respects in which Spencer's views drew on the divided currency of liberal thought—partly on the classical formulations of Mill but also on the revisions of classical liberalism effected by the post-Darwin development of the historical sciences.

13. I discuss these relations between the historical sciences and the historicization of character in providing a new template for governmental action on the social in greater detail in Bennett 2004.

14. For a fuller development of this point, see Bennett 2011b.

15. Spencer (1922:8) made a point of stressing how closely his and Gillen's books were based on the material evidence gathered from their expeditions and then stored in the NMV.

16. However, as Kuklick (2006) notes, Spencer did protest at some of the interpretations placed on his findings by such savants.

17. I draw here on Mulvaney, Morphy, and Petch 1997.

18. He was the Special Commissioner and Chief Protector of Aborigines in the Northern Territory in 1912 and prepared a number of influential reports on the administration of Aboriginal affairs.

19. These played a crucial role in Spencer's and Gillen's accumulation of, in Steinmetz's terms, "ethnographic capital." Spencer had become a Fellow of the Royal Society and a Commander of the Order of St. Michael and St. George by 1904. Gillen was made a Corresponding Fellow of the Anthropological Institute in London and in 1900 was the president of the ethnology and anthropology section of the Australasian Association for the Advancement of Science (see Mulvaney, Morphy, and Petch 1997).

20. I draw on the following sources in my discussion of these developments: Conklin 2002a, 2002b, 2008; Laurière 2008; L'Estoile 2007; Sherman 2004; Siebeud 2004, 2007. Although the institutions established in this period were described as ethnographic or ethnological, with important divisions of theoretical orientation between them, I use the more general anglophone term "anthropology" here to encompass all these institutional and intellectual tendencies, qualifying it as "social anthropology" to refer to the Durkheim-Mauss lineage, which rapidly became ascendant.

21. See also Peer 1998 on the conception of Greater France and its consequences within France and Lebovics 2004 for an assessment of the concept's longer-term legacies.

22. The discussion of these questions in the second part of Wilder 2005 provides a useful guide to the general issues involved, and Clifford's famous essay on "ethnographic surrealism" (1988) offers some indicators of their relations to the MH.

23. Spencer expressed this opposition in his criticisms of a paper presented by W. H. Rivers to the 1914 meeting of the British Association for the Advancement of Science in Melbourne, in which Rivers argued that Australia's Aboriginal population descended from a number of migrant streams from different origins (Kuklick 2006:565–567).

24. I draw here, in my reference to systems of distributed personhood, on the work of Marilyn Strathern (1999).

25. For some useful engagement with these questions, see Healy and Witcomb 2006 and Healy 2008.

26. I use the term "Aboriginality" here as the historically pertinent one, but in quotation marks in recognition of the criticisms of this concept that have been advanced and the preference for either more local (Koori) or more general (indigenous) designations.

3

Reassembling the London Missionary Society Collection

Experimenting with Symmetrical Anthropology and the Archaeological Sensibility

Chris Wingfield

In the corner of a display case in the Sainsbury African Galleries at the British Museum, an engraved ostrich eggshell (figure 3.1) stands on a glass shelf supported by a perspex stand, alongside a similarly engraved gourd. A short textual description attached to the shelf reads

Water containers	*The nomadic peoples of Botswana*
Incised ostrich egg with resin rim	*normally avoid pottery unless*
and gourd flask with vegetable-fibre	*obliged to settle in one place.*
carrying sling	
San people, Botswana	*Ethno 1910-363*
19th and 20th century	*Ethno 1976 AF 5.2*

Another label, describing just the eggshell, suggests a less precise geographical origin and a more specific temporal one:

Engraved ostrich egg flask
San people, southern Africa
Late 19th–early 20th century

This is followed by a longer text connecting the eggshell to an ancient tradition of decorating ostrich eggs and using them to carry food and water, which archaeological finds from South Africa have dated back sixty thousand years (cf. Texier et al. 2010). As well as making the eggshell representative of a series of similar objects from the ancient past, both labels assert a time and place with which the specific example on display is associated—the place and time of its manufacture. Though they exist in the heart of contemporary Bloomsbury, their enclosure in glass and their location in a gallery space dedicated to "Africa" suggest that they belong in another place, as well as another time. These technologies of enclosure and textual description combine to imply that the engraved eggshell belongs to the southern African past, rather than to the London present. In Johannes Fabian's (1983) terms, the eggshell is "allochronous"—its coevalness with those viewing it is denied. This is a fairly representative example of the ways in which many objects are displayed in museums. Indeed, until relatively recently, the labels of many ethnographic objects included only their place of origin, and museum databases and other textual forms of documenting these collections continue to make the place from which an object is supposed to have come especially prominent (Wingfield 2011). The temporal origins of ethnographic objects, when provided, tend to be calculated in relation to the date on which they were acquired by the museum. In this case, the "late 19th–early 20th century" date given in relation to the eggshell appears to be derived from the date (1910) when the eggshell was acquired by the British Museum (BM). This date has become central to the eggshell's institutional identity as a museum object, forming the first part of its acquisition number: 1910.363.

However, the British Museum did not acquire this eggshell from an anthropologist or explorer recently returned from southern Africa but purchased it along with a metal display mount and around three hundred other objects from the London Missionary Society (LMS) when that organization closed its museum. The LMS was a Protestant, but officially nondenominational, missionary society that was established in 1795. It was most active in the Pacific, southern Africa, China, India, and Madagascar, with some missions in the Caribbean, but expanded its operations into Central Africa and New Guinea during the later nineteenth century. The museum at Mission House in London was open to the public from 1814 until 1910 and was also drawn upon to supply missionary meetings and talks with items for display. A published catalog of the LMS museum, dating from 1826, mentions an ostrich egg "rudely carved and coloured by a Hottentot" (LMS 1826:13). An egg, "rudely engraved by a Hottentot," also appears in a subsequent catalog dating from around 1860 (LMS 1860:48). Although it cannot be conclusively shown that the engraved eggshell in the BM is the one that left a trace in both these documents, it seems very likely that it is.

FIGURE 3.1

Engraved ostrich eggshell, originally from southern Africa, now displayed in the Sainsbury African Galleries, British Museum (Af1910.363). © Trustees of the British Museum.

This suggests that when it entered the collections of the British Museum in 1910, the eggshell had already been in London since at least 1826 and possibly earlier. While the engraved ostrich eggshell may have been decorated in southern Africa, where it was presumably acquired by a representative of the LMS, it may have already been in London for around a century when it was acquired by the BM. The ostrich eggshell at the BM may once have been created as a water carrier in southern Africa, but for nearly two centuries, its primary function has been as a museum object in London.

SYMMETRICAL ANTHROPOLOGY AND THE ARCHAEOLOGICAL SENSIBILITY

By way of comparison, consider briefly the tomb of the poet Rupert Brooke (1887–1915) on the island of Skyros in Greece (figure 3.2). The text

FIGURE 3.2

Rupert Brooke's tomb in Skyros, Greece. © Dimitris Barbatsalos.

of Brooke's most famous poem, *The Soldier,* forms the main inscription on the tomb and begins with these lines:

> If I should die, think only this of me:
> That there's some corner of a foreign field
> That is for ever England.

Like the display case at the BM, the tomb uses a combination of spatial demarcation and textual inscription to suggest that the space it encloses belongs to a place and time other than those in which it currently exists. As containers, both tomb and display case use technologies of enclosure and inscription to link the spaces they enclose with the places and times in which their contents originated. Archaeology has largely grown up, as a discipline, among tombs and monuments, whether these have been prehistoric barrows, pyramids, or classical temples. It is not uncommon for ancient monuments to include textual inscriptions, so although Brooke's grave at Skyros is less than a century old, it offers a good example through which to explore the archaeological sensibility—the skilled way in which archaeologists have learned to approach the things they study. When approached archaeologically, the text becomes just one element in the larger material assemblage that forms Brooke's grave and can be considered in relation to the creation of the tomb by a Greek sculptor: a "medieval design adapted to Greek surroundings" (Maybin 2011).

In addition to the parts of the grave that are visible aboveground, an archaeological approach might attempt some degree of excavation—a strategic disassembling of the monument in order to gain insights into the processes by which it was assembled in the first place. This would presumably reveal that the structure now visible was added some time after the original burial, when stones were piled over the body and a simple wooden cross erected. Approached archaeologically, Rupert Brooke's grave would also need to be understood within the wider landscape. While the olive grove in which it is situated has become a place that is visited by literary pilgrims, the grave's presence on the island has also had an impact that extends beyond this location. In Skyros town, some distance away, a "statue of an ideal poet" has been erected in "Brooke Square" (Maybin 2011). Although the human body at the center of the tomb may have had its origins in England (the place that is referred to in the inscription), the tomb itself was materially constructed using locally sourced materials and labor, and its presence in Skyros has transformed the surrounding landscape to the extent that new sites have been created in the island's monumental landscape. Just as the tomb creates a space in Skyros for Brooke's English origins, the display case creates a space in Bloomsbury for the Africa of the eggshell's origins, suggesting that this object does not truly "belong" in Bloomsbury, unlike, perhaps, Rupert Brooke.

By juxtaposing the treatment of a nonhuman from overseas, encased in England, and a human from England, entombed overseas, and the similar technologies these involve, I hope to suggest some of the analytical and methodological possibilities offered by symmetrical anthropology. Bruno Latour developed the notion as a means of overcoming the "Great Divides" of the "Modern Constitution" (Latour 1993:103, 13)—between humans and nonhumans, on the one hand, and between "us," the moderns, and "them," the nonmoderns, on the other. According to Latour, these divides are created as part of projects of purification that seek to maintain the separateness of each category, at the very moment that hybrid forms are proliferating between them. Rather than reinforce these purificatory projects, a symmetrical anthropology would consider the processes of mediation and translation by which humans and nonhumans, as well as "modern" Westerners and others, become assembled into the hybrid assemblages that Latour has called actor-networks. In other words, symmetry is sought in the analytical treatment of human and nonhuman things, as well as of Westerners and others, categories that have frequently been treated separately by other anthropologies.

However, there is another sense in which anthropology needs a "complete overhaul and intellectual retooling" (Latour 1993:101) in order to become symmetrical. This relates to a project of purification that took place during the twentieth century within the discipline itself. A hundred years ago, anthropology was a subject that readily encompassed archaeological, ethnographic, ethnological, and biological approaches, but these have increasingly become separated from one another as a result of disciplinary projects of purification. The encompassing term "anthropology" has largely been claimed by those who conduct ethnography, who are concerned with documenting the unfolding processes of human life in the present (Ingold 2008a). Meanwhile, archaeology, primarily concerned with the past and its material remains, has become institutionally separated through the formation of separate institutional structures. This process is possibly best understood, at least in British universities, in relation to the development of social anthropology as a modernist project (Ardener 1985) with a peculiarly "presentist" approach (Fardon 2005). As well as neglecting the past, British social anthropology largely treated material things as markers of immaterial social relationships (Olsen 2007), rather than as the products of historical processes. Nevertheless, in "re-membering things" (Olsen 2003), it is not sufficient to conduct a "symmetrical archaeology" (Shanks 2007; Webmoor 2007; Witmore 2007) in parallel with Latour's "symmetrical anthropology." In order to become truly symmetrical, the center ground of a reunified anthropology needs to be reclaimed from asymmetrical ethnographers who, through a strong methodological commitment to engagement with humans in the present, have struggled to recognize the significance and agency of the nonhuman forms through which elements of the past remain present. When approaching something like the engraved ostrich eggshell at the British Museum, limiting one's focus of investigation to its contemporary context of social relations would be as restrictive as an exclusive focus on the South African past. Instead, it becomes necessary to regard the contemporary context as the outcome of processes of "incapsulation" (Collingwood 1946:114), in this case, literal ones, through which the products of past processes remain embedded in the present.

Nevertheless, reassembling archaeological and ethnographic approaches following a century of attempted purification is by no means straightforward. Andrew Sherratt (1993:128) has suggested that archaeology has two unique resources: "its access to the microstructures of daily life... and its ability to survey the grand sweep." By contrast, Alfred Gell (1998:10) has argued that anthropology has a particular depth of focus that is biographical and "attempts to replicate the time perspectives of...agents on themselves." He has also suggested that "the spaces of anthropology are those which are traversed by agents in the course of their biographies" (Gell 1998:11). At first glance, these two positions might seem to emphasize radically different orientations for archaeology and anthropology (or ethnography) as purified fields. However, they may be less contradictory than they appear if one considers how the "biographical" time perspective and its spatial correlate differ between human and nonhuman agents, given Gell's own arguments for the agency of nonhumans. While much ethnography has been shaped around the dimensions of space and time traversed by human agents in the course of their biographies, the archaeological sensibility has similarly been formed in relation to the temporal and spatial dimensions traversed by human-made things, or artifacts, in the course of theirs. Although human bodies have a biographical depth of focus that rarely exceeds a hundred years, artifacts can have biographies that, in the case of ancient stone hand axes, for example, have lasted well over a million years. At the same time, the lives of other, more fragile artifacts can be ephemeral and spatially limited. The archaeological sensibility, shaped as it is by a depth of focus specific to artifacts, is peculiarly able to consider the microstructures of daily life and the grand sweep in relation to each other, as Sherratt suggested, or the "act" in the context of the "life"—or more precisely, the "stage of life...of the agent," in Gell's (1998:10) terms.

In shaping my inquiry into the LMS collection around the temporal and spatial dimensions traversed by its objects in the course of their biographies, I have had to consider processes that operate over larger geographical scales and temporal depths than most temporally specialized historians or geographically specialized ethnographers would be comfortable with. Ethnography as a genre of writing and participant-observation as the method of study upon which it is based have considerable explanatory value when applied to the study of human "acts" and "lives," because of their biographical depth of focus. However, when we consider processes that operate on temporal and spatial dimensions that are beyond those traversed by human agents, this depth of focus can become restrictive. Whereas ethnography can be expanded spatially to become multi-sited (Marcus 1995), participant-observation cannot be expanded temporally beyond the life spans of the participant and observer. Although some anthropologists have attempted to address this by engaging with historical archives (e.g., Stoler 2009), I would argue that in order to engage with global processes that have unfolded over periods much longer than human lives, anthropology needs to reengage the archaeological sensibility. This allows a biographical depth of focus to be retained while the inquiry is expanded around the scales of time and space over which the biographies of artifacts operate. Considering the biographies of artifacts that were collected by the earliest LMS missionaries and that continue to survive in the present makes it possible to examine ongoing processes that have taken shape over the past two centuries.

Bringing an archaeological sensibility to the study of museums means being concerned with the material forms taken by these institutions, including their display cases, collections, and labels, and also with the processes through which these different elements have come to be assembled over time. It also means exploring the relationship between the publicly visible spaces of the museum and the hidden places where collections are stored. Approaching museums through an exclusive focus on their public display spaces would be like exploring an archaeological monument only in terms of the visible features that exist above ground. Bringing an archaeological sensibility to the study of museums means not only putting texts in their place as part of wider material assemblages but also excavating behind the immediately visible. It means being concerned with the ways in which museums operate in relation to processes that unfold over long periods of time and the ways in which past events impact the present. It also means considering the ways that museums and their collections are situated in wider landscapes, as "other" places, much like the burial places more commonly studied by archaeologists.

EXCAVATING OBJECTS

Museums, like monuments, tend to be fixed points in a landscape, but the things they contain, like the humans who visit them, are likely to have moved during the course of their biographies. Rupert Brooke was born in England, but by the time of his youthful death, he had already traveled to Germany, France, the United States, Canada, New Zealand, and Tahiti, where he lived for some time and may have fathered a child (Maybin 2011). Similarly, the engraved ostrich eggshell may have been originally laid and decorated in southern Africa, but it subsequently traveled to a number of other places before arriving at the British Museum in 1910. A great deal of work since the 1990s has attempted to locate the collecting of ethnographic artifacts in relation to colonial engagements and forms of exchange (e.g., Gosden and Knowles 2001; Henare 2005; Schildkrout and Keim 1998), just as other work has concentrated on the institutional histories of museums (e.g., Gosden, Larson, and Petch 2007; MacKenzie 2010; Penny 2003). Rather less attention has been paid to the lives of ethnographic objects between the time they were collected in the field and their acquisition by public museums. Michael O'Hanlon (2000:9) has proposed that in addition to the "scene of collecting" in the field, ethnographic collections have a "before," involving conditions of funding and prevalent attitudes at home, and an "after," which he suggested largely concerns their treatment at public museums. I would like to argue that in at least some cases, there may also be an important "in-between" stage. My attempt to reassemble the LMS collection is addressed at understanding the lives of objects following their arrival in Britain but before they became part of public collections. This has involved engaging an archaeological sensibility in order to tease out the surviving traces of these events. It has also meant attempting to develop a symmetrical approach that privileges neither their place of origin nor their contemporary location but attempts to trace the movement of things through the range of places and times in which they have been situated.

Uncovering the now dispersed LMS collection has involved treating individual objects from a range of contemporary museum collections as a series of related small-scale archaeological sites. This micro-excavation approach, which has been directed at the surfaces and appendages of museum objects, has made it possible to identify physical traces of some of the events in which different objects have been involved. This has suggested that, in many cases, much of the activity involving these objects occurred after their original manufacture. Some objects have holes in them where they were once tacked up for display (in some cases, the tacks are still in the holes). In many more cases, old labels are attached to or written onto these objects. Like other techniques and technologies, labeling is a form of action on matter that leaves traces that can be subsequently investigated. Excavating the LMS collection has involved trying to identify the physical traces that have been left on things by particular events in the course of their biographies and also the traces that particular things have left in documentary sources, whether textual or visual. Whereas some approaches have sought to understand "material culture as text" (Olsen 2003), I have approached texts and other documentary sources as, themselves, forms of material culture. Excavating these has made it possible to locate objects from the LMS collection in relation to particular events, during which they were associated with a range of other human and nonhuman things.

Archaeology has traditionally specialized in making sense of the traces of technological processes, and so it is to archaeological techniques that I have turned to help me make sense of the labels attached to objects from the LMS collection. In some examples, there are numerous labels attached to objects, and the overlapping edges of different labels have made it possible to establish the stratigraphic relations between them. The comparison of

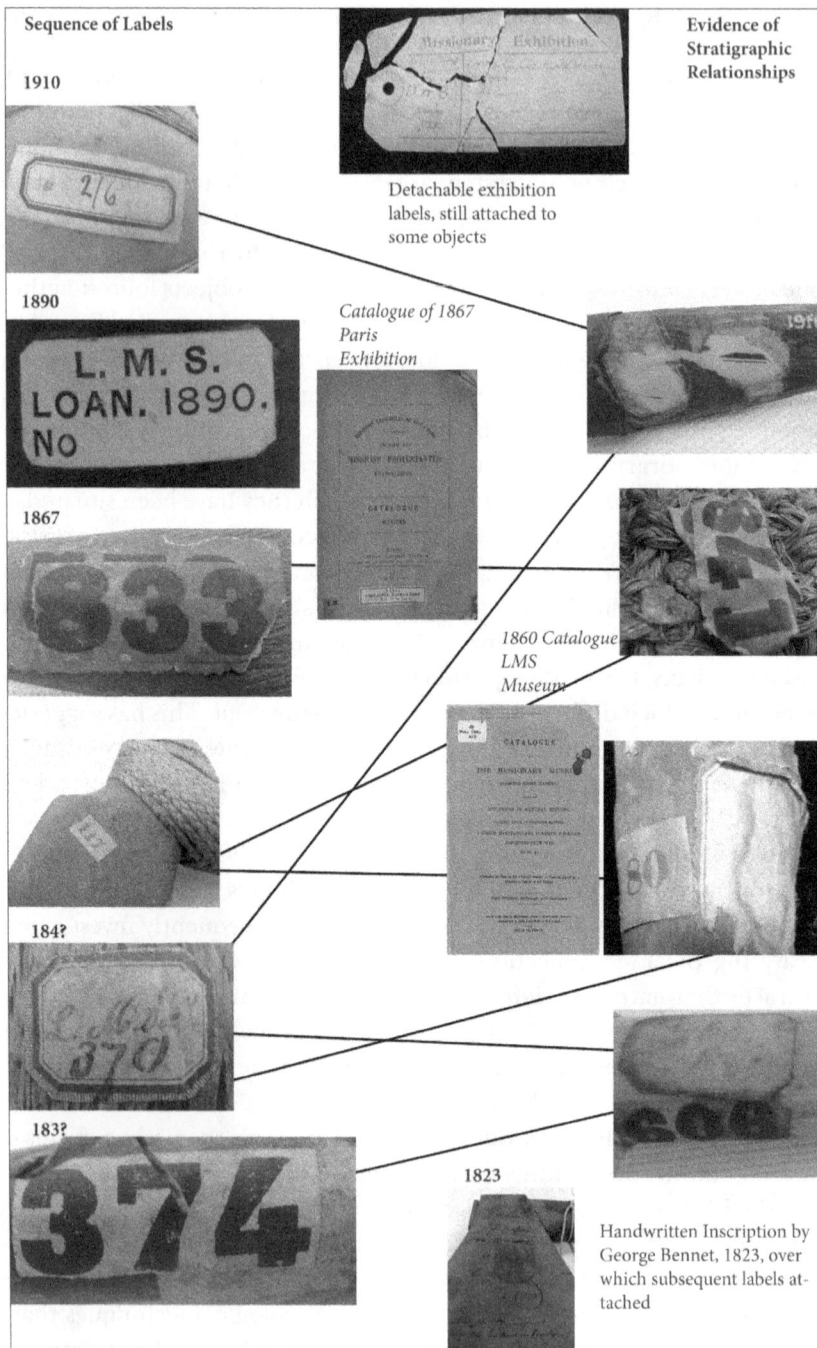

Sequence of Labels

1910

Detachable exhibition labels, still attached to some objects

Evidence of Stratigraphic Relationships

1890

Catalogue of 1867 Paris Exhibition

1867

1860 Catalogue LMS Museum

184?

183?

1823

Handwritten Inscription by George Bennet, 1823, over which subsequent labels attached

FIGURE 3.3

Diagram suggesting the sequence of and some of the relationships between key labels associated with objects from the LMS collection. © Chris Wingfield.

similar labels on different objects from the collection has also made it possible to establish a typology of these and to order them chronologically using archaeological techniques of contextual seriation (figure 3.3). By cross-referencing labels with surviving published catalogs of the LMS museum, it has been possible to secure absolute dates for a number of the key labels in the sequence. A catalog of the LMS museum, dating to around 1860, was associated with labels that were color-coded according to the mission fields from which the objects came, and many of these colored labels survive. Another set of numbered labels correlates with a catalog for an exhibition of 619 objects from the LMS collection that was mounted in 1867 at the Exposition Universelle in Paris in the Pavilion des Missions Protestantes Evangéliques (Vernes 1867). Some detachable labels are associated with exhibitions that were organized by the LMS across the British Isles during the first decade of the twentieth century, and another label type seems to have been added to objects from the collection immediately prior to their dispersal in 1910; many of these are marked with prices. Like the layers of reoccupation uncovered during archaeological excavations, successive labels reveal a series of instances when objects were reinscribed and put to new uses. Museum collections, like the places and structures studied in many fields of archaeology, are involved in ongoing processes of making and remaking, the traces of which can frequently be found overlaid on their original surfaces. Indeed, the sequence of identification labels attached to objects from the LMS collection is a continuous one and includes labels that have been added to objects comparatively recently, when they have been loaned to and acquired by public museums and private collectors. Nearly all the labels include a reference number of some kind, such as a museum accession number. This links the objects to the textual documents in which they were inscribed and allows them to be identified in relation to these traces. This number also frequently becomes central to the institutional identities of particular objects following their entry into museum collections.

MAKING MUSEUM OBJECTS

The biographies of things that formed part of the LMS collection provide a means of considering global processes that have operated over the past two centuries, and they also provide evidence of some of the smaller-scale events involved in shaping these. Anthropological accounts have long recognized that human biographies, although continuous, are marked by key events, when shifts in social position are ceremonially performed. Arnold Van Gennep (1909) famously described the structural patterns involved in rites of passage, which relocate human bodies from one social category to another, as involving three stages: separation through detachment, liminal isolation, and reincorporation or reintegration. Similarly, Igor Kopytoff (1986) has suggested that commodification might be regarded as a process that occurs during the biography of a thing, through which it is rendered "common," rather than "singular," and therefore exchangeable for other things. When the biographies of nonhuman artifacts are compared to those of humans, the ritual process and the commodification process appear to have much in common. Acts of exchange and rites of passage, symmetrically treated, appear to be analogous processes of transfer and transformation, and this suggests that just as rites of passage can be productively understood as a form of exchanging humans between groups (Allen 2000; Lévi-Strauss 1969[1949]), so transactions involving exchange can usefully be understood as forms of ritual.

In a consideration of the "objects of ethnography," Barbara Kirshenblatt-Gimblett (1998) has drawn on some of Van Gennep's terminology by describing collecting as a process of "detachment." If detachment is simply the first stage in any act of exchange, however, this makes it only a necessary rather than a sufficient condition for making museum objects. This is probably unsurprising, since the presence of a great many, if not the majority of, objects in museum collections is ultimately the outcome of transactions such as purchase or gift giving, which were not originally imagined as forms of collecting. Indeed, it is probably the accessioning of objects by museums, rather than their acquisition in the field, that involves the most clearly marked rites of detachment (Wingfield 2011). Most acts of exchange, after an initial detachment and possibly a period of isolation, subsequently involve reintegration, during which the things exchanged become embedded in new networks of relation. Might the donation of items to museums simply be understood as another instance of exchange, in which the museum's collection constitutes a new context into which they become reintegrated? At one level, this is the case. Nevertheless, by referring to the "objects of ethnography," Kirshenblatt-Gimblett (1998) is utilizing a distinction between "objects" and "things" that derives from the work of Heidegger (1962), in order to suggest that detachment plays a significant part in the "objectification" of particular artifacts. Chris Gosden has suggested that although "things" are embedded in the flow of life, an object is "an artefact separated from other associated artefacts and from people" (2004:39). While it is questionable whether any thing can truly become separated from the flow of life, which ultimately consists of much more than simply artifacts and people (Ingold 2011), the distinction between objects and things ultimately depends on the ways in which humans perceive and relate to them.

Many objects of ethnography are not the outcome of deliberate acts of field collecting involving detachment, but it is also the case that the majority of museum objects are not displayed and even those that have been on display do not cease to be "museum objects" when they are returned to the stores. Although the making of museum objects undoubtedly involves aspects of detachment, or alienation, in Marx's terms, and many museum objects do end up on display, both detachment and display are, arguably, relatively ephemeral events in the processes by which "things" become and remain "museum objects." In Van Gennep's (1909) characterization, one feature of the isolation phase in a rite of passage is that it includes humans undergoing some form of transformation. By attempting to detach something from the flow of life through ceremonial means and by locating this somewhere that is between one place and another, it becomes possible to regard both humans and nonhumans as isolated, alienated objects. This state is normally a temporary one that precedes their reincorporation into the ongoing processes of human life. What is peculiar about museum objects, as opposed to commodities for sale in shops and other contexts of exchange, is the expectation—or perhaps the fiction—that this period of isolation should be relatively permanent or at least long lasting.

In a consideration of commodity branding, David Wengrow (2008:21) has argued for a focus on the "concrete practices of marking and labelling." Commodities are goods that have been separated and packaged, ready for redistribution and reincorporation, and they are in a position that parallels human initiates who have passed through the separation phase of a rite of passage. Commodity brands mark these goods as uniform and substitutable, in the same way that the similarly substitutable bodies of initiates may be temporarily painted a uniform color or even marked more permanently by incisive practices such as circumcision. To use a familiar example, branded commodities are like pupils dressed in school uniforms, on which the institution stamps its authority through a school crest or logo. Whereas the commodity labels discussed by Wengrow are visually attractive, or at least striking, and are intended to display their uniformity—like the painted or uniformed bodies of initiates—this can only infrequently be said of the institutional labels applied to museum objects (figure 3.4). These have rather more in common with the labels applied to the bodies of inmates in institutions of confinement, such as prisons and asylums, where they are largely intended to facilitate institutional processing and tend to be more grimly bureaucratic.

It should be clear that what I have in mind are not the explanatory labels

that museums use to communicate information to visitors, such as those placed alongside the engraved ostrich eggshell on display at the British Museum, but rather the identification tags that are generally removed from museum objects when they are displayed. Whereas commodity labels, like those that accompany museum objects on display, frequently include a summary of information that is deemed to be significant, the labels attached to museum objects in storerooms frequently consist of little more than a number or code that allows the object to be identified when compared to a textual inventory. The presence of this label, even without the text to which it refers, suggests that the object in question belongs in an institution. Some institutional identity tags are designed to be easily removed, like the numbered wristbands attached to patients in a hospital, but others are intended to mark more or less permanently the surfaces of the objects to which they are attached. I hope I am not simply fulfilling Godwin's Law, that all discussions given enough time invoke Hitler and the Nazis (Godwin 1994), if I suggest the numbers permanently tattooed onto the skin of concentration camp inmates as an example of a permanent form of institutional marking. Electronic tags, barcodes, and computer databases are the latest of the bureaucratic technologies that are used to mark and also control the bodies of both human inmates and museum objects.

FIGURE 3.4

This carved figure, originally from Aitutaki, collected by the missionary John Williams and loaned to the British Museum in 1890, shows two London Missionary Society museum identity tags (Oc. LMS.38). © Trustees of the British Museum.

Although institutional identity tags, like commodity brands, are applied to things that have been detached and situated in "other" places, they nevertheless serve opposite functions. Commodity brands suggest that goods are equivalent and substitutable, or "common" in Kopytoff's (1986) terms. Identity tags, on the other hand, through the uniqueness of the number they include, suggest that the things they are attached to are unique and unsubstitutable, what Kopytoff calls "singular." Commodities generally pass through liminal "other" places on their way to reincorporation somewhere else, where their seals may be broken. The things that become incorporated in museum collections, on the other hand, may suggest themselves as suitable long-term residents of "other" places by being "matter out of place" (Douglas 2010[1966]). Some things become confined in museums as objects because of their removal from the place in which they were made, becoming Other through transportation. Some things become Other not through movement in space but because the passage of time allows them to seem "out of place" in the very locations at which they were made and used.

The numerous identity labels attached to the surfaces of museum objects from the LMS collection are suggestive of a series of rites of inscription, by which things have been continually reobjectified during the course of their biographies, most of which have been spent in museums. Just as it may be possible to read the marks of numerous ceremonial rites of passage from the various medals and badges attached to the dress uniform of a highly decorated soldier, so the numerous and repeated institutional confinements of certain museum objects can be read from their surfaces. As well as creating a stratigraphic series of labels that can be explored archaeologically, the repeated relabeling of the LMS collection has been a reiterative process by which things have been marked and inscribed as objects, or institutional inmates. This process can be understood as part of a purificatory practice through which the ongoing separation of these objects from the times and places in which they have existed has been ceremonially enacted. Technologies of inscription, such as labeling and cataloging, alongside the confinement of museum objects in locked storerooms and glass cases, have been part of an attempt to prevent the reincorporation of these objects into the flow of life at the locations in which they exist. Nevertheless, whereas rites of passage function as periodic enactments of particular social categories, in the case of human biographies, these rarely coincide with the physical processes of birth, maturation, and death, which they mark. Similarly, although rites of purification involving encasement, display, labeling, and cataloging have marked the surfaces of objects from the LMS collection, making their ongoing institutional separation visible, these enactments have not always been successful in restricting the engage-ments with objects in the LMS collection to those that have taken place in the controlled and liminal environments of museum display spaces.

REASSEMBLING THE ASSEMBLAGE

In arguing for a "renewed empiricism" as a way of reinvigorating the critical tradition, Latour (2004b:248) has suggested that "this would require that all entities, including computers, cease to be objects defined simply by their inputs and outputs and become again things, mediating, assem-bling, gathering." In many ways, this prescription describes a great deal of archaeological work, through which "objects," seemingly removed from the "flow of life," at least from a human perspective, become "things" that medi-ate an encounter with the past and around which people and things are gathered. While archaeology often begins with excavation, the strategic disassembly of things, it generally proceeds by reassembling them in order to understand the form they previously took. One example of this might be post-excavation work on the sherds of a pot. By refitting the different fragments, it can become possible to reassemble the pot into the approxi-mate shape it once had. By comparison with participant-observation, archaeological fieldwork may appear to be much more focused on docu-menting products than processes. Nevertheless, the work of archaeology involves the enactment of a whole series of processes in order to reassem-ble now disconnected fragments and to set them back in relation to one another. Whereas ethnography can be broadly defined as the documen-tation of processes as they unfold, archaeology generally begins with a product and attempts to resituate it in relation to the processes from which it was formed. Reassembling broken fragments of pottery can enable an archaeologist to understand the process by which it was shattered and also the processes of manufacture that gave it shape in the first place. In my research, the "pot" whose fragments I have excavated is the LMS collec-tion, and my attempts at reassembly have been directed at understanding both the processes through which it was created and those through which it was dispersed. Although labels have played a significant role in convert-ing things into museum objects, they have also become the means to reas-semble these objects with a range of other things by providing evidence of past associations. As traces of acts of inscription, labels become a means of demonstrating that, despite the ongoing institutional fiction that museum objects are detached specimens in "other" places, they have continued to be involved in a range of historical events.

In Latour's terms (2005), the LMS itself might be understood as an assemblage or actor-network, binding humans from around the globe together with a range of nonhuman entities. At the same time, the activities of this actor-network resulted in the creation of a material assemblage, to use this word in its more archaeological sense. The LMS museum collection was assembled in London from things that came from various locations around the world. While an archaeological assemblage may include a number of interesting things, the primary aim of careful archaeological excavation is not simply uncovering them. The disassembling of an archaeological assemblage through excavation is intended to reveal insights into its formation. This allows archaeologists to understand something of the involvement of humans in the processes that gave shape to what, at first sight, may appear to consist of only nonhuman objects. Imagine the excavation of a flint knapping site. By carefully recording the location of each of the fragments of stone and considering these in relation to the percussion marks left by the knapping process, it may be possible for a diligent archaeologist to reconstruct not only the sequence of human actions that created these but also the physical location in which these took place. Even without the finished axe that was the ultimate result of these actions, it may be possible to reconstruct its shape from the remaining fragments and thus gain an understanding of the intentions that shaped human actions in the remote past.

Approaching the LMS collection as an archaeological assemblage that can shed light on the operation of the LMS as a whole has involved attempting to reassemble it. Much of my research has been directed at excavating a number of contemporary public museum collections where objects that once formed part of the LMS collection can now be found. In the first instance, this has involved working with online museum databases. These are partial sources of information, and they privilege particular kinds of information, such as the "source" from which the museum acquired its objects (Wingfield 2011). This has made it relatively easy to identify 453 objects at the British Museum, the Pitt Rivers Museum, and the Horniman Museum that were acquired directly from the LMS in 1910, since the databases record the LMS as the source of this material. Other materials were acquired from the LMS collection by private collectors, and these have not always followed a straightforward itinerary into public collections. The majority of A. W. F. Fuller's collection is now at the Field Museum in Chicago, where database documents identify the source of this material as Fuller himself. By working with electronic and paper records, audio recordings of Fuller talking about his collection, and archival documents now located in Hawaii, it has been possible to identify 162 objects from the

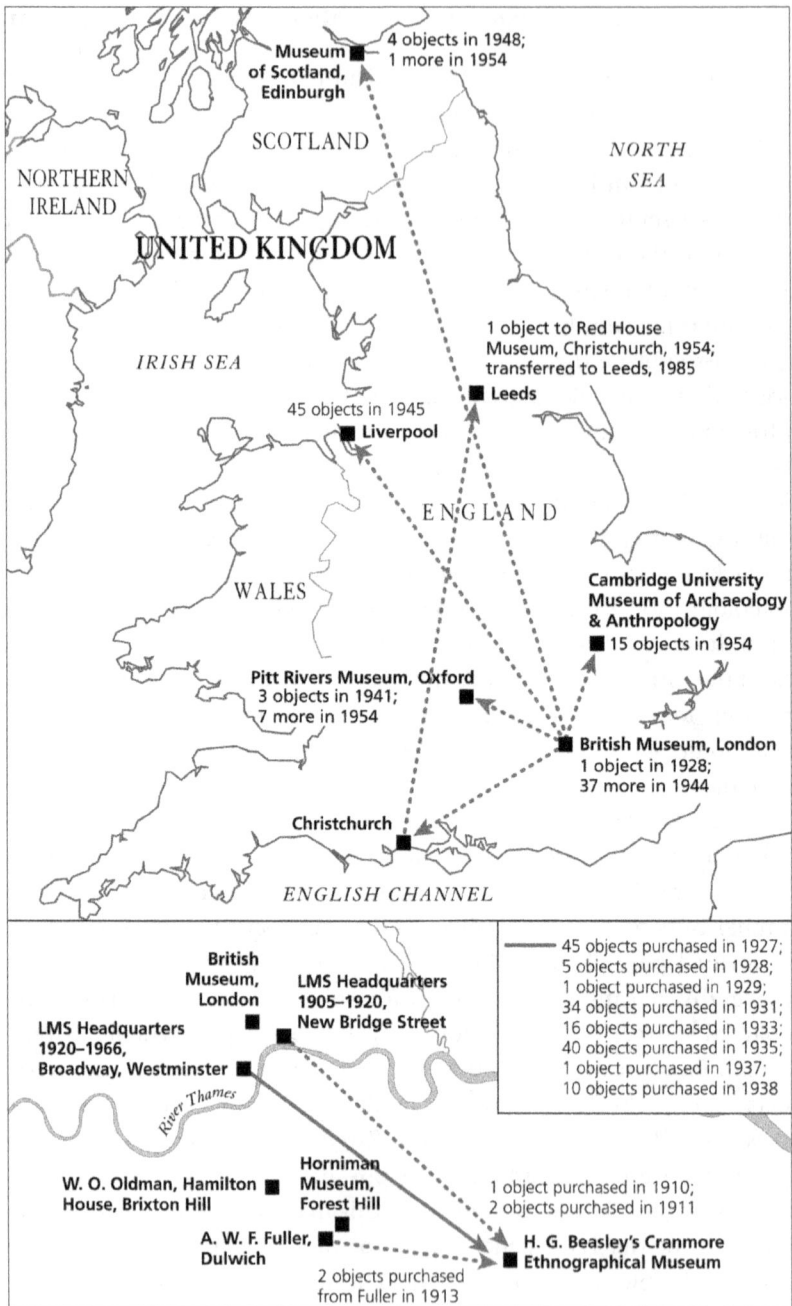

FIGURE 3.5

Maps showing the museums to which the collector Harry Beasley sent materials that had been in the LMS collection and the locations from which these materials were acquired. Information supplied by Lucie Carreau. Map by Molly O'Halloran.

LMS collection now at the Field Museum. At the same time, because Fuller acquired material from the LMS on a number of occasions during the first half of the twentieth century, it has been possible to definitively identify only 3 objects that were acquired when the museum closed in 1910. Other material from the LMS collection was acquired by Harry Beasley, whose collection was subsequently dispersed among a large number of public collections (see figure 3.5). The dealer W. O. Oldman also acquired material from the LMS collection, which he seems to have supplied to public museums around the world and to private collectors. Although documentary records of Oldman's purchases have made it possible to identify the materials he acquired in 1910, identifying their current locations has not proved possible so far. As with the reassembly processes involved in most other forms of archaeological work, not all the necessary components survive, meaning that the possibility of complete reassembly is limited by processes of survival and recovery.

COLLECTION AS PROCESS

As well as being concerned with processes of assemblage formation, the archaeological sensibility has been shaped by a concern with the processes involved in deposition—how it is that things came to be located where they have been found. The flint axe made at the knapping site discussed above might be discovered some hundreds of miles from the place where it was evidently manufactured. "Findspots" for particular artifact types are sometimes plotted on distribution maps, which are used in attempts to reconstruct the ways in which particular types of goods moved around a landscape. If a highly localized source of a material can be identified, such as with volcanic obsidian, then the distances of findspots from this source can be used as an indicator of the extent of regional networks of exchange. If the museums in which objects from the LMS collection are now found are regarded as "sites of deposition," or findspots, then their locations can similarly be used in relation to the places from which their objects originate, as indicators of the scale and direction of the processes by which these things were relocated from one place to another. When considering what has survived at particular locations, archaeologists are aware that not all things survive equally well. "Taphonomy" is the term given to the study of the processes by which things decay or are preserved in the archaeological record, and it seems that a consideration of taphonomic processes is no less important when considering what survives in museum collections. When developing an exhibition of objects collected by George Grenfell, an early

Baptist missionary in the Congo, at Birmingham Museum, I was intrigued by the absence of *nkisi* figures in his collection, as these are a characteristic feature of many other contemporary collections. When I spoke to members of the church where the collection had been stored for ninety years before being acquired by the museum, I heard stories about such objects being deliberately destroyed in the past.[1] It is this sort of taphonomic process that must be considered when approaching contemporary museum collections as archaeological deposits. Getting a handle on the range of events that can take place between the moment when an artifact is detached from its maker and the detachment involved in becoming part of a public museum collection is a step toward understanding these processes. Only then can any insight be gained into the degree to which museum collections are representative of the range of artifacts that were involved in the historic processes of exchange and encounter that unfolded between people from different parts of the world (Byrne et al. 2011a).

In the process of attempting to reassemble the collection of the LMS as a material assemblage and developing an understanding of the taphonomic processes by which disassembled elements have survived in various public collections, it has become clear that the LMS collection never existed in a finished or static form. Although a museum collection can be regarded as the product of the processes from which it has been formed, in many cases these processes have been continuous and ongoing. An archaeological assemblage provides a snapshot of things found together at a particular moment, but in attempting to reassemble the LMS collection, it became impossible to decide on a moment to "freeze-frame" this assemblage (Latour 2010:99). Instead, the documents in which objects had been inscribed at particular moments, as part of rites of inscription, became snapshots of the developing collection and of events that involved processes of assemblage but also dispersal. A large number of objects from the collection were dispersed when the LMS museum closed in 1910, but others were transferred into a loans collection, from which they continued to circulate as part of missionary exhibitions. Rather than the LMS collection existing as a finished product, both collection and dispersal processes took place alongside each other continually. When the LMS museum closed in 1910, a number of significant objects had already been on long-term loan to the BM for twenty years. However, even as the main museum collection was dispersed, additional collections continued to arrive in London, brought by returning missionaries. The closer my examination of the processes through which the collection had been assembled and dispersed, the more apparent it became that what I was documenting was not the formation of the collection as a single entity but rather the continuous movements of particular things in and out of a number of points of assembly.

Andrew Moutu (2007) has suggested that collection be thought of as a way of being, and it is precisely this way of understanding collection— as process rather than product—that I am proposing here. In addition, collection as a process needs to be considered alongside its counterpart, dispersal—assemblage alongside disassemblage—since they are parallel and connected processes. The disassemblage of the LMS collection contributed to the assemblage of private collections by Fuller and Beasley and public collections at the British Museum, the Pitt Rivers Museum, and the Horniman Museum. In the case of a dealer like Oldman, processes of collection and dispersal unfolded continually alongside each other, allowing him to make a living. At an archaeological excavation, the disassemblage of a site through excavation requires the assemblage of a team of excavators and their tools, places for them to sleep, and food to feed them. Archaeological excavation and the forms of documentation it uses enable the creation of a static snapshot of an assemblage that is in the process of undergoing gradual dispersal through decomposition and erosion. While the archaeological sensibility has been formed largely through the consideration of material assemblages at particular moments of excavation, the "archaeological imagination" (Shanks 2012) has developed as a means of attempting to situate these discrete snapshots in relation to the long-term processes from which they emerge. Although I have concentrated on describing some of the processes by which the LMS collection was assembled, the ultimate goal of this research has been to enable a reimagining of the longer-term processes of assemblage and disassemblage involved in the formation and dispersal of the LMS collection (Wingfield 2012).

HYBRIDITY, PURIFICATION, AND INDIGENEITY

When the engraved ostrich eggshell arrived at the BM with its stand, rather than being a "pure" African object as suggested by its current label, it had already been transformed: from a vessel for carrying water, into a museum object. Having been relocated to London and displayed in the LMS museum, it became involved in processes of mobilization that would ultimately gather and direct resources back to the place from which it had come. In being described only in terms of its manufacture in southern Africa, without its historic display stand, the ostrich eggshell had become a hybrid object, effectively purified at the British Museum. This suggests that museum technologies of labeling, display, and conservation might be usefully understood in terms of Latour's projects of purification. Approaching the engraved ostrich eggshell symmetrically therefore involves attempting to understand it as an object that has emerged from a long-term history of engagement between Britain and southern Africa, which is perpetuated through its ongoing display in the "African" galleries of the BM. It may seem that by arguing for the recognition of the hybridity of ethnographic objects, I am minimizing the ongoing claims that indigenous groups in different parts of the world may have on these things. This need not be the case, however, if the category of indigeneity is, itself, recognized as something that is the product of a similar project of purification.

James Clifford (1997:213) famously suggested that museums be thought of as "contact zones," both prescriptively and descriptively. The term, however, was coined by Mary Louise Pratt to reshape understandings of the frontier as "the space of colonial encounters, the space in which peoples geographically and historically separated come into contact with each other and establish ongoing relations, usually involving conditions of coercion, radical inequality, and intractable conflict" (Pratt 1992:6–7). Nevertheless, a number of issues arise when this concept is applied to the space of museums. In the first place, the contact zone's concentration on "people" is profoundly asymmetrical, privileging encounters between humans at the expense of encounters that took place between humans and nonhumans, sometimes at some remove from the geographical zone that was formerly described as the frontier. At another level, the notion of the contact zone emphasizes historical and geographical separation. Many of the encounters that take place in museums today occur between peoples who have long histories of contact, for whom material exchanges with one another have become an everyday occurrence. In these instances, the frontier, or contact zone, has moved on and "contact" has become an unremarkable event. In these cases, the museum space, where separateness is emphasized and the historical encounters of the contact zone are reenacted, is not a "contact zone" but a "purification zone."

When Gregory Bateson considered the possible long-term consequences of contact between two groups that had been historically and geographically separated, he suggested that theoretically this could result in three possible patterns: "(a) the complete fusion of the originally different groups; (b) the elimination of one or both groups; (c) the persistence of both groups in dynamic equilibrium within one major community" (1973[1935]:38). In many cases, the encounters that take place between different groups in contemporary museums are best understood in relation to Bateson's third alternative. They are engagements between groups that now form part of a single integrated field of social relations. These engagements play a role in maintaining an equilibrium of interaction that allows both groups to continue to exist, a process Bateson termed "schismogenesis." Although contemporary museum engagements may be staged to appear as contact between groups that are distinct, this is a performance and one that creates a particular illusion. It is an illusion much like that presented by a Möbius strip, whose opposite sides appear to be two different faces. By tracing the surface of a Möbius strip with one's finger, however, it becomes possible to see that what appeared to be two differently oriented surfaces form connected parts of what is ultimately a single plane. Similarly, when the groups that are performed in museum spaces are traced beyond the moments when encounters are reenacted, their degree of mutual involvement becomes much clearer. Many historically and geographically separated groups, through generations of interaction, have come to function as part of a single field of social relations. Nevertheless, their differences from one another continue to be ceremonially performed as part of events that are enacted in ritual spaces of purification, including museums. Bringing an archaeological sensibility to the study of museums may involve looking beneath the ways in which collections are displayed in public galleries, but when applied symmetrically to humans, it entails looking beyond the performances enacted in museum spaces.

Although processes of translation, blending, and mixing have proliferated at the intersection between indigenous peoples and settlers and between colonized and colonizers, the category of indigeneity asserts an essential distinctiveness that purifies these now blended categories. In South Africa, the imposition of apartheid (literally, separateness) graphically illustrates a state-led process of purification along similar lines, and some of the earliest areas targeted for destruction were the mixed urban neighborhoods of District 6 and Sophiatown. An engraved ostrich eggshell might, by contrast, appear to be an emblematic symbol of the indigenous speakers of Khoisan languages in southern Africa. My own experience of conducting fieldwork in the Kalahari, however, has suggested the numerous ways in which even the apparently "ancient" indigenous technologies involved in the processing of ostrich eggshells have become entangled with the wider contemporary world (Wingfield 2005). Indeed, many of the "indigenous" peoples of the Kalahari who make beads from ostrich eggshells have European ancestors. A category of pure, untouched indigenous identity, which exists "out of time" (Thomas 1989), beyond the influences of global historical processes, is one that few indigenous people, or the things they make, would be able to fulfill. In southern Africa today, many more people acknowledge a degree of mixing and blending in their ancestry and cultural traditions than those who maintain that they belong to a pure indigenous tradition. Arguing for the acknowledgment of the mobile hybrid lives of ethnographic objects can be a way of suggesting that they might be regarded as the legitimate heritage of people who do not live lives that are defined entirely in relation to one purified cultural tradition or another. At certain points in southern African history, groups with both European and African ancestors have proudly identified their mixed heritage. A symmetrical anthropology would be one in which these peoples, and the things they and their ancestors have made, would be taken seriously rather than be either politely ignored or pressured to identify themselves as "indigenous" and thus purify their identities.

At the same time, it would hardly be symmetrical to emphasize the hybridity that challenges the category of indigeneity without suggesting that the terms against which it is defined, whether settler, colonizer, European, or "modern," are similarly illusory. Achieving symmetry involves acknowledging that the proliferation of hybrids undermines the purity of all these categories. Moves have been made toward acknowledging the debts that colonial culture owes to encounters with indigenous peoples in settler societies in North America (White 1991), the Pacific (Thomas 1994), and southern Africa (Russell and Russell 1979). Nevertheless, the cultural practices of Europe have sometimes seemed to exist apart from encounters with other regions of the world (Johnson 2006), propelled by the unfolding of entirely internal historical dynamics. It is important that a symmetrical anthropology emphasize the real debts that cultural practices in Europe owe to exchanges with peoples from other places, although these exchanges were not symmetrical. Europe sent large numbers of humans to other parts of the world, where they created frontiers, or contact zones, until the period following the Second World War, but it was largely non-humans that traveled in the other direction. Tracking the movements of non-European artifacts to Britain as part of the LMS collection and their circulation in Europe is a way of exploring how Europe itself became enmeshed in the processes of hybridization that emerged from these conditions of exchange. It may seem that acknowledging the essential hybridity of cultural practices in all parts of the world would suggest a shapeless melange of homogenizing globalization. However, the promise of Latour's symmetrical anthropology is of the precise location in space and time of the flows, mediations, and assemblages that emerge from the proliferation of hybrids that has been one of the results of the ongoing interactions between humans and nonhumans, Westerners and non-Westerners, the past and the present.

CONCLUSION

Exploring the LMS collection through temporal and spatial dimensions that have been shaped around its artifacts, many of which were collected by LMS missionaries in the early nineteenth century and continue to survive in the present, has made it possible to consider processes of assemblage and disassemblage that have taken place over the course of the past two centuries. This has also made it possible to consider whether the presence of objects from the LMS collection has had an impact on the island of Britain in the same way that the burial of Rupert Brooke in an orange grove in Skyros has transformed that island in various ways. Despite institutional technologies that appear to confine and limit the movement of physical objects to within the controlled and purified spaces of museums, some objects from the LMS collection have circulated much more widely. The engraved ostrich eggshell at the British Museum has achieved a twenty-first-century circulation beyond the "African" galleries by illustrating the front cover of *Africa: Arts and Cultures* (Mack 2000), a book published for a popular audience.

Meanwhile, Steven Hooper (2007) has described the ways in which A'a, a Polynesian "god" from the London Missionary Society collection (figure 3.6), came to inspire both Henry Moore and Pablo Picasso, to the extent that each owned a cast of it. Although the prototype remained under lock and key at the British Museum, these indexes of the "fractal god" (Gell 1998:137) became associated with humans who were effecting the transformation of Europe in the name of "modernity." Like the rhizomes considered by Deleuze and Guattari (2004[1987]), elements of the London Missionary Society collection seem to have been able to overlap with other formations and throw out runners to root in fertile new ground. While missionaries and the things they took with them played a considerable part in transforming the areas of the world to which they went, the objects they brought back and the knowledge with which these became associated had a symmetrical impact on life in Europe. Although museum architecture may have been intended to create a purified, separated "other" space (Duncan 1995), in which things from other places and other times could be safely accumulated and maintained in conditions of separation (Foucault 1986), an approach to museums that builds on an archaeological sensibility needs to consider these monumental structures and the collections they contain in relation to the impacts these have had on their wider landscape.

If the heart of the LMS, as an actor-network, was in Britain, then from an anthropological point of view this is a heart of darkness. Much has been presumed about Europe as a source of Christianity, commerce, and

FIGURE 3.6

A'a, a deity figure originally from Rurutu (Oc.LMS.19), has had a complex subsequent biography, including as casts owned by Henry Moore and Pablo Picasso. © Trustees of the British Museum.

civilization, or even modernity (Chakrabarty 2000), but all of these notions have developed around perceived contrasts with other parts of the world.

Ethnographic investigations have revealed there to be more civilization, commerce, and, increasingly, Christianity in other places than missionary (and modernizing) rhetoric gave them credit for. Investigating the anatomy of the heart of the LMS by considering the ways in which things brought there from the periphery flowed through it to other parts of the network is a way of shedding light on a location that is probably better known through myths than maps at present. Nevertheless, the potential for anatomical investigations into a lifeless heart are limited, making it important to regard the LMS collection in relation to the processes of both assemblage and disassemblage, which moved objects around the network like the beating of a heart circulates blood around a body. Studying the London Missionary Society through reassembling its collection has meant considering the society in its "dynamic or physiological state" in order to "perceive what is essential, the way everything moves" (Mauss 1990:79–80).

Note

1. Grenfell's collection was kept in a memorial room at his former church in Birmingham from 1907, when a memorial was set up following his death, until 1996, when the church donated it to the museum. One person from the church remembered dressing up in some of the material but particularly recalled the spears. When I inquired as to where these were, since they were not in the collection I had examined at the museum, I was told that they had been stored in the old baptistry, which had been covered over with a new floor, presumably with the spears still inside.

4

Assembling and Governing Cultures "at Risk"

Centers of Collection and Calculation, from the Museum to World Heritage

Rodney Harrison

How large has the earth become in their chart rooms? No bigger than an *atlas* the plates of which may be flattened, combined, reshuffled, superimposed, redrawn at will. What is the consequence of this change? The cartographer *dominates* the world that dominated Lapérouse [*sic*].... A center (Europe) has been constituted that begins to make the rest of the world turn around itself. One other way of bringing about the same Copernican revolution is to gather *collections.* The shapes of the lands have to be coded and drawn in order to become mobile, but this is not the case for rocks, birds, plants, artifacts, works of art.... Thus the history of science is in large part the history of the mobilization of anything that can be made to move and shipped back home for this universal census.

—*Bruno Latour,* Science in Action

RISK, LOSS, AND THE ASSEMBLING OF "CULTURE" IN MUSEUMS AND HERITAGE REGISTERS

I begin by bringing together two statements, written just over a century apart, that present arguments for the formation of different kinds of collections. The first was written by Alfred Cort Haddon in his introduction to *Head-Hunters: Black, White, and Brown* (1901), a popular account of the Cambridge Anthropological Expedition to the Torres Strait, New Guinea, and Borneo. The expedition was responsible for the collection of thousands of objects and recordings of indigenous people (including photographs, films, wax cylinder recordings, quantitative observations of physiology, and volumes of handwritten field notes), which were subsequently removed and relocated to the University of Cambridge's Museum of Archaeology and Anthropology in England (and elsewhere).

In 1888 I went to Torres Straits to study the coral reefs and marine zoology of the district; whilst prosecuting these studies I naturally came much into contact with the natives, and soon was greatly interested in them. I had previously determined not to study the natives, having been told that a good deal was known already about them; but I was not long in discovering that much still remained to be learned. Indeed, it might be truly said that practically nothing was known of the customs and beliefs of the natives, even by those who we had every reason to expect would have acquired that information.

Such being the case, I felt it to be my duty to gather what information I could when not actually engaged in my zoological investigations. I found, even then, that the opportunities of learning about the pagan past of the natives were limited, and that it would become increasingly more difficult, as the younger men knew comparatively little of the former customs and beliefs, and the old men were dying off. (Haddon 1901:vii)

The second comprises two extracts from the proclamation of the listing in 2003 of *kusiwa*, the "Oral and Graphic Expressions of the Wajapi," on the register of UNESCO's Masterpieces of the Oral and Intangible Heritage of Humanity, which is stored, among other places, on a set of paper and digital files held at the UNESCO headquarters in Paris.

The Wajapi of the Tupi-guarani cultural-linguistic group are indigenous to the northern Amazonian region. Some 580 Wajapi live in 40 small villages on a specially designated territory in the state of Amapá. The Wajapi have a long history of using vegetable dyes to adorn their bodies and objects with geometric motifs. Over the centuries, they have developed a unique communication system—a rich blend of graphic and verbal components—that reflects their world-view and enables them to hand down knowledge about community life. (UNESCO 2011)

This graphic art is known as kusiwa and its designs are applied with red vegetable dyes extracted from the roucou plant mixed with scented resins.... Although the Wajapi live on their protected territory, their traditional lifestyle, including the practice of kusiwa, is in danger of losing its symbolic significance and may even disappear altogether. Such a loss would drastically alter the community's social and cosmological reference points. The principal threats stem from disinterest on the part of the younger generation and the decreasing number of Wajapi proficient in the kusiwa repertory. (UNESCO 2011)

What connects these statements, separated by both time and space, and the assemblages they describe, which are manifested in such different material forms, is the way in which both forms of collection are troubled by the specter of *risk*, an ominous, creeping threat of vulnerability to loss. In this chapter, I argue that it is this sense of risk and loss that haunts and helps account for the development of both late nineteenth- and early twentieth-century ethnographic museum collections and the various cultural heritage lists and registers that were created throughout the twentieth century and into the early twenty-first.[1] I suggest that both might be understood to represent centers of (and for) collection and calculation as defined by Bruno Latour (1987; see also Bennett, chapter 2, this volume). Latour uses this term in his model of the construction of scientific knowledge to describe the production and accumulation of "immutable and combinable mobiles"—objects, specimens, charts, maps, tables, field notebooks, and other recorded observations—which are collected from the peripheries (or "field") and returned to a center where they are combined and interpreted in different ways. This allows centers of calculation to "act at a distance" (1987:229) through the same networks of collection and distribution by which the mobiles are returned and through new networks that are created as a result of the assembling and reassembling of these mobiles at the center. In suggesting that both museums and heritage registers can profitably be viewed as centers of collection, I seek to draw the processes and forms of agency involved in the formation of ethnographic museum collections into closer conversation with those that have contributed to the development of the various UNESCO World Heritage Lists (including the UNESCO Lists of Intangible Cultural Heritage).[2] I argue not only that they share their raison d'être as assemblages brought together in response to perceived risk, but also that they are a product of a single genealogy, sharing intellectual and institutional histories. Similarly, both reflect anthropological debates about "culture" and ways of dealing with the relationship of the universal to the particular. In many ways, the shift from the physical accumulation of objects in museums to the virtual collection of places and practices in situ by way of registers and lists such as the World Heritage Lists is a reflection of a regulatory shift from colonial and imperial forms of governance to nationalist and transnational forms as a result of globalization processes.

This regulatory shift maps onto an intellectual shift from an anthropology dominated by the concept of "civilization," understood temporally, to one of "culture," understood spatially.

By reassembling the threads that connect international heritage preservation organizations and museums and by conceptualizing both as centers of (and for) collection and calculation, we can learn more about both the processes of heritage production in the late twentieth and early twenty-first centuries *and* the processes of ethnographic museum formation that took place a century before. This has broad implications not only for the way we understand the rise of intangible heritage in the late twentieth century in relation to forms of minority and indigenous agency, but also the ways in which we might locate indigenous agency in the formation of ethnographic museum collections in the past and present. In particular, I follow Tony Bennett's (1995) argument regarding the universal mission of museums to explore the ways in which indigenous peoples and other ethnic minorities have made counterclaims to representation in World Heritage since its introduction in the 1970s alongside the growth of international indigenous rights movements, which mirror earlier developments relating to their representation within ethnographic museums. I also explore the ways in which lists such as the World Heritage Lists "materialize" and stand in for objects, places, and practices and, in doing so, continue older museological forms of governance in categorizing and maintaining the boundaries between humans and "things."

THE TWILIGHT OF THE ETHNOGRAPHIC COLLECTION AND THE EMERGENCE OF THE HERITAGE REGISTER

When we consider the history of museum collections, we tend to consider them to be relics of specific collecting practices, rooted in a Western European tradition, that reached their zenith with the rise of scientific rationalism and the development of a new conception of the public sphere in the eighteenth and nineteenth centuries (e.g., Pearce 1995; Belk 1995; Bennett 1995, 2004; MacKenzie 2010:1–3). As noted in the introduction to this volume, the rise of ethnographic collections in museums in Western Europe was closely associated with the projects of colonialism (e.g., Thomas 1991; MacKenzie 2010) and imperialism (e.g., Coombes 1994; Barringer and Flynn 1998; Henare 2005) and the development of the professional field of anthropology (e.g., Hinsley 1981a; Stocking 1985; Sturtevant 1969). George Stocking (1985:7) has suggested that the high period of museum anthropology began with the foundation of Harvard University's Peabody Museum in 1860 and ended around 1920 (see also Jacknis 1985). This great age of museum anthropology in the Anglo American tradition coincided with a period of intensive ethnographic collecting (e.g., Hinsley 1981a; Schildkrout and Keim 1988; Coombes 1994; Küchler 1997; Herle and Rouse 1998; O'Hanlon and Welsch 2000; Gosden and Knowles 2001). The demise of museum anthropology and its associated collecting has been attributed to several factors, including the ascendance of functionalist approaches to anthropology (e.g., Stocking 1985), the emergence of participant ethnography as the favored anthropological research method (e.g., Buchli 2002:4), the shift from the museum to the university as a locus for the intellectual development of anthropology (Sturtevant 1969:623; Jacknis 1985; Stocking 1985; see discussion in Hicks 2010), and the shrinking of the former Western European empires through processes of decolonization, processes that accelerated with the achievement of independence by the various colonies and protectorates in Asia and Africa following the Second World War (Coombes 1994). With one or two notable exceptions (e.g., the 1948 American-Australian Scientific Expedition to Arnhem Land; see May 2010), intensive ethnographic field collecting expeditions had all but ceased by the 1940s.

The impetus for the development of such ethnographic collections derived from the relationship between natural history collections and emerging research in the biological sciences in the mid-nineteenth century in Europe (Herle 1998:80; O'Hanlon 2000); museums were to assemble complete sets of material culture with which to reconstruct the cultures that they were "modernizing" in the process of collecting. Johannes Fabian (1983) and James Clifford (1988:202, 1997) have drawn our attention to the fact that the narratives of ethnography rest on an allegory of modernity in which the non-Western world is always in decline, which defines the project of collecting cultures as one of salvaging the authentic in the wake of the modernization of the tribal world. These collections were the very essence of a colonial narrative that fossilized indigenous cultures by treating them as "pure," essential, uncreolized (Thomas and Losche 1999), placed firmly in the distant past (Thomas 1999b:109; Bennett 2004), and, most important, "doomed" to extinction (Griffiths 1996; McGregor 1997). Bennett's *The Birth of the Museum* (1995) has been particularly important in showing how museums were developed within the context of a new governmental relationship with culture in which particular artifacts and their representations could be put to work in developing normative notions of culture that could then be employed within regimes of social management. Museums thus had a function in providing an ordered model of culture that reinforced evolutionary notions of social and technological progress.

Integral to these notions of progress was the idea of "civilization," organized according to a temporal model. This is clearly reflected in the work of early anthropologists such as Edward Burnett Tylor (e.g., 1920[1871]) and in the typological schemes developed by Lieutenant General Augustus Henry Lane Fox Pitt Rivers and extended by Henry Balfour (Bennett 2004; Gosden, Larson, and Petch 2007).

The demise of museum anthropology is conventionally discussed in relation to the work of anthropologist Franz Boas, who rejected the evolutionary models of culture that dominated late nineteenth-century museum anthropology and developed the contextual or relativistic approach, which became central to anthropological notions of culture in the twentieth century (Sturtevant 1969; Jacknis 1985; Conn 1998; Bouquet 2001). Boas suggested that the principles of order, classification, and completeness upon which the ethnographic collection had been founded were not relevant to the development of anthropology, which should focus on the mental processes behind artifact production and not on the artifacts themselves (Conn 1998:108). Similarly, the notion of culture as a normative principle (i.e., as "high culture") and the evolutionary principles upon which the museum had been founded, which suggested that humans produced different artifacts based on different stages of cultural development, were rejected for a holistic notion of culture that acknowledged that each culture established its own standards and notions of value (Boas 1887). Following from this, Boas suggested that cultures could not be reduced to particular physical artifact "types," or forms (Boas 1940); hence, "cultures" could not be "collected." He argued that collecting and exhibition practices should focus on the regional diversity of cultures and the relationship between different forms of material culture and the broad domains of activity in which they figured within particular societies. His work drew the entire museological project into question and contributed to a shift from a focus on civilization, expressed temporally, to a focus on culture, expressed geographically.[3] This change in focus from a universal culture to multiple cultures "in place" had an important influence not only on shifting the location of the anthropological "laboratory" (cf. Bennett 2010) from the museum to the field but also on reorganizing forms of collection that, like Latour's atlases, required cultures to be codified and redrawn to make them mobile, collectable, and ultimately combinable (Latour 1987:224–225; see also Bennett, chapter 2, this volume) so that they could be put to use to other ends in the metropolitan centers.

The principles of cultural relativism articulated by Boas and his students had a major influence on notions of culture throughout the twentieth century, although it failed to find realization as a principle of moral relativism in the work of the United Nations Commission on Human Rights, which prepared the Universal Declaration of Human Rights (1948). Article 27 of the declaration made participation in the cultural life of one's community a universal human right:

> (1) Everyone has the right freely to participate in the cultural life of the community, to enjoy the arts and to share in scientific advancement and its benefits. (2) Everyone has the right to the protection of the moral and material interests resulting from any scientific, literary or artistic production of which he is the author.

This articulation of the universal human right to participate in the cultural life of a community had a major influence on the development of the Universal Copyright Convention (1952), the first international heritage safeguarding campaigns in Egypt and elsewhere after 1960, and the subsequent development of the Convention Concerning the Protection of the World Cultural and Natural Heritage (1972), which established the World Heritage List (see Harrison 2012).

Meanwhile, during the postwar period, the ongoing existence of ethnographic collections in museums became a source of anxiety and the stimulus for an increasingly exhaustive investigation and reimagination of the notion of the modern museum (e.g., Clifford 1988; Vergo 1989). In France, debates surrounding the museum's role in the expression of cultures as regionally distinctive and territorially defined in the Musée de l'Homme under the directorship of Paul Rivet (see Bennett, chapter 2, this volume) had an impact not only on the subsequent development of the *ecomusée* concept but also on the foundation in 1947 of an International Council of Museums (ICOM) under the auspices of UNESCO. The council played a major role in the subsequent globalization of museum practices, promoting education, exhibitions, and restitution as core museological concerns. It was also involved in linking up the practices of museum professionals with those in the heritage sector more generally through its relationship with UNESCO. This was also a period in which decolonized and indigenous peoples began to call for the repatriation of human ancestral remains and objects of national and local cultural significance from museums, a process that accelerated in the decades after 1970 (e.g., Greenfield 1996; Fforde, Hubert, and Turnbull 2002; Kramer 2006; Cuno 2008). The very nature of museums as collecting institutions was brought into question, and their ongoing role in late modern societies seemed increasingly uncertain. What was certain was that, by the early 1970s, the era of large-scale, museum-sponsored ethnographic field collecting expeditions had largely ceased (Sturtevant 1969) and the nature of the institutions that held collections arising from such activities was the source of intense debate.

In light of all this activity, which seemed overwhelmingly concerned with *not* collecting, it might seem strange to suggest that the rise of the heritage industry in the years following the Second World War, and particularly after the 1970s in relation to the development of the World Heritage Lists, might be seen as a continuation of the process of ethnographic assembling. However, I think that a very good argument can be raised suggesting that the impetus for developing a heritage canon, represented by the incredible proliferation of lists of heritage during this period, was similar to that which drove the ethnographic collecting "craze" in the late nineteenth and early twentieth centuries. As we have seen, collecting was framed as a process of salvage in the face of vulnerability to the loss of indigenous culture. In the quotation from the document announcing the inclusion of the "Oral and Graphic Expressions of the Wajapi" on UNESCO's Masterpieces of the Oral and Intangible Heritage of Humanity in 2003,[4] we see the list similarly framed as a collection motivated by the threat of loss of indigenous culture, although, in this case, the collection is an assemblage of cultural practices, not objects per se. This is typical of these nominations, almost all of which make some reference to vulnerability or risk of loss in their documentation (see also Harrison 2012). This concept of salvage and the threat of loss, which was so integral to the justification for ethnographic field collecting in the late nineteenth and early twentieth centuries, was also central to the development of lists of heritage, in particular, to the World Heritage List (see also Harrison 2010b, 2012). Indeed, the World Heritage Convention declares in its opening statement, "The cultural heritage and the natural heritage are increasingly *threatened* with destruction not only by the traditional causes of decay, but also by changing social and economic conditions which aggravate the situation with even more formidable phenomena of damage or destruction.... [The] deterioration or disappearance of any item of the cultural or natural heritage constitutes a harmful impoverishment of the heritage of all the nations of the world" (UNESCO 2010[1972]; emphasis added).

Elsewhere (Harrison 2010b:22, 2012), I have shown how the number of cultural heritage policy documents and associated heritage lists grew exponentially over the second part of the twentieth century: at the turn of the twentieth century, there were only two major international heritage policy documents in place, and by the end of the twentieth, there were more than seventy. Similarly, the range of objects, places, and practices that came to be defined as "heritage" also grew exponentially over this period (Harrison 2012). The development of national heritage lists was stimulated in countries that had not already developed their own by UNESCO's requirement that states prepare interim lists of cultural heritage after the adoption of the World Heritage Convention. The last few decades of the twentieth century could indeed be characterized as the great age of heritage listing and categorization. These lists now form vast assemblages of objects, places, and practices arranged, ranked, and rigidly graded according to status and value—from the global, national, and regional, to the local—and categorized according to an ever-expanding list of criteria, each one reflecting the perceived risk of a potential loss of "culture." It is not only the existence of these lists that is important but also their hierarchical structure. For example, World Heritage sites are assumed to be more "important" than sites listed on regional or local heritage registers. National heritage sites, such as those listed on federal registers in Australia and the United States, are considered to be more important than those listed only on local or city heritage lists. Similarly, a listing on such registers comes with the expectation of particular forms of action: conservation works, adaptation for reuse, public access, or even reconstruction, depending on the specifics of the listing and the nature of the list. The list itself is a compelling agent that appears to have the power to effect change on the places and objects collected together and listed on it, but "at a distance," in the way described by Latour.

COLLECTING AND CATEGORIZING AS A RESPONSE TO RISK

Mary Douglas's work on risk is helpful in drawing out some ways in which collections function in relation to managing the threat of cultural loss. Douglas sees the management of risk as bound up in cultural responses to the threat of transgression. In *Purity and Danger* (Douglas 2010[1966]), she identifies "taboo" as a universal social mechanism for maintaining purity and order, drawing on notions of danger and threat that are structured by a biological model of society in which matter that transgresses the boundaries of the body is perceived to be problematic. She defines dirt as "matter out of place" and the perception of uncleanliness as synonymous with those things that are ambiguous and do not neatly fit into social categories. Expanding on this work on risk and threat, which was largely developed with reference to nonmodern societies, she turned to explore the idea of risk as part of modernity and as a product of a perception of vulnerability resulting from globalization: "The idea of risk could have been custom-made. Its universalizing terminology, its abstractness, its power of condensation, its scientificity, its connection with objective analysis, make it perfect. Above all, its forensic uses fit the tool of the task of building a culture that supports a modern industrial society" (1992:15).

These ideas were central to Ulrich Beck's development of the idea of a modern "risk society" (1992; see also Giddens 1990), in which dangers are perceived to result from the conditions of modernity itself. Indeed, if classification is a method for ordering and managing risk and threat and if the perception of risk is heightened by the conditions of modernity, classification can be understood to be central to modernity as a project. In *Organising Modernity* (1994), John Law speaks of "modes of ordering" as expressions of the project of modernity; they are strategies for patterning the networks of the social. He shows how these modes of ordering not only characterize but also define and hence *generate* the qualities of different materials—including objects, texts, agents, and organizations—and their patterns of distribution and modes of representation. In this way, we might see the late twentieth-century process of generating lists and registers of heritage objects, places, and practices as a direct extension of the process of ordering and classifying objects that began in the late nineteenth-century museum as part of the modern project of organizing, defining, and creating its subjects (and by extension, organizing, defining, and creating modernity itself). As Barbara Kirshenblatt-Gimblett (2004:57) notes, the list becomes its own world: "Everything on the list, whatever its previous context, is now placed in relationship with other masterpieces. The list is context for everything on it."

Douglas's work also helps us reflect on intangible heritage as a category. In *Purity and Danger* (Douglas 2010[1966]), she notes that anomalies within classificatory systems are treated with distrust because they represent potential sources of disorder and threat. One way of dealing with such anomalies is to purify them by moving them to the realm of myth. Another is to build more elaborate systems of classification that can take account of them. I would suggest that we can see both processes operating in relation to intangible heritage. On the one hand, the development of the concept of intangible heritage allows the World Heritage Lists to reinforce their status as universal lists. On the other, the category itself renders those practices associated with it as folkloric and effectively nonmodern.

THE LIST AS COLLECTION

I have mapped out a series of broad conceptual and historical connections between ethnographic collections in late nineteenth- and early twentieth-century museums and the World Heritage and other heritage lists in the late twentieth and early twenty-first centuries, both of which can be defined as "cultural" assemblages whose collection is motivated by risk. This raises a number of questions about the agency of the list, how it is mobilized, the other agents with which it is connected via various networks, the processes by which the list assembles, and the ways in which the reformulation of notions of heritage moves expertise away from museums and toward heritage conservation agencies, reflecting shifting governmental practices and modes of ordering. Clearly, the lists themselves constitute a mechanism for drawing a whole range of objects, places, and practices toward a center and simultaneously developing a set of global interfaces for the distribution of different forms of governance and agency. Although this has very broad implications, I focus my discussion particularly on the implications for the exertion of and resistance to indigenous agency and the ways in which both forms of collection facilitate forms of governance in relation to categorizing and maintaining the boundaries between humans and nonhumans, or things.

Universality and Indigenous Agency

I turn now to consider the significance of the concept of "universal value" in relation to indigenous and minority agency with regard to the World Heritage Convention. The convention created a World Heritage Committee to advise on the nomination of places to a World Heritage List, which would contain "a list of properties forming part of the cultural heritage and natural heritage...which it considers as having *outstanding universal value* in terms of such criteria as it shall have established" (UNESCO 2010 emphasis added). Much space has been dedicated to unpacking the convention's text and its implications (e.g., Walsh 1992; Fowler 2004; Harrison and Hitchcock 2005; Kirshenblatt-Gimblett 2006; Leask and Fyall 2006; Smith 2006; Bandarin 2007; Francioni 2008). Instead, I want to focus on the principle of "universal value" and the way in which this opened up the question of representation on the list for indigenous peoples and other minorities.

The principle of universal heritage values embodied in the World Heritage Convention has been criticized by a number of authors. Byrne (1991, 1995, 2009; see also Lydon 2009; Gonzalez-Ruibal 2009) argues that the principle of universality should be read as hegemonic, representing the attempts of Western heritage organizations to push particular principles of heritage management that are not always compatible with non-Western and minority values and forms of heritage. Cleere (2001:22) suggests that the idea of a World Heritage List comprising places that have universal value is inconsistent with the global spread of World Heritage sites, which is overwhelmingly biased toward countries with monumental architectural traditions (Europe, Latin

America, certain Asian countries) to the detriment of sites from countries whose cultures were primarily nonmonumental (Oceania and sub-Saharan Africa, for example). Smith sees the principle of universality as part of the World Heritage Convention's authorizing heritage discourse (AHD), which both lists and defines heritage in narrow and specific ways, through the lens of a Western European tradition of heritage:

> Part of the authority of the European AHD...lies in its own legit-imizing assumptions that it is universally applicable and that there [are], or must be, universal cultural values and expres-sions. The whole discourse of universality is itself a legitimiz-ing strategy for the values and nature of heritage that underline the AHD. The discourse of universality makes a moral plea to a sense of "brotherhood" of "mankind...." This sort of appeal... add[s] to its persuasive power. (Smith 2006:99)

Clearly, the principle of universal value in the convention text is what gives it its hegemonic power. However, I argue that it was actually this very claim to universality that allowed the possibility for the indigenous, minority, postcolonial, and non-Western critique that was fundamental in transform-ing the practice of heritage in the later part of the twentieth century. I draw here on Bennett's argument in *The Birth of the Museum* (1995) about the con-tradiction inherent in the museum's claim to universality (based in turn on Paul Greenhalgh's [1988] discussion of the representation of women in the world fairs) and the ways in which this claim to be broadly representative of all human cultures meant that the museum could not ignore the demands of indigenous minorities and marginalized social groups to receive representa-tion equal to that of dominant cultures in museums:

> It was...only the museum's embodiment of a principle of general human universality that lent potential significance to the exclu-sion or marginalization of women and women's culture, thereby opening this up as a politicizable question. The same, of course, is true of the range of demands placed on museums on behalf of other political constituencies as the space of the museum has been subject to the constant process of politicization in being called on both to expand the range of its representational concerns (to include artefacts relating to the ways of life of marginalized social groups, for example) and/or to exhibit familiar mate-rials in new contexts to allow them to represent the values of

the groups to which they relate rather than the dominant culture (...for example, Aboriginal criticisms of the evolutionary
assumptions governing the display of Aboriginal remains and
artefacts in natural history museums). (Bennett 1995:103)

What I am suggesting is that only because the World Heritage
Convention was expressed as a universal declaration representing universal heritage values did the criticisms by minorities and marginalized
peoples—and indeed the question of representativeness itself—become a
problem for the World Heritage Committee to address. The engagement
of UNESCO with the politics of representation in heritage has had far-
reaching consequences and fundamentally shifted the official practices of
heritage in the late twentieth century. This point is essential to understanding the ways in which heritage developed in the decades after 1972, which
profoundly influenced heritage practices throughout the world by shifting
the focus away from practical issues of conservation to those of identity
politics and representation.

Cultural Landscapes, Tjukurpa, and the Uluṟu-Kata Tjuṯa National Park World Heritage Site

This process can be demonstrated by considering the influence of
indigenous Australians' criticism of the initial nomination of Uluṟu-Kata
Tjuṯa National Park to the World Heritage List as a "natural" heritage site
in 1987. Anangu people's protests, supported by Australian heritage professionals (e.g., Layton and Titchen 1995), successfully saw the park renomi-
nated under the newly created category of "cultural landscape" in 1994.
The outcry surrounding the nomination under the natural heritage category, which was seen as effectively denying the ongoing social and religious
importance of the place to Anangu people (Layton and Titchen 1995), had
a strong influence on the development of the cultural landscape concept
and the way in which it was subsequently deployed by UNESCO. It also had
an important influence on the ways in which UNESCO would subsequently
come to define intangible heritage.

The Uluṟu-Kata Tjuṯa National Park World Heritage Site nomination was submitted to UNESCO in 1986. As Layton and Titchen (1995)
point out, this nomination made the case for Uluṟu (Ayers Rock–Mount
Olga) National Park (as it was then known) on the basis of both natural
and cultural criteria (Australian National Parks and Wildlife Service
1986). However, the subsequent evaluation by the International Union for
Conservation of Nature (IUCN, also known as the World Conservation

Union) recommended its inclusion on the basis of two of the World Heritage Convention's natural heritage criteria: its demonstration of "ongoing geological processes" and "exceptional natural beauty and exceptional combination of natural and cultural elements." The International Council on Monuments and Sites (ICOMOS), which would normally advise UNESCO on cultural criteria, provided no evaluation of the park's cultural heritage values at the time of the nomination (Layton and Titchen 1995:176). The IUCN evaluation notes that "cultural values of the area are being reviewed by ICOMOS" (UNESCO 1987:9), but this appears not to have occurred. Uluru (Ayers Rock–Mount Olga) National Park was subsequently inscribed on the World Heritage List in December 1987 at the eleventh meeting of the World Heritage Committee as a "natural" heritage site, despite the IUCN noting that "the cultural values of the site are significant" (UNESCO 1987:12).

The listing of Uluru (Ayers Rock–Mount Olga) National Park as a "natural" site was met with concern by heritage professionals (e.g., McBryde 1990; Layton and Titchen 1995), Anangu traditional owners, and the park's board of management, which was pushing to receive more comprehensive recognition of the park's cultural values and for these values to be better integrated with its management as a landscape.[5] Since the early days of tourism to the park, visitors had climbed to the top of Uluru to enjoy the view from the distinctive monolith—indeed, climbing the rock had become one of a series of heritage "experiences" to be checked off on the Australian tourist's agenda. A handrail to assist with the process of climbing had been installed in the 1960s. However, Anangu people had long expressed concern about tourists climbing Uluru. Anangu people themselves do not climb it because of its spiritual significance: the tourist track over the rock followed the route of Dreaming ancestors, which was considered inappropriate to cross (Calma and Liddle 2003:104). Anangu people had requested closing Uluru to tourist traffic as one condition of management of the site when they were lobbying for its return to them in the 1980s. Although this was initially agreed upon, continued access allowing tourists to climb Uluru would eventually form one condition required by the Australian government prior to agreeing to return the deeds to Anangu people in 1983 (Toyne and Vachon 1984). Trying to find ways to discourage tourists from climbing Uluru by educating them about its cultural values was an ongoing concern to the board of management; the apparent lack in recognizing the park's cultural values as part of the World Heritage nomination was thus a serious cause of unease and agitation for Anangu people. Their protests were part of related criticisms concerning the separation of natural and cultural heritage significance in the World Heritage Convention, which would result in fundamental revisions to the convention's text in 1992, alongside the introduction of "cultural landscape" as a distinct class of World Heritage sites in the same year.

Problems with the strict delineation of natural and cultural heritage sites in the World Heritage Convention in relation to rural landscapes and "mixed" natural and cultural sites were raised as early as 1984. At that time, the World Heritage Committee requested that the IUCN consult with ICOMOS and the International Federation of Landscape Architects to put together a taskforce to develop guidelines for the identification and nomination of mixed natural/cultural properties (Rössler 1995; Fowler 2003:66ff.). A meeting was held in 1985 and guidelines drafted, but when the United Kingdom subsequently submitted a nomination for the mixed natural/cultural landscape of Lake District National Park in 1987, the committee did not feel able to make a decision on the nomination, with ICOMOS in favor of the nomination and IUCN undecided. The committee ultimately deferred its decision until criteria could be developed specifically for the nomination of cultural landscapes.

In 1991, the UNESCO secretariat presented a draft proposal for two new criteria for the nomination of cultural landscapes to the fifteenth session of the World Heritage Committee, in Carthage (Rössler 1995:43). The committee asked for further consultation on the revision of World Heritage criteria, and a meeting of experts was held in La Petite-Pierre, France, in October 1992 (Fowler 2004:17–18). At this meeting, definitions of various categories of cultural landscapes were proposed, as were revisions to the World Heritage operational guidelines to allow for the inclusion of cultural landscapes in the World Heritage List. These discussions were driven particularly by the criticisms of the separation of natural and cultural heritage, which had been leveled by Anangu people in relation to the classification of Uluru (Ayers Rock–Mount Olga) National Park and by Māori people in relation to the inscription of Tongariro National Park in New Zealand as a "natural" World Heritage site in 1990. These criticisms of the World Heritage List and the need to recognize the indigenous values of cultural landscapes were central to the discussions at La Petite-Pierre (Rössler 1995:44).

A number of participants with knowledge or direct experience of the Australian and New Zealand examples took part in the meeting at La Petite-Pierre (see UNESCO 1992:annex A). Significantly, no new criterion was created, but recommendations for redrafting the World Heritage Convention's cultural criteria were proposed. These gave particular consideration to the need to recognize the cultural values of landscapes to indigenous peoples and the value of "traditional" land management practices. (It seems fairly certain that Central Australian practices of managing the landscape using controlled burning were influential here.) The fundamental dualism between the categories of natural and cultural heritage value was maintained, but the revisions represented an important broadening of the concept of heritage as embodied in the convention's text.

The proposed changes (see appendix 1 at the end of this chapter), which were accepted at the sixteenth session of the World Heritage Committee held in Santa Fe, New Mexico, in December 1992, demonstrate the clear influence of Anangu and Māori conceptions of landscape, which had emerged in the debates surrounding the nomination of Uluṟu-Kata Tjuṯa and Tongariro as "natural" properties. The recognition of multiple cultures and overlapping landscapes in changes to paragraph 24(a)(v) and the emphasis on continuity of tradition in changes to paragraphs 24(a)(vi) and 24(b)(ii) appear to have been specific concessions for the Australian situation. The meeting also defined three types of cultural landscape (see appendix 2 at the end of this chapter). The inclusion of the notion of "continuing landscapes," which have an active role in contemporary society, and the category of "associative cultural landscapes," which acknowledges the spiritual connection between particular groups and the landscapes they occupy, was directly influenced by arguments raised by indigenous people in response to the "natural" heritage nominations of Tongariro and Uluṟu-Kata Tjuṯa (Fowler 2004:34) and, indeed, by the very nature of those landscapes, which were rugged, remote, and apparently undeveloped despite the complex spiritual connections and active regimes of landscape management that indigenous people applied to them.

These changes had important implications not only for Anangu people and the park's board of management but also in shifting and broadening the definition of heritage promoted by UNESCO. In 1993, at the request of Anangu people and the board, the name of the park was changed to Uluṟu-Kata Tjuṯa National Park. In the same year, Tongariro National Park was resubmitted for consideration under the revised cultural criteria as an associative cultural landscape, and it became the first cultural landscape to be inscribed on the World Heritage List at the seventeenth session of the World Heritage Committee in December 1993. The following year, Uluṟu-Kata Tjuṯa National Park became the second cultural landscape to be included on the World Heritage List when it was resubmitted for consideration as a living and associative landscape. The ICOMOS evaluation noted: "The cultural landscape...is of immense significance...a highly successful model of human adaptation to a hostile arid environment.... [It] also graphically demonstrates the intimate symbolic relationship between man and the landscape in this non-monumental culture.... [The park] is also worthy of commendation for its management system and policy...based on the perceptions and practices of the traditional owners of the land" (qtd. in Fowler 2003:107). This was an explicit recognition of the value of Tjukurpa (sometimes translated as "Dreaming")—the Anangu people's system of lore, which dictates the relationships between humans, animals, plants, and the environment; the relationship between past and present; and the methods for the maintenance of these interrelationships in the future—as an overarching philosophy in the appropriate management of the landscape, and the interrelationship of this system of management with the natural and cultural values of the park and Anangu people's well-being.

Uluru-Kata Tjuta National Park has consistently been seen as a model for defining and managing cultural landscape values. In 1995 it won the Picasso Gold Medal, awarded jointly by UNESCO to Parks Australia and the Uluru-Kata Tjuta board of management for outstanding efforts to preserve the landscape and Anangu culture and for setting new international standards for World Heritage management. The park's board of management has introduced a "Please don't climb" program that asks visitors not to climb Uluru, out of respect for its spiritual significance to Anangu people as the traditional route of the ancestral Mala men on their arrival at Uluru. This has had a significant impact on the number of tourists who choose to climb Uluru. In 2009 it was estimated that around 38 percent of tourists climbed Uluru, down from 74 percent in 1990 (Parks Australia 2009).

In this example, we see the ways in which the relationship between local actors and global processes creates "zones of awkward engagement" (Tsing 2005), creative spaces of friction that have long-lasting consequences both for local actors and for global institutions. The debates surrounding the listing of Uluru-Kata Tjuta National Park as a "natural" heritage site drew attention to broader issues relating to differences between the UNESCO World Heritage Convention's model of the separation and dualistic opposition of cultural and natural heritage and alternative models of heritage in which natural landscapes might be conceptualized as "cultural" ones. The convention's self-definition as a universal declaration representing all of human heritage meant that these alternative models had to be taken seriously and given equal consideration with Western ways of conceptualizing heritage. The outcome was a clear shift in the definitions employed in relation to World Heritage in the years that followed.

In the same way in which various individuals might be thought of as agents, the form of Uluru-Kata Tjuta and Tongariro as landscapes and the relationships between these landscapes and their indigenous custodians had a major influence on the definition of "cultural landscape" adopted by the World Heritage Committee. These landscapes subsequently affected the categorization, preservation, and management of other landscapes in the world. As a result of the complex social and physical networks demonstrated by their indigenous custodians in discussions about the form that their nominations and management should take, the landscapes themselves might be viewed as exhibiting forms of agency that have had a long-lasting impact on the ways in which heritage is defined and managed in the contemporary world. Indeed, we can think of Uluru as acting in these processes as an assemblage, or collective agent, that comprises not only its human advocates but also the whole range of its physical characteristics—its biodiversity, its prominence in the landscape, and the various texts, images, and other representations that had previously circulated to give it its renown and visitability as an "Australian icon." All of these worked in tandem to influence the specific changes proposed by UNESCO in the category of cultural landscape. In this example, we can see clearly how alternative models of heritage can be employed by indigenous and non-Western minorities to draw attention to particular local heritage issues, which are made global by tactically employing notions of the universality of heritage. Similar examples are evident in UNESCO's adoption of the category of intangible heritage (see Harrison 2012). It is the very notion of the universality of the World Heritage Lists that forces them to respond and expand to accommodate these varied viewpoints and critiques from the particular forms of heritage that they appear to sweep to the periphery.

Categorizing People, Governing Things

One significant problem that has arisen from the engagement of indigenous peoples in this process is the way in which the various lists require specific forms of indigeneity and a collusion with particular ways of understanding and expressing culture. These include the concepts of threat and risk previously discussed, which imply that, rather than be something produced out of the past as part of an ongoing engagement with the present, heritage and culture are limited resources that can be "lost" and were necessarily more "pure" in the past. This has often required indigenous peoples to emphasize the essential, primitive, and primordial aspects of their culture and to draw on notions of indigeneity that tend to collapse "culture" into "race" (e.g., Kuper 2003; Barnard 2006). In this way, the various World Heritage Lists' categories create a world in their own image; in relation to intangible heritage, they are a way of bureaucratizing and regulating indigenous and minority peoples and their cultural expressions. Nonetheless, it is also apparent that some minority and indigenous peoples have employed this essentialism "strategically" (cf. Spivak 1996; see Byrne 2003; Meskell 2009; Harrison 2010a)—they have colluded with these simplified and stereo typical representations of indigenous culture to achieve particular outcomes—in this case, as a way of bypassing the authority of (post)colonial nation-states and drawing attention to local issues by way of various global indigenous rights movements and the international publicity that inclusion on these lists provides. Duncan Ivison (2006) has discussed such engagements as a form of "emergent" indigenous cosmopolitanism, which blends an awareness of universal notions of justice with locally produced understandings of the ways in which this justice might be culturally expressed.

Notwithstanding these creative reconfigurations of indigeneity and the strategic use of transnational and universal discourses of human and cultural rights, the structure of UNESCO has tended to make it difficult for indigenous peoples and other minorities to use the World Heritage Lists as strategically as they might in drawing attention to issues of local concern. This is a function of UNESCO's requirement that nominations be made via state parties, thus prioritizing the agendas of nation-states over those of minorities (and indeed, somewhat contradictorily, over the "universal" principles upon which the lists purport to stand). Indigenous and minority critiques have often been marginalized as groups are subsumed within nation-states and as representations of their culture are employed within broader nationalist discourses (e.g., Benavides 2009; Askew 2010). Nonetheless, some indigenous groups have been successful in drawing attention to issues of local concern even when they have been unable to overcome this problem in the requirements of states' compliance for nominations to be made to any of UNESCO's World Heritage Lists. For example, Lydon (2009) discusses the case of the international campaign led by Mirrar people in the Kakadu region of northern Australia, who successfully prevented uranium mining on the Jabiluka mineral lease, even though the World Heritage Committee's member states ultimately voted against listing Kakadu on the List of World Heritage in Danger, against the wishes of Mirrar Aboriginal people but in line with the Australian federal government's lobbying of other states parties.

Categorizing Things, Governing People

It is clear that conceptualizing World Heritage as a form of collection allows us to productively connect the critical literature on museum collecting with recent developments in relation to heritage, revealing some of the ways in which indigenous and other minority groups have fundamentally influenced the nature of heritage conservation practices in the late twentieth and early twenty-first centuries. Yet, the increased emphasis on intangible heritage and culture in the work of UNESCO and other heritage agencies raises questions about the function of the list in categorizing and hence defining people, culture, and things and, in the process, governing the relationships between them. It is this question of the various World Heritage Lists as governmental assemblages to which I now turn.

I have suggested that the recognition of cultural landscapes and intangible heritage by UNESCO as categories of heritage have arisen at least partially as a result of the strategic operation of indigenous and minority agency in lobbying for the recognition of more diverse forms of heritage. This parallels the ways in which the representation of indigenous people in museums arose as an issue in relation to the museum's claims to universal representation in the late nineteenth and early twentieth centuries. In this way, the protection extended to monumental and canonical objects and places, which were assessed as having universal value under UNESCO's model, could also be extended to other, nonmonumental forms of heritage. Nonetheless, I have argued, this has had significant implications for indigenous people, as it has often come at a price, requiring them to strategically deploy essentialized and primordial representations of indigeneity in an effort to produce versions of "culture" that states and international organizations such as UNESCO will perceive to be at risk and hence worthy of listing or inclusion in regulatory heritage processes. Another significant implication is the way in which the categorization of certain forms of heritage as "intangible" in opposition to others, which are defined as "tangible," perpetuates a modern division between objects and people that is in some cases radically incompatible with indigenous ontologies. The World Heritage Lists must therefore be seen as specific modes of ordering and as governmental assemblages that define the boundaries between humans and nonhumans in ways that challenge indigenous perspectives on being in the world.

Indigenous ontologies can be understood generally to employ dialogical models of heritage in which heritage value emerges as a contingent quality of the relationship between humans, nonhumans, and material things, all of which may be held to be "animate" or act as "agents" (see Harrison and Rose 2010; Harvey 2005; Harrison 2012; Hays-Gilpin and Lomatewama, chapter 10, this volume). Much work in Australia, for example, has shown the ways in which "cultural" heritage issues are indistinguishable to Aboriginal people from "natural" heritage concerns, such as environmental health (e.g., English 2003; Rose, James, and Watson 2003; Byrne 2008), and that the "social" values of places are linked with the material expression of the landscape and archaeological sites within it (e.g., Harrison 2004b, 2010a). This Australian indigenous ontological position destabilizes the World Heritage Convention's anthropocentrism in its treatment of humans as preeminent and in regard to the dualism that sets nature or the nonhuman in opposition to culture or the human (see further discussion of these dualisms in Latour 2004a; Viveiros de Castro 2004). Within an ontology in which "culture" is everywhere, not only is there no boundary between nature and culture, but there is also no mind-matter binary (Harrison and Rose 2010). These precepts challenge both the idea that heritage meaning is made only by humans and the World Heritage Convention's underlying tangible-intangible dualism. Within this binary structure, objects and other tangible matter are made meaningful by being brought into a world of intangible meanings, which are the property of human culture and experience. In contrast, in Harrison and Rose (2010), we argued that indigenous Australian ontologies propose a philosophy of "becoming," in which life and place combine to bind time and living beings into generations of continuities in particular places. These generations are not only human; they also involve plants and animals, objects, and, indeed, whole ecosystems. In this way, it is not unreasonable to think of museum objects as kin (e.g., Hays-Gilpin and Lomatewama, chapter 10, this volume) or of stone artifacts from archaeological sites as the embodiment of long-dead ancestors (Harrison 2004b:198ff., 2010a; Colwell-Chanthaphonh and Ferguson 2006), for example.

DISCUSSION

This categorization and separation of humans, nonhumans, and things has major implications in determining contemporary museological and heritage practices. This mode of ordering produces a form of heritage that is perceived to be historical, bounded, inert, and finite. It becomes a threatened commodity, a property that requires and justifies its assemblage, categorization, and curation alongside its separation from the realm of everyday experience and the people who produce it in the present. Museum objects and cultural practices are simultaneously "protected" while being offered up for the consumption and enjoyment of those world citizens who are privileged and able to make use of globalized networks of tourism and travel, exploiting and commodifying the same cultures they purport to conserve in the process.

Nonetheless, it pays not to be too pessimistic about these modes of ordering and categorization as governmental assemblages. I would like to conclude with some observations about the challenges that are raised for heritage conservation and museological practice by this indigenous onto-logical position. As truth claims that integrate radically different concepts of time and space and that demand to be taken seriously, indigenous ontolo-gies are having a renewed impact on heritage practices (see Harrison 2012; Hays-Gilpin and Lomatewama, chapter 10, Knowles, chapter 9, this vol-ume). This indigenous model of heritage as emplaced, creative production involving human and nonhuman agents shifts our focus to the regenerative aspects of heritage *production*. Heritage emerges not as a process concerned with the past and present but as a future-oriented, emergent, contingent, and creative endeavor. It is not a process of meaning making, which exists only in the human mind, but one in which multiple actors, both humans and nonhumans, are equally implicated in complex processes that bind them across time and space (Harrison and Rose 2010). It becomes a sym-metrical process, in which curation involves not only protecting an object for future generations of people but also protecting people for future gen-erations of an object (and, indeed, for past generations of both).

This alternative model of heritage goes some way toward explaining the continued insistent politicization of the question of objects by indig-enous people in relation to both contemporary and past museum collect-ing (for example, by way of the repatriation debate) and allows us access to forms of indigenous agency that not only have some time depth but also continue to have relevance in contemporary settings. A number of studies have convincingly demonstrated an early awareness by indigenous people of their role as agents in the development of a colonial art-culture market during the late nineteenth and early twentieth centuries and the ways in which they expressed varied forms of agency in relation to this market (e.g., Taylor 1988; Thomas 1991; Torrence 1993, 2000, 2002; Gosden and Knowles 2001; Harrison 2006; Byrne et al. 2011b). In the same way that museum objects might be conceptualized as contemporary "ambassadors" (Knowles 2011) in relation to cross-cultural interactions, it is clear that they have also assumed similar roles in the past (e.g., Thomas 1991). Reassembling the connections between ethnographic collecting and the World Heritage Lists reveals alternative ways in which indigenous people have influenced the nature of collections of heritage over the past century and the ways of conceptualizing heritage itself at a global level since the 1980s.

In seeing heritage not as a discourse or process of symbolic meaning making but as an emergent property of the relationship between humans and nonhumans, in which the creative actions of things are recognized as existing in a mixed or shared relationship of symmetry with humans (Harrison 2012), the objects that form part of museum (and heritage) collections take on new forms of significance and agency in their ongoing, creative relationships with humans in the present. In part, they draw on their power as objects from the past, but similarly, they exist in a meshwork of relationships (both material and social) in the present. The challenge for museums thus becomes finding ways of engaging creatively with these objects so as to facilitate their ongoing relationships with people and the other objects around them in the future. This means opening up a dialogue with things as actors in their own right (Olsen 2010), rather than perceiving them merely as props that stand in for human cultures from the past, in the present.

CONCLUSIONS

I have mapped out a series of conceptual intersections between late nineteenth- and early twentieth-century ethnographic collecting and late twentieth- and early twenty-first-century heritage conservation practices, suggesting that both museums and heritage registers represent centers of (and for) collection motivated by a perception of risk of cultural loss. I argue that it is profitable to draw these phenomena into conversation for a number of reasons, not the least being the ways in which this helps us to understand a consistent thread of indigenous agency in relation to museums and heritage, both in politicizing the question of representation and in emphasizing the creative relationships between people and things (as agents) in indigenous perceptions of heritage. I suggest that the ways in which indigenous peoples and other ethnic minorities have made counterclaims to representation in World Heritage since its introduction in the 1970s and the growth of international indigenous rights movements mirror earlier developments relating to their representation within late nineteenth- and early twentieth-century ethnographic museums. These movements are connected in many ways, sharing a genealogy that links questions surrounding the relationship of the universal to the particular and the concept of cultural relativism. I also suggest that although indigenous people have been able to exploit notions of universal values and universal rights strategically in terms of World Heritage listing and the work of UNESCO, this has had implications for the ways in which the lists have continued older museological forms of governance in relation to the categorization of the boundaries between humans and things, which may run counter to indigenous ontologies. The challenge for heritage and museological practice in the future is to develop strategies to accommodate the varied local, emplaced forms of knowledge that arise from indigenous ontologies within what appears to be an inconsistent, modern notion of universal values and an ethic of producing and defining "cultures at risk," which underlies and motivates the processes of heritage and museum collection themselves.

APPENDIX 1

Below are the recommendations for redrafting the World Heritage Convention's cultural criteria, which were proposed at the 1992 La Petite-Pierre meeting. Additions appear in bold text.

Paragraph 24(a)

(i) represent a unique artistic achievement, a masterpiece of the creative genius; or

(ii) have exerted great influence, over a span of time or within a cultural area of the world, on developments in architecture, monumental arts, town-planning or **landscape design**; or

(iii) bear a unique or at least exceptional testimony to a civilisation or **cultural tradition** which has disappeared; or

(iv) be an outstanding example of the type of building or architectural ensemble **or landscape** which illustrates (a) significant stage(s) **in human history**; or

(v) be an outstanding example of a traditional human settlement **or land use** which is representative of a culture (**or cultures**), **especially when** it has become vulnerable under the impact of irreversible change; or

(vi) be directly and tangibly associated with events or **living traditions**, with ideas, or **with** beliefs, **with artistic and literary works** of outstanding universal significance (the Committee considers that this criterion should justify inclusion on the List only in exceptional circumstance or in conjunction with other criteria).

Paragraph 24(b)

(i) meet the test of authenticity in design, material, workmanship or setting **and in the case of cultural landscapes their distinctive character and components** (the committee stressed that reconstruction is only acceptable if it is carried out on the basis of complete and detailed documentation on the original and to no extent conjecture)

(ii) have adequate legal **and/or traditional** protection and management mechanisms to ensure the conservation of the nominated cultural property **or cultural landscapes**. The existence of protective legislation at the national, provincial or municipal level **or well established traditional protection** and/or adequate management mechanisms is therefore essential and must be stated clearly on the nomination form.

Assurances of the effective implementation of these laws and/or administrative mechanisms are also expected. Furthermore, in order to preserve the integrity of cultural sites, particularly those open to large numbers of visitors, the State Party concerned should be able to provide evidence of suitable administrative arrangements to cover the management of the property, its conservation and its access to the public. (Rössler 1995:45)

APPENDIX 2

These are the definitions of "cultural landscape" proposed in a revision of the operational guidelines for implementing of the World Heritage Convention as a result of the 1992 La Petite-Pierre meeting.

The term "cultural landscape" embraces a diversity of manifestations of the interaction between humankind and its natural environment.

The most easily identifiable is the clearly defined landscape designed and created intentionally by man. This embraces garden and parkland landscapes constructed for aesthetic reasons which are often (but not always) associated with religious or other monumental buildings and ensembles.

The second category is the organically evolved landscape. This results from an initial social, economic, administrative, and/or religious imperative and has developed its present form by association with and in response to its natural environment. Such landscapes reflect that process of evolution in their form and component features. They fall into two sub-categories:

A relict (or fossil) landscape is one in which an evolutionary process came to an end at some time in the past, either abruptly or over a period. Its significant distinguishing features are, however, still visible in material form.

A continuing landscape is one which retains an active social role in contemporary society closely associated with the traditional way of life, and in which the evolutionary process is still in progress. At the same time it exhibits significant material evidence of its evolution over time.

The final category is the associative cultural landscape. The inscription of such landscapes on the World Heritage List is justifiable by virtue of the powerful religious, artistic or cultural associations of the natural element rather than material cultural evidence, which may be insignificant or even absent. (UNESCO 1992:4–5)

Notes

1. I use the terms "lists" and "listing" throughout the chapter, but in other regional or national contexts, the terms "designation," "nomination," or "inscription" may be used. In all of these cases, what is meant is the identification and description of an object, place, or practice to convey a legal or procedural protection of some form.

2. Throughout the chapter, I use the plural to refer collectively to the World Heritage List, the List of Intangible Cultural Heritage in Need of Urgent Safeguarding, and the Representative List of the Intangible Cultural Heritage of Humanity (formerly, the Masterpieces of the Oral and Intangible Heritage of Humanity).

3. This also contributed to the developing separation of archaeology and socio-cultural anthropology (e.g., Gosden 1999).

4. The list of Masterpieces of the Oral and Intangible Heritage of Humanity, which was compiled between 2001 and 2005, was replaced in 2008 by the List of Intangible Cultural Heritage in Need of Urgent Safeguarding and the Representative List of the Intangible Cultural Heritage of Humanity.

5. In 1983, newly elected Labour prime minister Bob Hawke had announced an amendment to the Aboriginal Land Rights Act to allow for the return of the title for Uluru (Ayers Rock–Mount Olga) National Park to the Anangu traditional owners. It was agreed that the land would be leased back to the Australian National Parks and Wildlife Service and run under a system of joint management, an arrangement that had previously been put in place at Kakadu National Park. The park would be managed on the day-to-day level by the Australian Parks and Wildlife Service but would be overseen by a board of management with mostly Anangu members.

Part II
Indigenous Strategies
and Museum Collections

5

The Sorcery of Sweetness

Intersecting Agencies and Materialities of the 1928 USDA Sugarcane Expedition to New Guinea

Joshua A. Bell

It may seem strange to you that I should speak with such apparent wisdom—I, a little mortal grain of sugar...but please remember, if you care to follow my story, that I have knowledge because I am the embodiment and symbol of the principle of SWEETNESS.

—C. F. *Bardof,* The Story of Sugar

Though an authorial conceit written as part of an educational book about sugar, the quotation above usefully unsettles perceptions about the sentience and agency of nonhumans. Here, we have an example of nature speaking for itself or at least being imagined to (Latour 2004a). Though the thinking about nonhuman agency has been part of an interesting germination of ideas within the history of science and anthropology (Latour 1993, 1999; Haraway 2008), in this chapter, I do not engage in debates about the nature of agency or about what exerts force in the dance of humans and nonhumans. Rather, accepting the mutuality and entanglement of things and people, humans and nonhumans, I raise issues about what form the intersection of agencies takes materially within collections (artifacts, botanical and natural history specimens, text, still and moving images) and how these different materials, as they relate to the circumstances of the encounter in which they were made, can be used to better understand this dance. I invoke the voice of sugar to open up perspectives of agency discussed in this volume, since a central concern in this chapter is how to understand indigenous actions within this larger network of agencies. Posed a different way: how do we understand agency within collections from an external perspective without effacing or losing sight of communities' ontologies?

I focus on the collections made during the 1928 US Department of Agriculture (USDA) Sugarcane Expedition to the Territories of Papua and New Guinea (Bell 2010b, in press),[1] a partnership of national agricultural research institutes and private industry. Members of the USDA expedition spent four months collecting sugarcane varieties with which they sought to hybridize a cane resistant to mosaic, a virus ravaging the Louisiana sugarcane industry and the wider global industry (Brandes and Sartoris 1936).[2] Led by E. W. Brandes, the principal pathologist in charge of the USDA's Bureau of Plant Industry's Office of Sugar Plants, the expedition included Jacob Jeswiet, a Dutch sugar scientist who pioneered hybrid cane in Java; C. E. Pemberton, an entomologist employed by the Hawaiian Sugar Planters Association (HSPA) who specialized in sugarcane insect pests; and Richard K. Peck, a pilot, mechanic, cinematographer, and photographer.[3] Using a seaplane, these men visited some forty communities in eastern New Guinea, which resulted in extensive collections: 130 varieties of the "noble" sugarcane (*S. officinarum* L.) and a new species (*S. robustum* Brandes and Jeswiet ex Grassl) were collected as part of the more than one thousand botanical specimens; an unknown amount of other natural history specimens (birds, insects, mammals) were obtained; some 428 ethnographic objects and roughly two thousand photographs were taken; and 4,000 feet of 35mm film were exposed. These collections are now dispersed among the Smithsonian's National Museum of Natural History (NMNH); the National Anthropological Archives (NAA); the National Archives of the United States; the National Geographic Society Archives (NGSA); the National Herbarium, Wageningen, Netherlands; the Hawaii Agriculture Research Center; the Bishop Museum; and the homes of the descendants of expedition members.

As I have examined elsewhere, Brandes's 1929 *National Geographic* article, a report written by Pemberton to the HSPA, and the expedition's silent 35mm black-and-white film, *Sugar Plant Hunting by Airplane in New Guinea*, are all partial sources, which, though illuminating, individually fall prey to the period's self-aggrandizing narratives of first contact (Bell 2010b, in press). Bringing other aspects of the expedition's assemblage, namely the physical collections, into sharper view, I explore the "shadowy traces of local agency, relationships and settings" (Douglas 1998:70) that the collections inadvertently materialize, which are otherwise obscured textually and visually. Doing so, I work against the purification that has transpired by the collections' dispersal and movement into different institutions, which was further produced by researchers dividing natural from cultural materials.

Brought back into relationship with one another, the expedition's assemblages become a way in which to think through how one can write histories that in the words of Dening (1996) help give the past back its present, thus illuminating the nested sets of agency that lie within all materials. The question, as posed by Pinney (2004, 2005), is, how in the process do collections become reflective not just of histories found elsewhere but of counterhistories located in their materiality (Stahl 2010)? I conduct a critical forensic and contextual examination of the collections to understand the traces of indigenous communities, as part of the wider set of agencies within these assemblages, and to combat the silences that each material possesses (Trouillot 1995). By "critical forensic" (Edwards 2001), I am referring to the physical marks on things and their manufacture (patina, use wear, and so on) and the details in visual sources that disrupt an image's punctum. Complementing this analysis, I use a contextual reading of sources from the expedition, contemporaneous to it, along with both earlier and later sources. This material is drawn on critically and with full awareness of the dangers of flattening the transformations experienced by communities between 1928 and the present. However, in lieu of oral histories and fieldwork with communities from which the collections were obtained (a later project), these informed speculations are an attempt to understand the indigenous perspectives materialized in the collections.

In weaving together these materials, I follow Ginzburg (1980:16), who advocates for the role of conjectural knowledge whereby investigators use "signs and scraps of evidence" to build up arguments and connections to yield productive results. In this way, one is involved in placing the collections back within a meshwork of relationships through which a more indepth understanding of things and their source communities can begin to emerge (see the introduction to this volume). Doing so also mediates the ways in which archival materials and museum collections conceal as much as they reveal (Thomas 1999a; O'Hanlon 1999) and points to how engaging them can allow one to begin to reconstruct the micro-practices of their composition (Brown, Coote, and Gosden 2000:258) and thus recover otherwise muted stories, interactions, and ontologies (Bell 2010a). Here, I primarily focus on agencies found within materials from the Lake Murray–Middle Fly region as this area is where the expedition spent the majority of its time and where the bulk of the collections are from and the densest overlap of sources to date have emerged (Bell 2010b).

FORMS OF AGENCIES

Before turning to the collections and the traces materialized therein, I will make some comments on the agencies examined here, including their forms and scales. Within the material return of scholarship, objects or, more precisely, "things" have emerged as key participants (actants, agents, or actors) in the unfolding of human sociality. Setting aside the nature of this agency (Ingold 2007b), I understand things to be generative, compelling their human counterparts to act in certain ways in their shaping of sociality (Latour 2005; Miller 2005; Knappett and Malafouris 2008). This perspective brings the parts of the expedition into view and allows us to think through how the various entities—humans, mosaic virus, aphids, sugarcane, airplane, other nonhumans—influenced and shaped one another in their movements and translations. But there is a tension here—however productive—for in doing so, one risks potentially flattening differences as articulated locally (Strathern 1996).

In the absence of my own fieldwork, I draw on the ethnography of others for communities engaged by the USDA expedition, as well as on Melanesian theories of personhood (Strathern 1988). Doing so counteracts the tendency to create an overly Eurocentric model of agency that obviates indigenous perspectives and ontologies of what constitutes objects and subjects and thus what has and does not have agency, let alone what is material culture (Bolton 2001). Thomas (1991:108) notes that "to say that black bottles were given does not tell us what were received," and the same is also true of perceptions about what communities were performing through their giving of things. Sugarcane cuttings were not merely botanical samples for Melanesians but rather the beginning of what they probably hoped would be a prolonged series of exchanges. As Strathern (1990, 1992) has elaborated, in Melanesia, people and things are understood to be composed of the relations that they help engender, such that both are representations *and* performances. In ethnographies inspired by her formulation, things—whether stone axes (Battaglia 1990), wigs (O'Hanlon 1992), or slit drums (Leach 2002)—emerge as momentary condensations of flows of processes and as part of a wider network of human and nonhuman relations where agency is distributed (Bell and Geismar 2009). Would-be divisions between nature and culture, persons and things, are blurred, and things within a Melanesian perspective exert force. These perspectives are not to dismiss helpful corrective critiques that situate these engagements historically (cf. Thomas 1991), nor to reify distinctions between Melanesian and Western sociality (Scott 2007), but rather to draw attention to the ways these cultural entanglements may not conform to Western expectations (Strathern 1993). Being attuned to these differences and intersections usefully complicates our understanding of museum collections and the traces of agencies therein.

Collections thus emerge as being composed not just of things but also of people (makers, users, collectors) (Moutu 2007; Gosden, Larson, and Petch 2007; Byrne et al. 2011a). As meshworks (Ingold 2007a), collections are both arbitrary and purposefully made entities created out of a mix of happenstance, the actions of others, and the collector's criteria (J. Bennett 2010). Collections have embedded within them indigenous histories of manufacture, use, and disuse; the colonial histories or postcolonial power relations that facilitated their collection and movement to institutions; and, finally, the institutional histories they become part of. Collectively and individually, artifacts are materializations of particular moments and movements and thus can be understood to be the result of nested sets of actions, which are processual (Bell and Geismar 2009). The question is how to reassemble these processes while doing justice to their complexities.

REASSEMBLING THE USDA EXPEDITION'S ASSEMBLAGES
In 1929, Brandes wrote, "Primarily, of course, we came for cane; yet, important as that quest was, it was only natural that the strange tribes we bartered with were even more interesting than the plant life we found" (Brandes 1929:304). As his comment suggests, the collecting activities of expedition members quickly involved concomitant ethnographic collecting. While part of this appears to have been due to the pull of these exotic things, it was also done because of the recognition of the ways plants were being utilized. Arrows, which predominate in Brandes's collection, were easily obtainable but were also of interest due to the sugarcane and other grasses used as shafts. Collecting these objects thus fulfilled multiple agendas. Both still and moving images formed another broader strategy of collecting, enabling the documentation of aspects of science and the wider environment that were otherwise uncollectible (see Bell 2010b). Despite an interest in the ethnographic, however, the bulk of the expedition's collection is botanical. Numbering more than a thousand specimens, both live and dried materials were collected by expedition members. Live specimens of sugarcane were divided between Australia and the United States, with clones quickly circulating between research stations. The dried specimens appear to have gone primarily to the Wageningen branch of the Netherlands' National Herbarium,[4] where Jeswiet, who appears to have been the primary collector of these varied botanical materials, was by then the director. Jeswiet appears to have been collecting specimens to build up the herbarium's collection, as well as creating duplicates for trade. Though tracking down these materials is ongoing, the specificity of the locality and the temporal inscription of these specimens are proving critical in

Figure 5.1

Botanical specimens at Wageningen. (A) *Specimen that is a clone (28 N.G. 104 Imp 653) of* Saccharum robustum *Brandes and Jeswiet that was collected on the bank of the Kemp Welch River near Niuiruka.* (B) *Specimen 153 of* Gramineas, Coix lacryma-jobi, *collected by Jeswiet at Daviumbu Lagoon (27 July 1928). The inscriptions on the botanical specimens help situate the expedition in a manner not found with other collections. Photographs by Joshua A. Bell, courtesy of the Wageningen branch of the National Herbarium, Netherlands.*

contextualizing the expedition's activities in the absence of detailed textual sources (figure 5.1A, B).

The rationale behind the fauna collection is less clear, consisting as it does of the skins of four female common spotted cuscus (*Spilocuscus maculatus goldiei*; USNM M248956–59; figure 5.3) and one egg of the dwarf cassowary (*Casuarius bennetti*; USNM B37444). The idiosyncrasy of these materials collected by Brandes suggests that they are the result of opportunistic capitalization on the activities of the Papuans in the expedition's retinue. Pemberton collected a range of insects, now in the Bishop Museum, but the extent of these materials is unknown due to their not being databased. Further work needs to be done to determine what specimens he obtained (Brandes 1929:287; Gressitt 1971). It is clear from his report that Pemberton was interested in collecting insects that fed on sugarcane, as well as those that ate the first group. I pay attention to these materials here because if we are to understand the full range of the expedition members' movements and activities, these materials and their catalog data are important aspects of this reassembling.

Within the NMNH, the expedition's ethnographic material is in four accessions, the brief history of which is instructive. Brandes assembled the largest accession (NMNH 106509), consisting of 380 objects, which he donated on 25 July 1929. Brandes himself purchased or traded for the majority of the collection. As did the other expedition members, he used trade goods (fishhooks, safety razor blades, trade cloth) and cast-off objects (empty cigarette tins, tin film wrappers) to obtain these things (Brandes 1929:295, 323; Brandes and Sartoris 1936:568). A small number of objects (the exact number is unknown) were gifts from European residents, such as the drum (NMNH E344961-0) given by the district officer, Colonel H. E. Woodman, when Brandes and Peck visited the Ambunti police camp on the Sepik River. The drum was part of an array of objects that Woodman, a recent government officer but long-time resident of New Guinea, either bought or seized as part of his official or unofficial duties (Brandes 1929:318). The photographed display of Woodman's possessions and the subsequent gift are reminders of how objects were essential to colonial social relations (Gosden and Knowles 2001) and of the multiple histories within all collections. Brandes also collected things as personal mementos, which remain with his descendants. Though the full extent is unknown, both Jeswiet and Pemberton also collected objects, which remain in private hands.[5]

The second accession deposited by Brandes arrived in the museum on 23 November 1929. It helps to further illustrate how European residents accumulated objects in Papua and the personal networks they created through them. The accession's fifteen stone axes (NMNH 106585) belonged to Percy Robinson, the manager of Ogamobu Plantation in the Papuan Gulf, who sold the collection to the National Museum through Brandes. Resident in Papua since 1914, Robinson and his family were important plantation owners and labor recruiters (Hope 1979:144, 146–147, 182). These axes are most likely from the Tuman quarries in Aviamp, a locality in the Western Highlands, and they passed through a series of intermediaries until they reached coastal communities, where they were exchanged for shells, dogs' teeth, and other items (Hughes 1977; Burton 1985). During the fourteen years of his residence, Robinson was able to collect objects directly from communities and from Europeans as the functions of stone axes were being reevaluated and as communities were forced to raise funds to pay taxes. With the price of rubber down to 10 1/4 d. by April 1928, the Robinsons were facing bankruptcy when the expedition visited (Hope

1979:viii). Although failing to stave this off, the $300 sale undoubtedly helped their transition to New South Wales, Australia (NMNH 106585).

Peck's mother-in-law, Mrs. C. A. Kleinoscheg, donated the other two accessions on 15 October 1935 and 25 January 1936, following Peck's death (NMNH 137754, 131988). Totaling 216 objects, the bulk of Peck's collection came from localities in the northern area of Dutch New Guinea, which he visited as part of the 1926 Dutch-American Expedition (Taylor 2006). The approximately sixty-three objects obtained during the USDA expedition appear to have been collected purely for personal reasons. Correspondence indicates that Peck valued these mementos, which he stored "*sealed* in the cabinet, with disinfectants inside" (29 January 1936, Mrs. Kleinoscheg to Dr. Wetmore, NMNH 137754). While Peck did not record object localities, as Brandes did, he did purchase things at his own expense (11 July 1929, Letter to Dr. Hough, NMNH 106509).

Though Brandes and Peck took the majority of the expedition's still images (and all the moving images), Pemberton and Jeswiet also took photographs with an unknown Graflex camera model and a snapshot Kodak. In addition to the Smithsonian's 149 prints and glass plate negatives in the National Anthropological Archives (NAA 91-8), the National Geographic Society Archives contains 133 prints (of which 99 have been published) that Brandes sold as part of his publishing deal. Although Jeswiet's photographs are with his family (and as of this writing remain unseen), some forty prints appear as part of Pemberton's report to the Hawaiian Sugar Planters Association. Pemberton's daughter possesses two photographic albums of a mixture of images from all the expedition members. The only extant copy of the expedition's black-and-white silent film, *Sugar Plant Hunting by Airplane in New Guinea*, is in the NAA, but there are short extracts in the National Archives of the United States (see Bell 2010b).

TO NEW GUINEA IN SEARCH OF SUGAR CANE

Whereas a basic itinerary of the expedition can be found in textual sources (Brandes 1929; Jeswiet 1938; Pemberton n.d., 1930), the film illuminating these encounters is a confusing source due to its nonchronological editing (Bell 2010b). Indeed, the collections outlined above are what provide the most detailed information regarding localities visited, and it is only through bringing these sources together that a more complete account of where the expedition went, what it did, and thus the agencies of communities that were visited can begin to emerge. What follows is a synthesis.

Following several weeks with Brandes, "interviewing government officials in Sydney and Canberra [and] consulting [with] members of the

FIGURE 5.2

Film still from the film sequence of Ivan Champion drilling members of the Papuan native constabulary. Courtesy of the Human Studies Film Archive, Smithsonian Institution.

Colonial Sugar Refining Company," Pemberton and Jeswiet arrived in Port Moresby on 26 May 1928 (Pemberton n.d.:1). While waiting for Brandes and Peck, who arrived on 17 June with the expedition's plane, and for several days after their arrival, they collected botanical materials around the town (Brandes 1929:276).

Once acquired, the expedition's stores were loaded on the *Vanapa*, an auxiliary ketch, which set out for Everill Junction on the Strickland River, which would be the expedition's base of operations in the Lake Murray–Middle Fly region. The *Vanapa* also carried eight armed, unnamed members of the Papuan Constabulary and their commanding officer, assistant resident magistrate Ivan Champion, and the camp manager, Roy Bannon, who supervised eight Papuans, including Gano, the cook, Euki, the washboy, Emere, the airplane's crew, and Nape, Brandes's assistant (Brandes 1929:267).[6] These individuals and the infrastructure they helped create are temporarily foregrounded visually in the film through panoramic shots at Everill Junction, which are interspersed with a scene of the constabulary force carrying out drills (figure 5.2). The image attests to the performativity of colonialism and the negotiations it entailed (Gosden and Knowles 2001).

I draw attention to these participants because if we are to look for indigenous agencies and ontologies, a similar move needs to be made to think about the other intermediaries who were essential to the collecting endeavor. Too often, these collaborators are obscured (Jacobs 2006; Mueggler 2005). These individuals, particularly the armed Papuan constables and Champion, undoubtedly influenced the exchanges that took

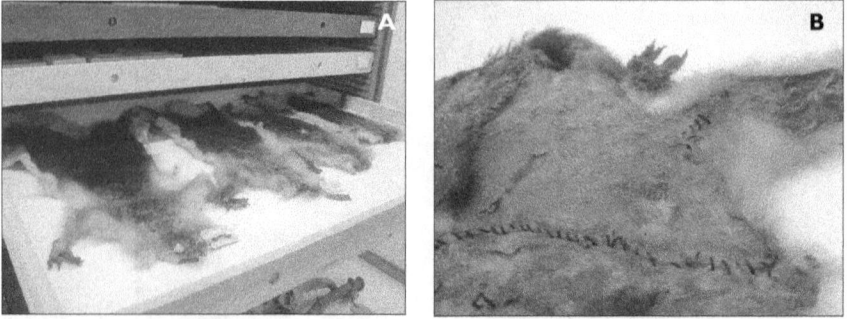

FIGURE 5.3

Four skins of female common spotted cuscus (Spilocuscus maculatus goldiei) *collected near Everill Junction (NMNH 248956–59) (A) and detail of the underside of one skin (B). Photographs by Joshua A. Bell, courtesy of the Division of Mammals, National Museum of Natural History, Smithsonian Institution.*

place and the willingness of communities to engage with the expedition. Besides the short film segments, these collaborators are present in photographs, such as the image captioned "Wussi River men collect cane for Expedition" (Brandes 1929:311). These photographs speak to what Raffles (2002) terms the intimacies of locality making, which infuse the making of collections. Defined as the "differential relationships of affective and often physical proximity between humans, and between humans and non-humans" (Raffles 2002:8), these relationships are present in the expedition's multiple collections and also obscured by them, as evidenced in the lack of named Papuan collaborators. Throughout the expedition, the knowledge of Papuans informed activities in the field and enabled certain collecting.

Such traces are found in the objects themselves. As noted, the fauna collection's small scope suggests that these objects were a result of opportunities provided by the Papuan crew. For example, the roughly treated underside of the four female common spotted cuscus skins suggests inexperience in preserving skins and work hastily done at the camp (K. Helgen personal communication 2010; see figure 5.3). Since they have no marks suggesting they were shot, I suspect that the cuscus were trapped by Papuans to supplement their food rations and the skins were subsequently obtained by Brandes. While conjectural, this example hints at the ways the collections emerged as the product of sets of knowledge and agencies worked out on-site between non-indigenous people, Papuan collaborators working for the colonial state, and those being engulfed by it.

Just as the intermediaries need to be acknowledged, the sheer amount of materials deployed by the expedition needs to be highlighted because it

FIGURE 5.4

Unpublished photograph by Brandes captioned "Natives looking at motor of seaplane, Sepik River, near Marienberg, August 26, 1928." National Geographic Society Archives, courtesy of the Brandes family.

shaped their engagements and thus the collections (Gosden and Knowles 2001; Bennett, chapter 2, this volume). The expedition's provisions consisted of "1,150 gallons of aviation gasoline…tons of tinned food and rice, 3 portable boats with outboard motors, 6 wall tents and 39 tent flies, and [the] usual complement of cots, blankets, fine-mesh sleeping nets, arms, ammunitions, hospital goods, and an assortment of scientific supplies, including still and motion-picture cameras" (Brandes 1929:267–268). Mytinger (1946:349, 378) notes further that the expedition possessed "three portable canvas canoes" for navigating shallow lagoons, two outboard motors, and "a trim little gramophone with [a] crate of shining records right out of a Washington store, and a whole box of sharp, unrusted needles." She also comments on eating "sun-downers [a cracker]…served with relishes, cheese, olives, [and] pickles" (Mytinger 1946:349). The attempt to retain aspects of colonial civility in the camp is seen in a posed photograph of the expedition members at a table, being served by Papuans (Brandes 1929:282).

The expedition's unpublished photographs in the NGSA collection provide other glimpses into the ways in which the members' experiences were mediated through an array of things. Critical forensic analysis of the images helps bring into focus details not originally intended by the photographer, which further situate the event at hand. In an unpublished image taken on the bank of the Sepik River near the Marienberg Mission Station (figure 5.4), we can see crates of Castrol motor oil on the photograph's left edge, which were part of the expedition's extensive aviation fuel depot.

The cloth laplaps around the men's waists speak to their enmeshment within the colonial labor system, as do the leaves of tobacco held by the man on the left. Tobacco was a common payment for labor provided to the expedition. Such details work against the purification of Brandes's textual and filmic narratives, which focus on the Europeans, and help reconstruct the practices and moments by which knowledge and the collections were formed (Bell 2010b, in press).

While waiting for the *Vanapa* to arrive at Everill Junction, the scientists collected cane in and around Motuan villages near Moresby (17 June–7 July, 15–21 July) and around the government station of Kikori in the Papuan Gulf (8–13 July) by means of their plane. On 21 July, the scientists flew to Everill Junction and began visiting different localities around Lake Murray–Middle Fly (21 July–7 August). The expedition then descended the Fly River, visiting communities (Orionio, Adura, Morigio, Weridai, Okani, Goaribari, Kunni-Kunni, Kairi, and Kikori) by boat and plane en route to Moresby (7–18 August). The group then divided, with Jeswiet, Pemberton, and Champion traveling to the Rigo district (Jeswiet 1938:427; Pemberton n.d.:10–14; Port Moresby 1928). With the help of some hundred carriers, they visited thirty-four communities, collecting botanical specimens. Pemberton's photographs reveal further collaboration with their Papuan carriers and the police and how they worked with community members to obtain specimens. Meanwhile, Brandes and Peck flew to Lae in the territory of New Guinea (24–25 August) and picked up a German priest, Father Joseph Kirschbaum, at the Marienberg Mission Station on the Sepik (26–28 August).[7] Kirschbaum would play a key role during the 1928–1929 Crane Pacific Expedition's trip up the Sepik (Webb 1995, 1996). His involvement is instructive. For example, at Bien, near the Sepik River's mouth, Kirschbaum asked "the chief to command the woman to pose for us [and then] intimated to the chief that we might be willing to purchase some trinkets. At once all the women scurried off into their houses and soon returned with all kinds of carved wooden images, drums, shields, etc., which they handed to the men to show us" (Shurcliff 1930:215–216).

Similar levels of mediation appear to have taken place during the USDA expedition's trip with Kirschbaum to Ambunti (29, 31 August–1 September), an unnamed village on the Upper Sepik (30 August), the western Iatmul community of Nyaurangai (31 August), and unnamed communities on the Lower Sepik River (31 August) before Brandes and Peck returned to Moresby via Madang (2–3 September). This is particularly evident in a staged sequence of sago processing near the Marienberg Mission, which was most likely arranged on the basis of Kirschbaum's personal relationships (Bell in press). Reunited in Moresby, expedition members prepared the sugarcane cuttings and traveled by steamer to Sydney and then to their respective homes (Brandes 1929:332; Bell 2010b).

Before I turn to Lake Murray–Middle Fly, I will make some general comments about the expedition's encounters with communities. Though the timelines varied, all the communities the expedition encountered had had some form of engagement with outsiders (Europeans, Indonesians, Chinese, or Malays) and thus had some expectations about what outsiders desired. That specific things were desired would have come as no surprise, given the extent to which relations were mediated by exchanges that transformed bodies through new labor regimes and local ecologies through the emerging plantation economy (Gewertz 1983; Gosden and Knowles 2001). The Middle Sepik is a case in point. More than twenty European expeditions replete with non-European carriers, crew, and police came to the region between 1885 and 1914 (Bragge, Claas, and Roscoe 2006:103). Things played various roles in both the peaceful and the violent interactions of these thousand or so visitors. Between 1909 and 1915, some 9,560 cultural objects left the Sepik River area, with thousands more undocumented (Bragge, Claas, and Roscoe 2006:103; see Buschmann 2009). Overmodeled skulls played a major role in this trade, with at least 466 being collected (Bragge, Claas, and Roscoe 2006:103), and it is no surprise that Brandes was also able to collect one (NMNH E344946).

Similar motivations influenced Brandes's and Peck's obtaining three rattan cuirasses found among the Yonggoms/Muyus of the Ok-Tedi and Upper Fly region. Two entered the NMNH's collection from Brandes (E344772) and Peck (E377483); the third remains in Brandes's family and is now a wastepaper basket in his son's home (E. Goldfaden personal communication 2000). These objects, along with the stuffed trophy heads Brandes obtained in the Lake Murray–Middle Fly, were iconic. Anthropologists mapped the distribution of these and other objects to articulate notions of violence and the constitutions of humanity, and these were sought after to fulfill personal and commercial desires (O'Hanlon and Welsch 2000). Such external desires inevitably fed back into local production, as has been demonstrated for obsidian objects in the Admiralty Islands (Torrence 1993), and created spaces for more productive ways for communities to rid themselves of spent objects, such as the *malanggan* in New Ireland (Küchler 1997). In this way, communities collected Europeans and Americans, and their things, as much as they found their things being collected.

Less certain is how communities understood the expedition's interest in sugarcane and other biological specimens. Until fieldwork with the communities encountered by the expedition is done, only tentative state-ments can be made. In all of the localities visited, the environment was understood to be a palimpsest of ancestral actions and to be inhabited by a range of nonhuman beings. More than this, people's quotidian actions—inspecting a fruit tree, harvesting rattan, gathering edible grubs—trans-formed localities into a "conduit of inscribed activity" (Weiner 2003:11) through which kin and property relations were negotiated (Moutu 2009). Sugarcane partook of this fluid realm of agencies as part of communi-ties' varied food sources and was something normally given to visitors to acknowledge their sociality (Busse 1987:68; Kirsch 2006). With the expedi-tion members' tropes of the wild and savage to describe the landscape and communities, it is clear that they had no sense of these relationships. It is unclear how communities would have understood the collecting of other botanical specimens. The gathering of sugarcane may have been seen by some as part of the normal establishment of relationships through food, and others may have seen it as an extension of the extractive industries of the plantation economy.

Other actions may not have been interpreted so straightforwardly. Although other nonhuman beings—cuscus, cassowary, flying fox, croco-dile—that the expedition collected or killed were in many instances locally consumed, they were also enmeshed in totemic systems. Most, if not all, entities were understood to be the result of mythic actions or to be poten-tial forms in which spirit beings resided. For example, cuscus, such as those collected by the expedition in the Lake Murray–Middle Fly region (see figure 5.3), were totems of the Kaukwin moiety (Busse 1987:236). Their killing, if witnessed, may have been understood as a demonstration of the group's non-affiliation to the totem. A similar analysis may have been made of their killing many crocodiles near Everill Junction (Brandes 1929:283). Such displays may have helped confirm a local name for Europeans—pu anim, which is derived from the sound of a gun (pu) and the word for people (anim) (Busse 1987:138, n. 28). These and other encounters pro-vided further information about the nature of the expedition's sociality.

Despite the impressions these actions may have given, the photographs and film show that many local people had no problem engaging with the expedition. Prints in the National Geographic Society Archives show men standing alongside expedition members with sugarcane, as well as crowd-ing the airplane (Bell in press). Indeed, recognizing the expedition as a source of desired trade, these men may have been trying to monopolize the relations they saw unfolding (Strathern 1992). Except for the Rigo trip, the airplane also shaped their impressions. Though a novelty, any supernatural aura that Brandes thought the Papuans attributed to the vehicle may have just as likely been wariness, given Peck's tendency to dive-bomb canoes and fly low around villages. The plane's limited storage capacity shaped what could be collected, and the expedition members' fear of possible violence or theft induced them to remain in its immediate vicinity. With few exceptions, much of what was collected had been preselected by communities (Schindlebeck 1993). Finally, due to the perishable nature of the sugarcane, these engagements lasted only a few hours or days (Brandes and Sartoris 1936:568).

PERSPECTIVES ON ENGAGEMENTS IN THE LAKE MURRAY–MIDDLE FLY REGION

The issue for communities was not whether the expedition was supernatural, as Brandes (1929:290) presumed, but rather what capacities the members possessed and how they could be productively engaged with.[8] The time spent in the Lake Murray–Middle Fly area was the most sustained and thus is illuminating. The rhetoric of pioneering exploration ignored the global network of relations by which Zimakani- and Boazi-speaking communities were connected to an array of human and nonhuman constituents, the articulation of which in 1928 was shaped by fifty-two years of interactions with Europeans and Asians (Bell 2010b). On the main body of Lake Murray, the USDA expedition visited Maravu and Kaundoma, and on the Strickland they visited Devam. They also ventured to Daviumbu and Avu Lagoon and "discovered" Wam Lagoon, which they named Lake Herbert Hoover (Brandes 1929:259, 314–315). On the basis of identification of objects in the film footage, filming appears to have been confined to either Devam or Daviumbu community and Kaundoma.

Various intersecting histories predated the expedition. Most significant perhaps were the bird of paradise hunters, who from 1908 to 1914 came looking for the greater bird of paradise (*Paradisaea apoda*) and the Raggiana bird of paradise (*Paradisaea raggiana*). To stem the decline of birds, the territory of Papua outlawed their hunting in 1908, but men routinely came across the border from Dutch New Guinea to hunt in the Lake Murray–Middle Fly and the Upper Fly (Busse 1987:139–140; Schoorl 1993:149–156; Swadling 1996:188–199). They were a source of desirable trade, though violence did shape these encounters (Schoorl 1993:150–151; Busse 1987:140–142).

More immediately relevant was the establishment of Everill Junction as a police camp in November 1927 with the goal of finding and punishing two to three hundred Suki and Zimakani men for their raid against the

Kiwai community of Weredai on the Lower Fly River before the expedition's visit (Daru 1927a, 1927b). This was the largest site of sustained government presence in the region, and it is hard to imagine that the expedition's reoccupation of Everill Junction did not continue certain associations. The expedition began on 10 November 1927 led by patrol officer Zimmer, who was joined sixteen days later by the resident magistrate, E. R. Oldham, with sixteen police and twenty long-term prisoners from Daru, who assisted in clearing the site known locally as Gaumapa. During 27–28 November, "over a hundred men visited the camp," with several assisting in exchange for tobacco. Several men accompanied Oldham to Daru on 29 November (Oldham 1929:19), as did another twenty-three during a subsequent visit by Zimmer in April 1928 (Oldham 1929:19). During the later police action, however, one man was shot and fifty-one men from several communities were arrested and taken to Daru (Oldham 1929:19; Busse 1987:151–152). Although Zimmer returned these men in 1929, during the expedition's visit they remained absent, with their fate a source of speculation. Two days after Champion's arrival on the *Vanapa*, several men "paid him a friendly visit... and asked when the men at Daru would be returning" (Oldham 1929:20).

Caroline Mytinger and Margaret Warner, American artists and travelers who hitched a ride on the *Vanapa* to Everill Junction, appear to have reinforced the expedition's association with the government's earlier actions.[9] They did so by revealing a nearly life-size portrait of Tauparaupi, one of the imprisoned men from the Weredai massacre, whom they had painted earlier in Daru (Mytinger 1946:268–269, 270–279). Wishing to complete the painting of Tauparaupi's shorn hair, Mytinger showed the portrait and mentioned her model's name (1946:383–384). While one can only speculate as to the Zimakani men's understandings of this portrait, it likely provoked gossip about the arrested men's fate and perhaps confusion about what the image of Tauparaupi was and why they were being shown his image now. Here, we have an example of the enchantment of technology (Gell 1992): the men may have understood the portrait to be Tauparaupi's body transformed in a fashion analogous to their own acts of transformation, through headhunting and the making of stuffed trophy heads and decorated skulls. This is perhaps why, when the men encountered the image, they "stopped in their tracks and stared with a wild-eyed expression" and, when induced to come aboard the ship, examined the painting's back and "scratch[ed] at the paint with a fingernail" (Mytinger 1946:383).

Boazi oral histories about Europeans, obtained by Busse during his fieldwork in the 1980s, help to further frame this and other encounters. Boats such as that which the Italian naturalist and explorer Luigi D'Albertis traveled on in 1876 and 1877 were believed to be "huge catfish which belched smoke from their dorsal fins," shirts were understood to be removable skin, and white men themselves were thought to be *givagiv*, malicious spirits with supernatural powers (Busse 1987:132). Similarly, in 1914, men from the Wamek village of Duand believed a government party to be *givagiv* (Busse 1987:145). While it is not clear the extent that such interpretations permeated perceptions in 1928, it is likely that this was part of the array of possibilities that Europeans presented. Much of the fear that Mytinger and the expedition members perceived people as expressing may very well have been wonderment at the communities' capacities to elicit strangers with whom relations could unfold. Indeed, what was at stake was how to turn these encounters into productive conduits for exchange (Strathern 1990, 1992).

Still and moving images reveal that despite any wonderment or hesitation, trade was swiftly established (Bell 2010b). Arrows with sugarcane shafts and bows form roughly half of the 105 objects obtained from the eight communities visited in this region. Though some of the bows appear used, all the arrows, each displaying technical and artistic detail, are unused. At Kaundoma, a community on the northeast shore of Lake Murray, the film footage documented a series of exchanges that transpired on 27 July. Later, men and women gathered around the plane, on the pontoons of which Brandes, Peck, and Pemberton appear to have stayed. Community members are seen moving back and forth, carrying birds of paradise plumes, tobacco pipes, arrows, and blocks of sago (figure 5.5A and B), all of which previous visitors had wanted, and indeed the expedition collected those things. A bird of paradise ornament similar to those offered by the men appears in Peck's collection (see figure 5.5C), and the same men appear with different objects in other sequences filmed at Kaundoma, showing that they offered a series of things in their attempts to learn what the expedition wanted (figures 5.6–5.9). In another sequence, a man holds a painted skull, which Peck obtained (NMNH 377581). This skull is one of three collected from Miwa and Devam on the Strickland River, where two necklaces of human jaws were also obtained. Skulls and stuffed trophy heads were key products of the regional headhunting complex and were tokens by which men transformed others in the constitution of themselves. Whereas some of these things became inalienable parts of men's cults (Busse 1987:103, n.26), others, such as those collected by the expedition, circulated. Jawbone necklaces were important valuables used in bridewealth and peace payments. If Brandes's comments are to be believed—that their arrival by plane caused everyone to flee and remain hidden for two hours (Brandes 1929:284)—it is possible that the jawbones were offered to appease the startlingly new

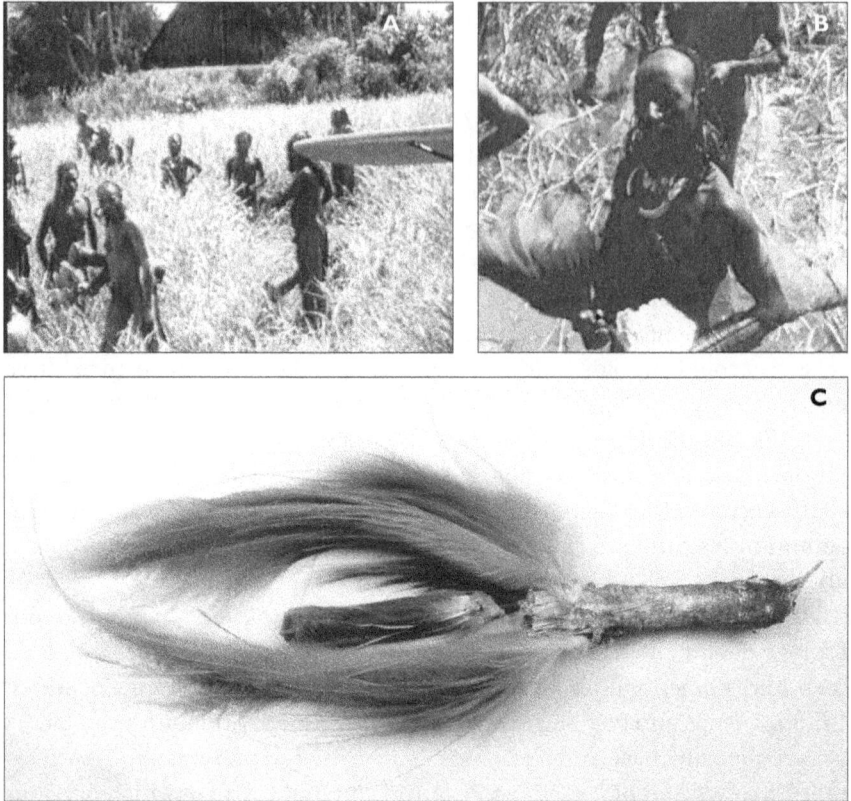

FIGURE 5.5

(A) *Opening screen shot of Kaundoma on Lake Murray, where men approach with bird of paradise feathers and* (B) *blocks of sago, among other things.* (C) *Peck purchased a bird of paradise skin and plumes (NMNH E377619), which appear to be very similar to those being held by men in the film footage. Film still courtesy of the Human Studies Film Archive, Smithsonian Institution; photograph courtesy of the Department of Anthropology, National Museum of Natural History, Smithsonian Institution.*

forms that had arrived by air and through their offering show these strangers that the communities were also human (Justin Shaffner personal communication 2010).

Returning to interactions at Kaundoma, in the film footage, one sees expedition members' pointing hands or the passing of trade goods, thus assisting with linking things back to communities and to specific, though unnamed, individuals (see figures 5.6–5.8). In one segment, Brandes selects a bamboo pipe (NMNH E344803) and perhaps some arrows by pointing

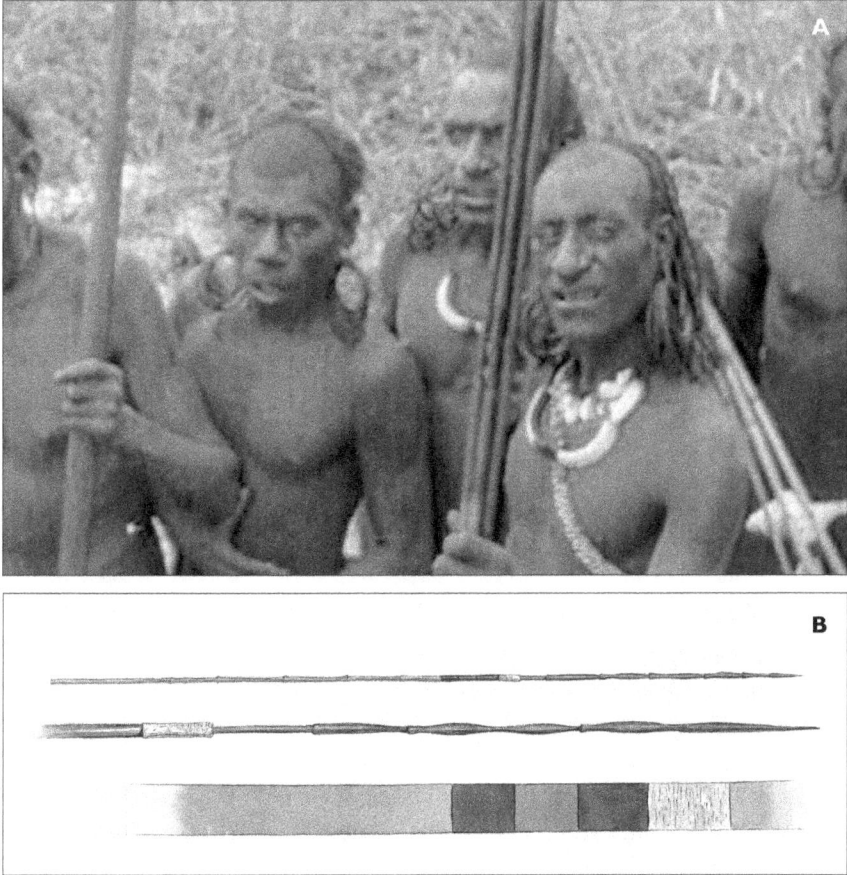

FIGURE 5.6

(A) *Film still of another scene of exchange at Kaundoma, where the same man in figure 5.5B is visible. He and his companions hold arrows with black palm tips similar to arrows Brandes collected in Kaundoma (see NMNH 344798, illustrated in B). Film still courtesy of the Human Studies Film Archive, Smithsonian Institution; illustration courtesy of Alexis Demetriades.*

from the plane's pontoon. An older man hands the material in a basket to a youth, who then approaches. This footage provides glimpses of the wider sets of negotiations within communities as men move around, talking about what to trade, assessing what they are receiving, working within their own group dynamics.

Another example is similarly illuminating. At Kaundoma, a man was filmed looking up at Brandes while offering several feather ornaments (see figure 5.8). A small knife is filmed being passed to the man. A subsequent

FIGURE 5.7

(A) *Brandes's arm, visible to the left in the film still, points toward a man as he passes to a boy arrows and a fiber basket in which is a bamboo tobacco pipe.* (B) *This pipe may be one of three collected by Brandes at Kaundoma (NMNH E344803). Film still courtesy of the Human Studies Film Archive, Smithsonian Institution; illustration courtesy of Alexis Demetriades.*

photograph shows him post-transaction, holding the knife and trade beads, without his headdress and boar's tooth necklace, and with a caption that attributes the man's look to his being befuddled by the plane and the expedition's array of things. For communities used to selling and buying knowledge,

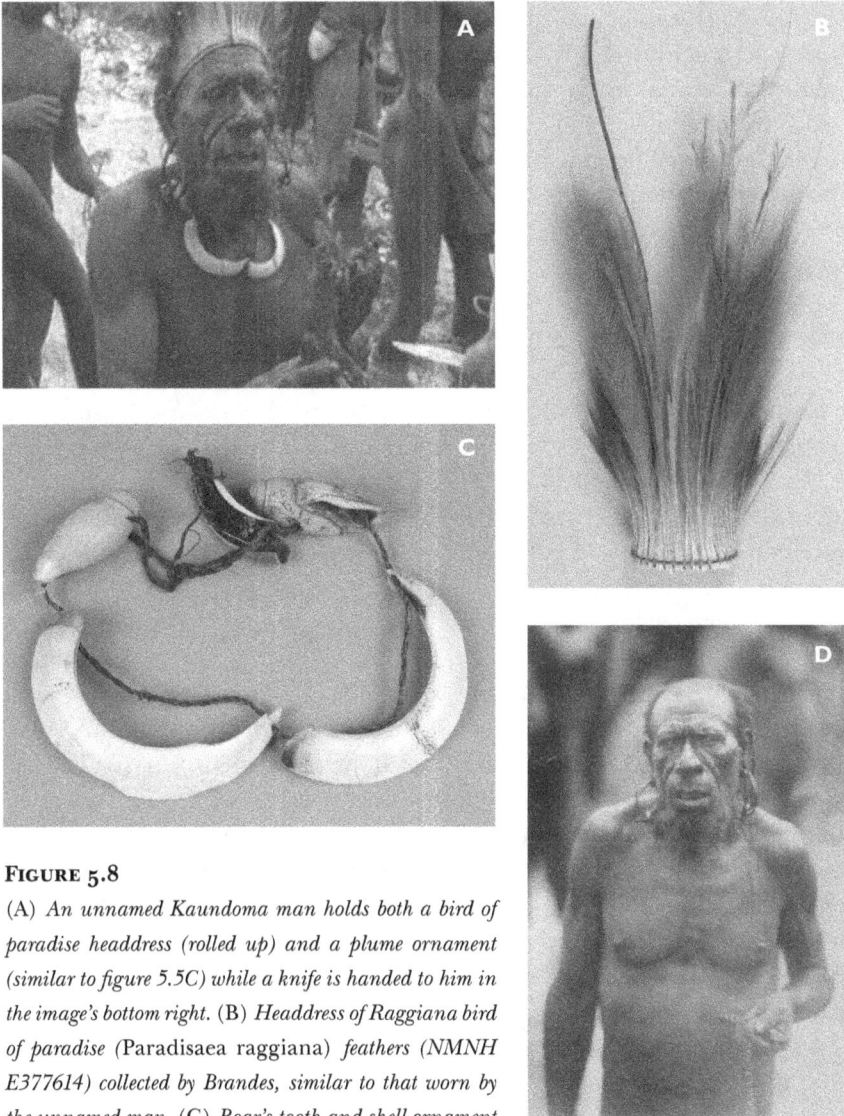

FIGURE 5.8

(A) *An unnamed Kaundoma man holds both a bird of paradise headdress (rolled up) and a plume ornament (similar to figure 5.5C) while a knife is handed to him in the image's bottom right.* (B) *Headdress of Raggiana bird of paradise* (Paradisaea raggiana) *feathers (NMNH E377614) collected by Brandes, similar to that worn by the unnamed man.* (C) *Boar's tooth and shell ornament worn by the unnamed man (NMNH E344811).* (D) *The same man without his headdress and boar's tusk necklace. This unpublished image in the National Geographic Society Archives is captioned "Wild Lake Murray native holding beads and knife just given him by Dr. Brandes. The man is struggling to think what these strange white men are." Film still courtesy of the Human Studies Film Archive, Smithsonian Institution; photographs courtesy of the Department of Anthropology, National Museum of Natural History, Smithsonian Institution and the Brandes family.*

rituals, songs, and objects (Harrison 1989), these exchanges were a means to extend relationships. What the images reveal are the ways in which community members traded what they had physically on them and what they brought to the plane. The ethnographic collections that resulted were not due to the expedition members' obtaining whatever they desired; instead, the collections were infused by a series of choices and negotiations, the traces of which can begin to be teased out when these materials are brought together.

WE ARE ALL SORCERERS

My larger interest in the expedition's recursive loops and the ways the expedition connected both real and imagined American consumers of sugar, cereal, and coffee to the seemingly distant island of New Guinea is nicely brought forward in a quote from one of many short articles that appeared in 1928 and 1929: "One of these days you may be sweetening your cereal, or your coffee, [with] an entirely new brand of sugar—scouted for by airplane, found by a searching party crashing through the brush of New Guinea wilds, and brought back to this country" (Popular Science Monthly 1929). While certain aspects of the expedition's movement and the assemblages and their afterlife were made visible, others were obscured by this and other narratives. Absent is any mention of the role of European and Papuan colonial intermediaries, let alone the Papuan and New Guinea people themselves, from whom and with whom the sugarcane and other things were collected. Throughout its unfolding, the expedition engaged agencies on multiple scales and temporalities that, depending on one's position within this meshwork, possessed and elicited different effects. To understand this dance of agencies, both insider and outsider perspectives need to be examined, with an eye toward how the former usefully complicates the latter.

In concluding, I will briefly discuss an image by Brandes. Taken on 27 July at Kaundoma, the photograph shows an older man at some distance; he squats in the grass with a wing of the airplane visible above (see figure 5.9). Before the man lies a paddle, and in his hands, just visible, is some dark object, perhaps a steel blade, a stone axe, or a parcel of some sort. Squinting, the man looks back at Brandes. The caption reads, "Sorcerer, squatting, the evil genius who apparently urged violence…. This man kept up a guttural chatter to others, and Dr. Brandes could tell by his actions and gestures that he tried to persuade them to attack the party. Enlarge by about two diameters. Important."

The photograph's cardboard mount includes a number of penciled

FIGURE 5.9

Mounted unpublished photograph in the National Geographic Society Archives of a supposed sorcerer, taken by Brandes on 27 July 1928 in Kaundoma. Photograph by Joshua A. Bell, courtesy of the Brandes family.

annotations made by an unknown member of *National Geographic*'s editorial staff. The marks indicate the image's status as a duplicate, arrows indicate spots to be removed, and lines point to where the plane's wing should be bracketed out to focus on the squatting man. This image and Brandes's interpretation condense much of what I have explored in this chapter about the ways in which some agencies were exalted and others obscured by the expedition and the trajectories of its materials. The penciled marks on the photograph's mount are a reminder of the sets of movements by which the agencies involved in the expedition, and the participants, were bracketed and subsequently altered in the transformation of things into specimens and their ongoing performances in different institutions.

The image also usefully recalls some of the uncertainty on both sides of the expedition's encounters: What form would the others' actions and intentions take? How could the expedition elicit sugarcane, and in turn how could the communities elicit the things they wanted in a generative fashion? Whether or not the man was urging his companions to attack, or indeed was a sorcerer, the invocation of this designation is interesting and provides a final way to think about agencies. Within Melanesia, magic is broadly understood to be foundational and a critical way of eliciting relationships with a range of human and nonhuman Others (Weiner 2003). Central to the people's creative engagement with the world and its many agencies, magic was, and remains, a form of analysis and understanding (Kirsch 2006) akin to the technologies materialized in the expedition's cameras and plane and in Mytinger's paintings. Both groups were involved in sorcery as they sought to make sense of their encounters with each other and to shape the terms of engagement (West 2007). Bringing the dispersed aspects of the expedition's assemblage back together, I have tried to signal the agencies at play, the different acts of conjuring that were involved, and the perspectives they entailed (while being explicit about my own magic). I have sought to work against the tendency to bracket out the messiness of the expedition's encounters in the hope that a richer understanding of the expedition, its artifacts, its images, and the communities involved can emerge when they are completely engaged.

Notes

1. This chapter is part of a larger project to connect contemporary New Guinea communities encountered by the USDA Sugarcane Expedition with the heritage materials collected by the expedition. The aim of this project is to understand the historical moments materialized in the expedition's collections and how these materials can be used to understand cultural and environmental transformations in contemporary Papua New Guinea. So far, the focus has been to complete an inventory of the artifacts collected by the expedition before new fieldwork is commenced and another level of narratives obtained (see Bell 2010a).

2. At present, these collaborations are understood to have involved the Celotex Company of Chicago, the Hawaiian Sugar Planters Association, the Colonial Sugar Refining Company of Sydney, the Dutch sugar industry in Java, and the administration of the territory of Papua (see Bell 2010b, in press).

3. Aspects of these men's broader biographies are worth briefly noting. A plant pathologist for the USDA until his retirement in 1951, Elmer Walker Brandes (1891–1953) was essential to research addressing problems caused by mosaic, the curly-top disease of sugar beets, and the leaf disease of Pará rubber trees. Jeswiet (1879–1960) served as chief of the Division of Cane-Breeding of the Experiment Station for Java Sugar Industry at Pasoeroean in eastern Java (1912–1925) before becoming a professor of taxonomy and plant geography at Wageningen Agricultural College (1925–1946).

Before his dismissal due to his Nazi allegiances, Jeswiet played a transformative role in global sugarcane operations through the creation of new hybrid canes (Cramer 1952; Galloway 2005). Cyril Eugene Pemberton (1886–1975) worked for the Hawaiian Sugar Planters Association (1919–1953) and on retiring became an honorary curator at the Bishop Museum (Bianchi 1977). Peck (1896–1931) notably participated in the 1926 Dutch-American expedition to Dutch New Guinea, serving as the expedition's pilot and as a still and motion-picture photographer. He was later killed in a test flight (Taylor 2006).

4. Wageningen lists a thousand specimens, but few are currently in its electronic database. In 1934, specimens obtained from clones of sugarcane collected by the expedition and grown in Guayama, Puerto Rico, were also sent to the US National Herbarium in the NMNH (cat. nos. 128, 152, 177, 895, 908, 1100).

5. At the time of this writing, these collections have not been studied, though preliminary conversations with Pemberton's descendants indicate that he collected 54 objects from the Lake Murray, Ok Tedi, Kikori River, Middle Sepik, and Rigo areas.

6. Though further details about the Papuans have yet to be located, Ivan Francis Champion, OBE (1904–1989), was renowned for his trans–New Guinea crossing up the Fly River (Champion 1932). Born in Oakland, California, Bannon (1892–?) worked as a miner for the Bulolo Dredging Company and later as a warrant officer, and he served during World War II (Bradley 2010:97).

7. Father Franz Joseph Kirschbaum (1882–1939) was a pastor in the Society of the Divine Word, which had been active in former German New Guinea since the 1890s. From 1907 or 1908 until his death in an air crash, Kirschbaum was a pioneer missionary in New Guinea (P. Roscoe 1988:516; Welsch 1998:92–93).

8. I thank Justin Shaffner for calling this dynamic to my attention.

9. The two traveled throughout the Solomons and eastern New Guinea (1926–1930), with Mytinger painting portraits (Mytinger 1946:347–392).

6

We'wha Goes to Washington

Gwyneira Isaac

The story of We'wha in Washington is an intriguing one because it coincides with the formative years of anthropology in the United States and because We'wha herself was a remarkable individual. No simple frame or label could contain or describe her, nor the artifacts she created, nor the indelible impression of Zuni diplomacy that she left with Washingtonians during her six-month stay in DC. While much has been written about her as a berdache, or what Zunis refer to as a *lhamana*—the third gender or "man/woman" (Babcock and Parezo 1988; Lanmon 2006; Roscoe 1991)—little is known about the role she played as an informant during her 1886 visit to DC with the anthropological couple Colonel James and Matilda Coxe Stevenson.[1] According to newspaper accounts, the material contributions she made during this time consisted of pottery, looms, prayer feathers, woven belts, textiles, and photographs—all of which were reportedly accessioned into the Smithsonian collections of the US National Museum, the entity now known as the National Museum of Natural History (NMNH). Unfortunately, if these objects were accessioned, they were never attributed to We'wha, resulting in a significant gap between the accounts of her visit and her material legacy at the Smithsonian.

Sorting through the records of her time in DC raises a number of interesting issues, starting with the question of the anonymity of her accessioned

FIGURE 6.1

We'wha weaving on the National Mall, 1886. National Anthropological Archives, Smithsonian Institution (SI 3644).

contributions. The only mention of her by name in the accession ledgers for the National Museum refers to a photograph of her planting prayer feathers—an image that cannot be found—although a number of other photographs do survive of her and are now housed in the National Anthropological Archives in Washington, DC. In another strange twist, We'wha may also have "remained" in Washington in the form of a mannequin titled "belt-maker" that was produced for the Smithsonian anthropological exhibits shown at the Chicago World's Fair in 1893. This mannequin is now a cast-off but not wholly forgotten ghost of an earlier era of life

FIGURE 6.2

We'wha setting up a loom in the National Museum. National Anthropological Archives, Smithsonian Institution (SI 03641).

groups and dioramas, which have fallen out of favor and have been relegated to the basement of the NMNH.

These starkly different inscriptions of her visit reveal that individual or social agency is created according to its specific telling or, as explored here, is manifested or lost through the particular arenas of anthropological practices—the means and boundaries (i.e., institutional practices) in and according to which histories are retained and reproduced. As with any historical telling, the newspaper accounts and the images of We'wha weaving on the Mall (figure 6.1) and in the museum (figure 6.2) prompt us to consider the performative nature of these events and how this specific aspect may have affected their inscription. In particular, we need to ask, what was being performed beyond the technology of weaving? If We'wha was being presented as someone with innate artisan skills specific to her culture and region, what new relational dynamics occurred when this knowledge was relocated to Washington? A tension can be found between a form of indigenous knowledge valued by anthropologists for its groundedness in a specific environment (see further discussion in the introduction to this volume) and the public or popular value of it created by its mobility—seen here as embodied by We'wha's presence in the nation's capital. Questions arise about the ways in which indigenous knowledge is defined not solely through its point of origin, but also through its repositioning in the Smithsonian and the US capital.

Through these questions, we open up an interrogative space in which to look at how individual creative dynamics combined with institutional practices affect the processes of historical inscription. Who are the main players, what are their interrelational dynamics, and through what means was their story inscribed? I stress creativity here because, although we are prying into the formative years of the science of anthropology, with its heavily structured classificatory schemas, the main characters of our story—We'wha and her anthropological collaborator, Matilda Coxe Stevenson—are the unique agents and subjects of this history due to their unconventional and, more important, creative thinking. In individual ways, each was passionate about the specific means by which cultural history and knowledge should be recorded. We'wha took tremendous risks in her unwavering commitment to ensure that her cultural traditions were transcribed at the national level. Stevenson was obsessed with accuracy, which would enable her ethnographic texts to stand the test of time (Isaac 2005; Parezo 1993).[2] While many have speculated on the nature of their friendship, there can be no doubt that their shared intellectual passion for the study of cultural knowledge (both theirs and others') forged a lasting union between them.

We turn now to a series of arenas in which our storytellers perform. We start in the Pueblo of Zuni with James and Matilda Stevenson's introduction to We'wha, exploring the beginnings of this collaboration around the sharing of cultural knowledge. We then shift to We'wha's visit to Washington, her navigation of Washington society inside and outside the museum, and Matilda's role as her host and scribe. Our third and last exploratory arena is the current configuration of the collections and archives and how these provide insight into the means by which their stories have been retained.

LIKE-MINDED INDIVIDUALS: WE'WHA AND MATILDA COXE STEVENSON IN ZUNI

Our story begins in the Pueblo of Zuni, New Mexico, where We'wha was introduced to members of the 1879 Bureau of American Ethnology (BAE) expedition to the Southwest. This was the first fieldwork project under the auspices of the BAE and, in many ways, the first of its kind, in that it included an in-depth anthropological study of indigenous peoples of the United States. During their stay in Zuni, the expedition photographer, John K. Hillers, chose to photograph the students at the new Presbyterian

FIGURE 6.3

We'wha with the students of the Presbyterian school, Zuni Pueblo. Photograph by John K. Hillers, Smithsonian archives (22251d2).

school that had been opened in the pueblo a year earlier (figure 6.3). In the center of the image, standing halfway between the girls gathered on the left and the boys on the right, is We'wha, who by this time was wearing full female attire. According to expedition members, We'wha was working for the Presbyterian school as a matron for the children and as overall domestic help (Roscoe 1991).

While records indicate that, traditionally, lhamanas were an important and integrated component of Zuni life (Stevenson 1904; Parsons 1916; Benedict 1934; Roscoe 1991), non-Zuni visitors to the pueblo had difficulty in translating or understanding this practice. In the first years of encounter, the expedition members did not recognize We'wha as a man in women's clothing—a fact that, in hindsight, many historians found hard to believe. In effect, once her male sex was known more widely among Euro Americans, the female identity was taken to be unbelievable. In a thoughtful portrayal of We'wha, Will Roscoe explores which of the members of the BAE and subsequent expeditions understood that We'wha was a lhamana. He notes that Frank Hamilton Cushing—the BAE ethnologist who remained in Zuni after the rest of the expedition returned to DC—recorded We'wha

147

in his census of the pueblo as a hermaphrodite and later, in 1920, George Wharton James described her as a man dressed in women's clothes:

> She was a remarkable woman, a fine blanket and sash maker, an excellent cook, an adept in all the work of her sex, and yet strange to say, she was a man. There never has been, as yet, any satisfactory explanation given...of the peculiar custom followed by the Pueblos of having one or two men in each tribe, who foreswear their manhood and who dress as, act like and seemingly live the life of, women. Wewha was one of these. (James 1920:64)

We'wha's unconventional role guaranteed her placement in Euro American historical accounts in photographs with annotations as to the complexity of her gender. The inclusion of her pottery and weaving within the Smithsonian collections, however, does not stem from this, but rather from the early recognition by the expedition members of her artistic talents. According to James, "she excelled all other of the Zuni women in the exercise of her skill in blanket and pottery making. Her blanketry was noted far and wide, and her pottery fetched twice the price of any other maker" (qtd. in Roscoe 1991:51). The Stevensons commissioned We'wha to make pottery for the National Museum, and Cushing, who facilitated this transaction, wrote back to Washington: "The articles which you have ordered from We We are not even begun. I have called on her twice relative to them since your departure.... I desire you to say to Mrs. Stevenson that I have done everything to get We We at the work.... Today she informed Miss Hamakin it was too cold to begin" (Southwest Museum 1879).

While much has been made about the fact that initially Matilda Stevenson did not question We'wha's female identity, following the revelation that she was a lhamana, Stevenson appears to be the only anthropologist or historian to provide an ethnographic explanation for her important social and ceremonial role. Stevenson had previously recorded the supreme deity in Zuni as being made up of both male and female genders, and she may have linked this particular duality to lhamanas, giving We'wha a level of efficacy not recognized by any of the other anthropologists working at Zuni. She also wrote of the acceptance in Zuni of lhamanas and the positive aspects for mothers and other women in the family in being able to keep their sons in their household. In line with the matrilineal practices of Zunis, men would leave their mother's house to live with their wife's family. In 1904 Stevenson noted the following:

> Men who adopt female attire do so of their own volition, having

from childhood hung about the house and usually preferring
to do the work of women. On reaching puberty their decision
is final. If they are to continue woman's work they must adopt
woman's dress; and although the women of the family joke the
fellow, they are inclined to look upon him with favor, since it
means that he will remain a member of the household and do
almost double the work of a woman. (Stevenson 1904:37)

Perceptions about transvestites in Euro American culture were rigid
and their treatment punitive. Correspondence from Clara True, an associate of Stevenson with whom the anthropologist later fought a bitter court
case, reveals the prejudices against which Stevenson would have been working in the years following recognition of We'wha's role as a lhamana. In a
biography of Stevenson, Lurie suggests that her "forthright acceptance of
We'wha illustrates a degree of scientific and personal sophistication noteworthy for her time and sex" (1966:57).

Since the 1990s Stevenson has gained recognition as one of the first
women to conduct fieldwork in the United States (Miller 2007; figure 6.4).
The daughter of an educationally progressive Washington/Philadelphia
family, she studied geology, mineralogy, and chemistry under Dr. Mew of
the Army Medical School. In 1872 she married Colonel Stevenson, "a self
taught geologist, naturalist and anthropologist," who was the executive officer for the Hayden Geological Survey (Parezo 1993:40). Before their joint
work at Zuni, she accompanied him on expeditions to Colorado, Idaho,
Wyoming, and Utah and with his guidance began her first ethnographic
investigations among the Arapahos and Utes. In 1879, when he was put in
charge of the BAE expedition to the Southwest, Matilda joined him and
became a member in her own right of the expedition (Parezo 1993:40).

It has also been noted that the Stevensons were the first husband-and-
wife team recorded in the history of anthropology (Parezo 1988). Together,
they were able to provide a more holistic account of life within the pueblos
than if they had worked separately. They were complimented for these collective methods by Edward Burnett Tylor, the first professor of anthropology at Oxford University, who had visited them at Zuni. In 1885 in a lecture
to the Anthropological Society of Washington, Tylor extolled the benefits
of a husband-and-wife team: "And one thing I particularly noticed was this,
that to get at the confidence of the tribe, the man of the house, though he
can do a great deal, cannot do it all. If his wife sympathizes with his work,
and is able to do so, really half the work of investigation seems to fall to her,
so much is to be learned through the women of the tribe which the men

FIGURE 6.4
Matilda Coxe Stevenson. Photograph dated 1872. National Anthropological Archives, Smithsonian Institution (SI 01144900).

will not readily disclose" (Tylor 1885:93). Stevenson took Tylor's method-ological recommendations to heart, seeking insight into both female and male aspects of a society. In a description of We'wha gathering and prepar-ing clay for pottery making, Stevenson recorded the ceremonial aspects, as well as her own ability as a woman to gain entrance to a process withheld from the male members of the expedition:

> On passing a stone heap she [We'wha] picked up a small stone in her left hand, and spitting upon it, carried the hand around her head and threw the stone over one shoulder upon the stone heap in order that her strength might not go from her when carrying the load down the mesa.... When she drew near to the clay bed she indicated to Mr. Stevenson that he must remain behind, as men never approached the spot. Proceeding a short

distance the party reached a point where We'wha requested the writer remain perfectly quiet and not talk, saying "should we talk, my pottery would crack in the baking, and unless I pray constantly the clay will not appear to me." She applied the hoe vigorously to the hard soil, all the while murmuring prayers to Mother Earth. Nine-tenths of the clay was rejected, every lump being tested between the fingers as to its texture. After gathering about 150 pounds in a blanket tied around her forehead, We'wha descended the steep mesa, apparently unconscious of the weight. (Stevenson 1904:374)

On appraising We'wha's status as a lhamana, Stevenson would have appreciated her ability to share knowledge of both male and female realms, as well as her nuanced understanding of the relationship between the two.

Although We'wha may have initially been introduced to the expedition for her domestic skills, these were not what curried favor with Stevenson, who quickly engaged with her intelligence. Subsequently, We'wha became important, if not *the most* important, informant or collaborator in Matilda's documentation of Zuni life. She wrote that We'wha was "the most intelligent person [in] the pueblo," who possessed "a good memory, not only for the lore of her people, but for all that she heard of the outside world" (Stevenson 1904:37). She also noted that We'wha's oratory skills were recognized by Zunis and that "owing to her bright mind and excellent memory, she was called upon by her own clan and also by the clans of her foster mother and father when a long prayer had to be repeated or a grace was to be offered over a feast" (Stevenson 1904:310–311). In acknowledging We'wha's significance in Zuni ceremony, Stevenson wrote that she was "the chief personage on many occasions" (1904:310–311). We'wha's accuracy appealed to Stevenson, who saw her own contribution to anthropology as her ability to open up the religious societies and practices—or as she referred to them, the "storehouses of memory"—to scientific analysis (Isaac 2005). Because knowledge was passed down orally in Zuni, her connection to an erudite and companionable Zuni man/woman who enjoyed demonstrating and discussing Zuni culture would have been a defining relationship for Stevenson. Similarly, for We'wha, her time in Washington and the recognition gained through Stevenson for her artistic skills and ceremonial knowledge would have widened We'wha's perspective on the world beyond Zuni.

The fortuitous pairing of these two intellects resulted in Stevenson and We'wha working together during Stevenson's return visits to the pueblo in 1881, 1884–1885, 1891–1892, 1895, and 1896, the year in which We'wha died. Of interest to this particular inquiry is the request from both of the Stevensons for We'wha to join them in Washington. This invitation served Matilda's desire to popularize anthropology and to encourage political backing and funding from Congress, which supported the Smithsonian Institution. Second, it also provided her with the means to work in an environment where We'wha might be more open to sharing knowledge, "in close companionship" and away from the prying eyes and ears of Zunis, who might have intervened in the sharing of religious knowledge (Roscoe 1991:62). For We'wha, it appears to have satisfied her own appetite for learning, including gaining insight into Euro American society. As Stevenson noted, We'wha had an "indomitable will" combined with an "insatiable thirst for knowledge" (1904:310).

PRINCESS OR PRIESTESS? WE'WHA TAKES ON WASHINGTON

In 1886 We'wha accompanied the Stevensons as they traveled from Zuni to their house near Logan Circle in Washington, DC. She remained there for six months until a suitable chaperone could be found to accompany her back to Zuni. Following the noted success of Cushing's introduction of a delegation of Zuni leaders to East Coast society a few years earlier, Roscoe posits, Matilda Stevenson invited We'wha with the intention of increasing the visibility of her research among influential Washingtonians. The numerous newspaper accounts attest to the high level of publicity We'wha received. The terminology used to describe her, however, is perhaps more ambiguous than Stevenson intended: "Society has had recently a notable addition in the shape of an Indian princess of the Zuni tribe. This is the princess Wawa. She is the guest of the wife of Col. Stevenson of the geological survey. Princess Wawa goes about everywhere at all the receptions and teas of Washington wearing her native dress" (*Washington Chronicle*, 18 April 1886).

Although the reporters chose to label We'wha as an Indian princess, Stevenson consistently introduced her as a Zuni priestess. In a letter of introduction to President Grover Cleveland, Stevenson wrote, "We'wha a Zuni Indian priestess...has been spending the winter with me for the purpose of Ethnological study" (qtd. in Roscoe 1991:70). In reporting this event, however, one newspaper stated, "We wha the Zuni princess, walked up the broad entrance to the White House yesterday, and in company with Mrs. Col. Stevenson, was shown into the Green Room. She was dressed in her aboriginal costume and wore a headdress of feathers" (*Washington Post*, 24 June 1886). Reporters looking for a story of epic proportions most likely heard "princess" or replaced "priestess" with it. Whereas a priestess was an unfamiliar concept to Washingtonians, a visiting princess was bound to pique the interest of the social circles for which these articles were written. The idea of an Indian princess may also have ignited nineteenth-century fascinations with kingdoms/chiefdoms that had ceded to invading settlers, perceiving that their presence gave the Euro Americans the right to claim their own American-born "royal" lineages (Deloria 1969).

The inscriptions of We'wha's visit to DC—at least in the popular press—had little to do with her scholarly intentions or her Zuni or anthropological identity. She was depicted according to how the press wanted to see her. Her abilities for cultural adaptation, however, were adept, and the papers noted in great detail this admirable trait. They described how she quickly set about learning English, the correct social protocols for meeting and greeting visitors, and how to find her way around town by following the tracks for the streetcars (Roscoe 1991). Stevenson observed in her ethnography that We'wha "acquired the language with remarkable rapidity, and was soon able to join in conversation" (1904:130). A revealing account from the *National Tribune* recorded her mastery of Washington social etiquette:

> It is surprising how quickly she learned to know how to greet visitors when they came to Mr. Stevenson's house and to recognize those whom she had met once. The writer hereof was introduced to her there at one of Mrs. Stevenson's Friday afternoon receptions, when the others were calling, yet, on repeating the visit three or four weeks later, We'wha, who was alone in the parlor at the time, at once recognized the voice and stepped to the door, saying, as she held out her hand to shake hands, "How do you do? Walk in. Sit down." All was said in a cordial tone and with a very bright smile. (*National Tribune*, 20 May 1886)

The records of We'wha's role in Stevenson's exploration of Zuni art, technology, and ceremony are sparser than those of her social appearances in the popular press, leaving us to consider that publicity was a key element of Stevenson's plan. Twelve newspaper articles chronicle the social activities of We'wha, but only two refer to their joint ethnological activities.[3] In a paper written for *Science*, Otis Mason, the curator of ethnology at the National Museum, stated, "For six months this woman has taught her patroness the language, myths, and arts of the Zunis—now explaining some intricate ceremony, at another time weaving [a] belt or blanket under the eye of the camera" (Mason 1886:24). Among the Zuni origin stories published in Stevenson's ethnography, two are attributed to We'wha.

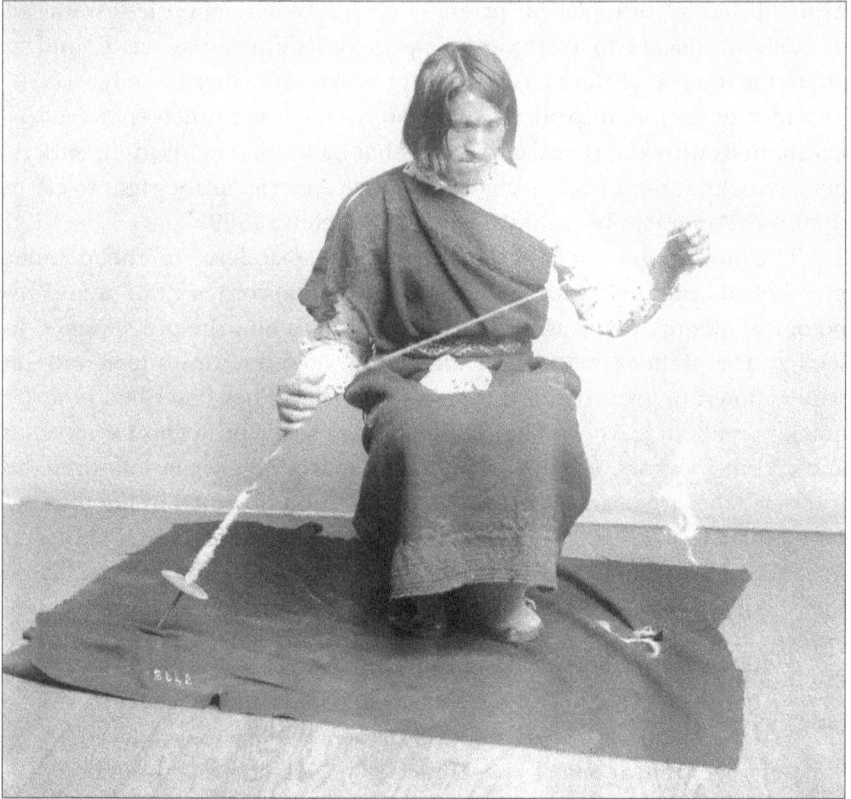

FIGURE 6.5
We'wha demonstrating spinning. National Anthropological Archives, Smithsonian Institution (SI 03642).

According to Will Roscoe, "the source for much of the material used in her version of the origin myth may have been We'wha," including controversial "details on the berdache kachina which other accounts do not have" (1988:132). This makes sense if Stevenson focused on the information provided by We'wha.

One of the most detailed visual records of We'wha in DC is a series of photographs taken of her preparing wool to spin, setting up the large suspended loom, and weaving on a back-strap loom. Formally posed images show her placed against a studio backdrop (e.g., figure 6.5). The photographs that are the least staged show her making herself at home, building a loom out of what was available from the collections, and balancing it upon collection boxes and stools (see figure 6.2). A newspaper reporter documented this, stating that We'wha was there "to weave [a] blanket on the loom and to explain the use of the implements" (*Evening Star*, 12 June 1886). He also pointed out that the loom and attachments had come from the Smithsonian collections: "The loom, the spindle on which she twisted her yarn, and the long reeds, or sticks, upon which her yarn, or worsted, was wound, and the long flat stave, or 'beater,' which she thrust now and then through the strands in the loom, were all specimens of Zuni handiwork taken from the collections of the museum."

It is noteworthy that only after the loom had arrived in DC and was reengaged with We'wha was its manner of use wholly documented. We learn from historic accounts that the Stevensons were known for the large quantity of items they collected, but their early materials, more often than not, were accessioned into the collections with little accompanying documentation. Bringing We'wha to Washington enabled Matilda to revisit the objects and provide more information. We'wha was also encouraged to tour the Zuni collections at the Bureau of Ethnology, where she looked at a detailed model of Zuni that the Mindeleff brothers had constructed for the National Museum and pointed out her house; she also assisted in the arrangement and description of "various masks, dance rattles, and other objects" (*National Tribune*, 20 May 1886). She is recorded as being protective of Zuni esoteric knowledge. It is likely that beyond identifying these masks, she would not have divulged the more secret aspects of their use. The *Evening Star* reporter noted, "[The loom that We'wha was using] with the blanket upon it will be placed in a case in the museum, together with the photographs of Wa-wah at work upon it, which will illustrate the mode of weaving employed by the Zunis" (*Evening Star*, 12 June 1886). Although her image was being used to make exhibits, as explored in the subsequent section, her individual identity and name were often lost or omitted during these institutional processes of inscription.

COLLECTIONS AND THE (DE)SCRIPTION OF KNOWLEDGE

Despite the strong media interest in We'wha's presence in Washington in 1886, few museum records and material traces remain of the time she spent at the Smithsonian. The ethnography collection's records at the NMNH consist of microfiches of correspondence from the collectors (the originals are kept at the Smithsonian archives), the accession ledgers noting the transfer of objects from the collectors to the institution (along with their original ownership details), card catalogs that were started as the overall record system after the ledgers, and, finally, the current electronic database (EMu), which was built from the catalog cards—not the ledgers.

Cross-referencing between these is the only means by which connections between the origins of objects and their institutional identities can formally be established.

No search of the database or the ledger books enabled me to link We'wha to any objects in the museum. By looking at all the related ledgers, I was able to find one reference to her for a photograph that was accessioned in 1887. Accession number 19373 is listed as "Photo of Wah-wah the Zuni priestess setting up prayer plumes. Bureau of Ethnography. Colored by A. Z. Shindler." As all ethnographic-related photographs are now housed at the National Anthropological Archives, I searched there for this image, only to find that it no longer appears to be in the collections, although it may have been deposited in papers or files elsewhere in the institution and therefore is lost only to the current catalog system. Similarly, the search for the loom that had been in the collections prior to We'wha's visit, which she put together and used, did not produce a definitive artifact. The Zuni or Southwestern looms seem, from the start, to have been dismantled for transport and later housed as separate parts (reeds, beaters, frames). It appears that the loom We'wha used was also disassembled after her demonstration and put back into the collections as separate parts. My hopes of finding the "loom with the blanket upon it," as described in the *Evening Star* article, were thwarted. Certainly, none of the loom parts had labels or associated documentation that identified them as the ones used by We'wha. A search for textiles made by We'wha also did not turn up anything.

Careful research by Dwight Lanmon (2006) has allowed him to tentatively identify a series of pots he thinks were made by We'wha. This includes the prayer meal bowl, catalog number 425653, held by We'wha in the portrait of her sprinkling corn (figure 6.6). Lanmon also argues that the inscription on another pot, "Ma-Meh/Male," is most likely her signature: "We'wha Made" (catalog no. 111343). According to Lanmon, this is possible if the fact that she was not familiar with writing English is allowed for and if we assume the *M*s to be inverted *W*s. The information that the looms used by We'wha may have come from other weavers in Zuni, however, leaves me wondering about claims that things We'wha is holding in the pictures were actually created by her. Ultimately, Lanmon's attribution of the pottery to We'wha through stylistic analysis is more convincing.[4]

The discovery of a single card catalog record eventually uncovered the series of prayer feathers made by We'wha. Although no attributing information for her was in the ledgers or database for these objects, someone had added information to the card catalog records for these prayer feathers, which were collected by Stevenson (catalog no. 176540). The annotation

FIGURE 6.6

We'wha holding a pottery bowl with sacred cornmeal. National Anthropological Archives, Smithsonian Institution (02440800).

states, "Zuni offerings of feather plumes, to the sun god—a prayer for rain. Made in Washington City, at the summer solstice, by Wewa, a prominent member of the tribe. The plumes, in proper positions, were afterward carefully secured for the U.S. National Museum." The current collections specialist for ethnography, Felicia Pickering, noted that this information was probably the result of the prayer feathers' being used in an exhibit and, once they were taken down and rehoused in the collections, the exhibit label that accompanied them had been copied into the card catalog.[5]

The story behind the creation of these prayer feathers can be found in Otis Mason's 1886 article in *Science* titled "The Planting and Exhuming of a Prayer." Mason (1886:24) described how, after We'wha decided she would produce prayer sticks for the summer solstice, she set up criteria in her search for suitable feathers, pigments, and wood: "Wa-wah was all excitement to make her preparation of meal, sticks, paint and feathers. All of these were abundant enough in the stores, but nothing of the kind would suffice. Various diplomatic schemes were tried, but her heart was fixed. The prayer must be right to infinitesimal particulars, or she would have nought to do with it." We'wha's disinterest in purchasing the materials in local Washington stores most likely stemmed from Zuni practices prescribing that the creation of religious paraphernalia should not in any way be tied to monetary economies. Mason explained that eventually, as with the loom, We'wha solved the problem of locating the right materials by reusing those brought back from Zuni by the Stevensons on earlier expeditions: "the treasures of the national museum" were opened and "the very pieces of yellow, blue and black pigment collected in former years by the Bureau of Ethnology" were "laid under contribution" (1886:24). They also enlisted the help of other divisions, making use of fauna collections also possibly from Zuni: "Mr. Ridgeway's department of ornithology was invoked to supply feathers of the golden eagle (*Aquila chrysaetos*), the wild turkey (*Meleagris mexicana*), the mallard (*Anas boschas*) and the bluebird (*Scialia arctica*)" (1886:24). Although We'wha allowed the ceremony of planting the prayer feathers to be observed and recorded, she did not pass on the information about the correct circumstances under which the materials must be obtained outside a monetary economy, which most likely directed her decision to reclaim the materials collected from previous expeditions to Zuni.

In creating these prayer feathers, We'wha asserted her cultural values upon the collections, reconfiguring the pigments and feathers as cultural, rather than geological or ornithological, artifacts. While adapting the social mores of Washington society, We'wha drew a line at the modification of her religious practices to suit the ideas of curatorial convention held by her hosts. The result was a set of prayer feathers that bound We'wha's efficacy as a diplomat, a priestess, and an educator with her idea that the museum collections were malleable and socially responsive storehouses. This is akin to the co-curation scenarios presented by today's collaborations between museums and communities. Interestingly, these prayer feathers are the only known creations that were originally attributed to We'wha by name within the museum records.

One of the more ambiguous but nonetheless significant remnants of We'wha's six-month working tour of DC is a mannequin likely to have been based on the photographs of her using the waist-strap loom (figures 6.7 and 6.8). Although I had been impeded in my search for documentation

FIGURE 6.7
The "belt-maker" in the exhibition hall of the National Museum of Natural History.

FIGURE 6.8
We'wha weaving a belt (in Stevenson 1904). National Anthropological Archives, Smithsonian Institution (SI 2261c).

leading to the identification of objects made by We'wha, I did find an observable trail of records about the NMNH mannequins, which had been gleaned from the Smithsonian archives by interns Gillian A. Flynn and Lynn Snyder in 2001–2002, when the mannequins were initially dismantled and removed from the exhibit halls. The museum began experimenting in 1873 with using mannequins to illustrate cultural artifacts. By the 1890s, an identifiable team of curators was working with exhibit designers to produce life groups for the 1893 World's Columbian Exposition in Chicago. These life groups took the form of life-size dioramas with human "figures arranged in tableaux" demonstrating cultural activities (Glass 2009:94). Parezo and Fowler (2007:25) attribute the decision to produce these to W. H. Holmes, a Bureau of American Ethnology curator who was influenced by natural history habitat groups, as well as "by the life groups exhibited at the 1889 Paris Exposition." Holmes worked alongside his colleagues at the BAE—Cushing, George Brown Goode, and Walter Hough—to produce exhibits for numerous expositions, including those of New Orleans (1883–1884), St. Louis (1889), Madrid (1892), and Chicago (1893) (Parezo and Fowler 2007).

The manufacture of museum mannequins was a highly experimental process during the early years of ethnographic exhibit development. The museum's first attempts centered on depicting named individuals. Elisha Kent Kane produced two mannequins in 1873 based on Inuit individuals—Joe (Ebierbing) and Hannah (Tookoolito)—using wax to produce life-like heads and appendages. By 1893, however, assistant secretary G. Brown Goode regarded these as rudimentary and sought alternative techniques. The museum then hired French sculptor M. Achille Colin in 1881 to produce portraiture busts of named Native Americans who visited DC, such as Good Road Woman, a Yankton Sioux, and The Hawk That Hunts Walking, a Mdewakanton Sioux. A. Zeno Shindler, the same artist who colored the photograph of We'wha, was hired to paint the sculptures and produce life-like appearances. Later on, facial casts were made of the pupils at the Indian School in Carlisle, and, in one recorded case, the cast from Rosa White Thunder, a Brule Sioux girl, was used by U. S. J. Dunbar to create a full-figure mannequin with a wig and movable arms.[6]

In preparation for the Chicago World's Fair, the curator of ethnology, Otis Mason, set out to arrange the exhibits according to cultural regions, seeing this as a way to unite the work of the bureau in a cohesive and engaging manner, bringing knowledge about subsistence and the linguistic, technological, and physical attributes of each culture to life (Ewers 1959:520). These particular figures were not modeled from named life subjects but were composites made up from photographs and through consultation with curators. In the museum's 1893 *Annual Report*, it was noted that the decision to create the less detailed mannequins for the World's Fair was due to the time frame in which the large numbers of figures had to be made. These particular groups, however, were noted as unique because they were "shown in the cases surrounded by proper environmental accessories and engaged in the occupations peculiar to the tribes which they represented" and therefore were "no longer pieces of sculpture, but pictures from life" (National Museum 1893:54). This project brought together Holmes, Cushing, Walter Hoffman, and James Mooney, who determined the cultural groups, their occupations, and the appropriate poses. The curators were also photographed posing for the figures themselves.[7] Cushing helped reenact Zuni ceremonies and assisted in the creation of four other Zuni groups: "bread-makers and millers, a potter, a basket-maker [and] a belt-maker" (National Museum 1893:54). He must also have offered to help with the life groups of the Apaches, Sioux, and Powhatans, since there remains a sequence of photographs of him posing as a Dakota warrior (Isaac 2010). Alongside photographic materials from the field, these posed studio photographs were used to produce plaster cast mannequins, which were painted and clothed using materials and objects from the collections. In the *Annual Report*, the curators emphasized the authenticity of the mannequins, suggesting that without their expertise, it would be "very dangerous to try [to] make such groups except under the eye of an ethnologist who has been among the people to be represented" (National Museum 1893:54).

Reenactments of archaic or indigenous technology were, by the late nineteenth century, becoming an integral component of museum-based research. Gosden and Larson (2007) point out that Lieutenant General Pitt Rivers believed that Oxford students of anthropology should obtain "a practical knowledge of the manufacture of flint implements, flaking, secondary chipping," and "boring holes" (qtd. in Gosden, Larson, and Petch 2007:124). Because objects were seen to manifest specific historic and cultural ways of knowing the world, by experiencing how to make them, curators could embody "a form of intellect generated through physical actions and interactions" and participate in "a scheme aimed at training the body as well as the mind" (qtd. in Gosden, Larson, and Petch 2007:124). Tylor also followed this philosophy, feeling that "the best way to understand a primitive craft was to practice it" (qtd. in Gosden, Larson, and Petch 2007:127). Significantly, Hinsley (1981b) also attributes the National Museum's life groups to the practice of reenactment. This process involved the "minute examination of artifacts to determine material and process of manufacture," and "having analyzed the product, the anthropologist then proceeded to reenact the process" (Hinsley 1981:104). Hinsley attributes to this process Mason's careful taxonomies of North American basketry, as well as Holmes's pioneering work on the Piney Branch site. Cushing was also recognized as the leading investigator in what he termed "experiential reproduction" (McGee et al. 1900:363), a method through which he learned the techniques needed to create stone tools, manufacture pottery, and smelt copper, eventually linking these to the evolution of "manual concepts" in humans (Cushing 1892). Significantly, his paper articulating these methodologies appeared exactly a year before the NMNH curators started using the mannequins to reproduce cultural and physical attributes.

According to the *Annual Report* for 1893, the origin of the Zuni belt-maker mannequin can be traced to Cushing and these experimental reproductions. This mannequin was most likely a composite of various sources, including the photographs of We'wha, because these had been created for the sake of exhibit manufacture seven years earlier and were probably in the hands of the technicians. Cushing was also noted as having used field notes and observations from his time in Zuni (National Museum 1893). The result is a figure that is masculine in body and facial features but highly feminine in facial coloring and rosy blush (figure 6.9). This would appear to be Cushing's translation of We'wha more than an actual duplication or reenactment of her in mannequin form.

What we do not know, however, is the role of Stevenson in this reproduction. She is listed in the papers in the National Anthropological Archives (NAA) as receiving a medal for her contributions to the Chicago World's Fair, but nowhere is she listed in the museum's annual reports describing the project. Cushing's work in Zuni, his long-term interest in heuristic knowledge, and his artistic interests place him at the center of the mannequin-making domain of the museum. Stevenson's absence, however, is harder to explain, especially given that she had arranged for We'wha's demonstrations of weaving. Possibly, posing for these mannequins, as the other curators had, was not an acceptable endeavor for a woman. Plus, she had at one time referred to Cushing as a "charlatan" weighted down by so much Zuni "toggery," implying that his anthropological approach impaired his judgment.[8] Ultimately, she did not have a permanent position at the BAE but was largely paid on contract. Her absence in this part of the story may have been due to her peripheral status during these years, but it is also fair to suggest that none of the surviving records provides the full story. Stevenson's relationship with the BAE staff was often fraught, in part because of her gender and in part resulting from her obsessive behavior

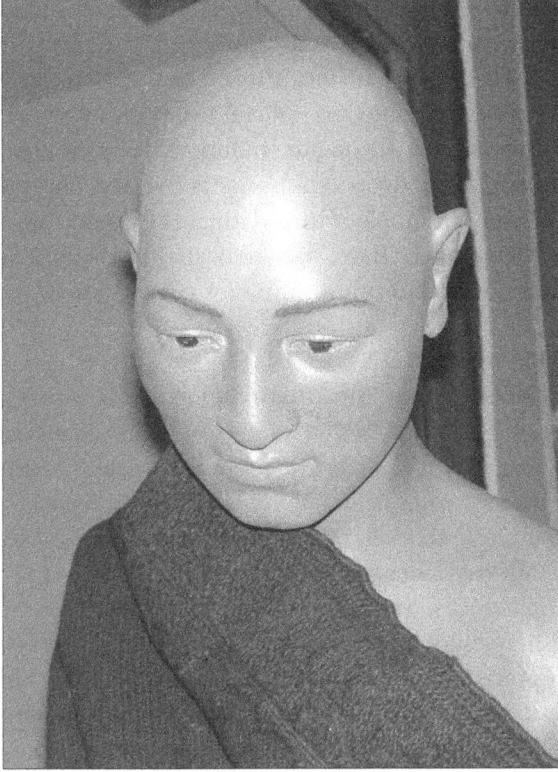

FIGURE 6.9

The "belt-maker" mannequin. National Museum of Natural History.

(Parezo 1993). Either way, her involvement in the World's Fair is missing from the Smithsonian annual reports and the correspondence about the mannequins.

Eventually, the "belt-maker" not only was exhibited at the 1893 World's Fair but also went on to be used in the 1901 Pan-American Exposition in Buffalo, New York (National Museum 1901:pl. 30), the 1909 Alaska-Yukon-Pacific Exposition, and the 1935–1936 California Pacific Exposition in San Diego, and she remained on display in the NMNH exhibits for forty years, from 1961 to 2001. According to Flynn and Snyder (2002), she has traveled to more locations and been on display the longest of all the mannequins. In a disposition report, Flynn and Snyder noted that there were more than 128 mannequins, many of which had lost their original identities as life groups or been broken and damaged beyond repair, and they recommended that some be retained due to their importance as part of the material culture embodying the institutional history of the NMNH. An interesting debate arose in the anthropology department between those who believed that these were historically interesting objects worth keeping and possibly accessioning into the collections and those who saw them as exhibit props that, beyond the documentation of their creation in the nineteenth century and early twentieth, no longer served any useful purpose and should be disposed of. As of this writing, the remaining mannequins, including the "belt-maker," have been relocated to the basement, and the debate over their final disposition continues (figure 6.9).

DISCUSSION AND CONCLUSION

Let us explore further the different media in which these stories have been inscribed. I am thinking about storytellers bringing history and cultural knowledge to life, giving it presence, vocality, and substance— through text, pottery, song, and, latterly, mannequin form. The tragedy of the Smithsonian's retelling of We'wha's and Stevenson's stories, however, is that our two main narrators and their individual stories—the objects, pots, sacred belts, field notes, and unpublished manuscripts—were often separated from their identities, coming back to life only through subsequent historical interpretations. As described previously, We'wha's objects became anonymous once accessioned. Similarly, Stevenson's papers were taken over by her colleague John P. Harrington after her death and were used as data for his own work, largely without attribution to her. Ultimately, both We'wha's and Stevenson's work became subject to institutional forces more influential than their individual voices. It is worth noting that in the series of photographs of We'wha weaving on the Mall, the last image depicts only the loom, and We'wha is no longer in the picture. Although We'wha and Stevenson forged new social connections, the treatment of their contributions reveals not only the capricious nature of historical inscription but also the dynamics of interference or noise—the social practices that may distort the individual voice.

We'wha's stories find identifiable historical traction when, as in the case of the prayer feathers, she reconfigured—or reclaimed, if you will—the Zuni collections at the National Museum, eschewing preexisting museum-based biological and geological categories. This unique reuse was recorded and eventually inscribed in the records. It was at these moments, when We'wha operated independently from Zuni and Washingtonian expectations, that she revealed her own insights into the limits of cultural translation. The mannequin is more complex, however, for neither the storyteller nor her story is retained per se. It is, however, a recognizable vestige of her physical presence. The "belt-maker" was created six years after she left DC, and it remains captive in the museum, unaccessioned and held within an ambiguous space in the basement. I am reminded of Berger's description of photographs as traces (Berger and Mohr 1982). I see the "belt-maker" as a recursive tracing created from photographs and from memory, evoking but not duplicating We'wha. The mannequin has a different power, not as We'wha's own memory but as the memory of her. It is a biographical, as opposed to an autobiographical, inscription. In this unconventional yet revealing twist to the story, her agency, as an "indigenous" subject, becomes divergent and uncontrolled. De la Cadena and Starn (2007:3) struggle with these mutually dependent yet conflicting perspectives in their exploration of indigeneity: "recognizing it as a relational field of governance, subjectivities, and knowledges that involve us all—indigenous and non-indigenous—in the making of its structures." As such, the mannequin stands in for an identity; it is physically present and, at the same time, disembodied from its implied personage. These autobiographical and biographical inscriptions instruct us that "indigenous agency" in museum collections is often chimerical, but more important, it is relational when viewed through co-constructed forms and objects.

The different inscriptions of We'wha and her stories take disparate paths according to the type of media examined. For example, photographs, through their indexical qualities, have allowed her visually inscribed identity to remain intact, associated, affective, and well remembered: her name is often written on the backs of these images. The objects and the mannequin, however, have become disassociated from We'wha. The pottery and weavings are no longer unique creations associated with their creators. Because they were recorded in the card catalogs as "Zuni," We'wha loses her named identity and association with these creations, and they are absorbed into an ascribed cultural group or ethnic category. The NMNH is not unusual in this: the early function of most ethnographic museum accession books was to record information about cultures, not individuals.

Objects in and of themselves are not histories. Stories that surround or engage with them require interpretive methodologies that establish the nature of these inscriptions and their associated meanings. I agree with Greg Dening's (1996:xiv) perspective that it is in their performances that objects and stories find historic traction: "We find different ways to make sense of what has happened according to the different occasions of our telling and the different audiences to which we tell it." He goes on to suggest that "we are culturally astute in knowing how these different ways are to be interpreted," yet, in a world of cross-cultural arenas such as the

Smithsonian, co-constructed historic inscriptions require further analysis, especially in regard to institutional versus individual inscriptive practices, as well as the particular cultural inscriptive practices and translations (e.g., We'wha's prayer feathers, which converted museum categories and meanings back into Zuni ones, although this process was institutionally recorded only via exhibit labels, not accession records).

Making sense of how objects tell stories has been an ongoing preoccupation in anthropology (Cruikshank 1995; Edwards 2005; Hoskins 2006[1998]; O'Hanlon 1999; Thomas 1999b), cultural studies (Clifford 1997; Hall 1997), and history (Ulrich 2001). Critics of the anthropological practices that have detached objects from their creators have sought to reconnect them to their communities of origin (Brown and Peers 2003) and to explore how objects become active parts of social networks (Gosden 2005; Joyce 2000; Mills and Ferguson 2008). Objects have also been credited with animacy and voice: "Objects are used not only to represent experience but also to apprehend it and to interpret it and to give it meaningful shape.... Objects do speak and should be heard as significant statements of personal and cultural reflexivity" (Babcock 1986:317–318). Alternatively, storytellers and stories have been privileged over objects, such as in Clifford's (1997:189) account of the consultations that took place in the Portland Museum of Art with Tlingit elders: "The objects in the Rasmussen Collection, focus for the consultation, were left—or so it seemed to me—at the margin. For long periods no one paid any attention to them. Stories and songs took center stage." Ultimately, each form of inscription—photograph, pottery, ledger book, and so on—plays a different role in how stories are performed and retained, requiring us to understand how each form operates, as well as how they play off one another. As Handler (1992:21) suggests, collections are about relationships: "Objects must be surrounded by other objects, by words, by human activity. Without meaningful human activity...objects are meaningless" (see also Byrne, chapter 8, Knowles, chapter 9, Hays-Gilpin and Lomatewama, chapter 10, this volume).

The interrelational dynamics that shape these histories are key. We have We'wha and Stevenson—two pioneering individuals who were pushing the boundaries of their generations in terms of gender and education—and, more important, their articulation of their interest in cross-cultural translations. Their unconventional approaches guaranteed them both a place in history, but the loss of their authorship appears due to similar institutional practices of inscription.

The significant number of photographs of We'wha and the written accounts of her visit prompt me to ask, what do these say about an anthropological project in which Native Americans were brought to the National

Museum to work as informants and intermediaries for the political entities of DC? This kind of project became standard practice in museums by the turn of the nineteenth century, with visiting Zunis as some of the earliest examples. Herman Viola's (1981) work on the diplomacy of these visits reveals a complex mix of commercial, exploitive, and opportunistic aspects of Euro American agendas. Interpreting the vestiges of We'wha's visit in this light also reveals how visiting dignitaries have been viewed, treated, or memorialized in the history of the National Museum and political arenas of Washington.

Today, there is another relational element to this story—the establishment of the National Museum of the American Indian (NMAI) as a culturally performative space highlighting and celebrating both the tribal and individual identities of artists. As such, the introduction of the NMAI changes the dynamics of the national spaces of and expectations about the tellings of Native American histories in Washington, DC. In regard to how Native identities are inscribed in museums more generally, as both material and immaterial forms, Cruikshank (1995:27) states: "Increasingly, indigenous peoples in North America are making oral tradition and material culture central to their definitions of culture. In public speech, for example, performance of verbal artistry and the display of ceremonial regalia have become standard ways of demonstrating both ethnographic authority and the central place of words and things in socially reproducing culture." As a visiting dignitary from Zuni, We'wha's activities were recorded as she reconfigured collections and learned the English language and Euro American ways of life. If we compare this process with current institutional dynamics, we see that visiting artists at NMAI, in the same way, are encouraged to connect with and at times to reuse objects. No doubt, this new/old practice is explored by artists in ways that are in reaction to a prior lack of recognition of individual authorship. These current museum practices promote the idea of visiting community delegates, but now as a means to transform the meanings of collections through their contributions as individual authors.

Comparisons between the original context of We'wha's visit and those of today highlight interesting interpretive strategies. First, they suggest that transformations associated with the increased efficacy attributed to individual artists as authors are not about *giving* people agency—they have always had this—it is about acknowledging the ways it can be inscribed and, therefore, recognized and made visible. The meaning and significance of the collections are now measured according to authorship, whereas in earlier ethnographic museum contexts, meaning was located in geography, ethnic category, and tribal affiliation. The politics of power or, as explored here, the politics of agency have shifted, not in their meanings per se but according to where meaning itself is located within this process of seeking agency. For example, in the nineteenth-century context, We'wha had agency as a Zuni (writ large), whereas today, she is recognized and given agency and meaning as We'wha, the Zuni lhamana artist and storyteller. Locating meaning in her individual persona can, in part, be attributed to art history's hierarchies of value based on artist recognition. Certainly, the NMAI works within this model, yet it also bridges indigenous cultural and aesthetic value systems. In a broader contemporary frame, however, meaning is also ascribed to We'wha as a lhamana, identifying him/her according to newly configured gender politics. Thus, We'wha's story spans Zuni and Euro American categories of power and illuminates the relational dynamics of individual creativity and the disciplinary and institutional practices of inscription.

Notes

1. For more on Zuni interpretations of lhamanas, see Roscoe 1991. In many of the first accounts, We'wha was described using feminine pronouns (Stevenson 1904; James 1920). In the late twentieth century, however, masculine pronouns were used (Babcock and Parezo 1988; Roscoe 1991). In writing about We'wha's visit to Washington in 1886, I have chosen to use feminine pronouns to correspond to the terminology and perceptions of We'wha's time frame. I use both feminine and masculine pronouns in the conclusion, however, as this is a study of inscription and how We'wha's gendered identity has changed over time.

2. Stevenson was recognized for her determination to obtain the most accurate and comprehensive information possible; her approach included interviewing numerous informants about the same topic and not accepting anything as "truth" until she had the same information from at least three people (Parezo 1993).

3. The press coverage of We'wha's visit included the following articles: *Washington Post*, 21 March, 1 April, 4 April, 11 April, 9 May, 14 May, 24 June 1886; *Evening Star*, 31 March, 14 May 1886; and *Washington Chronicle*, 18 April 1886. Only the *National Tribune*, 20 May 1886, and the *Evening Star*, 12 June 1886, discussed We'wha's anthropological endeavors.

4. Lanmon (2006) attributes a total of four pots to We'wha: 111343 and 134557 (which he analyzes as possibly signed by We'wha), 425653 (the pot included in the photograph of We'wha sprinkling cornmeal), and 111986, which is associated with We'wha through stylistic analysis.

5. An additional handwritten note adds, "11 found 1/4/79 formerly mislabeled 156540."

6. The list of artists and sculptors at NMNH working on these mannequins over the past century was compiled by Gillian A. Flynn and Lynn Snyder (2002), interns who assisted JoAllyn Archambault, the director of the American Indian Outreach Program, and Deborah Hull Walski, the collections manager. A series of binders now held by the Collections and Archive Program contains the notes, off-prints, and photographs that cover this history.

7. See images in the NAA of Hoffman as the Crow Indian painter and Cushing as the Dakota warrior. These are discussed in more detail in Isaac 2010.

8. A photograph of Cushing is held at the National Anthropological Archives with a handwritten annotation by Stevenson: "This man was the biggest fool and charlatan I ever knew. He even put his hair up in curl papers every night. How could a man walk weighted down with so much toggery?" (Roscoe 1991:9).

7

Creative Colonialism

Locating Indigenous Strategies in Ethnographic Museum Collections

Robin Torrence and Anne Clarke

ETHNOGRAPHIC COLLECTIONS AND SOCIAL RELATIONS

Over the course of the nineteenth century and into the twentieth, thousands of objects made and used by indigenous people were gifted, bartered, and looted as Western nations expanded their colonial enterprises across the world. The material culture of colonized peoples was transferred from the realm of local cultural practice to a globalized capitalist marketplace and transformed into a commercial commodity. Not only did objects acquire monetary values far removed from their original contexts of production and use, but they also gathered symbolic capital through the practices of collection, classification, and display in public and private spheres alike. Many of these indigenous objects now form the nuclei of the extensive ethnographic collections housed in public museums and private collections around the world. Rather than be viewed as simply a product of the desires of Western consumers or an outcome of asymmetries in power, these collections are better understood as the consequences of complex and entangled social relationships (commercial, personal, official) between collecting and producing communities (e.g., Byrne et al. 2011b; Gosden, Larson, and Petch 2007; Newell 2006; Gosden and Knowles 2001; Thomas 1991). A new culture primarily grounded in the specifics of the local context

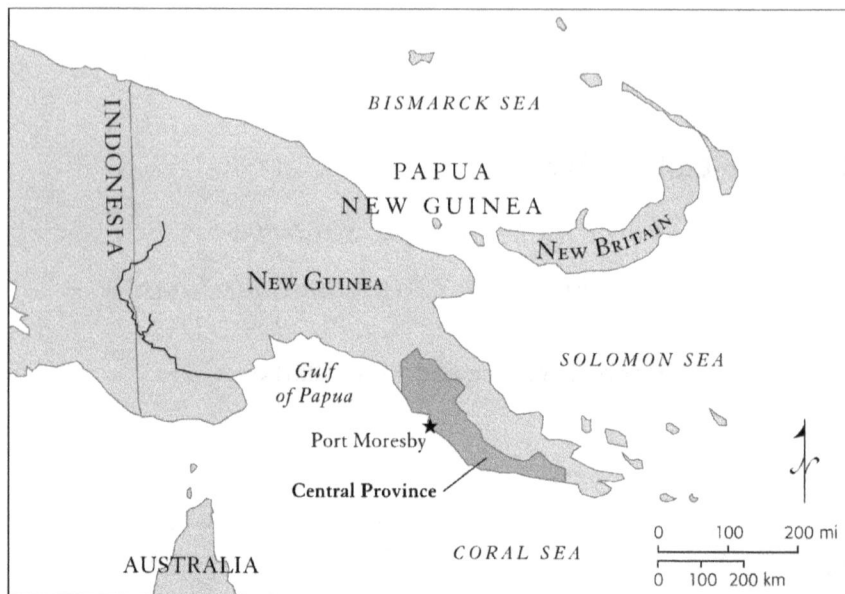

FIGURE 7.1

Map of Papua New Guinea, showing Central Province (shaded area) and Port Moresby. Map by Molly O'Halloran.

resulted from the trade and exchange of objects (Thomas 1994), although the social relations were also subject to the ebb and flow of larger economic, political, and historical forces (Bennett 1995, 2004). Given the dynamic role that museum collections played in past societies, it is no longer useful to envisage them as static entities. By adopting new theoretical and methodological approaches, they can be converted into rich sources of information about historical processes. Through tracing how the contents of these assemblages of ethnographic objects changed over time, we can witness the ways in which unique cultural practices and social relations emerged in specific colonial settings as a result of webs of interactions in which material objects played a central role (Clarke and Torrence 2011; Gosden, Larson, and Petch 2007; Gosden and Knowles 2001:59).

Our case study of ethnographic artifacts demonstrates the power of museum collections to draw out the complexities of social relations in colonial society. Following ideas and methods proposed by Gosden and Knowles (2001) and Thomas (1991), we use museum collections from Central Province (figure 7.1) to illuminate processes underlying the construction and creation of colonial society in British New Guinea. Based on patterns expressed in these museum collections, in terms of relative quantities, presence and absence, and material properties and decorative styles, our chapter identifies strategies adopted by indigenous communities to create, sustain, or avoid social interaction with Westerners and also considers how objects were used in the creation of new indigenous self-identities. Our approach focuses only on the indigenous side of the "collecting encounter" (Adams 2009:17), a necessary counterpoint to previous detailed historical analyses of Western traders and collectors in the Pacific region (e.g., Buschmann 2009; O'Hanlon and Welsch 2000; Peterson, Allen, and Hamby 2008; Quanchi and Cochrane 2007). Even when divorced from their makers and users, objects now hidden from public view and shut away in museum storerooms provide a new and important source of information about the societies in which they circulated (see also Byrne et al. 2011a).

ARCHAEOLOGY AND ETHNOGRAPHIC COLLECTIONS

Since the goal of our research is to understand how entangled social relations in colonial settings led to the generation of new cultural behaviors for both Western and indigenous participants (Gosden and Knowles 2001), it is important to hear the voices and track the behaviors of these two groups. Given the biases inherent in written texts, achieving this aim demands new concepts and approaches. The much quoted observation by Thomas (2000:274)—"it is striking just how difficult it is to recover and characterize indigenous agency in any specificity, from the historical record"—sets out the basic methodological and theoretical challenge for those interested in identifying the role of indigenous communities in the formation of museum collections. To tackle this challenging task, our research on ethnographic collections and nineteenth- and early twentieth-century auction and sale catalogs uses an object-centered approach central to archaeological research (see the discussion of "archaeological sensibility" in the introduction to this volume; see also Clarke and Torrence 2011, 2012; Torrence and Clarke 2011; Torrence 1993, 2000). We argue that museum collections share important characteristics with materials retrieved from an archaeological excavation in that many museum objects are accessioned with little or no accompanying documentation about who made them, what they were used for, how they were made, what they were called, or how they were perceived by their original owners. For archaeological and ethnographic museum artifacts alike, the major variables available for study are the material properties of the objects themselves and their associations with other items.

A key archaeological concept relevant to the analysis of museum collections is the "assemblage," which refers to "an associated set of contemporary artifacts that can be considered as a single unit for record and analysis" (Darvill 2008; see Gosden, Larson, and Petch 2007 on the museum as a "field site"; also see the introduction to this volume). We argue that since the groupings of ethnographic objects found on the shelves of museums (i.e., collections) share many of the same properties as archaeological assemblages (e.g., they were collected from the same region or by the same person), it is appropriate to use archaeological principles to link the material attributes of objects to behavior and on this basis to infer the broad social processes that underpinned the exchange of material culture in colonial Papua New Guinea.

Following archaeological principles, our use of inference is based on the assumption that both individual objects and assemblages are the consequences of human actions. In our case study, the behaviors took place within the local context of negotiations between the indigenous people who made and offered the objects for exchange and the explorers, scientists, missionaries, traders, government officials, anthropologists, collectors, and other outsiders with whom they interacted. Consequently, we assume that museum assemblages are representative outcomes of the different kinds of material exchanges between local groups and Western outsiders. Through a number of case studies, our collaborative project has developed a range of archaeological approaches for reconstructing social relations from ethnographic museum collections/assemblages. These include analyses of (1) assemblage composition in terms of the relative proportions of artifact types or the presence or absence of key types, (2) artifact production and decoration, and (3) one-off exchanges identified through a biographical approach (Kopytoff 1986; Clarke and Torrence 2011, 2012; Kononenko et al. 2010; Philp 2009, 2011; Torrence 1993, 2000; Torrence and Clarke 2011; see also Harrison 2006, 2011a).

Crucial to making inferences about historical processes from artifacts in museum assemblages is the simple observation that the movement of an object between two individuals or social groups requires some form of social interaction. In fact, as discussed in Sahlins's (1972) foundational study, the exchange of objects is widely used to create, mediate, sustain, and negate social relations within and between different groups. In the cross-cultural setting in which items from Central Province were exchanged, negotiation between strangers was likely to have been the main form of social interaction since physical violence and stealing were relatively rare. Writing about a similar colonial setting in Australia, McBryde (2000) elegantly showed that in contact situations in which there was a wide disparity of power relations, such as in the early days of the Port Jackson colony in Australia, indigenous people used items of material culture, such as hats, to mediate their interactions with the British colonists, choosing how and in what social contexts they were exchanged. In another case study, Torrence (2000) discussed how the Admiralty Islanders from Papua New Guinea made changes in the way obsidian-tipped spears and daggers were made and decorated, in order to attract and make material profits from exchanges with European traders.

A useful framework for linking negotiation to material items can be found in Humphrey and Hugh-Jones's (1992) argument that the process of bartering creates equality. As they show, neither side wins or loses, because successful exchange can occur only if both parties are satisfied with the outcome. For example, Gammage (1998:58) records how European and Papua New Guinea participants were equally delighted with the outcomes of their bartered transactions: "The Europeans thought food cheap, shell worth two or three shillings buying a thousand pounds of *kaukau* or a fair-sized pig. Enga thought the line paid amazingly well: a *kina* for a big pig, priceless salt for mere vegetables…. The profits were enormous. People took care not to show that they were being overpaid, but fifty years later they recalled the trading gleefully." In the same vein, Strathern (1992:248) describes an occasion when local people from the Hagen area of the New Guinea Highlands would not exchange their stone axes, spears, or pigs with the newly arrived and highly perplexed Australian explorers because the shells, steel axes, and other trade goods the latter had brought were just not desirable enough. The Hageners were prepared to engage in barter only when they were convinced that these white strangers were actually human beings, as was demonstrated when the latter offered the culturally appropriate gold-lip pearl shells.

In Central Province, bartering was probably the most common, but not the only, form of exchange between indigenous groups and Westerners. The spheres of interaction proposed by Sahlins (1972)—generalized, balanced, and negative reciprocity—are a useful way to start thinking about the multiple kinds of negotiation that might have characterized indigenous-outsider interactions. Sahlins made the insightful observation that although each of these forms of exchange generally operates within a particular class of social relations (respectively, family, various kin groups, and strangers), a common strategy is to use exchange to reduce social distance and draw people into a more intimate social sphere. In other words, exchange creates the ties that bind. So, for example, the presentation of a "pure gift" with no expectation of return (generalized reciprocity) is a common way to establish a closer social tie with someone outside the immediate family and create the social obligations that come with being close kin.

In this chapter, we focus on the way local people in Central Province negotiated social relations within an early colonial setting by making, offering, and withholding objects in their dealings with outsiders. Since, as is well illustrated by the Hagen example, the material properties of an artifact are instrumental in shaping the character of the exchanges that create and maintain social relations, we have reconstructed past social interactions by studying the museum objects used in these transactions. Following this basic principle of inference, we have detected strategies used by Papua New Guineans to engage in and profit from Western trade, which in turn contributed to the formation of new identities within this colonial society.

SITUATING THE COLLECTIONS

The choice of Central Province, Papua New Guinea, for our case study is a deliberate one. As the region surrounding the British and Australian government headquarters in Port Moresby, it provides an excellent place to monitor social interactions during the history of this colony. Negotiating social relations through exchange with various kinds of "strangers" has been integral to both the ancient and recent history of cultural groups in this region. Well-known prehistoric trade links stretched north and south along the coast and between coastal and inland regions (e.g., Irwin 1985; Allen 1977), and communities not far to the west had long been in contact with bird of paradise traders from Southeast Asia (Swadling 1996). The well-known, long-distance *hiri* exchange system, which linked Motu groups residing near Port Moresby with trading partners in the Papuan Gulf to the west, was still flourishing when Westerners first arrived (e.g., Barton 1910; Dutton 1982; Groves 2011:26–29).

Our exploration of the entangled social relations (Thomas 1991) that characterized colonial life in Central Province focuses on a series of ethnographic collections for which we have good chronological control. Analyses were made of a substantial collection of approximately twenty-five hundred items housed at the Australian Museum (Sydney), which were supplemented with information from collections at the Macleay Museum (University of Sydney), the Queensland Museum (Brisbane), and the British Museum (London). The data enabled us to compare and contrast historical accounts and government records with changes in the strategies used by the indigenous communities to create social relations with the wider range of outsiders they encountered between first contact and the first decades of the twentieth century.

We begin with a brief summary of the key historical processes that formed the background to the social relations forged through the exchange of artifacts. The first period, 1875–1884, includes the early explorations by scientists, prospectors, and adventurers; the beginnings of commercial trading; and the founding of Christian missions. At this time, Western superiority over the local population was not at all well established. Outsiders visiting or attempting to establish settlements in the region would have been highly outnumbered in any conflict. Perhaps more important, explorers were heavily dependent on the local population for basic resources, including food, water, and shelter. In the second phase, 1884–1900, the British began to exert authority over the region by making a formal claim to the British territory of New Guinea in 1884 and by establishing a crown colony in 1888, supported by the formal presence of an administrator based in Port Moresby. In these early years of the colony, inland regions of Central Province barely experienced the effects of Western contact (Groves 2011:30–59). Furthermore, there was very little physical control over the indigenous population, although the establishment of a Native police force in 1888 (Groves 2011:52) began to play an important role in colonial governance. During the third phase, 1900–1925, the Commonwealth of Australia assumed authority over the newly established territory of Papua. It was not until the end of this period, however, that Australian authorities effectively exerted control via censuses and a head tax (Ryan 1972; Oram 1976). After 1925 very little material from Central Province was accessioned by the Australian Museum.

It is highly significant that 93 percent of well-dated artifacts from Central Province in the Australian Museum were collected during the first two phases, before social relations became formalized within the context of a wage-based economy, as, for instance, in the description of exchanges between plantation workers and anthropologists by Gosden and Knowles (2001). In contrast, when the artifacts in the Australian Museum were collected, what are now typically envisaged as ethnographic items played such a central role in the negotiations between local communities and Westerners (cf. Barker 2001) that their physical attributes reflect the nature of these ongoing interactions.

STRATEGIC GIFTING

Although the trade in artifacts in Central Province was partially driven by external factors, such as the high demand for ethnographic objects and curios by collectors and museums in Europe, the exchange of objects between source communities and outsiders was also integral to successful communication and peacemaking, especially prior to the creation of the pidgin language, Police Motu. Gift giving played an important role in initiating

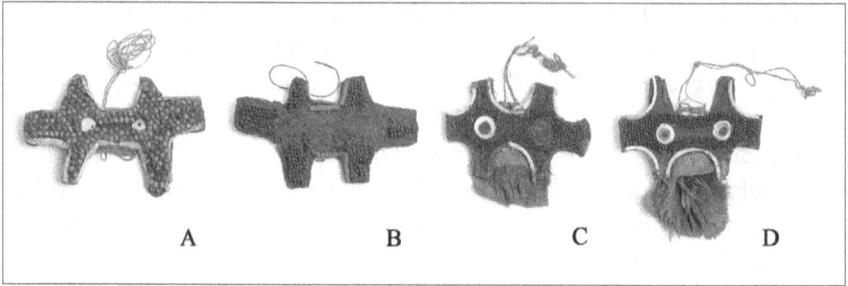

FIGURE 7.2

Fighting or mouth ornaments from the Australian Museum collections. A (B.6297) and B (B.6298), obtained by Liljeblad, may be copies of the traditional types shown in C (E.348) and D (B.6419). Photos by Emma Furno, reproduced with permission from the Australian Museum.

and shaping interactions. Papuans in Central Province and elsewhere offered gifts as a way of initiating or strengthening ties with an outsider because these new social relations could enhance their status locally, open up avenues to desirable commodities, or even provide a way to rid the community of unwanted and potentially dangerous goods, such as objects used in sorcery, in much the same ways as described by Barker (2001) for the early history of Oro Province.

Objects known as "mouth" or "fighting" ornaments, known in a local language as *musikaka*, appear to have been very popular with Europeans, possibly because these combined the traits of "exotic," "colorful," and "bizarre" with "savage" and "war-like" (figure 7.2). During warfare, these sorcery objects were supposedly held in the mouth by grasping a thick woven ring mounted on the back, but at other times they were suspended from the neck by a cord (e.g., Stone 1880:116–117; Murray 1912:231). They were first described by early visitors such as Turner (1878) and Stone (1880:116–117) and were illustrated in the influential catalog of Pacific objects published by Edge-Partington (1996[1890–1898]:1:274), which soon became a key guide for collectors.

The Australian Museum's examples of musikaka from Central Province are made of either turtle shell or wood that was cut into a shape with three opposing arcs and then outlined with boar's tusk. The surface was decorated with red or black seeds (*Abrus precatorius*) in various patterns, and shapes resembling "eyes" were usually created with shells. Many also have a pouch fashioned from plant material to which parrot feathers and other materials used for sorcery were attached; it hung below the body of the ornament (e.g., see figure 7.2C, D). Similar mouth ornaments appeared in contemporary British sale and auction catalogs (e.g., Oldman 1976:no. 56, object 14 [15029]; Webster 1895:objects 210, 465), but compared with other types of objects, they are relatively rare in museum collections. The Australian Museum has nine extant artifacts of this type, with eight acquired between 1883 and 1887; four additional specimens obtained in 1878 were destroyed in a fire, and two more purchased in 1883 have been de-accessioned or are missing.

It seems likely that the two mouth ornaments in the Australian Museum's Central Province collection in which turtle bone (rather than wood) was used for the foundation were strategic gifts offered to people with whom it was beneficial to forge social ties (see figure 7.2C, D). Both of these objects were donated to the museum by ministers from the London Missionary Society: Rev. William George Lawes and Rev. William Wyatt Gill (see Chalmers 1886). Such rare objects with spiritual power may have been gifted to create social ties with the men who were actively involved in the barter of trade goods, which were used by the church to obtain necessary supplies of food (Lawes 1876–1884). Although the missionaries may have been eager to demonstrate the savagery of their converts by collecting objects involved in sorcery, it also seems highly likely that their trading partners made a strategic decision to present these gifts as a way to improve their local status through connections with outsiders, to better position themselves in terms of access to supplies of trade goods, or possibly to remove potentially dangerous objects from the community. The presence of other objects used in magic and ceremony—which are absent from other contemporary assemblages—in the assemblage acquired from Lawes at the Australian Museum indicates that local people gifted or offered different objects to a long-term resident whose social ties were useful and valuable than they did to passing traders (cf. Clarke and Torrence 2011).

ATTRACTING INTERACTIONS

As in other parts of the globe, even during the earliest encounters, creativity and experimentation were fundamental indigenous strategies for negotiating with Western explorers, traders, missionaries, and government officials (e.g., Thomas 1991; Meleisea and Schoeffel 1997; Torrence 2000; Harrison 2002, 2004a, 2006; Kononenko et al. 2010). The communities in British New Guinea were clearly eager to barter for European trade goods, such as cloth, beads, and metal objects (Davies 2011; Philp 2009). Analysis of the museum collections reveals a number of strategies used by indigenous producers to attract and increase the volume of trade: (1) manufacturing copies of well-known objects; (2) devising acceptable substitutions for popular goods; (3) inventing items that would appeal to Western tastes; and (4) enhancing traditional artifacts to attract attention. Innovative trade objects were cleverly created to appeal to the desires of outsiders. Based on observations over time, the producers created goods that conformed to European imaginings about "savages," or they altered "traditional" goods and motifs to be compatible with the buyers' specific requirements (cf. Silverman 1999; Schildkrout and Keim 1998:5–6; Graburn 1976).

Abundant examples of these four kinds of creativity and experimentation characteristic of colonial interactions are represented in the Central Province assemblages sold to the Australian Museum by Captain Hillel Fredrick Liljeblad in 1885 (seventy-four objects) and 1890 (eighty-three objects). The historical record has not captured much information about Liljeblad, except that he was born in Finland in 1849, captained ships in the early colony from about 1884 when he navigated the British "annexation squad" to Port Moresby (Artifact 2009), applied for a land grant in Port Moresby in 1891 (result unknown), and died in Sydney in 1924 (Liljeblad and Lillieblade 1993:29). We know that he was present at the ceremony when Britain officially claimed the new colony on 7 November 1884 (Artifact 2009) and that he was master of the London Missionary Society ship *Ellengowan* when it arrived in Sydney in February 1885 (State Records Authority of New South Wales n.d.). He is also referred to as an "informed local" (Edelfeld 1887:127). Liljeblad collected objects from Central Province and other parts of British New Guinea, and in 1906 he sold the Australian Museum a drum from German New Guinea. We can imagine that Liljeblad was typical of many early travelers to the region whose aim was primarily to profit from trade. As a ship's captain, he traveled widely and presumably had many opportunities to barter and perhaps, through repeated visits, to establish longer-term "business" relationships with some local communities. Many of the objects Captain Liljeblad collected conform to other contemporary Central Province material in the Australian Museum, but his assemblage provides especially good evidence for the experiments typical of the bartering that characterized cross-cultural interactions in Central Province. We use a selected sample from Liljeblad's assemblage to illustrate some of the creative strategies used by indigenous artifact makers to increase their engagement in barter with outsiders.

Beginning with fighting mouth ornaments, the two examples sold to the Australian Museum by Liljeblad (see figure 7.2A, B) are radically different from the published examples noted previously and from the remainder of the collection. We propose that Liljeblad's objects represent poor-quality copies made specifically for sale to outsiders. It is possible that supplies of used items had run dry by the time Liljeblad purchased these, as the traditional items are unlikely to have ever been available in large quantities, unlike the numerous spears, bows, and arrows that were freely bartered around the same time. Neither of Liljeblad's mouth ornaments is surrounded by boar's tusks. In one case, unmodified plant fiber is used to frame the object (see figure 7.2A), whereas in the other example, small pieces of wood are preserved around only part of the outline and may never have been applied to the entire periphery (see figure 7.2B). In addition, the pouches on the backs of the objects are quite small, and the parrot feather decorations are absent. The base of the larger object is a piece of metal (see figure 7.2B), whereas the other is made from a much softer wood than what was used in the more traditional objects (see figure 7.2A). The selection of metal is important. Was this material specifically chosen to increase the value of the item, since metal was highly prized among indigenous communities, or was the metal intended by the maker to appeal to Western tastes?

The second creative marketing technique exhibited in the Liljeblad collection is the substitution of an artifact type or style for one that required much less effort or skill to produce. Good examples of this strategy are Liljeblad's two lime gourds: neither is decorated, unlike all the other contemporary artifacts of this type in the Australian Museum collection and widely known from Central Province (e.g., Cranstone 1961:pl. 23a). Furthermore, both of the lime gourds he collected have an unusual shape compared with the majority of the decorated examples in the Australian Museum's Central Province assemblage. In these cases, we hypothesize that someone took advantage of an opportunity to make an exchange and offered his or her own gourd (both have lime in them), because at that particular moment, he or she did not have a decorated one to hand.

Sometimes, substitutions were expedient, as in the case of Liljeblad's lime gourds, but over time the community might devise a whole new artifact form just for the purpose of increasing their access to barter. Representing the third way of attracting opportunities for trade, Liljeblad's collection includes several new object types specifically made for sale (e.g., figures 7.3 and 7.4). The most well-known are the "man-catchers" outed by Michael O'Hanlon (1999) as recent inventions (cf. Cranstone 1961:fig. 32). Although possibly derived from tools used to hunt pigs, they are flimsy and clearly nonfunctional since the loop, which was supposedly for capturing the victim, was rarely large enough to fit over a human head. There are twenty-seven man-catchers in the Australian Museum's Central Province collection; there are relatively secure collection dates for sixteen of them, and all but two of these belong in our first phase. Man-catchers

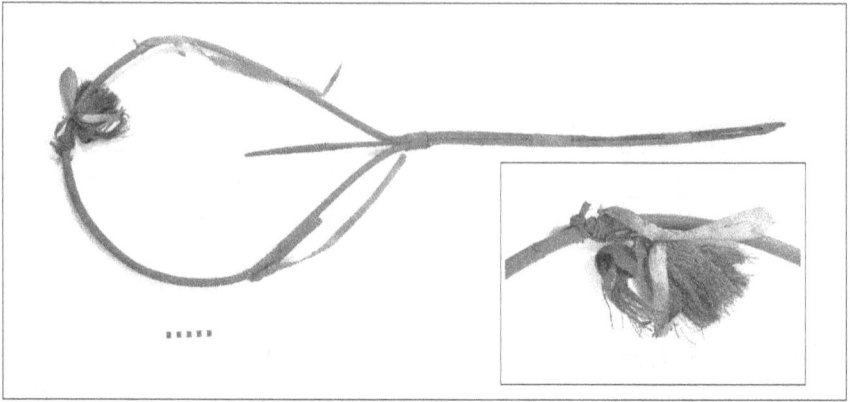

FIGURE 7.3

This short-handled, decorated man-catcher, collected by Liljeblad (Australian Museum B.6321), was much more portable than the more common, larger objects of this type. The inset focuses on the nonfunctional plant material banners and the cluster of fibers and nuts tied to the sides of the hoop. Photos by Finton Mahoney, reproduced with permission from the Australian Museum.

are also present in auction and sale catalogs of the late nineteenth century (Torrence and Clarke 2011). They were made in the region west of Central Province as well, but the documentation for the collections does not enable precise proveniences. Their manufacture and sale were relatively short-lived (Torrence and Clark 2011:46–47). The earliest example (now missing) in the Australian Museum register was accessioned in 1880. Man-catchers were probably not produced much after 1885, possibly in line with the overall shift in emphasis at this time from weaponry to body ornamentation (Clarke and Torrence 2011).

Liljeblad sold ten man-catchers to the Australian Museum in 1885 (B.6321-001–003; B.6320-001–007). Seven are typical examples with long handles in the range of 2.5–3.0 meters and ornamented with strings of plant material and seeds. Although these decorations might have detracted from their role as a killing implement, the buyers were perhaps more interested in attractive ornaments. Three, however, have very short handles, approximately 0.6–0.7 meters long, and may represent a further innovation involving miniaturized copies of the original concept (figure 7.3). A number of scholars have shown that items produced mainly for sale to tourists or travelers are often made to be easily transportable (cf. Torrence 2000; Graburn 1976; May 1977).

A fourth strategy for attracting barter was to increase the object's appeal in the eyes of potential collectors. A tobacco pipe collected by

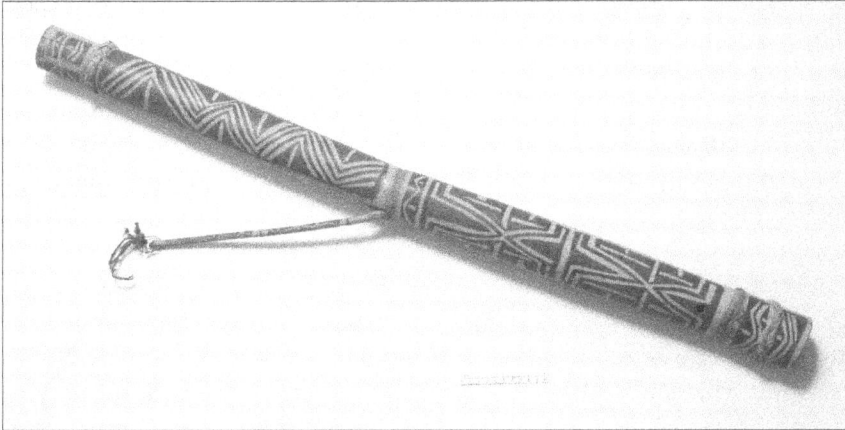

FIGURE 7.4

Strategies to attract buyers included enlarging the size of the object and enhancing it with elabo-rate attachments, as in the case of this large tobacco pipe (1 meter long), which was decorated by burning, from the Liljeblad collection (Australian Museum B.6173). Photograph by Lauren Fuka, reproduced with permission from the Australian Museum.

Liljeblad is a good example because of its large size and the addition of decorative elements (see figure 7.4). Not only is this by far the longest item in the Australian Museum's Central Province pipe collection, but it also has an extra appendage, in the form of a branch off the main stem of bamboo, that was deliberately not removed and that was even decorated in the same fashion as the main body of the pipe. A string banner dangling from this unusual appendage was also added to ensure that the artifact captured everyone's attention. A very similar example from Central Province is in the British Museum; feathers are tied to a similar appendage (Cranstone 1961:pl. 22a). One described as a "very curious specimen" is presented in Webster's sale catalog (1897:object 151). Perhaps the maker had noticed that some buyers were especially fond of large and gaudy artifacts, a con-cept that fits with the common desire in England for objects to decorate the walls of public rooms in grand houses (cf. Torrence and Clarke 2011). Enlarging the size of the decorations to attract buyers was a strategy employed also by makers of Admiralty Island obsidian-tipped spears and daggers in nearby German New Guinea (Torrence 2000:118).

ASSERTING IDENTITY

Another useful illustration of the complexities surrounding the ways in which Papuans used items of material culture to attract and create social relationships with outsiders is the production of bamboo tobacco pipes. The decoration of these objects also shows how the process of exchange with outsiders folded back on itself and played an active role in the way indigenous communities reshaped their own local identities as a reaction to colonization. Like the other inventions discussed previously, bamboo tobacco pipes helped open up new avenues for trade with Westerners, but at the same time these items also provided a means by which locals asserted their own cultural identities.

A. C. Haddon's extensive treatise *Smoking and Tobacco Pipes in New Guinea* (1946) comprises an analysis of 250 pipes based on materials held in the Cambridge Museum of Archaeology and Anthropology and the British Museum (Haddon 1946:1). This seminal study sets out the basic methods of manufacture, the types and regional styles, the methods of decoration, and speculations on the origins and timing of tobacco smoking in Papua New Guinea. The main methods used to produce the mostly geometric designs were identified as carving, incising, burning, scraping, and intaglio (1946:9–10). Haddon (1946:13) made the interesting comment that on many pipes the decoration is "carelessly executed." The symmetry of the geometric designs is often skewed because they do not match around the circumference of the pipe, and in many cases the lines are poorly made and uneven. He proffers the explanation that this may be due to a lack of skill, slovenly workmanship, or "influences which can or cannot be traced" (1946:13).

Haddon's observations about the poor execution of the designs on many of the pipes he examined are well supported by our own study of the Central Province assemblage in the Australian Museum. Many pipes display design elements that are mismatched in the round, lines that are poorly incised or burned, or designs that appear to be incomplete. It seems that artisans were still learning to convert an existing set of designs to a differently shaped surface. Once again, an artifact collected by Liljeblad illustrates the experiments people were undertaking to increase their opportunities for trade. One of the earliest pipes Liljeblad sold to the Australian Museum has a small area that is crudely decorated by incision (figure 7.5). Surprisingly, among the irregular scratched designs are two poorly executed human figures. They are slightly reminiscent of scrimshaw designs, which were perhaps observed by someone who had participated in European or American whaling expeditions. In any case, the crudeness of the decoration shows that it was made by someone with little experience in the technique of incision and who also lacked a clear conception of what elements should be placed on a pipe. Overall, the poor quality of much of the decoration on tobacco pipes suggests manufacture by unskilled

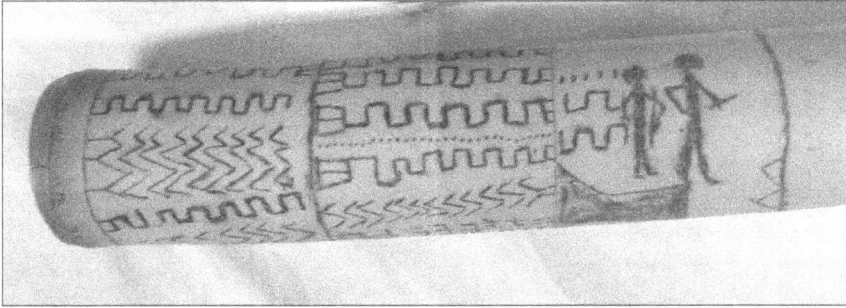

FIGURE 7.5

A crudely incised design on a tobacco pipe collected by Liljeblad (Australian Museum E.27469) exemplifies the experimental nature of early ornamentation. Photograph by Robin Torrence, reproduced with permission from the Australian Museum.

producers or by people who were experimenting with a new medium in order to increase opportunities for exchange.

Another possibility is that tobacco pipes were made quickly and with minimal attention to detail because they were produced for sale rather than personal use. Many of the pipes appear to be nonfunctional because they are so long and large that drawing the smoke to fill the pipe would have been extremely difficult, if not impossible (Deveni Temu personal communication 2010). In fact, most of the pipes in the Australian Museum collection bear no evidence in the form of smoke stains or residues that they had ever been used. Some are clearly unfinished: for instance, the hole for placing the tobacco is absent, or the pipe stem is blocked because the internal septum of the bamboo was not removed.

The date of the earliest decorated pipes from Central Province supports the proposal that these objects were specifically made for sale to outsiders. Undecorated pipes of a relatively small size are well known from photographs of people apparently placed in seemingly natural situations, as opposed to those dressed up and posed for the occasion. For example, a line drawing and short article entitled "Native of New Guinea" that depicts a man called Mayr, who was brought to Sydney by the trader Andrew Goldie (*Sydney Mail* 1879), contains a long description of the method for using these new and unusual artifacts. Importantly, this early depiction of a pipe in the personal possession of a Papuan man is plain and undecorated. This makes a direct contrast to the Australian Museum assemblage of seventy-five pipes, of which only one is plain.

Having discovered that plain bamboo pipes were not attractive to

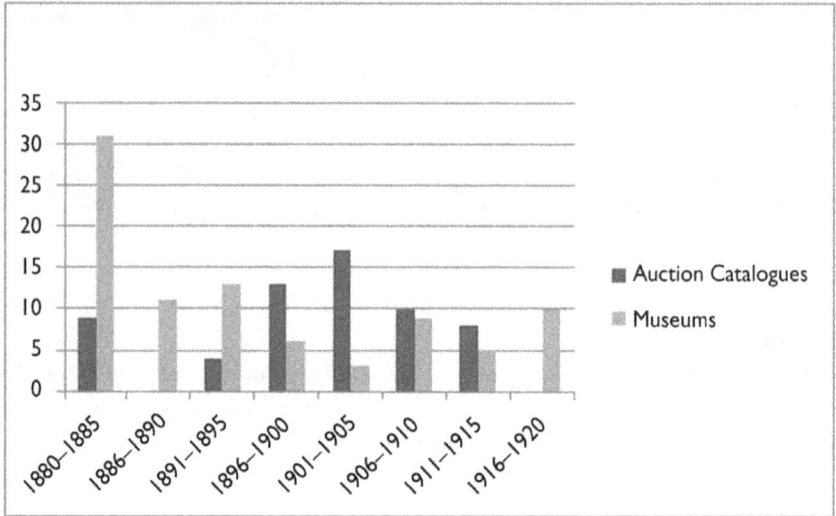

Figure 7.6

Summary of the chronological distribution of well-dated tobacco pipes from Central Province now held in the Australian Museum, Queensland Museum, or British Museum or offered for sale in the contemporary Webster and Stevens catalogs.

Western buyers, the indigenous makers made a calculated experiment devised to attract social relationships with strangers. Registration data from the Australian, Queensland, and British Museums, together with information from the Webster, Oldman, and Stevens auction and sale catalogs (as discussed in Torrence and Clarke 2011), show quite clearly that tobacco pipes only began to appear in museum collections from around 1880 onward (figure 7.6). Significantly, there are no tobacco pipes in the British Museum from the exploratory journey of HMS *Rattlesnake* along the south coast of New Guinea in 1849–1850 (Philp 2009). The earliest Central Province collection in the Australian Museum, donated by Lawrence Hargrave in 1876, does not contain tobacco pipes, nor does the collection of 246 objects purchased from Andrew Goldie, which was registered in 1878. There is only one tobacco pipe in the Goldie collection in the Queensland Museum. Although the exact collection date is unknown, it is not prior to 1880 (Susan Davies personal communication 2010). As figure 7.6 shows, the number of tobacco pipes entering museum collections peaked between 1880 and 1885. The smaller amounts between 1896 and 1910 largely represent a lag effect of objects that were recycled through the auction houses and artifact sellers.

In addition to being a pragmatic strategy to attract trading opportunities, the tobacco pipes introduced a new element in early colonial society. The ornamentations applied to these artifacts show that the makers were finding ways to assert their local identities as part of their negotiations with the new colonial society. In a description of tobacco pipes from Sogeri in Central Province, Haddon (1946:167) notes that one of the "flagged" designs is "a variant of the design frequently tattooed on the shoulders and in the armpits of coastal women." He further notes that heavily burned designs on some Central Province pipes "[were] identical with patterns tattooed on Hula and Motu women, and some [were] found as burnt patterns on lime gourds" (Haddon 1946:183; cf. designs on pipe in figure 7.3). The use of traditional tattoo designs cut or burned into the skins of bamboo can be read as an assertion of local identities in the face of the flux and uncertainty that characterized social relationships in the early colonial period. By using body designs, Papuans were inscribing themselves and their local cultural identity onto the objects offered to Westerners. Although the decoration was selected to enhance an item intended for sale, the choice of particular designs that represented clan affiliations can also be interpreted as a forceful assertion of local group identity and as a way to enforce a divide between the makers and the outsiders with whom they were interacting in a purely commercial sphere (cf. Silverman 1999).

At this stage in the history of intercultural negotiations, the designs did not become generalized or pan-Papuan but instead signaled specific localized identities, paralleling the function of the tattoos on which they were based. Haddon (1946) easily identified regionally specific designs on the tobacco pipes in the collections at the Cambridge and British Museums, and these also stand out among the variety of examples in the Australian Museum collection. The choice of tobacco pipes as an object for experimentation in exchange relationships was a particularly strategic response to the challenges of negotiating with outsiders, who also smoked tobacco in pipes, albeit using a different technology and technique, and among whom tobacco was a common trade item. The reconfiguration of the plain pipe of everyday use by the addition of culturally specific body designs can be seen in this context as a Papuan declaration of difference and demarcation.

Decorated bamboo tobacco pipes were created to fill a niche in the newly established market for curios, fulfilling the criteria of being both easily portable and exotic enough to represent the purchasers' adventures in a far-flung colony (e.g., Graburn 1976). The early and brief appearance of decorated tobacco pipes shows that Papuans recognized the value of everyday objects in establishing and consolidating their relationships with colonial outsiders. Working out which objects and which attributes of the objects best served to underpin and consolidate social relationships may explain in part the short time period for pipe production. The idea of experimentation and strategy extends to the transference of tattoo designs to pipes as artifact makers recognized that although everyday objects could be bartered for trade goods, decorated items had greater value. The late introduction of decorated tobacco pipes in Central Province, their relatively short period as a collectible item, and the overwhelming predominance of poorly executed decorated examples in the collections all point toward the pipe's being an object that Papuans actively and strategically reconfigured in response to the demands of colonial collectors. It is important to stress that from the perspective of the producers, asserting local identity through these items achieved a great deal more than simply increasing their access to trade goods.

The transformation of ordinary objects into sale items is also reflected in the history of the boat models depicting the traditional outrigger canoe (*vanagi*) and multi-hulled sailing boat (*lakatoi*) (Haddon 1937:220–231). Over time, accurate replicas that were used within traditional society to teach others how to make boats (Dairi Arua Heri personal communication 2011) were transformed by mixing the two different kinds of boat into a single item for sale to tourists. The makers selected a key element of each boat type: crab-claw sails, which are iconic of the lakatoi, and the outrigger of the vanagi. These were then combined in a way that represented the peoples of the region as a whole, as opposed to a focus on the variations among types and local groups, as was the case with the tattoo designs on the tobacco pipes. In this way, the model boats sold in the market in Port Moresby today (figure 7.7), just like the tobacco pipes of the past, are not just souvenirs, but for the makers, these provide a symbol of who they are and a means for broadcasting their identity more widely (cf. Phillips 1999:48; Silverman 1999:59; Graburn 1999:353).

SIGNIFICANT BY THEIR ABSENCE

Although local groups were eager to engage in trade with outsiders, they were also careful to control the nature of the social relations created through the exchange of objects. For example, in discussing whether people from the south coast of New Britain should sell an armband, Gosden and Knowles (2001:20) note, "Transactions with outsiders were thus influenced by a range of complex considerations covering attachment to the item to be given up, the nature of the relationship desired with the transactor, and the lure of the items to be obtained through exchange." Unlike in the Highlands of Papua New Guinea (Hughes 1978; Strathern 1992:248) and many other areas of the world where European traders were either forced

FIGURE 7.7

A boat model collected in 1974 (Australian Museum E.66183) incorporates the properties of an outrigger canoe (vanagi) *with the sails of the multi-hulled* lakatoi *and reflects the role of souvenirs in identity-forming processes in modern Papua New Guinea. Photograph by Emma Furno, reproduced with permission from the Australian Museum.*

into or took advantage of using local forms of currency in their interactions with the local community (e.g., Schildkrout and Keim 1998:26), communities in Central Province had a very different attitude about the use of local valuables. Restricting the circulation of these items to within traditional trading partnerships and ceremonial contexts helped maintain a separate indigenous social sphere.

H. M. Dauncey (1913:72–73), a long-term missionary at Delana in Hall Sound (west of Port Moresby), used a photo of items from a local man's personal collection, which he called "a friend's store box," to illustrate the objects used as valuables in this region (figure 7.8). An analysis of the

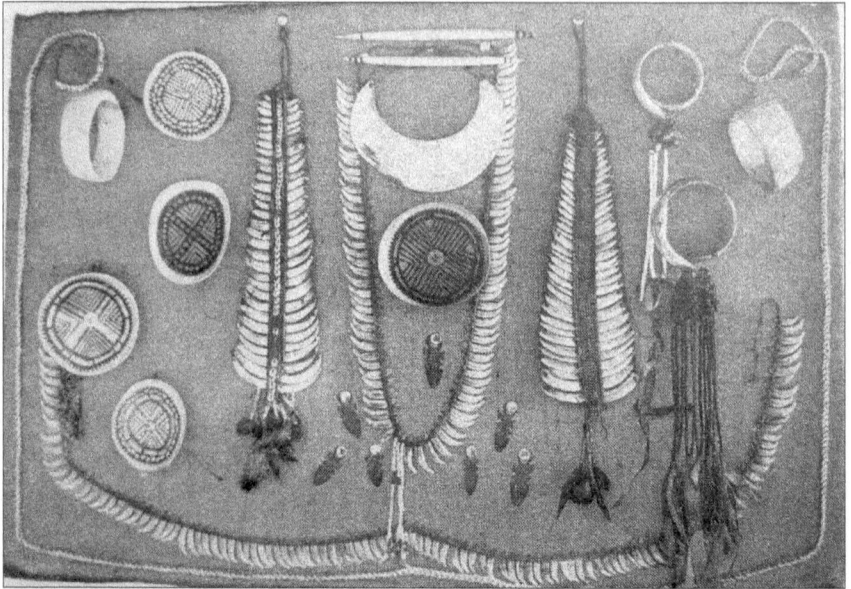

FIGURE 7.8

The content of what Dauncey described as "a friend's store box" illustrates the quantities of the main forms of valuables used in Central Province in the hiri trade network and in other types of exchange that were owned by a single person (Dauncey 1913:36, 73).

material in this box provides a good example of how people in Central Province withheld certain items from circulation with Westerners. For coastal groups in Central Province, the most important valuables were armbands called *toea*, which were made from cone shells and obtained from trading partners to the southeast, particularly in the Mailu area. These objects maintained high value within Papuan groups well into the colonial period (e.g., Barton 1902–1903:18–20; Seligmann 1910:88–89). For example, Dauncey (1913:37) observed that one man was willing to pay nearly half his annual income to obtain a large toea. Consequently, the name of these highly valued objects was later transferred to one of the main units of currency in independent Papua New Guinea. As also noted by other studies of museum collections (e.g., Gosden and Knowles 2001; Barker 2001:362; Davies 2011) and auction catalogs (Torrence and Clarke 2011), objects that served as valuables in local cultures were often difficult for Westerners to obtain because the owners would offer them only to people with whom they desired an enduring, special relationship.

The calculated strategy of withholding valued objects in interactions

TABLE 7.1

Comparison of the Occurrence of All Central Province Valuables in the Australian Museum with the Private Collection of a Single Individual from Delana

Valuable	Australian Museum	Delana Chief
toea shell armlet	3	4
(toea with decorations)	(0)	(2)
tautau, movio/mobio string of nassa shells	3	1
koiyu cut turtle shell mounted on shell	7	5
mairi crescent pearl shell neck ornament	3	1
Total	**16**	**11**

Source: Dauncey 1913:73.

with Westerners is also well expressed within the Australian Museum's Central Province museum assemblage. Table 7.1 presents an interesting comparison of the total number of objects in the collection that were traditionally used in exchange with the quantity of valuables found in the single store box (Dauncey 1913:73; see figure 7.8). Surprisingly, the museum collection is barely larger than what was in the possession of one individual. Only three toeas with adequate documentation to ensure that they were collected in Central Province are present in the Australian Museum assemblage. These were sold to the museum in 1903 on behalf of Milton Flood, who collected them in British New Guinea. In contrast to two of the toeas in Dauncey's photo, which have strings of beads or trade cloth attached, the Australian Museum shell armbands are very small and none are decorated. The collection also contains three armbands resembling toeas that were collected by Margaret McArthur (2000) in the mid-1950s from the Kunimaipa region, inland from Port Moresby. By this date, however, these objects had lost their original function as trade valuables and had acquired specific local significance as pig magic.

A second type of valuable, seen placed around the edge of the grouping in the box in figure 7.8, is represented by three examples in the Australian Museum. These strings of beads, made east of Port Moresby at Hula by sewing split *nassa* shells onto a thin woven backing, are known as *tautau* (*taotao*) by the Motu and *movio* (*mobio*) by Roro-speaking groups to the west (Seligmann 1910:89; Dauncey 1913:36). Third, the crescent-shaped, polished pearl shell neck ornament shown in figure 7.8 is called *mairi* in the Motu language (Seligmann 1910:89). There are three examples of mairi from Central Province in the Australian Museum collection, but only two were actually used; the third is unfinished, with one side of the shell left unpolished.

Elaborately carved turtle shell fretworks mounted onto shells, known as *koiyu* (*koio*), were made in the Roro-speaking region that stretches from Hall Sound up to Waima/Maiva. According to Dauncey (1913:36) these were "the greatest treasures of all" for these particular groups. Seligmann (1910:204) reports that they were used in exchanges for taro with groups in the Papuan Gulf area, but no mention is made of their trade eastward toward Port Moresby. The Australian Museum has only seven examples in the collection, compared with five in the single private collection (see figure 7.8).

The scarcity of valuables in the Australian Museum collection is particularly significant because these items continued to be used to cement social links within Papuan groups long after initial contact with Europeans. Clearly, this function was rarely transferred to their relationships with the new outsiders. Even as late as 1913, Dauncey made it clear that valuables were not easy for Westerners to obtain. "It is often reported that anything may be bought from the simple savage for a few beads, a bit of red cloth, or a mirror, but much as you might wish to purchase this collection, nothing you could offer would persuade the owner to part with it" (Dauncey 1913:36).

The paucity of valuables in museum collections raises two issues. Perhaps, since most Westerners just passed through the region briefly, locals did not feel that it was worth investing such valuable objects in establishing formal social relations with them. Gosden and Knowles (2001:95–96) report that only the Japanese trader Komine, a permanent and powerful resident, was able to acquire the gold-lip shells used in ceremonial exchanges on the island of New Britain, although other collectors had tried to obtain them. If we examine the sources of the valuables in the Australian Museum collection more closely, we can find good evidence for the importance of social relations in the exchange of objects. For example, the single short strand of tautau collected by Milton Flood is very small compared with the multiple strands obtained by Rev. Lawes, who was a long-term and prestigious resident with whom local people were likely to have attempted to establish close social ties. Interestingly, the three toeas sold to the Australian Museum by Flood are also small and undecorated. Flood (1902) wrote to the Australian Museum that he obtained his objects from an indigenous agent who acquired curios for sale to European residents in Port Moresby as part of a hiri voyage. It seems clear that even when dealing with an indigenous trader, if the exchange took place within a commercial context that would not create long-term social ties, local people were only willing to exchange "valuables" that were clearly substandard.

Second, the deliberate decision to restrict valuables to exchange within an indigenous network clearly shows that not all aspects of traditional Papuan culture were considered open for negotiation or change during the emergence of the new colonial culture. Consequently, one notable aspect of the emergent colonial culture was the creation of separate cultural spheres for locals and colonizers that existed alongside the shared economic sector. In fact, the withholding of local valuables was another strategy used by the indigenous population to actively create a new identity for itself within the developing colonial society.

CREATIVE COLONIALISM

Ethnographic collections are crucial elements for understanding the social relations of exchange in colonial contexts because they represent the tangible evidence of how indigenous people themselves selected, created, and reworked their material culture strategically and pragmatically. Our assemblage-based analysis of museum collections made in the formative years of the colony (c. 1875–1925) reveals a period of flux, uncertainty, experimentation, and creativity as indigenous Papuans and Europeans alike negotiated the cultural, social, and political challenges posed by colonial rule. Our analysis supports and builds on the model of colonial society in Papua New Guinea set out by Gosden and Knowles. In *Collecting Colonialism: Material Culture and Colonial Change* (2001), they outlined how cross-cultural relationships in colonial society during 1910–1940 on the island of New Britain revolved around forms of exchange. Their key conclusions that "colonialism in New Guinea created a new culture which joined all parties through continuing social relations" and that "objects were crucial to these relations" (2001:10) are echoed in our study. Although our analysis has identified strategies adopted at an earlier time period and in a different region of Papua New Guinea, the study of museum collections has provided specific examples of how emergent colonial culture is locally situated within negotiations over material objects.

Although our analysis supports the emphasis by Gosden and Knowles (2001) on the nature of colonial culture in Papua New Guinea as a shared rather than as an imposed or hybrid entity, the earlier collections in Central Province highlight some key differences with the New Britain colony. The collections that Gosden and Knowles studied were made well into the colonial period, when relations between the indigenous population and white government officials, plantation owners, and managers had become quite formalized and, as they note, were often focused around performances whose procedures and rules had evolved over time. By that stage, the two sectors of society were carefully segregated, and much cultural work was focused on maintaining differences. In contrast, in Central Province in the late nineteenth century and early twentieth, the local people and new arrivals were still sizing each other up and trying to find ways to interact. The early visitors were also heavily dependent on local populations for the basic necessities of life, such as food and water, and for access to land for exploration or exploitation. At this stage, material culture constituted an important medium of exchange that opened up other avenues for interaction. Consequently, the initial stage of social interaction was characterized by experimentation on the part of both groups.

The strategies employed by indigenous groups in Central Province, Papua New Guinea, to extend their opportunities for engagement with foreign traders (i.e., attraction, assertion of identity, and withholding) illustrate the material pragmatism that characterized the social relations surrounding trade and exchange in early colonial culture. What is especially interesting is that many of the experiments and innovations we have documented in this chapter took place as early as the 1880s, not long after Westerners began systematic trading in the Central Province region. The creation of totally new items of material culture together with the copying of valued items may have had further implications for the indigenous societies that were engaging in active barter with outsiders. Both the inventions and the replicas are likely to have been manufactured by people who lacked experience, perhaps because they did not possess the traditional rights to make or use the artifacts that they were substituting, such as the mouth ornaments used in sorcery. In this sense, then, the innovations represented in the Central Province museum collections might have caused disruptions to patterns of traditional social life. Furthermore, the use of tattoo designs to decorate items like tobacco pipes shows that there was a self-conscious attempt to assert particular local and probably clan identities. The application of these designs to new materials might also have reflected back on traditional practices and local conceptions of identity. Even if the practices we have recognized had only minor local effects, they opened the way for further changes, such as the construction of new identities within the emerging colonial culture.

Were the innovations and experiments illustrated in the museum collections initiated solely by indigenous people, or did traders such as Captain Liljeblad play a role by perhaps suggesting items to copy, particular substitutions, or even new objects to manufacture? Probably this question can never be fully answered, but identification of the specific origins of the innovations, while intriguing, is not essential. What is more important is the simple observation that increased interaction and negotiation through barter contributed to the beginnings of a new culture in Central Province that was shared by both colonizers and locals and that this was character-ized by many forms of innovation and experimentation.

The starting point for our research was the somewhat obvious, but none-theless profound, observation that ethnographic objects in museum collec-tions owe their origins to the indigenous artifact producers and those who offered them up for barter or sale to various Western explorers, scientists, missionaries, traders, government officials, and adventurers. The creator communities are the ones who, through interactions with outsiders, made decisions about what social links were desirable, which items were appropri-ate for exchange, and, increasingly through time, how trade goods should be manufactured and decorated. If we capitalize on the simple notion that museum collections are just as much the tangible outcomes of indigenous action as they are a product of Western activities of classification and col-lecting, then analyses of these intriguing assemblages will produce richer histories of cross-cultural engagement and negotiation.

Acknowledgments

Funding for our project was provided by the Australian Research Council, Univer-sity of Sydney, and Australian Museum. We thank the School for Advanced Research for a delightful week of stimulating debate, warm hospitality, and great food. We are especially grateful to our colleagues Jude Philp and Erna Lilje for their encouragement, suggestions, criticisms, many delightful hours of discussion and debate, and particularly Jude's wise choice of Central Province for the project case study and her assistance with understanding the early history of the colony. We also thank Susan Davies, Peter White, Deveni Temu, Dairi Arua Heri, Lauren Fuka, Finton Mahoney, Nina Kononenko, Jill Hassell (British Museum), and Vanessa Finney (Australian Museum archives) for infor-mation, assistance, and advice.

Part III
Objects, Agency, and the Curatorial Responsibility

8

Exposing the Heart of the Museum

The Archaeological Sensibility
in the Storeroom

Sarah Byrne, with comment by Evelyn Tetehu

Where is the heart of the museum? Many people would say that it is the space in and around the displays, between the cases and corridors of collections, texts, images, and objects. It is where the people are. Yet, the heart of the museum for many others is away from these crowded and carefully constructed spaces, located at an almost antithetical kind of place—the museum storeroom. Here, restricted access maintains a largely unpeopled and silent space, punctuated only by the endless rows and shelves thronged with objects—objects found juxtaposed in many weird and wonderful ways, reflecting the museum's past practices and simultaneously feeding the exhibitions that define it today.

The museum storeroom is no longer a domain inhabited by just a handful of collections staff and visiting researchers or specialists; increasingly, museums are opening their storerooms to other visitors. Indeed, this is particularly true in collaborations with source communities in relation to ethnographic collections. The amount of material culture of any given community on display is likely to be only a fraction of what a museum actually houses. Therefore, it is commonplace for consultation and collaborative collections research to take place at the museum storeroom, transforming it into a specific "site of translation" (Clifford 1997). Ethnographic objects and collections have been described as both contact zones (Clifford 1997) and field sites (Ouzman 2006; Gosden, Larson, and Petch 2007; Allen and Hamby 2011) into which curators, researchers, and communities enter, but as of yet, museum storerooms have not received the critical attention they deserve in terms of how they frame and facilitate such collaborative research.

In this chapter, I argue that the application of an "archaeological sensibility" provides new insights into ethnographic collections and a renewed understanding of the spaces in which they are stored, which can lead (perhaps unexpectedly) to more productive collaborative research between source communities and museum curators. This proposition might at first seem paradoxical. The idea that archaeology, a discipline more conventionally associated with the deep past, can contribute to the study of ethnographic collections, the majority of which were accumulated much more recently, with many of the objects still active within the memories and practices of the communities that made them, might seem misaligned. But I argue that conceptualizing the museum collections as assemblages and considering the field skills needed to negotiate and work within museum storerooms provide an alternative way of both thinking about and working within museums. This chapter draws on my experiences of working with source communities in a storeroom setting as part of the Melanesia Project at the British Museum between 2006 and 2007.

ARCHAEOLOGICAL SENSIBILITY AND THE ETHNOGRAPHIC MUSEUM

Applying an archaeological sensibility to museum collections can entail the application of both archaeological concepts and methodologies. I am not suggesting that archaeological methods or ideas can be directly applied to a study of ethnographic collections, but some of the discipline's central sensibilities can be of relevance to museum ethnography. Michael Shanks (2008) distinguishes between the "archaeological sensibility," which "refers us to the perceptual components of how we engage with the remains of the past," and the "archaeological imagination," which "refers us to the creative component—to the transforming work that is done on what is left over." In this chapter, I do not follow this distinction but rather see "archaeological sensibility" as a term adequate enough in itself to reflect both the disciplinary perception and the process, thereby encompassing the archaeological imagination. The archaeological sensibility includes a variety of methods and concepts for analyzing temporality, the relationship between objects and place, and different approaches to scale, space, and landscape. In short, it applies some of the central tenets of the archaeological discipline not to conventional sites of study but rather to the museum itself.

Employing an archaeological sensibility in respect to ethnographic collections unearths and creates a number of tensions. These tensions are not about whether archaeological methods and theories are suitable for the study of these collections but are instead linked to two interrelated factors: first, the politics of representation surrounding the collection, storage, and display of ethnographic materials and, second, the relationship between anthropology and archaeology.

DISCIPLINARY DIALOGUES

At the end of the twentieth century, Chris Gosden (1999:8–9) remarked, "In Britain, there is currently a closeness between anthropology and archaeology which has not been seen since the 19th century when the two disciplines were one, within an overall evolutionary framework," and "Archaeology and anthropology have overlapping subject matter, so that ideas and evidence from one can feed into the other." The relationship between the disciplines had, of course, a very different history in the United States. Arguments put forward by Lewis Binford and others from the 1960s posited that archaeologists and anthropologists shared a common focus on human behavior, social organization, and evolution and therefore forged an integration specific to the US context. While these essentially "processual" approaches continue to carry weight in some (but not all) of the archaeology carried out in the United States, anthropology has more consistently moved away from a concern with such large-scale goals. The closeness between the disciplines at the turn of the twenty-first century, which Gosden alludes to, was the result of quite different trends in academia. The post-processual agenda in archaeology from the 1990s onward was largely unified by attempts to repeople the past. This resulted in the application of a wide range of new methodologies and theories primarily aimed at drawing out human agency and the meanings of past objects and landscapes (Barrett 1994; Tilley 1997[1994]; Dobres and Robb 2000). The emphasis on meaning represented a new phase of archaeology's entwinement and engagement with anthropology. Equally important at the time was the "material turn" in anthropology and Danny Miller's (1987:112) call for "an independent discipline of material culture" (for a good historical overview, see Hicks and Beaudry 2010), which produced new frameworks for the interpretation of material culture and human–object relations, influenced by both disciplines (cf. Tilley et al. 2006).

Anthropology's renewed emphasis on materiality has generated a whole series of new reflections relevant for museum ethnography, including the concept of objects having biographies (Appadurai 1986; Kopytoff

1986; Hoskins 2006[1998]) and the manner in which ethnographic objects have the potential to generate personal and communal narratives (Peers and Brown 2003), unpack past social networks (Larson, Petch, and Zeitlyn 2007; Byrne 2011), and broker new relationships between researchers, curators, and source communities (Fouseki 2010; Bonshek 2009). These internal developments and the gravitation toward the "material" have clearly reemphasized the potential of the "overlapping subject matter" between archaeology and anthropology. But what I would like to suggest here is that whereas archaeologists have readily and extensively incorporated and engaged with both evidence and ideas from anthropology, anthropologists have been more likely to engage with archaeological evidence only, rather than its ideas. Anthropologists still, in the main, turn to archaeology as a way of providing a long-term context for their study, largely subscribing to the notion that "anthropology needs archaeology if it is to substantiate its claim to be a genuinely historical science" (Ingold 1992:694). But it has been pointed out that even this role of archaeology in providing "evidence of longer-term historical processes to contextualize contemporary anthropological concerns is still open to critical evaluation" (Rowlands 2008:482). The proponents of material culture studies have gone to significant lengths to counter this trend by advocating for the integration of archaeological approaches into anthropology (Tilley et al. 2006; Hicks and Beaudry 2010), but more still needs to be done in order to emphasize and draw out ways in which archaeology can contribute to anthropology.

POLITICS OF REPRESENTATION

The rise of indigenous politics called the museological endeavor itself into question (Jones 1993; Kreps 2003; Smith 2006) and stimulated alternative, non-Western models of museums and curatorial practice (Simpson 1996; Stanley 2007; Peers and Brown 2003). The American civil rights movement in the 1950s and 1960s, although primarily focused on the rights of African Americans, also brought attention to the inequalities experienced by Native Americans. This kick-started a call for museums in the United States and Canada to reconsider, reorient, and reevaluate how they engaged with and represented their indigenous populations (Cameron 1971; West 2004a; Cooper 2008). Increasingly, museums elsewhere became important platforms through which indigenous concerns and postcolonial politics could be voiced, most fervently in settler colonial contexts such as New Zealand (O'Regan 1994; Butts 2002; McCarthy 2007), Australia (Anderson 1990; Bennett 2004; Simpson 2008), and post-apartheid South Africa (Davison 2005; Witz 2006; Bakker and Müller 2010). Museums have responded to these engagements by transforming conservation, collections management, curatorial practices (Clavir 2002; Ogden 2004; Sully 2007), and modes of display (Stone and Molyneaux 1994; Ames 1999; Jessup and Bagg 2002).

The application of any form of archaeological sensibility within this process understandably carries with it the weight of negative history. The positioning of ethnographic and archaeological objects together during the Victorian period was instrumental in upholding and propagating social evolutionary and racist viewpoints (Chapman 1985; Stocking 1985, 1987; Bennett 2004). Institutions such as the Horniman Museum and the Pitt Rivers Museum regularly displayed European prehistoric stone tools in relation to ethnographic examples from regions such as Australia and Melanesia in order to emphasize the primitive nature of those societies. The legacy of these practices still resonates today. Indeed, Rowlands (2008:482) acknowledges that anthropologists engaging with archaeologists today are "anxious still to avoid charges of evolutionism, [and] have tended to concentrate on the knowledge that people in the present have of historical events and processes, rather than on the substantive nature of their historical effect." But just as anthropology and archaeology were once unified in the promotion and construction of an identity that was embedded (albeit misguidedly) in colonialism, it is fitting to consider whether they have any potential to complement each other in the promotion and construction of identities in the postcolonial world.

MUSEUMS AND COLLECTIONS AS ASSEMBLAGES

I will now focus on one specific element of the archaeological sensibility by considering whether the notion of the assemblage, a concept that has acted as the backbone of archaeological inquiry over the past fifty years, can bring with it a renewed understanding of the way in which ethnographic collections are viewed, studied, and disseminated (Torrence and Clarke 2011). The term "assemblage" is conventionally defined in two ways, either as "an associated set of contemporary artefacts that can be considered as a single unit for record and analysis" or as "a group of artefacts found at the same site" (Oxford English Dictionary online). Although the concept of an assemblage has had some presence in other fields, such as art, paleontology, and geography, it has generated the most concentrated debate within archaeology.

From the 1960s onward, processual archaeologists scrutinized the idea of an assemblage as an analytical unit, attempting to decode the cultural meaning of assemblage variability (Binford 1973, 1982; Sackett 1986) and to unpack what assemblages might reflect about social structure and change (Binford 1962). Behavioral archaeologists were simultaneously preoccupied with the formation and taphonomic processes responsible for the creation of assemblages in the first instance (Schiffer 1987, 1999; Shott 1998). It is not surprising that post-processual archaeologists focused less attention on assemblages as they moved from a site-based, analytical archaeology to an interpretive, landscape-oriented one. That said, in many fields, particularly in regard to lithic (Odell 2004) and faunal (Katzenberg and Saunders 2008) assemblages, archaeologists still return to the perennial question of whether assemblages are adequate analytical units for solving behavioral questions (Vaquero 2008). As part of a broader material turn in social theory and in attempts at finding a language that can better express human–object relations, a number of prominent social theorists have also embraced the concept of the assemblage (Latour 2005; Deleuze and Guattari 2004[1987]; De Landa 2006a). In this chapter, I draw on both established notions of assemblages from the archaeological literature and some of these more recent approaches in social theory.

ASSEMBLAGE AS CATEGORY

A number of central qualities inherent in the concept of the assemblage need treatment here. Innate to the idea of an assemblage as a category is the notion of objects found together in unexpected combinations. Binford (1982:18–19) points out, "It is perhaps shocking to realize that a recurrent pattern of association among artifacts may derive from regularities in the history of site use. The demonstrably associated things may never have occurred together as an organized body of material during any given occupation." In more recent times, as part of a Theoretical Archaeology Group session in 2009, "The Theory of Assemblages," Michael Shanks (2009) made a very similar point about the nature of assemblages on his blog: "These things were not intended to go together—a collocation of oyster shell, situla, ox scapula." This essential quality of an assemblage as a material collocation, how objects are situated or juxtaposed in relation to one another, is pertinent when thinking about ethnographic collections. The actual physical collocation and relationship between objects, be they in storerooms or on display, obviously bear little reality to the way in which these objects were used or assembled by source communities or, indeed, collectors.

In cultural historical and early processual archaeology, there was an assumption that archaeological assemblages directly equated with culture, a view that was later criticized, given that assemblages, by their very structure, reveal substantially more about the cultural deposition of an artifact than about its use. Hodder (1979:452) pointed out, "It is therefore invalid to tot up the numbers of cultural similarities and differences between archaeological assemblages, erect 'cultures,' and assume that these have some ethnic, linguistic, or other significance." Although referring to an archaeological setting, this point highlights something important about how ethnographic collections are viewed, used, and understood. It emphasizes that the fragmented nature of collections needs to be read carefully before assuming underlying cultural patterns. Indeed, to garner a better understanding of cultural meaning within collections, we need to understand the taphonomic processes that created the assemblage in the first place.

Lucas (2010:354) has pointed out that an "assemblage is therefore what constitutes the residue of past events, not individual objects, if by assemblage we understand a set of material relations or organization evident in the archaeological record." Indeed, the events, the agency through which objects became separated from source and deposited, in storerooms or in soil, rather than the objects per se, constitute the nature of the assemblage. In situ archaeological assemblages tend to be more clearly bounded by place and time. Although museum assemblages are equally located and reflect particular eras of collecting, they are often more open-ended, consisting of objects gathered together from multiple locations by multiple agencies at multiple times with the potential to be added to at any point in the future.

MUSEUM STOREROOM AS FIELD SITE

It is at the museum storeroom where conceptualizing collections as assemblages is particularly pertinent. Embedded within a concern with assemblages is a concern with the sites in which objects are located and translated (see also the introduction to this volume). Binford emphasizes the close relationship between assemblages and places:

> Archaeological sites yield assemblages. Assemblages are sets of artifacts (both items and features) which are found in clustered association (normally defined stratigraphically) at or in archaeological sites.... The archaeologist "sees" the past segmentally from the perspective of fixed positions in space. The "fallout" from the events that "moved across" fixed places establishes the character of the archaeological remains on sites. To understand the past we must understand places. (Binford 1982:5–6)

Conceptualizing ethnographic collections as assemblages forces a more detailed consideration of the spatial relationships between objects themselves but equally of the spatial relationships between those engaging and interacting with one another in respect to the objects. Whereas the grouping of objects in galleries provides insights into curatorial commitments and perspectives current at the time of installation, the physical relationships between objects in museum storerooms reflect deeper processes of time, the material manifestations of myriad separate, interweaving, and overlapping relationships between people, things, time, and place, much like an archaeological site.

Objects that once belonged together have been split up, pulled apart, and given new identities according to the trajectories of Western museum practice, most commonly according to their geographical region, form, or material. For example, objects related to a traditional practice of dancing from a particular community are often found spread across different museum categories: masks may have their own category, objects worn in the same dance can be found in a section on personal ornaments, related skirts will reside in a category of dress, related dancing staffs will sometimes be found mislabeled among a collection of canoe paddles, and so on. Equally, relationships between objects that were amassed by particular collectors (reflecting collecting priorities or strategies at any given moment in time) are frequently broken down in storeroom assemblages. Different museums have obviously different storage procedures and structures in place, and these can be subject to change through time. But in many instances, the categories set up when a museum was originally established are either still in place or continue to significantly influence how the material is housed. The movement of an object into the storeroom not only severs the internal logic of a given collection but arguably also transforms the collection into an assemblage; the object now becomes part of a group of materials, defined not in relation to the social practices it was once used for or the collecting criteria it fulfilled but in relation to the space it now occupies.

Other researchers have pointed out the significance of considering the spatial aspects of museum collections. Rebecca Duclos (2004) employs the term "cartographies of collecting" in order to map the processes of collecting (somewhat along the lines of Clifford's [1997] notion of the anthropologist as "traveler") rather than map the spatial imprint of what has been collected and deposited at the museum itself. In a similar vein, Jude Hill's (2006, 2007) research emphasizes the spatial relationships created by the dispersal of Henry Wellcome's collection. Both Hill's and Duclos's useful mappings of museum collections originate from a cultural geography perspective. I would argue that the examination of object circulation and deposition patterns at museum storerooms can particularly benefit from an archaeological approach, due to the specific methods archaeologists have developed for analyzing the relationships between objects and place.

Visiting and Engaging with Storeroom Assemblages

So what happens when storerooms are visited and interacted with by those outside the museum? There is a perceptible tension between the public and the museum storeroom. In January 2011, there was a call in the UK press, urging museums to show more of their hidden material (e.g., BBC 2011). It is no coincidence that this came at a time when visitation figures to national museums in the United Kingdom had more than doubled: from 7.2 million in 2000 to nearly 18 million in 2010.[1] Visitors are becoming more sophisticated and interested in what goes on behind the scenes at museums. The call for museums to open up their storerooms to new communities forms part of a much wider trend demanding social responsibility and accountability within the museum, what Kahn has defined as the "need to represent culture as adaptable, dynamic, and evolving rather than fixed and bounded, and to include multiple and diverse voices, opinions, and perspectives rather than rely on curatorial authority" (2000:57–58). The intense debates in the twenty-first century about how museums should engage with community development (Kreps 2003; Crooke 2007) and involve communities in meaning making (Hooper-Greenhill 2000; Peers and Brown 2003; Karp et al. 2006) have highlighted the museum storeroom, transforming it into an important site of translation.

Although many museums are now moving to the model of open storage (rather than being boxed out of sight, objects are stored on open, more accessible shelves) and facilitating public visits, storerooms were never designed to be accessible to large numbers of people. They are by their nature controlled, restricted, and often intimidating places. Kingston (2007:53) points out that "one of the store's normal roles is, after all, security, the preventing of the unauthorized escape of heritage from the approved network." Such parameters set particular challenges for curatorial staff in terms of how to manage and facilitate these engagements to make them worthwhile and relevant to visiting communities.

How does the structure of storeroom assemblages frame and define these interactions? Museum staff "know," or at the very least can trace (through institutional registers, records, photographs, collectors' journals, and databases), many of the site-formation processes that have created the assemblages now present in the museum storeroom, that is, why certain objects appear together in boxes, in drawers, or on shelves. Yet, visitors who are confronted with these assemblages often lack such knowledge. Indeed, piecing together the historical relationships manifest in these assemblage structures can require meticulous, time-consuming research. Databases reveal some of these relationships but of course not all. In addition, databases are physically separate from the tangible engagements that occur between curators, collections staff, and visitors at storerooms. In many ways, the visitor interacts with the assemblages in the storeroom as an archaeologist might do at a site. The visitor encounters the museum assemblages not within a historical framework but from a contemporary, materialist position.

Although the dissemination of objects from museum storerooms is now being orchestrated virtually, through online databases, there still is a vital need for physical engagement with objects and for community visits to museum storerooms. These issues are of particular concern when we think about how museums facilitate visits from source communities. On the one hand, storerooms are very appropriate places to work collaboratively with source communities. Lacking the embellishment of curatorial narrative or metaphor that ordinarily frames exhibition spaces, objects are at their rawest state, often marked only with a simple label. As a result, visitors and curators can more effectively explore the collections together. On the other hand, institutional practices, the weight of history, and the various interactions that created the assemblages in storerooms can be hard to penetrate and ultimately still frame the process of collaboration at these sites.

Field Skills

What field skills are needed to negotiate and work within the space of the museum storeroom? Arguably, museum collections can represent a challenging field site for the social anthropologist. The silence emanating from the objects, their acute detachment from related social practices, the notable gaps and absences—all mean that human–object relations cannot be easily observed but have to be teased out of the material and historical data. Museum collections are sited, fragmented, partial, convoluted representations of people and things, similar to the contexts commonly frequented by archaeologists. Indeed, archaeological field skills are specifically designed to grasp what the material traces left behind in particular places might mean. Shanks (2008) points out, "As well as remains, archaeology deals in traces or tracks, impressions and footprints, impacts and imprints that witness the non-presence of the past, and that require an 'ichnography'—a science of traces."

But archaeological field inquiry also differs from social anthropology in pertinent ways. Rather than be immersed in one field topic or field site, archaeologists are encouraged to be mobile, to move between both temporal and spatial contexts in order to build an understanding of the connections and patterns between things; in doing so, they commonly operate on different scales of inquiry from those of anthropologists. This could potentially be of benefit when working across time periods and cultures within the storeroom setting. More significant still is the way in which archaeological fieldwork is carried out in teams. Although some anthropologists use teamwork in the field (cf. Kuhlmann 1992), the majority still largely carry out fieldwork alone, what Reimer (2008) describes as the "lone wolf" researcher. One of the core defining characteristics of the archaeological discipline is the way in which it gathers people of different specialities around the same assemblage so as to unpack and analyze it from different perspectives. Such a process creates not only new frameworks of knowledge but also new social and professional networks. This resonates with bringing varied communities and specialists into museum storerooms to unpack and subvert the established relationships within assemblages.

Archaeology is, at its heart, interventionist (see Edgeworth 2006; Lucas 2010). It intervenes with (and often destroys) things in one context by dragging them into another context. When archaeologists excavate assemblages, various stages of post-excavation analysis essentially reassemble component objects in relation to the questions being asked and the people asking them. In this way, archaeological assemblages undergo various stage changes. Schiffer (2010:38) points out, "For many artifacts, archaeological context is only a temporary state. That is because reclamation processes transform artifacts from archaeological context back to systemic context." This process of reassemblage occurs at different places, or sites of translation. First, excavated objects are reassembled on-site; then, they are reassembled at a new location during post-excavation analysis and at yet another when ascribed meanings are disseminated. Working with communities in the context of the museum storeroom is equally interventionist: it facilitates a process of transforming objects from one context into another by reassembling the collection in relation to different knowledge, conceptual, and ontological frameworks, which effectively moves the objects outside the museum, connecting them to other times and places.

Interventions and Transformations

In the introductory chapter to this volume, Harrison emphasizes how the concepts developed by assemblage theorists Manuel De Landa, Gilles

Deleuze, Félix Guattari, and Bruno Latour are pertinent within the broader project of reconfiguring museum collections. In the context of this chapter, a number of these ideas warrant consideration, including De Landa's (2006a:5) point that assemblages are "wholes whose properties emerge from the interactions between parts." This suggests that assemblages essentially defy and resist internal definition. Therefore, it may be less important to define museum assemblages as structures per se than to concentrate on the external qualities and relationships their emergence suggests and can create. Furthermore, De Landa (2006a:11) says that "these relations imply, first of all, that a component part of an assemblage may be detached from it and plugged into a different assemblage in which its interactions are different." Indeed, it is this inherent quality of assemblages, the ability to effectively "detach" objects from their current assemblages and "plug" them into new ones that is central in archaeological research and underlies much of the recent collaborative research on ethnographic collections.

Also important here are some of the ideas in Bruno Latour's actor-network theory (ANT). ANT is conceived largely as a tool through which social scientists can explore and trace the "social." Latour's (2005:7) definition of the social "not as a special domain, a specific realm, or a particular sort of thing, but only as a particular movement of re-association and re-assembling" is fitting here. It reiterates the fact that the social is something that emerges out of the movement of people and things. While Latour's work is by no means focused only on material things but also on entities such as institutions and governments, the relevance of his ideas within a museum setting has been noted (see Byrne et al. 2011a).

If we are to follow the ideas of museum collections as assemblages and the social as something emergent, it is useful to consider what constitutes a "reassemblage" in a museum context. I see the process of reassemblage as both the physical and conceptual movement of the objects within a collection. Beginning at the point of collection, ethnographic museum objects have been part of an array of different reassemblages, passing through the hands of collectors, dealers, traders, missionaries, and auction houses until the point of entry into the museum. And it is of course blatantly evident that the reassemblage process by no means stops there. Indeed, reassembling objects in relation to one another for display is one of the main jobs of any museum curator. Reassembling collections in exhibitions is a carefully controlled, coordinated, editorial process with clear public outputs aiming to educate, entertain, enthrall, or induce reaction and interaction. This chapter, however, is specifically concerned with the reassemblages that emerge when curators work with source communities in a storeroom setting (a form of excavation really), which is almost an antithesis to the reassembling involved in museum exhibitions. Reassembling collections in museum storerooms with source communities is essentially a more private, sometimes haphazard, and less predictable process. I will now discuss some work I was involved with as part of the Melanesia Project at the British Museum in order to consider how some of these processes of reassembling emerge and what ramifications they might have for museum and curatorial practices more generally.

THE MELANESIA PROJECT AT THE BRITISH MUSEUM

Between 2005 and 2010, the Melanesia Project took place—"Melanesian Art: Objects, Narratives and Indigenous Owners," an endeavor funded by the Arts and Humanities Research Council and a joint initiative between Goldsmiths College, the Cambridge Museum of Archaeology and Anthropology, and the British Museum. The project's goal was to research the British Museum's Melanesian collections with a particular emphasis on the meaning these collections have within and for source communities today. There were three main objectives:

> Objects: to study the British Museum's Melanesian collections, providing new provenances, new contextual information drawn from archival work as well as recent ethnography, insights into technical and stylistic aspects, and collection histories.
>
> Narratives: to contextualize the collections by analyzing the relationship between objects and personal historical and political narratives. Illuminating their varied and changing significance and meanings for indigenous individuals and communities, past and present.
>
> Indigenous owners: to explore the dialogues between museums and indigenous individuals and communities around the past and present significances of historic Melanesian collections, to generate more sophisticated understandings of what such dialogues and collaborations involve, establishing bases for future work, specifically around upcoming exhibitions. (Melanesia Project 2005)

Given that this project was set up to study neglected Melanesian collections and to draw in and engage with new stakeholders, the British Museum facilitated visits of delegates from different parts of Melanesia. I was involved in two programs with the Melanesia Project. In 2006, I helped facilitate a visit of four Solomon Islanders to the museum for three weeks: Evelyn Tetehu (originally from Santa Isabel, now living in Brisbane), Michael Kwa'ioloa (from Malaita, now living in Honiara), Kenneth Roga (from New Georgia), and Salome Samou (originally from Santa Cruz, now living in Fiji). On occasion, we were joined by some Solomon Islanders who were resident in the United Kingdom: Mazula Head, Annie McArthur, and Vicky Glass. I worked with all of the delegates but more closely with Evelyn Tetehu throughout the process. After interacting with the collections, the delegates provided recommendations and insights about their meaning and social significance at a workshop held as part of an international conference, "Art and History in the Solomon Islands: Collections, Owners and Narratives," 4–5 October 2006. The second program I worked on, in 2007, involved three media professionals from Melanesia: Walter Nalangu from the Solomon Islands Broadcasting Corporation, Ambong Thompson, a film and radio program organizer at the Vanuatu Cultural Centre, and Peter Solo Kingap, a newspaper journalist from Papua New Guinea. The aim of this was to produce a radio program about Melanesian material culture and *kastom* (customs) that would be broadcast in the delegates' home countries.

The Melanesians who visited London over the course of five years all spent time at the British Museum storeroom. Indeed, the storeroom was one of the main locales of collaboration and sites of translation for the project. These storeroom visits activated the Melanesian collections into new phases of movement, circulation, and reassemblage, the likes of which had not been seen since the objects were first collected and accessioned into the museum.

Selecting Solomon Islands Objects

The British Museum holds one of the biggest and most important collections of Melanesian material in the world, almost twenty thousand objects overall with approximately thirty-eight hundred objects from the Solomon Islands alone. Given the scale of the collections, organizing the visits of the Solomon Islanders presented challenges for the curatorial and collections staff in terms of deciding in what sequence the collections should be presented to the delegates. Prior to the visit, my colleagues and I asked the delegates to indicate what objects they were interested in seeing, and they told us they wanted to see all of the material from their respective regions. The number of objects from each delegate's region averaged between two hundred and three hundred. It is important to note that this process happened before the British Museum put its collections online and, therefore, delegates had access only to textual lists of the collections. In addition,

FIGURE 8.1

(Left to right) *Michael Kwa'ioloa, Ben Burt, Evelyn Tetehu, Sarah Byrne, and Kenneth Roga examine drawers of ornaments from across the Solomon Islands. Photograph by Liz Bonshek.* © *Trustees of the British Museum.*

many of the Solomon Islands objects were photographed for the first time during this project. Today, accessible photographs online could potentially facilitate a different process, whereby visitors would be able (if they have access to the Internet) to look at the associated information and photos (if present) before actually visiting the museum. The Melanesian collections at the British Museum are stored primarily by place (with the exception of the Malinowski collection) and then loosely by object type. The storage is not open shelving; instead, the majority of objects are stored away from sight in variously sized wooden boxes, most of which were packed in anticipation of a storage move that never happened but is currently planned for 2014. This kind of storage is not particular to the British Museum; for example, the storeroom at the Cambridge Museum of Archaeology and Anthropology is similarly arranged. Some of the larger boxes have a wide range of objects stored together. These assemblages contain artifacts used in a range of cultural practices, originating from a variety of different areas, and acquired by an array of collectors. Initially, we questioned whether the objects should be retrieved and presented to the visitors by place, object type, or use. In the end, two days were spent looking at ornaments (figure 8.1), one day on figurative sculpture, one day on objects related to household and betel chewing, another day on weapons and tools, and the final day on textiles and barkcloth. Deciding on the itinerary for these days and in what order we would show this material was mainly influenced by the structure of the storeroom itself and the size and spatial locations of the assemblages therein.

During the planning stage for this project, I found myself walking the corridors of the Oceanic storeroom with location list in hand, feeling completely overwhelmed by row after row of the same pine-colored boxes, which I knew contained a bewildering array of colorful, complex, and creative manifestations of cross-cultural contact with Melanesian people from different times and places. Compounding the situation was the fact that although I had worked with Papua New Guinea collections previously, I was less familiar with Solomon Islands material culture. Therefore, each time I opened a box, I was experiencing many of the objects for the first time. Those days spent in the storeroom were intellectually stimulating, and it is no overstatement to describe them as sublime. Anyone who has carried out research in a museum storeroom should empathize with the largely inexplicable, heart-pounding feeling of revealing and interacting for the first time with objects that one is interested in. There is something about the overlay of generations of human lives from places and times far removed, all squashed into one space, that is exhilarating. Indeed, during this process, I became aware of how reminiscent this was of working on an archaeological site for the first time, troweling back the soil expectantly in the hope of revealing things from the past and simultaneously creating new relationships for the future. I do not relay this feeling to digress, but to make an important point. Museums should not be complacent about the power of their storerooms. Experiencing the assemblages of materials within the storeroom site has the potential to bring the visitor straight to the heart of the museum, in terms of not only its history but also its raison d'être.

Lamentably, due to practical constraints of time, the Solomon Islands delegates did not partake in the process of recovering these objects from the storeroom. Most objects were brought to them in a study room one floor down from the main storeroom, although they did visit the storeroom on occasion to look at the larger objects and those on storage racks. The delegates were therefore dislocated from the storeroom itself. It is increasingly common for visitors to museums to be housed in such a neutral space. For example, the new development at the Pitt Rivers Museum followed this model by constructing a study room at the museum itself, a considerable distance away from the storeroom. While the presence of these kinds of rooms does not necessarily preclude a visitor from going to the actual storeroom, the important point is that collaboration in these separate spaces is becoming the more common practice. Such dislocation may well be beneficial for the collection and its staff, who can maintain a carefully controlled environment and minimize health and safety risks, for example. But if museum staffs want to create dialogue with source communities, translating what it is museums do and why they do it and exploring how this complements or contradicts how materials are viewed and translated by particular communities, they might think about how the storeroom can act as a particularly powerful site of translation in this regard. One of the most important and positive shifts, somewhat countering the dislocated study room model, is the move within many museums toward open storage, enabling curators to bring visiting source communities into and around the stacks and shelves and hence to the heart of the museum.

Reassembling the Collection

In looking at, inspecting, and holding the objects from the storeroom, the perspectives of the Melanesian visitors circulated, animated, and intersected with the objects in a variety of ways, breaking down established assemblages while creating new ones. As the visitors vocalized memories and opinions about the objects, a series of both physical and conceptual reassemblages emerged.

The physical structure of Solomon Islands assemblages in the British Museum storeroom is governed by type. Therefore, the majority of the assemblages presented to the delegates were groups of the same type of object: all fishhooks together, all grass skirts together, and so on. The organization of objects by type has its historical roots in nineteenth-century museological practices of collecting and displaying objects, often within social evolutionary frameworks (cf. Stocking 1987). Indeed, assembling objects by type has continued to be a popular methodology for storing, displaying, and researching museum objects. In particular, research and exhibitions that situate ethnographic material as art objects have considerably reinforced and upheld the validity of studying objects in this way; it is a form of regulatory curatorial practice (see the introduction to this volume). A good example of this is the existence of countless books on masks in which the main focus is on the variation between mask types as art pieces (e.g., Herzog et al. 1998; Finley 1999; Nunley et al. 1999).

One of the most interesting things about the interactions at the storeroom during this project was the way in which the delegates' conversations reassembled the collections by moving objects out of the typological constraints imposed on them by the museum. One such assemblage of objects (which had been grouped by type) that Annie McArthur and Evelyn Tetehu inspected were eight lime flasks from Santa Isabel. These flasks are containers for the lime powder used in betel-nut (*areca*) chewing; all are made of bamboo with incised and blackened geometric designs. Five of the flasks (Oc.1938.1001.12–16) were collected in 1938 by J. K. B. Lister, two were donated by Julius Brenchley (Oc.6421, Oc.6419), likely collected in 1865

Figure 8.2

Lime flask (Oc.7647) and its contents of small, black, fragrant seeds known as rugupole
(Roviana) and white seeds that may be rekiti *(Roviana). © Trustees of the British Museum.*

during his cruise on the HMS *Curacao* in the Solomon Islands, and the last
(Oc.7647) was donated by Charles. F. Wood in 1872 and may have been
collected on one of his voyages in the region in the late 1860s. It was this
potentially earliest flask that garnered the most attention and kicked off a
conversation between me and the two women that lasted well over an hour.
Interestingly, this conversation focused not on the object itself but on the
contents within it.

Although many of these flasks still have lime powder in them, this
example also contains two kinds of seeds (figure 8.2). Annie McArthur
identified the small, black, fragrant seeds as *rugupole*, which helped to prevent the burns commonly experienced when using lime powder in chewing
betel nut. She was not exactly sure about the species of the lighter-colored
seeds but thought they might come from a small reed, locally known as *rekiti*,
that may have functioned to prevent the lime from clumping together. The
presence of the seeds led to a lengthy discussion about other traditional
items commonly mixed with betel nut. Evelyn Tetehu spoke about how people in Santa Isabel often chewed ginger (*papase* in the Zabana language),
betel nut, and lime powder together to heal sore throats or so that the
mixture could be placed on the body to heal ailments such as headaches.
This prompted further discussion on the uses of ginger in traditional spells
(*basa* in Zabana; *baha* in the Roviana language). Tetehu also mentioned
what she thought might be a more recent practice: putting ginger beside
one's bed or in a beam or wall of the house to encourage well-being in the

Oct., 1915.]　　　　　　MAN.　　　　　　[Nos. 84–85.

ORIGINAL ARTICLES.
With Plate L.

Solomon Islands: Ethnography.　　　　　Edge-Partington.
Fishing Appliance from Ysabel Island (Bugotu).　*By J. Edge-* **84**
Partington.

Among the ethnological specimens brought home by my son from the Solomon Islands is a very interesting, and to me quite new, appliance (Fig. 1) for catching the crustacean (*Lysiosquilla maculata*), which buries itself in the sand before the tide recedes. The appliance is made by attaching one of the raptorial claws of the male Squilla to the end of a strip of cane, or the mid-rib of a coco-palm leaflet ; a few inches above the claw, a small fish (*Periopthalmus*) is lashed on as bait. The native takes this down to the beach at low-water, and when he finds a hole in the sand, which denotes the whereabouts of his prey, he inserts the appliance into the hole, whistling or singing at the same time. If the "fish" is at home it moves up to secure the bait. It will be noticed that the claw is fixed on with the barbs facing upwards ; when the native feels a bite he strikes his fish, which is then easily drawn to the surface. A full account by Mr. Stanley Kemp of this species of crustacean is to be found in the *Memoirs of the Indian Museum*, Calcutta, iv. No. 1, 1913, page 113, Plate viii, from which I have copied Fig. 3.

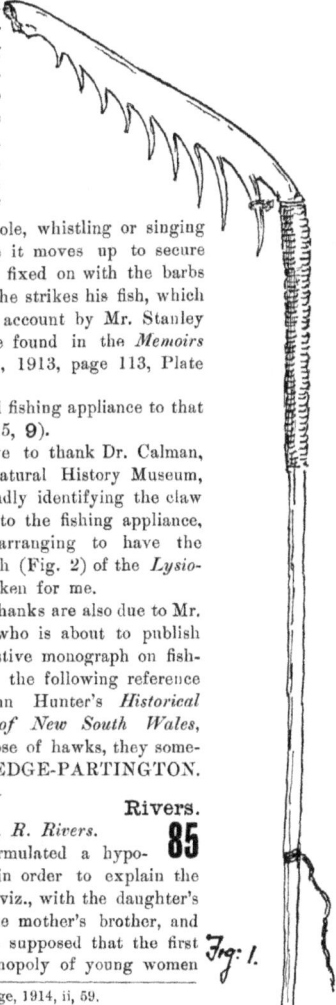

This will add another instance of a natural fishing appliance to that described by Mr. Henry Balfour in MAN (1915, **9**).

I have to thank Dr. Calman, of the Natural History Museum, for so kindly identifying the claw attached to the fishing appliance, and for arranging to have the photograph (Fig. 2) of the *Lysiosquilla* taken for me.

My thanks are also due to Mr. Beasley, who is about to publish an exhaustive monograph on fish-hooks, for the following reference from John Hunter's *Historical Journal of New South Wales*, 1793, page 63, " The talons of birds, such as those of hawks, they sometimes made use of " (as fish-hooks).　　J. EDGE-PARTINGTON.

Melanesia.　　　　　　　　　　　　　　　Rivers.
Melanesian Gerontocracy.　*By W. H. R. Rivers.*　**85**
In a book recently published I have formulated a hypothetical scheme of early Melanesian society* in order to explain the occurrence of three peculiar forms of marriage, viz., with the daughter's daughter of the brother, with the wife of the mother's brother, and with the wife of the father's father. I have supposed that the first form of marriage was the consequence of a monopoly of young women

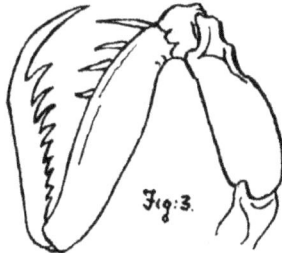

* *History of Melanesian Society.* Cambridge, 1914, ii, 59.

[145]

FIGURE 8.3

Article by Edge-Partington (1915) that illustrates the hinganatarika *(Zabana) that reminded Evelyn Tetehu about her childhood. © Wiley & Sons Ltd.*

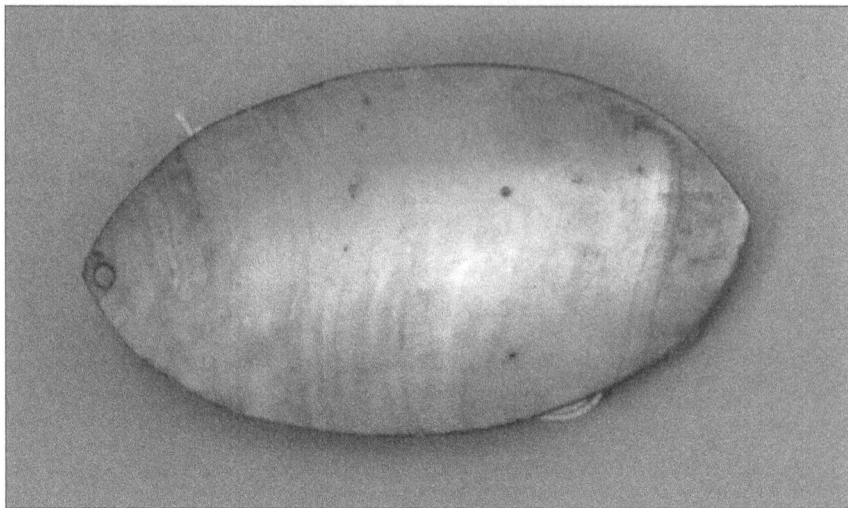

FIGURE 8.4

Golden mother-of-pearl spoon that Evelyn Tetehu thought may have been used for weaning babies during a special ceremony known as vasido *(Zabana). © Trustees of the British Museum.*

household. She also warned that although ginger planted near your house is essentially "good ginger," spells or curses could easily turn this ginger "bad." It was particularly interesting that, unlike what curators or research-ers might do, the women spent very little time discussing or comparing the typology, morphology, or designs of the objects. Instead, the conversation was much more oriented around their use, which led quite organically to a discussion of betel chewing and the role of betel in kastom magic and medicine. Although prompted by the lime flasks and the contents of one flask in particular, the conversation included discussion of other betel nut–related objects, such as mortars and pestles. It was the practice of using the object rather than the materiality of the object itself that became the main focus of attention. The object had effectively become reassembled in a broader conceptual framework and narrative: it moved out of the museum and its typological setting to engage with related social practices. It also underwent a temporal reassemblage: the contents of a lime flask from the 1860s became connected to cultural practices some 150 years later. This emphasizes De Landa's (2006a:11) point about out how "a component part of an assemblage may be detached from it and plugged into a different assemblage in which its interactions are different."

The temporal relations enacted in the process of reassembling also deserve further attention. For instance, Evelyn Tetehu had lived away from the Solomons for more than thirty years and thus relied on memories from her youth to interact with the collections, but equally she has maintained a strong relationship with her homeland and visits Isabel regularly. In one case, a seemingly unremarkable although rather strange-looking object consisting of a midriff of a coconut leaf with a mantis shrimp's claw attached at the bottom (Oc.1919.16) reminded Tetehu of her youth. She told us that she and her sister had used this type of shrimp claw, known as *hingana-tarika*, as a sort of fishing lure, which they poked into a hole to catch live shrimp (probably *Lysiosquilla maculata*). This object, collected by Thomas Edge-Partington and donated to the museum in 1919, was the subject of a brief article by Thomas's father, James Edge-Partington (1915; figure 8.3), the renowned collector of Pacific Island material culture. Tetehu was equally excited about an object that she had heard about but never seen. She had been told that this golden mother-of-pearl spoon (Oc.4008), collected circa 1860–1869 (see figure 8.4), was used for weaning babies during a special ceremony known as *vasido* (Zabana), during which a stick of mustard (the same type used in betel-nut chewing) was put down the throat of young babies until they vomited, after which they were fed their first solid food. Vomiting was an indication that the child was ready for solids. Traditionally, mashed-up taro was used to wean the child, but now sweet potato is used and the shells have been replaced by spoons. Although this object was only labeled generically as a "shell ornament" and it did not even have a specific Solomon Islands provenance attached (it was found among other Solomon Islands shell ornaments), Tetehu displayed a strong connection with it. The contrast in the narratives about an object that Tetehu herself actually used and one she had memories about was not as marked as might be expected; both were detailed accounts and both objects elicited her attention and excitement. It is typical that such encounters move from the remote past to "lived" or more recent experiences. Again, what unites these objects is the way in which Tetehu contextualized them in relation to recent and ancestral practices. Although, on occasion, the delegates' narratives related to the material and construction properties of particular objects and therefore directly inscribed the physical objects with new meaning, more often the narratives drew away from the objects toward a discussion of related social practices—a pattern that was replayed throughout the process of engaging with all kinds of objects.

Identifying connections between objects in a museum collection in terms of practice can reveal details of the structure of the collection itself. One of the most interesting things in the collaborations between communities and museum collections is the focus given not only to the objects that

FIGURE 8.5

Peter Solo Kingap inspecting the green stone adze from the Western Highlands, Papua New Guinea. Photograph by Sarah Byrne. © Trustees of the British Museum.

are present but equally to the objects that are missing. Like any assemblage, museum collections are samples—far from a complete record. One particularly animated encounter during the Melanesian broadcasters program was when Peter Solo Kingap was discussing a group of green stone adzes from the Western Highlands in Papua New Guinea. He identified one ceremonial adze used in dancing (see figure 8.5) but became frustrated that he could not fully explain the typical ensemble of objects worn together during traditional dancing, because they were missing from the collection. We were able to locate certain objects but not all that he spoke about. Absences mark significant points of engagement with collections, and as Baudrillard (2005[1968]:113) points out, "even though objects may on occasion lead into the realm of social discourse, it must be acknowledged that *it is usually not an object's presence but far more often its absence that clears the way for social intercourse*" (emphasis in original). For Kingap, the adzes were only part of the story; the desire to find and reassemble these collections in relation to how they were once worn together seemed very strong. He sought a physical reassemblage toward something more socially meaningful.

Absences are naturally more noticeable when one attempts to reassemble collections in relation to practice, because objects are being interacted with as related groups rather than as individual objects or groups of objects of the same type. Indeed, these absences can reflect the agency of the people involved in assembling the collections: a collector's preference, the reluctance of local communities to part with certain items (cf. Davies 2011; Torrence and Clarke, chapter 7, this volume), differences between objects collected or available at different points in time, or gender differentiation. The absences identified through communities' engagement with collections can provide new angles by which to research the collections and indeed might even encourage collaboration with other institutions to investigate whether these absences are similar or different elsewhere. It is also important to note that Kingap's account of dancing was stimulated by an object that the museum had classed merely as a "tool."

PRACTICE AS PRIORITY?

While it may be obvious that the relationships between objects in museum assemblages bear little conection to assemblages of objects used in social practice, the main questions here are whether this pattern of reassembling museum collections in relation to practice, which emerges out of collaborative encounters, should be of concern to the museum and what the ramifications might be. Museum staff have often been criticized for being too object centered, and collaborative collections research has revealed this fetishization of material culture (Macdonald 2002; Fouseki 2010). Indeed, the gap between cultural practice and the object-centered focus of the museum is particularly challenging and important in the Melanesian context, in which, more often than not, kastom is something that is enacted, not looked at in a museum (cf. Bolton 2003).

Assemblage theory and ANT both offer interesting perspectives on the relationship between objects, social practice, and social structure that are relevant when thinking about the emergent reassemblages that occur in collaborative collections research and how this might impact the structure of the museum and related practices. Latour (2005:64–65) points out: "For ANT, as we now understand, the definition of the term [social] is different: it doesn't designate a domain of reality or some particular item, but rather is the name of a movement, a displacement, a transformation, a translation, an enrolment [sic]. It is an association between entities which are recognizable as being social in the ordinary manner, except the brief moment when they are reshuffled together."

This idea that social meaning is born out of the "reshuffling" of things (Bennett, chapter 2, this volume) suggests that structures can emerge at any point depending on the movements of the actors (both human and nonhuman) involved. This is similar to De Landa's (2006a:10) contention that social assemblages are characterized by "relations of exteriority" and external movements rather than any internal structure *per se*. In a similar way, collaborative collections research in a museum context is less concerned with tracing the known structure of the collection and instead is focused on the creation of new meanings and relationships through actions of reassembling and reshuffling. These processes can actively destabilize, impede, and alter the spaces in which they occur. De Landa's concepts of "territorialization" and "deterritorialization" are significant in this regard:

> So in the first place, processes of territorialization are processes that define or sharpen the spatial boundaries of actual territories. Territorialization, on the other hand, also refers to the non-spatial processes which increase the internal homogeneity of an assemblage, such as the sorting process[es] which exclude a certain category of people from a membership of an organisation, or the segregation processes which increase the ethnic or racial homogeneity of a neighbourhood. Any process which either destabilizes spatial boundaries or increases internal heterogeneity is considered deterritorializing. (De Landa 2006a:12)

If the museum storeroom and its assemblages comprise a territory of sorts, then it is useful to think about how the dual processes of territorialization and deterritorialization might play out. In many respects, the homogenizing process of territorialization is carried out by the museum staff, who are involved in defining and sharpening the spatial boundaries of an assemblage through practices of classifying and sorting. De Landa (2006a:15) also emphasizes the centrality of classifying (which he terms "coding") as a way of stabilizing assemblages: "While territorialisation provides a first articulation of the components, the coding performed by genes or words supplies a second articulation, consolidating the effects of the first and further stabilizing the identity of assemblages." Furthermore, he suggests that within a bureaucracy (such as the museum), this "coding is performed by narratives establishing the sacred origin of authority." Alternative claims by indigenous communities on museum assemblages and processes of physical, digital, and knowledge repatriation enact not only destabilization but also deterritorialization within the museum: a power balancing act. The spatial aspect of this process is significant. The way in which these engagements move the objects out of old relationships and assumptions and into new relationships and interpretations creates new assemblages and decodes established ones.

I suggest that paying closer attention to the social practices of which objects once were a part and to the relationships between objects in such practices has the potential to create longer lasting, more embedded collaborations. This translates into a better understanding of the social context in which the objects were created and used and of the subsequent processes that transformed them into museum collections, revealing their contemporary meaning for curators and communities alike. Reassembling collections in relation to practice is not an attempt to return to some semblance of an "origin point" when these objects were used and made. Instead, it draws our attention to the different practices to which the objects and collections were subject through time: the practices related to their making and use, the subsequent museum practices that transformed them into ethnographic objects, and, perhaps most important, their relationship to social practices today.

RAMIFICATIONS INSIDE AND OUTSIDE THE MUSEUM

On a practical level, reassembling storeroom collections in relation to practice could be better facilitated by following a number of steps: first, the curators and community representatives should access the museum's databases and analyze all the material from the area in question (and, perhaps, neighboring areas for comparison); second, key social practices should be identified, for example, cooking, feasting, dancing, fishing, hunting, and gardening; and, third, it should be decided which collections will be viewed on what day. Effort should also be made to allow visitors some mobility within the storeroom and the flexibility to view objects that complement any emergent narratives.

As museums can facilitate only a certain number of representatives from any given community at one time, the onus is often on the visitors to then communicate the information they have gathered about the collections back to the community they represent. One other benefit from reassembling and researching collections in relation to practice might well be to provide a more meaningful structure for how the material can then be disseminated back to communities, especially when collections are large and access to the Internet is restricted.

Reassembling collections in relation to practice means that objects become animated, are less likely to be viewed as art objects, and therefore more easily can move out of their museum context and assume a more active social function. Contextualizing materials in locally meaningful categories might also help consolidate reflections on the legacy of traditional practices and recent changes and, as a result, what role museum objects have for communities today. I have already pointed out that reassembling collections in relation to practice can help reveal some of the absences within museum collections and, as a result, provide new insights into the structure of museum collections. Focusing on social practice in the process of collaborative collections research also has the potential to contribute to new modes of display and to the development of creative and interactive events.

There is a long history of debate about how museums can account for the particularities of social practice while still maintaining a general overarching narrative or theme suitable for display. In the late nineteenth century, Boas argued for the installation of dioramas showing museum objects in use (see Hinsley and Holm 1976), his way of countering the popularity of social evolutionary or typological modes of display at the time. Although both dioramas and typological modes of display became unpopular by the middle of the twentieth century, the ethos of the "ecomuseum" from the 1970s onward (for history, see Davis 1999) and the development of the "new museology" discourse in the 1980s (see Vergo 1989) also foregrounded the need to represent the specific identities and cultural practices of particular communities more clearly. More significant still has been UNESCO's Convention for the Safeguarding of the Intangible Cultural Heritage (2003), which has called on museums to place more emphasis on the rich traditions of music, dance, and orality from the communities whose tangible objects they hold. Article 2 of the UNESCO convention states that intangible cultural heritage "means the practices, representations, expressions, knowledge, skills—as well as the instruments, objects, artefacts and cultural spaces associated therewith." In many respects, Article 2 could apply to every single tangible item within a museum setting, but what is important is its emphasis: tangible objects are deemed significant only in relation to the intangible values they represent.

The meaning of intangible heritage and its ramifications for the museum have been widely debated (Kirshenblatt-Gimblett 2004; Alivizatou 2006; Kreps 2009), but one of the most significant implications is how its focus encourages community collaboration and consideration of not only the history of a particular community but also its contemporary context. As Deacon and others (2004:13) point out, "intangible heritage consists of vibrant cultural practices that will require creative approaches to safeguarding that are driven by the practising community." This focus on practices both contemporary and past can feed into the interpretation and display of cultural objects within the museum context. The full impact of this turn to the intangible has yet to be seen in museum displays. Indeed, it depends on the ethos of the institution as to what extent these values influence display practices. Richard Kurin (2004:8) writes, "Museums can encourage and promote cultural diversity, the continuity of tradition, and ongoing cultural creativity. Not all museums will want to do this, nor should they." There is still quite a way to go in terms of working out how to incorporate the intangible into a project largely focused on tangible heritage, but multimedia and new technology are clearly important in disseminating such nuances (Alivizatou 2006). I posit that if we are serious about representing intangible values in the museum, then the reassembling of collections in relation to practice at the point of collections research and in the collaboration stage, as suggested in this chapter, could reveal new relationships and feed into new and creative displays, effectively allowing the deterritorialization enacted by source communities in the storeroom to more directly influence displays.

Another benefit of this turn to intangibility is the increased presence of staged events at museums (often but not exclusively in conjunction with exhibitions). A good example of this was the spectacular Day of the Dead event held at the British Museum in November 2009 in conjunction with the temporary exhibition "Moctezuma: Aztec Ruler." During the event, the public was treated to a vibrant procession of performers, musicians, and dancers and was introduced to traditional foods and cooking practices from Mexico. Jonathan Jones (2009) of the Guardian wrote: "Skeletons on stilts danced in the smoke that wafted from fiery braziers. Babies wore skeleton costumes and children feasted on sugar skulls while a Mariachi band played. Elsewhere, a musical anthropologist had people singing along to an Aztec dirge. And most of all, wherever you looked there were people—thousands and thousands of participants in what must surely be one of the most extraordinary public events ever staged in a museum." In the music workshops, replica instruments from the British Museum collections were played by musicians and audience members alike. These kinds of interactive events are important mediums through which the meaning of the museum's collections can be communicated to a mass audience.

The status and suitability of the museum as a performative space has been long discussed (see Pearson and Shanks 2001). Indeed, the potential of these events not only to disseminate knowledge but to also contribute to social development through participation and representation is the backbone of the ecomuseum philosophy (developed by Rivière and de Varine in the 1970s), which has been subsequently developed by many museums worldwide (see Davis 1999). These museum events often rely on setting museum objects in motion, that is, contextualizing them in relation to the social practices of which they were and continue to be a part—and, in so doing, encouraging a more holistic form of heritage practice. Pearson and Shanks highlighted the role of the archaeological sensibility in this process when they wrote: "Both performance and archaeology attend to detail, focusing tightly but sensitively upon particular conjunctions and instants. Their substance is local, whatever may be done with relationships to more general settings" (2001:57).

Paying closer attention to the reassembling that takes place within storerooms during collaborative research (its own kind of performance) has the potential to create an interesting dialogue and movement between the more private, haphazard "conjunctions and instants" that happen within the storeroom setting and those that are communicated within the museum public arena and displays.

CONCLUSION

This chapter explores certain processes of collaboration that take place between source communities and museum staff when working in storerooms. I have suggested that the application of an archaeological sensibility and the conceptualization of museum collections as assemblages open up new ways of thinking about the formation and location of ethnographic collections. On the one hand, the chapter highlights how the spatialization and structure of the storeroom can dominate and frame collaboration, but equally I have acknowledged that the storeroom acts as an important site of translation (cf. Clifford 1997)—a space in which source communities can gain some territory by processes of reassembling and where museum staff can communicate the history and current goals of museum practices. Museums are not static institutions but rather places of continual movement and renegotiation. Reassembling museum collections in relation to practice is one creative strategy helping to break down the hegemonic structure of the museum assemblage and opening up new pathways of collaboration and new ways of disseminating and displaying collections, hence bringing both community and curator closer to the heart of the museum.

COMMENT BY EVELYN TETEHU, 17 APRIL 2011

Working with the author at the British Museum examining artifacts from my home island forced me to think about why my ancestors would have given artifacts to collectors: as a gift or sometimes because the visitor showed keen interest in an item. This would have been the first step in the disassembling of a personal collection of artifacts—later to be reassembled in a museum or private collection.

After I returned from the British Museum, a village elder showed interest in what I had to say about my visit. He asked me, "Did you see a spear that my grandfather gave to a white man?" He had never seen this spear, but his grandfather had told him its story. This story gave the spear so much importance that the elder expected that the "white man" would also have appreciated its importance, such importance that it must be known worldwide! His grandfather would not have parted with this symbol of his, or his group's, identity easily. This was no tourist item; this was a part of his history.

My late mother once presented to a "white man" shell arm rings of a type that no longer was made. Knowing how scarce and valuable these rings were, the "white man" declined her offer. I advised him to accept, as she was giving this from her heart and she intended that he interpret this as a memory of her, the giver. Again, the item was something of such high personal value that the giver was expecting that it would be recognized by the recipient as such. And, in this case, it was.

These are examples of the creation of socialities between villagers and visiting foreigners who, though they may have been collectors, were not seen as such. However, since there are usually differences of perception between the giver and the acquirer regarding the value and meaning of these items, those socialities in most cases remain poorly developed.

From what I have learned in searching out old artifacts held in households in the villages of Santa Isabel, I find that these always have strong personal meaning. That is why they were assembled as a household collection in the first instance (though some such collections are not always physically located in a house; sometimes they are hidden in caves or buried). These assemblages of artifacts are often indicators of a particular tribal or clan group.

Many items are those that can also be worn as body decoration. I believe that the primary reason for wearing them, however, was not decoration. It was to show the social status of the individual wearing them. Sometimes these assemblages of artifacts are produced in a local court as evidence that the holder of these items is the true representative of a certain landholder group. When I see similar items in museums, I feel that my people would have been very reluctant to give or to sell these. Were some items collected under pressure, perhaps even under threat, or were some "spoils of war"— taken from other islanders and passed on to collectors by people for whom they had no special meaning?

The author describes museum collections as "fragmented, partial… representations of people and things." They definitely are. The household artifact collections that I have been examining in the course of a Santa Isabel Cultural Heritage Programme at first also appear to be fragmented and partial. The difference here is that these items have stories attached to them. In some cases, these are myths, though mostly they are historical accounts of their origin and relationship to the holder. These artifacts are connected through their stories.

Being focused on the physical appearance of an artifact, most collectors failed to recognize the importance of an artifact's social "place," so this information did not accompany the artifacts on their way to museums. However, I believe that much can still be done to give these museum collections life. Information we are collecting in Santa Isabel, through empowering and training village cultural investigators to seek out and photograph the artifacts held by village households and to document their stories, is being fed back to the British Museum to better inform its holdings.

I agree with the author's idea that ethnographic collections could be reassembled or reclaimed by paying closer attention to the social practices of which they were once a part. However, to get the best from that step described by the author for "reassembling the collection," I feel that the association with community should be through a continuing exchange of information, as we are doing through links between our Santa Isabel Cultural Heritage Programme and the British Museum (and, of course, our own Solomon Islands National Museum).

Acknowledgments

Warm thanks to Michael Kwa'ioloa, Kenneth Roga, Salome Samou, Mazula Head, Annie McArthur, Vicky Glass, Walter Nalangu, Ambong Thompson, and Peter Solo Kingap. A special thank you to Evelyn Tetehu for sharing her knowledge and insights with me and for writing a response to this chapter. I would like to acknowledge the help of staff from the Melanesia Project, Jill Hasell, Liz Bonshek, Lissant Bolton, and Ben Burt. And a final thanks to Annie Clarke, Rodney Harrison, all SAR participants, and two anonymous reviewers for helpful comments on this chapter.

Note

1. For visitor figures, see http://www.culture.gov.uk/what_we_do/museums_and_galleries/3375.aspx and http://www.guardian.co.uk/culture/2011/dec/01/national-museums-double-numbers-free-entry.

9

Artifacts in Waiting

Altered Agency of Museum Objects

Chantal Knowles

The museum is a repository for artifacts, where they can be stored, preserved, cared for, researched, and exhibited; through these systems and processes, they acquire value (Clifford 1988; see also the introduction to this volume). When museums actively acquire objects, enabling them to become part of a collection, the things are inscribed with categories and classifications and are frequently presented as authentic representations of a place, time, people, or culture. The classificatory system imposed by the museum may be alien to the makers or to previous owners, but it implies scientific value, research potential, and authenticity. The resultant cumulative collection is a product of the museum's history and the individuals, in particular the curators, who work within its institutional framework. When scholars examine the history of research or display at a particular museum, the same artifacts are regularly brought to the fore, and consequently many other artifacts remain in waiting for a change in fashion or circumstance, for when a different curatorial gaze is turned on them.

Taking as a case study A.UC.767, a Māori *waka*, or canoe (figure 9.1), in the National Museums Scotland (NMS), I will examine the encounter between the artifact, artist, conservators, and curator during its restoration for exhibition in the new Pacific Gallery in 2011. This large sculptural piece had resided in the stores for at least a generation, and as curator of the Pacific collections and lead curator for the gallery, I was keen to see it go on permanent display.

FIGURE 9.1

The waka A.UC.767 as she was examined in September 2006. The absence of a stern post and her degraded state are clearly visible. © *National Museums Scotland.*

It soon became clear that it was badly damaged, lacking a key feature of any war canoe—the *taurapa* (stern post), an intricately carved fretwork piece that rises high above the canoe hull and at the base of which would be seated the chief when the vessel was at sea. In the conservation workshops, a series of questions about the genesis of the canoe and its early history were raised, and it became apparent that the canoe was not what it was thought to be. The archival record suggested that its inherent complexities had led to its being overlooked by visiting researchers and the museum curators, and I therefore looked to members of the Māori community to better understand the object and find a solution that would enable its display and interpretation for a wider public.

This object is a conundrum; it survived nearly two hundred years of being ignored. The canoe was not reminiscent of other waka, being an ill-fitting assemblage of component parts, and hence did not fit the received museum categories. It has required active participatory engagement with the object to get beyond that. This project confronted the canoe as a marginalized object (Douglas 2010[1966]; the introduction to this volume), which was therefore unstable in its anomalous state. Rather than abandon the object in favor of something more complete and simpler to display, by bringing it back into place within Māori culture and museum practice, I sought to challenge people to engage with it, which became a key strategy of the project. The new gallery presented a unique opportunity to confront this artifact's ambiguity, address its historical importance, and make it accessible to a wider audience.

KNOWLEDGE AND CLASSIFICATION: WORDS AROUND THINGS

Early in the development of the new Pacific Gallery, the Māori canoe was identified as a key artifact. Principal drivers in choosing to include it were the fact that it had not been on display within living memory and would therefore be new to the public and that it was a large object, thus considered to be a striking visual "hook" for the gallery. The canoe, described in the museum database as a war canoe, was incorporated into the gallery's brief and themes as such. The catalog also recorded that, at only twenty feet in length, it was considerably shorter than other known examples of Māori war canoes, which could reach up to a hundred feet in length, and was damaged to the extent that it would require significant conservation prior to display.

Museum Words

Analysis of the documentation, classification, and cultural context of the canoe became the starting point for the project that eventually unfolded. The original, undated, handwritten register entry read: "A.UC.767. *War Canoe*, Maori. Prow highly carved: upper portion of sides carved with grotesque figures in which the eyes are inlaid with mother-of-pearl and lashed to the boat by strong cord. Wood. L. 20'6." W. 2' (Damaged)." The entry provided an early date for the object by labeling it "A.UC.," indicating that it was part of the Edinburgh University Collection, which was the founding collection for the national museum in 1854.[1] The damage suggested a need for conservation or repairs, which, given its age and purpose for use in warfare, was not unusual. There were three supplementary notes, each attributed to visiting researchers from New Zealand. The earliest reads: "According to Mr Duff, of Canterbury Museum, Christchurch, N.Z., Jan. 1948, this is probably a small river canoe converted into a canoe model by the addition of top strakes of a full size canoe."[2] This suggested that the original museum category of "war canoe" might be flawed and misleading. The second note provided a regional provenance and also queried the original entry: "Milled[?] planks, prow of stern too small, hull may be a real one-man canoe which has been remodelled by flattening the keel. Gisborne area: D. Simmons, June 1978."[3] The most recent reads: "2 July 1998: War canoe. c. 1830s/1840s: Roger Neich, Auckland Museum, N.Z."[4] Each scholar had visited the collection before commenting on the canoe, and it is believed that they saw the canoe firsthand. None of these scholars singled out the object as an item of note, nor mentioned it in their diaries or notes pertaining to their trip.[5] Although several Māori visitors had come to the museum between 1997 and 2002 and could have seen the canoe in the museum stores, no response to the canoe was attributed to them.[6]

The regional card index was checked for further information, and information about the artifact was found to be filed under the region "New

Zealand" and object type "canoes, paddles," with the card for the canoe additionally recording in pencil "above case" and "58–61," notes that most likely located the canoe above the numbered wall cases within the ethnography gallery at some point before 1940.[7]

As stated above, the canoe had originally come from the Edinburgh University Museum as part of the founding collection of the National Museums Scotland, and on consulting the daily record books, I found an entry dated 29 November 1827: "Yesterday arrived from Kelso a large New Zealand Canoe," followed three weeks later on 22 December with the entry "The New Zealand Canoe Repaired" (National Museums Scotland Archives 1827a, 1827b). Although not described in these records as a war canoe, it seems likely that this referred to A.UC.767 as both its size and damage merited comment.

This new archival evidence, which had not previously been associated with the canoe, created a potential link with Sir Thomas Makdougall Brisbane (1773–1860), a former governor of New South Wales (1821–1825) who retired to the Scottish Borders town of Kelso. Thirty-seven additional ethnographic artifacts in the National Museums Scotland collections are directly attributed to him, all of which came from the Pacific. Two of these objects, a feather box (*wakahuia*, A.UC.503+A) and a "staff of office" (*taiaha*, A.UC.518), originated in New Zealand, and there is evidence that Brisbane, in his role as governor and through his own scientific interest, collected for various institutions in Scotland (Morrison-Low 2004; Saunders 2004). Henare (2005:91–92), in documenting exchanges between Māori people and Europeans, cites an instance in 1823 when the Māori leader Te Ara wrote to Brisbane, offering a "New Zealand Matt" in exchange for a "fowling piece to shoot birds for food." Brisbane had the intellectual curiosity, the means, and the opportunity, in his role as governor and residence in Sydney, to access many artifacts through his acquaintances and through curio traders in Sydney (e.g., Harrison 2011a). Given his associations with New Zealand and the university museum, the probability is that this canoe was acquired by him.

I inspected the canoe further to supplement the information available in the museum documentation, repeating the measurement of the object's dimensions and undertaking a series of photographs of specific elements of the canoe. In 2006, I sent some of the photographs to Roger Neich, requesting further clarification as to the function of the canoe in an attempt to clarify the conflicting notes in the registers. In response, he wrote:

> The carvings are all you would expect of a war canoe, although

20 feet is quite small for a war canoe. The side strakes [*rauawa*] and prow are carved in the very specific form for a war canoe—you would not see these compositions on a fishing canoe.... I would say it is definitely a war canoe, probably from the Bay of Plenty, and looks to date from about the 1830s to 1840s period. The stern post would have been quite tall and completely composed of open-work carving, with a small figure at the base facing into the canoe. It would probably be the largest war canoe in an overseas museum. (Roger Neich personal communication 15 September 2006)

Accepting this as confirmation of the object's status as a war canoe, with three diagnostic attributions to the Bay of Plenty region, Brisbane, and the unexpectedly early date of 1827, I began to reflect further on the canoe's Māori history in order to envisage how it could be displayed.

Māori Histories

Māori artifacts in museums are described by the Māori people as *taonga*, which Tapsell defines as

> any item, object or thing which represents a Maori kin group's (whanau, hapu, iwi) ancestral identity with their particular land and resources. Taonga can be tangible, like a greenstone pendant, a geo-thermal hot pool, or a meeting house, or they can be intangible, like the knowledge to weave, to recite genealogy, or even the briefest of proverbs. As taonga are passed down through generations they become more valuable as the number of descendants increase[s] over time. All taonga possess, in varying degrees, the elements of ancestral prestige (mana), spiritual protection (tapu), and genealogically ordered narratives (korero). (Tapsell 2000:13)

It was essential from the beginning of working with the waka to consider it both as a canoe and as an item of ancestral importance.

The Bay of Plenty, Te Moana ā Toi, is situated on the west coast of the North Island of New Zealand, and the Māori *iwis* (nations) resident in the area trace themselves to three ancestral canoes (Te Arawa, Tākitimu, and Mataatua). Since the region in the early nineteenth century had increasing access to European trade and a thriving carving tradition, the canoe or its various components could have been produced by carvers from one or more of these associated iwis (McKinnon 2009). Unfortunately the limits of the archival record do not allow us to associate the canoe with a specific iwi.

In Māori culture, the canoe in all of its forms is of great significance. Every Māori will trace his or her *whakapapa* (genealogy) back to an ancestral canoe, the large vessels that brought their ancestors to New Zealand (Cooper 1989:24). Who the Māori are, their spirit, their past, present, and future, are inextricably interwoven with their ancestral canoes. After their Polynesian ancestors settled Aotearoa (New Zealand), Māori people developed a series of dugout canoes for specialized purposes. *Waka tīwai* (river canoes) lacked ornamentation and were used for river and lake transport. *Waka tētē* (fishing canoes) were used at sea for fishing and for travel along the coast; these could reach up to twelve meters in length and had side strakes but minimal carving on prow and stern (Best 2005[1925]; Hamilton 1896:9–16; Howe 2007:240). The large kauri tree of the North Island enabled canoes of great size to be made, and the *waka taua* was the largest and most impressive. Carrying up to a hundred warriors, it held an important place in the Māori culture. War canoes were essentially people carriers, designed to move war parties to battle, and they were cleverly constructed to allow easier portage between lakes and rivers and dismantling into their component pieces for storage. The stern and prow were each carved from a solid log, and the hull and side strakes connected these carvings. The side strakes were lashed to the sides with a batten running the entire length of the hull. Decorative streamers of feathers and bindings were added to the prow and stern, with feathers interwoven into the bindings on the hull to give the finished canoe an impressive, animated visual appearance. Each waka taua would be individually named at the final part of the process of assembling the materials and then making and carving the canoe. There is a clear distinction between the *tapu*, or spiritual status, of a war canoe for certain members of the community, such as women and children, and the free access for the whole community to a river or fishing vessel.

The canoe was of such significance in Māori life that it helped form the representation of the Māori as a particularly "warlike" people. The canoes are the focus of many early writings describing the contact experiences. Captain Cook praised the "great ingenuity and good workmanship" of the canoes, the largest of which he noted were "built wholly for war" (qtd. in Thompson 1997:113). Yate (1835:163), relating a visit to the region, described the emotion evoked by the sight of a full war party at sea: "A fleet of a hundred New Zealand vessels is a dreadful sight, inspiring, from the shouts of the warriors whilst paddling along, the utmost terror in the minds of those whom they are about to attack. None can view unmoved a hundred of these canoes in action."

The role of war canoes in the popular imagination embedded and reinforced the outsider's assumption of what it meant to be Māori. The overriding view of the Māori culture and identity at that time, as being rooted in war, was continually played out in their representations in the British and colonial press (see, for example, Sydney Gazette 1830). As a consequence, artifacts such as weapons and preserved heads, representative of a warrior race, were sought by Europeans (Henare 2005:93; Thompson 1997:116), and it is therefore no surprise that what was thought to be a war canoe was bought by a collector such as Brisbane.

Since waka taua were named canoes with an important role in a community, it is unlikely that they would be traded often. However, in the 1820s, when the museum's canoe was most likely to have been constructed, the Māori in New Zealand were engulfed in intertribal warfare. Inter-iwi battles stretched between the North and South Islands. This period is known as the "Musket Wars" because it was characterized by the introduction into war raids of muskets acquired from Europeans through trade. While the first use of muskets in a Māori battle dates back to 1807, the wars intensified in the following years as sporadic contact and trade with Europeans increased access to firearms. It is against this background of disruption and warfare that our waka quite probably came into the hands of Governor Brisbane. The prospect for trade represented by the desire of Europeans to acquire "curiosities" and Māori people's need to acquire European arms led to a convergence of motives and opportunity that may well have created the circumstances under which the canoe was crafted expressly for trade and sold.

Through the uncovering of this multiplicity of evidence relating to its origins, the waka taua at the NMS gradually began to emerge as a complex artifact. Its history within the museum included numerous conflicting attributions and categories, which changed as each subsequent researcher viewed it. An initial visual appraisal with museum conservators had also identified a series of ambiguities in the artifact, not least its size and scale in relation to its purpose. A review of the contextual history reconfirmed these uncertainties and suggested that the canoe was unlikely to have been strategically valuable to an iwi in warfare. Nonetheless, in Māori terms, it remained inextricably linked to the diagnostic features of a war canoe.

The more I researched the waka in my role as curator, the more difficult I found it to understand and categorize in Māori *and* museum terms. Nevertheless, in discussion with conservators and colleagues, I began to consider ways of restoring the canoe for public display. From the museum's perspective, the physical absence of the taurapa (stern post) became an influencing factor in how the project unfolded, because without this component part the canoe was incomplete and its poor overall condition was likely to impede visitor engagement and an aesthetic response. Neither the conservators nor I felt comfortable with pursuing the repair and restoration of the canoe without expert guidance; we therefore agreed that a replacement stern post should be produced by a Māori carver. This would be entirely consistent with Māori practices of renewal and repair (Sully 2007). As we could not approach a particular iwi for guidance, we initially turned instead to the British Māori community. In September 2006, I invited the Māori artist George Nuku to view the waka in the museum collections. This allowed us the opportunity to view the canoe together and discuss the appropriateness of a new stern post for the waka being carved by him.

ARTIFACT PRODUCTION

The arrival of Nuku at the museum stores provided the impetus to marshal sufficient staff to move the canoe out of its storage niche and into a space where unconstrained access was available. During the subsequent inspection of the canoe—involving conservators, curator, and artist—it became apparent that the task before us was not the simple addition of a new taurapa to an existing artifact. Observed in its entirety, the artifact's many different components presented us with several notable problems. To begin with, the side strakes were bound low along the sides of the hull,[8] and it was not clear where one element of the canoe ended and another began. Moreover, the carved insets for the thwarts, which are so characteristic of a war canoe, did not correspond with each other across the hull and thus could not actually have accommodated the thwarts. The photographs that had previously been taken to document elements of the canoe had in fact presented a distorted view. Each photograph had captured a limited aspect of each element (because of the waka's scale), such that these led to the interpretation that we were looking at a war canoe. However, the moment we unwrapped the canoe and began to look at the proportions and overall shapes, it immediately became clear how misleading the individual photographs were in providing a true sense of the whole piece. Thus, the comments of Duff and Simmons, though not their conclusions, in the accession register were the most accurate reflection of our canoe: this was a composite artifact that was difficult to categorize, describe, interpret, and exhibit. Consequently, this waka also presented singular difficulties in our efforts to restore it.

FIGURE 9.2
The hull stern interior, showing what is presumed to be the museum repairs documented in 1827.
© *National Museums Scotland.*

Material Encounters

Our engaging with the canoe visually and through touching and moving around it exposed the limitations of the archival sources, so often the backbone of a museum curator's research. The elicitation of diagnostic features and the categorization of the artifact, which on paper clearly defined the canoe, had provided only fragments of knowledge rather than a true representation of the physical whole. In sharp contrast, the material approach that we then began to pursue allowed the object to be researched in its entirety. This further study was undertaken by a small project team consisting of George Nuku, me, and conservators Charles Stable and Sarah Gerrish, who had expertise in ethnographic artifacts and wood conservation, respectively.

At this early stage, our appraisal of the canoe enabled us to identify three separate component pieces: a modified hull that most likely derived from a river boat; well-worn side strakes, which appeared to originate from a full-sized war canoe and had been cut and bent to fit the hull; and a scaled prow that was badly damaged, possibly suggesting a prior use on a large-scale model canoe. In addition to these three Māori components, there were uncarved wooden additions, or repairs, which had been tinted to mimic the Māori components. Closer examination of the hull stern

237

revealed it to be a later addition that was tapered to a V and thus resembled neither the shape of a war canoe stern nor that of a fishing canoe hull. When viewed externally, the hull stern appeared to be a linear continuation of the hull; however, an internal view showed an agglomeration of battens and screws that belied the clean lines of the exterior (figure 9.2). Additional smaller pieces of wooden infill had been stained and bound into the canoe. There were several types of cordage used in the binding and a proliferation of different nails and screws. Nuku examined the Māori elements and commented on the various signifiers that pertained to each carved element. At the same time, he asked museum staff a series of probing questions about the waka's condition and history. Most of these proved extremely difficult to answer, and we therefore began to develop a series of new hypotheses relating to the genesis of this artifact.

The proposed project began to change shape as we examined the canoe further, and it became apparent that we could not simply commission a new stern post but would have to allow Nuku to work on-site with museum staff to facilitate the removal of the museum additions and the incorporation of a stern onto the existing hull. At this stage, as the complexities of the project were revealed, we could have decided against proceeding, but the canoe had resided within the museum stores for nearly two hundred years, waiting for an appraisal and engagement. Therefore, despite the problems and ambiguities that the object exposed, the importance of the canoe in terms of its age and size compelled me to act. I believed that if we did not engage with the canoe now, when funds, time, and the willingness to do so were there, when would we ever do so? This project presented a unique opportunity to bring the canoe out of the storeroom and into the light—to make it "alive," as we began to say. We finally had a chance to position this waka in the public gaze and allow our visitors to be drawn to and engage and interact with it.

In pursuing this goal, the project group felt that we would be continuing the intent of the original maker(s), whether Māori, European, or museum, to create a war canoe to trade. In doing so, the maker(s) had brought together and juxtaposed through the assembling of all the component pieces the work of several different Māori artists. Each piece of the assembled whole had a history before it was traded to Brisbane, making each piece potentially considerably older than the 1827 date of arrival at the museum. Therefore, repairing and renewing the existing parts and sympathetically adding contemporary carvings to substitute for missing elements made sense from a Māori perspective (Wijesuriya 2007:64). Furthermore, this endeavor felt ethically correct from a museum perspective as we would be preserving the canoe, stabilizing it, and ensuring that all of our actions were documented and, if necessary, reversible (Stable 2012).

Making the decision to proceed raised the possibility of criticism within each separate discipline or culture for all members of the group, particularly from our peers. Because of the partial images and fragmented documentation, I had requested further information, which resulted in some attention from scholars, especially as it was the largest canoe known to exist outside New Zealand. However, when confronted with the complexities of the whole artifact, the interest and engagement of researchers faltered. I considered that, if stored separately, the hull, side strakes, and prow ornament might have provoked research, yet the unique, complex nature, indeed the very existence, of the canoe denied each component a fair appraisal. I perceived this as a sidelining of an important historic artifact and was therefore determined to provoke interest and a greater understanding of and engagement with the canoe by those who would encounter it in the gallery in the years to come.

Unfolding Creative Responses

George Nuku was invited to work at the museum in the conservation workshops in order to be in close proximity to the waka. This enabled daily interactions with the canoe and also encouraged discussion and debate between artist, curator, and conservators. Nuku made four extended visits to the museum, and a number of additional pieces were added to the canoe. In his work at the museum, Nuku drew not only on the canoe's attributes but also on his own Māori approach and knowledge. At the moment of embarking on his work with the canoe, he brought the team together to address it. Although aware that he was not working with an actual, categorized, classified waka taua, he acknowledged the power and effect of the component parts, their long history, and their biographies. He named the canoe Te Tūhono, which means "To Join," a name that recognized and gave consequence to the composite nature of the vessel, accepting its existence as a hybrid. Although never a war canoe, unable to seat warriors, Te Tūhono's iconography and diagnostic features meant that we would continue to address the object as a war canoe. At this point, we began to personalize the canoe and refer to "it" as "her," addressing her as she would have been in the Māori context. This created a closeness between those working on the canoe and the canoe; thus, the collaboration was among all the agents on the project team, including the canoe herself.

I commissioned Nuku with a very specific brief: to create a new stern post for the canoe and work with conservators to repair the loss and damage to the other parts of the canoe. Nuku chooses to work in a modern material, acrylic, which has a myriad of uses across museum displays, such as mounting or casing artifacts. In selecting Nuku as our artist, we were responding to the object as a composite work to which we were adding a new strand. The acrylic would provide a visual distinction between the old and the new, defining the canoe in our own terms yet displaying it in an honest way that could engage with the public and with Māori people. We understood that there would be practical complexities in doing this, which involved the binding of two materials of differing densities, weights, and characteristics, but Nuku was keen to use this material to create a sense of both continuity and change within the work. He explained:

> My mother's people came to New Zealand from the Pacific, and when they came to New Zealand, it was a world of trees. They were able to define their world through the trees, their houses were made from trees, and the canoes and all the weaponry and implements were largely made from wood, and in fact the people called themselves trees. However, we don't live in the world of trees any more. We live in a plastic world now, where our currency is plastic, even parts of our body are plastic, and plastic is all around us. And my concern is that we consume the plastic in an unconscious manner and that my role is to introduce that consciousness to the plastic to enrich it, enriching our relationship with the plastic as we do with the trees. (Nuku, interview with Maia Jessop 2010)

Nuku began his work by drawing the canoe, familiarizing himself with her form, size, and style. He then carved in polystyrene a design for the stern post and a template for the hull stern on which it would sit. This allowed him to test scale and experiment with the proposed changes to other elements of the canoe. Accommodating the taurapa required the development of a specific shape for the stern end of the hull, distinct from the style seen on a fishing canoe and not achieved by the museum repair decades ago. Yet, the existing museum repair was integrated and integral to the current canoe structure and made it sound and relatively stable. Any addition or change would reverberate along the whole structure, requiring a reconfiguration and realignment of the rest of the canoe, including the lifting of the side strakes so that they sat on the hull sides rather than overlapped them and the raising of the prow. The absent thwarts would be needed to provide stability to the raised side strakes.

At the beginning of the conservation project, we painstakingly stripped the canoe and took her apart, preserving each piece, documenting it, photographing it, and bagging samples of nails, wood, and other materials for analysis. To understand the origin of the modifications, we needed to undertake further research into the background of the canoe and to compare her with full-size canoes in existing collections, such as Te Toki-a-Tāpiri in the Auckland Museum. Nuku examined this canoe on a visit to Auckland but also obtained a series of photographs, which we were able to use as a basis for deciding how to conserve the NMS canoe. We attempted, with little success, to engage in a wider discourse of the project through presentations on the New Zealand museum's website and to the public in Edinburgh and Canberra.[9]

The process of dismantling and rebuilding the canoe in order to replace and repair specific elements of her made us feel at once comfortable and uncomfortable about the trajectory of the project. This level of intervention into an object that was already part of the collection, although acceptable in the past when previous invasive repairs had been made, was now highly unusual. In particular for museum staff, there is normally an obligation to preserve objects as they are on arrival at the museum because at that moment they "represent" something and are considered "authentic." Our attempt to intervene to change and adapt our canoe challenged the central ideas of our curatorial and conservational responsibilities. For Nuku, there was a responsibility to his own culture and his art, although renewing and creating were part of his daily practice. Of key importance in helping us to address our experiences during the project were our weekly team meetings, which we recorded and filmed. At these times, significant pieces of the object would be unbound or unscrewed, so we could all watch and participate in discussing the often confusing story that was unfolding. At these moments, we would discuss the work, including any new research or discoveries from the written records or from examining the canoe herself. We also discussed the next steps, what we hoped to achieve, and any problems, technical or ethical, that these might present for us.

The distinct disciplines in which we worked became more explicit at these meetings; for example, when it came to removing and taking apart the prow, we spent several hours examining the component pieces, trying to work out what was original and what was museum made, discussing the purpose of a complete reworking and whether we had the skills to embark on it. When we were unable to agree, we each went away to research and think through options before coming back to the canoe and working through the viability and benefits of any change. The canoe herself often demanded change, as each incorporation of new work threw other, seemingly more stable aspects of the existing canoe out of line and changed the structure. In the case of the prow, we eventually decided to continue to incorporate a blank addition to the prow hull—inserted by museum technicians probably more than 150 years ago—in order to provide stability for the prow carving. Inserting additional new carving was felt to be unnecessary, and in this instance, we had an opportunity to recognize the work of the museum technicians, who had undoubtedly had a key role in the canoe's preservation. Despite the reassurance throughout this process that each of our interventions was reversible and none affected the integrity of the whole, the nature of the project meant that the canoe's assembled form would change dramatically.

In our deciding to act—or being provoked into action by the canoe and the sense of curatorial responsibility that she engendered—the methodological approach to the artifact was transformed. The paucity of documentation, the singularity of the object, and its lack of clear cultural "fit" made inevitable a physical encounter. A forensic, investigative approach to the object was taken to seek out embodied and embedded knowledge. The materials, tool marks, abrasions, and wear all offered up clues for further investigation and, in turn, influenced and limited the parameters and goals of future action, moving the process inexorably from straightforward restoration to a reworking of the artifact.

Repair and Renewal

In the work on Te Tūhono, there was a novel series of challenges, of which the most apparent was the creation of a new stern for the hull to support the new stern post. Nuku's rough form in polystyrene gave our conservator, Stable, a template from which to work in creating a new hull stern to replace the early nineteenth-century repair. However, the action of creating such a striking stern post, and thus modifying the hull, exposed the overall damage and wear to the remainder of the canoe. There was a sense among all involved in the project that this was the opportunity to return to the waka her dignity. Due to the extensive additions and repairs required, the work constantly challenged our levels of knowledge and practice in our chosen field (see Stable 2012).

Nuku was very keen to see each missing piece replaced, and although the flat sheets of acrylic mimicked planks of wood, from which the stern post could be carved, the loss on some elements challenged the limits even of modern sheet acrylic. Of particular concern were the complex 3D sculptures on the prow and stern; however, Stable was able to bring his skills as

FIGURE 9.3

Charles Stable uses custom-made metal frames to hold the side strakes in place in order to model a new stern for the hull. © *National Museums Scotland.*

a conservator and combine them with Nuku's understanding of the canoe form and his preference for clear plastic. To create the stern end of the hull, Stable constructed a metal frame (figure 9.3) to hold the side strakes in their new position, then created a plaster former, from which a putty stern was modeled. This was carved by Nuku (figure 9.4) before being cast by Stable in resin, then returned to Nuku to be inlaid. This process was replicated for the legs and feet of the prow figure.

The new positioning of the side strakes allowed Sarah Gerrish to measure the loss, then infill and consolidate the side strakes so that large gaps would not be left on either side of the battens. Areas of loss were filled and strengthened with wooden blanks tinted to match the existing pieces; this was structurally important in order to rebind the canoe. Each intervention reverberated along the canoe, creating new alignments and the need for further work. Above all, there was a need to harmonize the historic pieces with Nuku's modern additions in order to facilitate the reconstruction or reassembling of the canoe as Te Tūhono.

At times, our group expertise was not sufficient to carry out all the elements of the project; for example, the realignment of the canoe pieces

FIGURE 9.4
George Nuku carving an acrylic stern post for A.UC.767, September 2009.
© National Museums Scotland.

required a specialist's knowledge of canoe binding. A fortuitous encounter between Nuku and Tahiarii Pariente, a Tahitian boat maker and navigator, gave us the opportunity to bring him to Edinburgh. A skilled canoe binder, he worked on the canoe for a day, binding the prow pieces together and teaching the team how to secure the binding along the battens securing the side strakes and hull in place (figure 9.5). As Nuku had done, before beginning his work, Pariente brought everyone working on the canoe together, addressed the waka, and encouraged her cooperation. His knowledge of the properties of wood instilled a confidence in the team to bend and bind the wooden components and integrate the feather decoration. Again, among the group there was the sense that the canoe was a willing participant in the process, her dry ancient wood becoming pliant to accommodate her new configuration. Pariente's knowledge of the tolerance of wood and his skill in binding enabled each piece of the canoe to be repositioned accurately. The result belied the painstaking efforts of the project team: it was simply as if the canoe had finally had the opportunity to push back her shoulders and sit up straight. Over two days, the prow, side strakes, and finally the stern were bound to the hull, each using existing holes and incorporating white feathers.

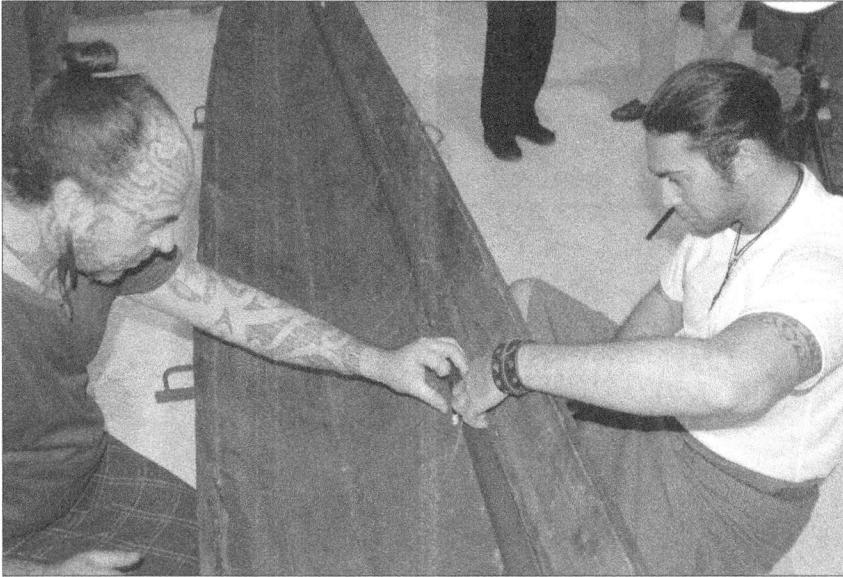

FIGURE 9.5

George Nuku and Tahiarii Pariente binding the side strakes to the canoe hull, February 2011. © National Museums Scotland.

The properties of plastic differ to the properties of wood, so when I am binding these two elements together, it is more of a collaboration than a restoration. From my experiences as a Māori artist, we are taught to do this anyway...for example, with wood, inlaying it with shell and binding it with feathers is bringing together three forms of divinity: from the land, from the forest, from the trees, from the shell of the haliotis, the abalone, the paua shell from the ocean, and the feathers from the domain of the air. And the plastic fits perfectly in line with that. It is a match made in museum heaven, it really is. (Nuku, interview with Maia Jessop 2010)

The production of Te Tūhono took place in front of our eyes and at our fingertips, echoing the collaborative forces that had brought together the original canoe so many years before. As each piece was repositioned and Nuku's stern post attached, there was an emotional journey, a revival and reawakening of the original parts. Within the project team, we acknowledged our respect for the canoe and her original carvers and makers;

we discussed her carvings, their meanings, and the circumstances under which they were made. Through the process of rebuilding, we felt, each accretion to the object was a reinforcement of the original intent for this to be a "war canoe."

The purpose of Nuku's final visit was to bind acrylic thwarts on top of the side strakes. These had been initially conceived by the museum as important to the structural integrity and positioning of the side strakes, but after the completion of the rebinding, it became clear that they were no longer necessary in structural terms. At this point, there was a discussion about the validity of continuing to add to the canoe; some of us felt that we had been swept along by various forces, and we paused to reflect on whether we had moved the project beyond its original scope. From the museum perspective, we believed we had, but Nuku reminded us that this had become more than a restoration process, that we were *making* something, and from his perspective the inclusion of the thwarts was essential to the completion of Te Tūhono. The thwarts were added to the canoe in January 2011.

This discussion about the validity of the thwarts, after their structural need had been obviated, was indicative of much of the process of the project. Nuku carried a Māori vision of the waka taua and a clear sense of the end point. He was formally making Te Tūhono, creating her in a form that was prescribed by generations of ancestral Māori carvers before him. Although never explicitly discussed, it became clear that there were agents at work whose influence resonated through the centuries to the project in the present day.

The canoe was finally raised into the gallery in May 2011. Immediately prior to her being hoisted into position, a feather decoration bound by Rosanna Raymond and George Nuku and including feathers from Scottish birds of prey was suspended from the stern; this type of decoration would have been essential if she had been launched in the waters of New Zealand.

COMMUNITIES OF ENGAGEMENT: CATEGORIES, RESPONSIBILITY, AND AGENCY

In a discussion of exhibitions of Māori works, McCarthy (2007:12) notes: "Display in the late twentieth century should be seen, not as 'inauthentic' but as a creative recoupling, or rearticulation of constituent elements in response to social and political forces in settler colonies" (see also Clifford 2001; the introduction to this volume). This provides a context for understanding the genesis of the NMS waka in the colonies and her later re-creation in Scotland. In fashioning the original composite waka two centuries ago, the makers created something outside the frames of reference of both European and Māori communities. At that specific moment in time, individual artifacts were brought together to create something unique yet undeniably Māori. The composite whole altered the perception of these parts or at least prevented their merits from being recognized. When assembled in this way, the natural trajectory of the component parts (for which there are prescribed actions) was interrupted and a unique artifact created, but this distinctiveness was uncomfortable and, in this state, the canoe was sidelined by the museum as a distortion of Māori material culture. This also explains why, despite her age and rarity, non-Māori scholars and Māori people alike never lingered on this object but were attracted to artifacts that conformed to a known set of diagnostic characteristics and could be read within cultural, art historical, or ethnographic taxonomies.

Objects in Place

The tension in museum categories that caused the canoe to slip into obscurity was even more troubling within the Māori system; the tapu status of a war canoe conflicted with each of the canoes whose elements were combined to make the waka. This was exacerbated by the poor workmanship that was obvious in the assembly, which affected indigenous pride and the importance of taonga (see Sully 2007). This waka represented "matter out of place" (Douglas 2010[1966]), and her hybrid nature deterred interaction or research because it prevented any Māori from approaching the canoe in a known, culturally prescribed way. The damaged nature of each element, especially the losses in the side strakes' binding points, the missing limbs on the prow, and the uneven cut of the keel, suggests that the component pieces had ended their useful lives and were actually intended to be left to rot away and go back to the earth. Whereas in other instances carvings have been recycled into other uses (see Tapsell 2000:68–77, which documents perhaps the most famous example of this, Pukaki), it seems likely that the level of damage suffered by the waka components meant that their collection and composition into a canoe arrested their decay, interrupting the natural cycle and thus preserving them out of their place and time. Their repurposing as a model, curio, or souvenir created a problematic artifact that obscured the knowledge, value, and workmanship that lay at the heart of the production of each component part. In effect, the canoe became a conundrum, resonating down the centuries. Museum staff had initially repaired the canoe and displayed her, but out of reach and partially obscured by lower display cases. She had then been put into storage, where visual and physical access to her was limited. Due to her size, she was even kept remote from other Māori carvings, thus separating her from other taonga, or ancestors, and sidelining her from future research.[10]

For some objects, the transition from source community to museum is relatively straightforward. Although the context of use changes and therefore its classification or category is transformed, the object sits comfortably in both. For other objects, the transition into a museum is incorporated in an acceptable trajectory of artifacts for the source community. Although the New Ireland *malangan* figures should be destroyed after use, it has been argued that trading them to visiting Europeans was viewed as equally appropriate because they were no longer accessible to the community and their removal was similar to their ritual dismantling (Küchler 1988). However, I would argue that the NMS waka never existed comfortably in either a Māori or museum space because it was fabricated on the margins at a moment of great upheaval. The vessel could never reside within the Māori community in the Bay of Plenty without role or purpose, and the inherent power of the component pieces may have troubled the order of things. Once in Brisbane's collection and then in the museum, her Māori/non-Māori status limited her interpretation as an authentic representation of Māori art, as an example of the warlike nature of the Māori, or even as an example of daily life, and she therefore could not be accommodated within the didactic themes of the NMS galleries.

The project, and in particular the initial naming ceremony by Nuku, addressed Te Tūhono as a war canoe and reengaged with her transformation into a war canoe, begun in the nineteenth century. Her acceptance as such placed her within a category that the participants in her restoration could accept and explain to others. Furthermore, this repositioning and redefining as a war canoe fit her back into Māori taxonomy, reconnecting her with her ancestral past and acknowledging the Māori engagement in the production of her parts, if not the resulting whole. In realigning the component pieces, replacing the loss, and creating new artworks, Nuku fashioned an object that was new but nonetheless rooted in a long-standing tradition, thus restructuring the museum's view of the canoe and the Māori and non-Māori public's view of it. Today, in the gallery interpretation, the museum describes her as a war canoe. Yet, Te Tūhono is also an art object that can be enjoyed by the public. The inherent ambiguities of the canoe, her unique status, and her researched biography have become primary documentation whose very existence establishes the canoe wholly within the museum space. She is no longer on the margins of the museum collection and consequently can fulfill a role: center stage in the new gallery.

The constraints imposed by the ways in which objects are codified and understood in their cultural contexts create a liminal space in which certain objects exist (Douglas [2010]1966:119–120). The NMS waka is one of these objects, the embodiment of an encounter between Māori people and Europeans at a moment of great change in both communities. These origins made the waka at once unique and anomalous, an object to which both contemporary Māori culture and museum culture found it difficult to ascribe meaning. Importantly, it was this very instability that set the stage for a new encounter in the twenty-first century. While I use Douglas's theory to understand our responses to the canoe now, I regard Te Tūhono as being unique but very much *in her place* within a specific historical context. Not only did this turbulent period of change and disruption for the Māori community provide the opportunity for Governor Brisbane to acquire a war canoe, but it also produced the circumstances and unique moment in time when this particular, peculiar war canoe was made.

It is as essential to preserve and display the waka, despite her complex nature, as it is to display artifacts that conform more closely to notions of authenticity with regard to Māori material culture. My responsibility as a curator is to care for and research objects in my collection and, by doing so, make them available to others. Nevertheless, some objects demand, or even command, attention (Gell 1998; Wingfield 2010), and others remain in stores, waiting for the right set of circumstances to trigger a renewed focus upon them. As a custodian, I have to consider the objects and their original makers and descendants, all of whom may have a continued association with them.

When George Nuku stated, "No Māori made this canoe," he meant that the assembling of the pieces could not have been carried out by a Māori. He suggested instead that they were brought together outside New Zealand in the store of a Sydney curio seller (e.g., see Harrison 2011a). While I agree that this is a probable source for our waka, I would argue that the evidence is not conclusive. Moreover, the actions of individuals are not necessarily those of a group acting within the constraints of tradition and consensus. There are many histories of enterprising Māori and Europeans in this period, as well as of Europeans who took up residency in or married into Māori communities (Salmond 1997; Tapsell 2000). This evidence of the complexities of the period means that on one level we must simply accept the canoe for what she is. In order to preserve this history of development and change, I had to ensure that we remained true to the component pieces of the canoe *and* the assembled whole. In deconstructing and then reassembling the canoe as a war canoe, we respected and preserved the original intentions of its creators while respecting Nuku's agency and that of

Te Tūhono herself. Throughout this process, I was aware that we could have, and perhaps should have, left the canoe as she was. However, as her curator, I felt strongly that the possibility of the waka finally being on public display made such reappraisal essential. This was the moment for Te Tūhono to receive the focused research that would allow her to be placed once more in the gaze of multiple audiences, in particular, Māori people and scholars of Māori material culture. To have abandoned this process simply because of the ambiguities presented by the canoe would have been to abandon my responsibility as a curator. Reengagement and renewed interest in the canoe may provoke a reappraisal of her interpretation in our gallery, but, following the principles under which the project was undertaken, we have documented the whole process from source material to the integration of the contemporary artwork. As a result, we have an archive from which further dialogue can be encouraged.

Curatorial Responsibility

I remained true to aspects of my curatorial praxis by placing certain constraints on the project, above all, that our interventions had to be reversible. As a consequence, every action was recorded in detail, and a system of documentation was established that is as yet unparalleled in any other NMS project. Maia Jessop, a Māori filmmaker and scholar of Pacific ethnography, recorded over forty hours of film, including interviews, of our work in the museum. The museum photographers and project participants took several hundred photographs, and Gerrish sampled six separate materials for scientific analysis. The paper archive now includes two curatorial notebooks, the reports and minutes of meetings, and two file boxes of research notes and correspondence—a record of the project and a tangible legacy for future researchers. Stable was concerned about the differing rates of deterioration of acrylic and wood, so, for the first time, the museum commissioned a 3D scan of all the canoe's component pieces, old and new (figure 9.6). This not only facilitated the rebinding and repairs, since we were able to model the process on a computer, but also allows access to each of the individual elements by researchers even though these are now bound back into the whole. Where once only a series of register entries existed, A.UC.767 now has her own significant archive.

The lack of documentation for this artifact at the outset of the project was both constraining and liberating. We were forced to appraise the physical object itself; we were pushed to examine, take apart, and contemplate the waka. This continual reassessment of our objectives was in many ways due to the physicality of the canoe *coercing* our actions. By limiting our

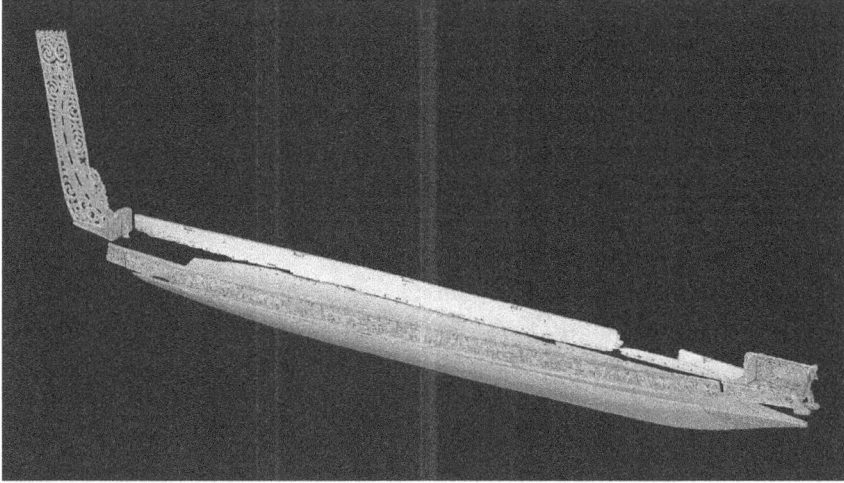

FIGURE 9.6

A virtual reconstruction of the canoe with additional pieces by George Nuku, modeled from 3D scans. © National Museums Scotland.

options and taking us out of the museum's comfort zone of minimal intervention, the situation forced us toward a creative response, with the materiality of the canoe a key agent in the project.

In September 2006, the canoe had sat slumped in the stores due to the aged binding, which slung the side strakes low along its length, and the considerable damage to prow and stern. My curatorial responsibility was to draw attention to this object and provide a space for the canoe in the museum, both physically and intellectually, thus giving those that encounter her an opportunity to engage with her, despite the problematic history of her fabrication. In order to do this, I had to engage with the systems that both Māori and museum had created, which had preserved the artifact in her current form. Uppermost in my thoughts were the agency of the object, the intent of the original creators of both the component pieces and the vessel that arrived at the museum in 1827, and the crucial need to preserve the trajectory, however unusual, that brought the canoe into being.

Within the team, Nuku was most at ease with the trajectory that the project began to take, because he had a very clear sense of his personal goals within the endeavor. A war canoe would have been taken apart, remade, and rearticulated during her lifetime in the community. When stored, a war canoe was often unlashed and dismantled and the hull stored in a special canoe shed; one hull could over its lifetime have various sets of carvings. Furthermore as meeting houses became the community focal point and war canoes gradually stopped being made, carved elements of war canoes were repurposed and reused in meeting houses (Neich 2008[2001]:174–175). Gerrish, who was familiar with the extensive restoration required to preserve European furniture within the museum, was often surprised by Stable's and my conservative responses to the changes the addition of a new stern post had provoked; we were used to minimal intervention in order to stabilize objects, rather than creating or combining works. Despite our common "museum" perspective, our responses remained individual, and at times tension arose in the group about how best to proceed while respecting what had gone before. These debates took place in the presence of the canoe and across and around her as new solutions were tried and tested.

Fragments of Agency

As a consequence of the complexities of its creation, this artifact embodies a dialogue that crosses time, space, and disciplines. It is an artifact of encounter, with its origin at a time of flux when several interests coincided in its creation. In the assembling of the original component parts, people *and* things with different histories came together at a moment in time and created the canoe (see the introduction to this volume). In doing so, their interaction became part of the canoe, and in reassembling the canoe, in the creation of Te Tūhono in the museum for display, a new community of participants (new things and different people) engaged with one another. Across the centuries, the canoe represents the work of several artists acting together to pay homage to a continuing tradition while being responsive to the changing demands of collector, curator, and museum. The dialogue between makers, curators, conservators, and canoe is bound into the fabric of the waka; their actions and intent marked Te Tūhono as clearly as the tool marks on the wooden hull, the inlay in the carvings, the knots in the bindings. The set of relationships—the communities of engagement that have circulated and included the canoe—required to create the object in the 1820s and its remaking in the 2000s contributed to the decisions and actions we undertook. The component parts of the composite canoe come together or collide, engaging their past lives and inventing new ones. The ambiguity of the canoe, her tendency to avoid classification, even clear description, meant that working with the canoe, physically getting to know each element and how it shaped future additions and accretions, changed the way we think about the object and feel emotionally about Te Tūhono. The agency of those involved in the process over time is ever present, even though the trajectory that the canoe's component pieces have traveled is not necessarily what was originally anticipated, or hoped for. Understanding this and working with Nuku brought a power to the whole object, which was conveyed through the detailed tool marks of the carving despite being belied by the physical whole.

The juxtaposition of new pieces with old now plays out not only across the whole but also where wood and acrylic meet. There is a visual distinction between the original encounter and today's, which is also a contrast of weight, texture, and hue. Although this doubtless creates new ambiguities, the reworked canoe draws the eye, invites engagement, and grabs attention. This has been evident from the public interest in the project (Edinburgh Evening News 2008, 2009) and the widespread use of the image of the canoe in press coverage leading up to and immediately after the opening of the new gallery.

In comparing the history of the waka with Pukaki (Tapsell 2000), a gateway sculpture created by Māori people for their own use and then gifted away before being returned, the trajectory and agency of the sculpture were quite distinct from those of the canoe, which never had a home in the community (since it was composed of fragments of other things). Therefore, I question whether it could have followed a cultural trajectory that Tapsell likens to a comet (being sent out, transformed, and then returned), or did the museum become Te Tūhono's orbit? At the outset of the project, the trajectory that the artifact has followed was not predictable, although it has certainly been a transformative process.

In taking a single object and making clear how the artifact itself shaped the multiple human agencies and responses to it, I hope to provide food for thought and discussion. In rooting this chapter in a project that involved a practical undertaking, that involved *making things*, I hope to reveal that objects do have the power to shape and change our responses (Gosden 2005:196).

CONCLUSION

Despite many of the ways to describe the role of objects in everyday life and in social networks across time and space, objects alone cannot influence behavior. Circumstances arise that trigger the production of an artifact—the availability of materials, the context, and the people—and the factors involved interact in such a way as to create a network of influence that produces a particular thing. The example of the Māori canoe demonstrates a very specific moment in time when a series of influences connected and created a unique object alien to two cultures (Māori and colonial) yet inalienable to both. Two centuries later, the desire to display the canoe provided the catalyst to reconstruct and re-create the artifact, precipitating a new cross-cultural encounter in the museum.

The making of Te Tūhono started out as a simple restoration; however, in revealing the waka's history and by engaging a Māori artist, this production became a new dialogue between the museum culture and Māori culture. An understanding of each other, including the limitations of our practice, our ethical codes, and our culture, was necessary in taking each stage forward, creating a forum for new agents to work together and new pathways for the future. The guidance from Nuku enabled the waka to be reclaimed and repositioned as essentially Māori, yet her complex history remains part of her essence, inscribed in her component parts and the histories that created her and made explicit through her naming as Te Tū hono. As Te Tūhono, she remains a unique reminder of the complexities of European and Māori engagement, evidence of the skill and artistry of Māori people, and a testament to museum endeavors to preserve artifacts in perpetuity. Bell (2006; chapter 5, this volume) and Edwards (2001) discuss objects and photographs as "sites of intersecting histories": Te Tūhono is a site of many continuing intersecting histories. Complex and diverse, these histories have helped carve a new place for Te Tūhono in both Mā ori culture and museum culture, and through this project, renewed and beautiful, she can participate in both our worlds again.

The canoe now mounted in the new gallery (figure 9.7) is interpreted by an object label and a series of short films addressing aspects of the project, including the creation of the "war canoe" displayed. In opening up the history of the object, the background to the project, and the cultural significance of canoes, we hope that the artifact will engage the public. So far, observations show that Te Tūhono is attracting significant dwell time from those who choose to visit the gallery, suggesting that she is encouraging interaction and engagement. Thus, the canoe has become a portal, engaging with an unusually complex world very different from the concrete, uncontested facts usually experienced in the museum. The interaction between canoe and museum visitor is a sensory encounter of body and object, a shared experience that is a crucial part of engagement with collections (Dudley 2010). Te Tūhono's written label is simultaneously too complex, fragmentary, and incomplete for visitors, so instead we have to encourage their visual encounter, their personal perspective and engagement with the artifact. We have to elicit their response and provoke their imagination, rather than use the object to tell a story.

FIGURE 9.7
Te Tūhono in the Pacific Gallery called "Facing the Sea," July 2011. © *National Museums Scotland.*

Te Tūhono is ripe for further research, ready to be reassembled, rearticulated once again, creating new events, new debates, and new encounters (Clifford 2001). The voyage of this particular canoe is ongoing and will be influenced by things as calamitous as the degradation of the acrylic or as prosaic as tourists photographing their moments of encounter. Each moment illuminates fragments of the agency of those involved in the waka's creation, who set her upon her voyage, journey with her, and interact with and transform her.

Acknowledgments

Although I am the sole author of this chapter, I have tried to give voice to George Nuku through direct quotes from interviews, and I hope I have represented fairly both his thoughts and those of the museum staff involved. Without the participation of Nuku and Charles Stable, the project could not have happened. Stable challenged his own working practices in order to participate in the project and also brought a technical knowledge that allowed the pieces of the canoe to be brought together. I am wholly indebted to him. Other key members of the team included Maia Jessop, who created a fabulous film archive of the project, and Sarah Gerrish, who consolidated all the restoration on the original pieces and provided advice and expertise for Nuku's reinstatement of the paua shell. Many other staff members, in particular the staff of conservation and the Department of World Cultures, were instrumental in the project's success, especially

Neil McLean, Rachel Smith, Kylie Moloney, and Brenda McGoff. I dedicate this chapter to Brenda, who tragically passed away before seeing Te Tūhono completed and the gallery open. Support also came from Henrietta Lidchi and Jane Carmichael in agreeing to the initial commission; both recognized the risks in the project but supported and championed it. Many other colleagues worldwide commented, queried, and critiqued the project as it progressed, but particular thanks go to my colleagues at the SAR seminar, who encouraged me to reflect on the project, and the volume editors, Sarah Byrne, Rodney Harrison, and Annie Clarke, who helped marshal my many diverse thoughts into this chapter. Any errors that remain are my own.

Notes

1. The National Museums Scotland was founded by an act of Parliament in 1854 under the name the Industrial Museum of Scotland; in 1862 its collections were opened to the public in a temporary home; by 1866 the first phase of a newly built museum was completed and the collections, including the recently transferred natural history collection, opened to the public. The University Collections include both natural history collections and "natural curiosities," which includes the ethnology collections and A.UC.767.

2. Dr. Roger Duff, the director of Canterbury Museum, visited various UK museums in 1948, funded by a British Council scholarship.

3. David Simmons, a former curator of ethnology at Auckland Museum, New Zealand, visited the museum to review the collections in 1978.

4. Dr. Roger Neich is a former curator of ethnology at Auckland Museum and a professor of anthropology at the University of Auckland.

5. Roger Neich personal communication 5 September 2008. Neich kindly confirmed the absence of any mention of the canoe in his own or Simmons's notes; his experience of working with Duff's notebooks suggested that they would not prove particularly fruitful.

6. In 1998 the British Museum curated a special exhibition called "Maori." Several artists were invited to demonstrate their skills in the exhibition, others attended the opening, and many took the opportunity to visit other collections while in the United Kingdom. Those who visited National Museums Scotland included Lyonel Grant, a leading carver.

7. A photograph captioned "West Wing Looking South c. 1895" in the National Museums Scotland picture library shows a series of tall wall cases filled with Pacific artifacts. Large-scale objects are displayed in the space between the tops of the cases and the ceiling, and there is a possibility that the NMS waka was part of this display.

8. For consistency, I have used Neich's translation of *rauawa* as "side strakes," although they can also be referred to as "top strakes."

9. See http://www.nzmuseums.co.nz/news/the-waka-presents-a-mystery-to-us; http://www.nma.gov.au/audio/transcripts/vaka/NMA_ocean_crossings_20090826. html; and http://fruitmarket.co.uk/education/past-projects/barclay-seminar.

10. The NMS stores cultural objects from the same communities together whenever possible. Māori artist Lyonel Grant was keen for a new work of his acquired by the museum in 2002 to stand in the store with the other Māori carvings so that the ancestors could be with one another (Lyonel Grant personal communication May 2003).

10

Curating Communities at the Museum of Northern Arizona

Kelley Hays-Gilpin and Ramson Lomatewama

> This fusion of the profoundly spiritual with the otherwise purely physical, this
> primacy of the process of creating an object over the beautiful object itself,
> this utter inseparability of the object from the conduct of daily life—all are
> Native ways of viewing objects that arguably are significantly different from the
> paradigms of Western knowledge.
>
> —*W. Richard West Jr., "Keynote Address: The National Museum of the American Indian"*

The Hopi people of northern Arizona are renowned for their arts, particularly katsina dolls, pottery, silver overlay jewelry, and basketry. Hopi art and artifacts began to enter museum collections and curio markets in large numbers in the 1880s as a result of salvage ethnography and a growing tourist art market. The Hopi collections at the Museum of Northern Arizona (MNA) are unique because MNA has taken an active and collaborative part in developing Hopi arts since the 1930s. For more than seventy years, MNA collected Hopi material culture and actively worked to shape the production of Hopi art and outside markets. In the early twenty-first century, MNA moved toward collaboration and the inclusion of Hopi consultants in virtually all decisions and policies that involve collections, education, research, and collections care (Museum of Northern Arizona 2005). Representing the internal diversity of Hopi identities to the public and preserving this record of diversity for future Hopi generations are challenging tasks because of the need for Hopi people to differentiate themselves from other tribes in a vibrant Native American art market supported by non-Hopi collectors and at the same time to educate future Hopi generations about clan identities and responsibilities, keeping certain proprietary clan knowledge within the kin group and avoiding the public exposure of culturally sensitive objects and information.

In an earlier article (2011), Kelley Hays-Gilpin focused on ethnic and community identities and the mutual constitution of Hopi and MNA identities from a museum perspective. Studies of MNA collections and their associated documentation and discussions with Hopi artists show that Hopi art emphasizes the makers' social identities at many levels: ethnic group, village, clan, membership in ritual associations, gender, and age. In this chapter, Hopi artist, scholar, and community member Ramson Lomatewama joins Hays-Gilpin to explore Hopi ontology—basic precepts about how the world is, which Hopi people recognize as very distinct from Western ontology and which are beginning to reshape curation practices. The primary data come from conversations among museum professionals and Hopi community members about the curation and exhibition of MNA's Hopi collections. We explore how Hopi views of Hopi-made artifacts in museums are distinct from the views of most museum professionals, including scientists, collections managers, conservators, and educators, and what these differences imply for curation practices.

To begin, we will clarify our positions and some terms we have chosen to use. We draw on about five years of collaborative research and planning at MNA and on personal experience as a Hopi community member, respectively. But we do not speak for others here. We would like to remind museum professionals that there are clan, village, gender, and generational differences in how Hopi people think museums should care for Hopi-made artifacts. Likewise, not all museum employees have the same views, experience, training, and responsibilities. All of us act within constantly changing meshworks of relationships, not just networks that connect people and things (nodes), but entangled lines of action, and of processes, not just products (see Alberti and Marshall 2009:348; Ingold 2007a). Our main point is that what we are calling "artifacts" also act within meshworks and thus act as members of communities. We focus here on artifacts that are now members of museum communities but still have relationships with those who made them, their descendants, or both. We use the term "artifact" to refer to something made or modified by humans, because this term implies relationships in ways that "object" does not. Thus, we are using the term more broadly than most archaeologists would. What Hopi speakers would do is to call it what it is—a rain sash, a katsina doll, a water jar—not invent superordinate terms like "textiles," "carvings," "pottery," or "objects." So "artifacts" still is not a perfect term, and there may not yet exist a perfect term in English. In short, we are not talking about passive, inanimate objects whose primary use is to serve as evidence or data for past lifeways, although educating humans in that way is often among their many active roles.

We focus on Hopi perspectives in this chapter, but Hopi people's participation in the care and exhibition of MNA's Hopi collections has raised concerns that also are mentioned by other American Indians working in and consulting with MNA and other museums nationwide (see, for example, Cooper 2008; Isaac 2007; West 2004b). We therefore suggest that some aspects of Hopi views of appropriate collection care are shared by members of other indigenous communities in the Southwestern United States, other Native North American communities, indigenous communities throughout the Americas, and indigenous peoples throughout the world.

CURATING HOPI COLLECTIONS AT MNA

Hopi consultants tend to strongly support the curation of Hopi collections at MNA and have asked for very few items to be repatriated. They nonetheless would like to see changes in collections care and display that would better reflect their values and multifaceted connections to the collections. These connections are primarily emotional and spiritual, although there are also, of course, connections we would characterize as psychological, physical, and intellectual.

Collaboration is necessary, fulfilling, and also challenging for both museum and Hopi participants. Except in matters of repatriation mandated by federal law, most of the power and money is in the hands of the museum. For example, many Hopi people are certain that the museum makes money on admissions, publications, grants, donations, and booth fees charged to Hopi artists at the annual Hopi Festival of Art and Culture. Museum employees know that MNA has run a deficit almost every year of its operation, so they see Hopi views about "outsiders making money at Hopi expense" as a misconception (Kilborn 2009). Yet, it is true that museum employees have higher incomes and more secure employment than most Hopi artists. Museum curators have the time and expertise to write successful grant proposals, and most Hopi community members do not. The curator of anthropology earns a few hundred dollars a year in publication royalties, which she reinvests in other publications. That money and the power to choose what to do with it are in her hands, not in those of the Hopi people who contributed to her success by sharing their knowledge. This is duly noted. Other concerns include different views of oral versus written agreements, time schedules, priorities, perceived deference to representatives of other tribes, questions of who within the Hopi tribe has authority to make various decisions, and other matters of procedure and personality. Another challenge is that American Indians hold some stereotyped views about what we might call (based on our personal experiences serving as "culture brokers") "the unchanging insensitive scientist," though not as many as Euro Americans have about "the unchanging noble Indian." Many scientists still seem to think that Hopi culture is simple and uncomplicated, that Hopi people are isolated from world events, and that they are trying to hide knowledge that should be freely shared. In other words, many scientists think of Hopi people and their knowledge and culture as "data." At the same time, purveyors of New Age religions mystify and romanticize Hopi life as spiritual and close to nature. All underestimate Hopi abilities to live in two worlds, to be educated in two ways. What we have to say here will not smooth over tensions in day-to-day interactions, but we hope to reveal the roots of some important cultural differences.

Hopi and other Native consultants generally perceive the museum, and scientists generally, as privileging rational thought over emotion and secular over spiritual concerns (see White Deer 1997 for a Choctaw view of archaeology that expresses many of the same concerns that MNA staff hear from Hopi, Zuni, and Navajo consultants). These hierarchical dichotomies were constructed by science and for science. They are recognized by Hopi people and many other American Indians as "how science is" but not "how the world is." That many archaeologists and anthropologists now also question these inherited Cartesian dualities is surely a sign that we are moving toward common ground (see, for example, Harvey 2005; Ingold 2000, 2006), but recognizing dysfunctional frameworks is much easier than transforming entrenched practices.

A MODEST PROPOSAL: COULD WE BORROW THOSE BACK?

We begin with a story that illustrates some Hopi concerns about MNA collections. We would like to acknowledge helpful individuals by name, but it is not appropriate to reveal the identities of individual consultants in the context of this publication. Many consultants working with MNA on exhibit and curation planning were uncomfortable speaking on behalf of their communities when they did not feel they had the authority of community consensus or an appointed leadership role. Our conversations were intended to help MNA personnel understand some Hopi people's concerns about particular collections at particular times, and consultants sometimes preferred that their comments not be generalized. Western scholars and Hopi people value ownership, expertise, and individuality differently. We discussed whether to use names and quickly reached the conclusion that the process was more important than the individuals. We had different relationships to the collections, to the museum, and to one another, and these relationships shaped the roles we played in the actions and decisions taken in the subsequent episode. We decided to use titles here (including "artifacts") instead of names, because the roles are more important.

At the 2010 Hopi Festival of Art and Culture at MNA, one of the museum's most active Hopi community members and regular consultants approached the director with a request: he wanted to borrow certain artifacts in the museum's ethnographic collections for use in preparing for a katsina ceremony in his home village. The person in charge of the preparations for the ceremony foresaw a shortage of this particular item and asked the community member (CM) to visit MNA and find out whether the museum would be willing to loan certain artifacts to the village. The CM then discussed the request with the director. The director invited the curator of anthropology and the registrar, one of the Collections Department personnel charged with the proper storage and security of collections, to take part in the discussion of the proposed loan. He asked the CM to explain to the employees that Hopi people and museum staff do not look at collections the same way.

The community member, director, registrar, and curator gathered in the collections storage area and brought out trays holding many of the items being considered for the loan. The CM first asked the registrar what she knew about Hopi life, whether she had ever visited his community, and what she thought about it. She admitted that she had visited once or twice and was not very familiar with Hopi culture but expressed interest in learning. This exchange opened the way for further instruction. The CM explained that before asking for a decision about the loan request, he wanted MNA personnel to understand how the items in question were made and used and how Hopi people feel about these and other artifacts in the collections. He explained that this information was not to be written down as research data,[1] so we will relay the important concepts without identifying the artifacts and their functions, except to say that the artifacts were made in the CM's village about fifty years ago, they are drab and undecorated, not what curators might call "charismatic objects" (Wingfield 2010), and they have never been exhibited.

The CM asked whether any of us were familiar with the work of theologian Martin Buber. Some of us were not, so he explained Buber's "I–it" and "I–Thou" relationships (Buber 1958). Scientists and museum professionals usually enact I–it relationships with artifacts (objects) in their collections. Significantly, there is an absence of I–it relationships for Hopi people;

for them, every relationship is enacted as an I–Thou dialogue. There is a relationship of mutuality between humans and what Western scientists and museum professionals call objects, and that is why in this chapter we are calling them artifacts instead. By "objects," we simply mean items we relate to as "its." The conventional archaeological definition of an artifact, as something "made, modified, or used by humans," emphasizes some kind of relationship with humans.[2]

CM. What is this you have here?

Registrar. A camera.

CM. What is the camera made of?

Registrar. Plastic and metal.

CM. Where do plastic and metal come from?

Registrar. The earth.

CM. There you go!

We recognize that anything we use in a modern technological society has lost that connection to the earth. The relationship is disconnected. We do not recognize the history of the origins of everyday artifacts. But to Hopi people, the artifact's history is parallel to the life cycle of a person. If you have an understanding of the life cycles of things, the history of anything begins prior to its manufacture.

If the CM is representing a common Hopi point of view, and we think he is, then for Hopi people, everything in the museum is a "Thou" and nothing is an "it." Every artifact was made with specific intentions from materials gathered from the earth, which already had life force but were given particular form, use, and meaning by the maker as informed by his or her cultural values and understandings. The English words "art" and "artist" have no Hopi equivalent. The closest word to "art" is *tutkya*. The maker infuses the artifact with his or her ingeniousness, which is implicitly culturally located and which can be apprehended and appreciated by the viewer as an infusion of skill, care, thought, intention, and emotion. Some artifacts, particularly those made for ceremonial use, are given names and are fed with cornmeal, the quintessential Hopi food—as is true for all the Pueblos, most Mesoamerican cultures, and many others (see Johannesson and Hastorf 1994, particularly the chapters by Ortiz and Ford). Artifacts that have relationships with humans can feel sad when not allowed to fulfill their purposes, do their jobs, or be with their communities (see Wingfield's discussion of objectification and institutional inmates in chapter 3, this volume). Therefore, the CM suggested, some museum artifacts should be allowed to return to their source community to be used, to take part in community activities. "Taking part" is a phrase one hears often in Hopi discourse; it refers to being a participating member of ceremonial events. If what the museum professionals define as "damage" occurs in this process, it is acceptable to Hopi people because alteration is a normal part of function and life cycle. Alteration, even "damage," would not disturb many Hopi people, though the CM appreciated that the possibility of damage would make museum personnel uncomfortable, perhaps because it would compromise their effectiveness in doing *their* jobs. This is the crux of the contradiction between Hopi ideas about the proper care of artifacts, which is analogous to the proper care of all community members, not just humans, and the museum's mission, which is to preserve objects intact by removing them from the flow of time, separating them from their contexts of use or post-use repose.

Each participant in the ensuing discussion represented his or her concerns as a stakeholder. The CM had been selected by ritual facilitators in his community to serve as an intermediary due to his expertise in both Western and Hopi knowledge and philosophy and to his long-term relationship with the museum. The director wished to preserve, and if possible enhance, the museum's positive relationship with the Hopi community. The registrar enacts policies and procedures meant to protect against damage and prevent loss. The curator represents the research interests of archaeologists and other scientists. (At MNA, the Collections Department is responsible for the physical care of collections, and curators are responsible for intellectual care. This division unfortunately replicates a Western dichotomy we argue against here. The policy was the product of a particular situation and has, as we see here, unforeseen consequences.) Curators easily accept that items are broken and damaged in the course of use. For archaeologists, research value is increased by material evidence of use. A damaged, or otherwise use-altered, artifact has higher research value than an intact one that has not been used, because we can study the raw materials exposed in broken edges, detect use wear, and identify residues.[3] For curators, use includes study, exhibition, educational activities, and other actions that remove museum artifacts from their storage trays (and can make an artifact into an "it" or a "Thou," depending on the relationships enacted). Museum staff are already accustomed to tensions with researchers who wish to handle, measure, photograph, and take analytical samples from museum artifacts that collections staff would prefer never be moved or exposed to light. Research use and preservation often conflict, and this requires researchers and collections managers to compromise. We suggest that cultural use may be viewed as another point along this continuum from use to conservation and that the term "preservation" signifies an ideal state that even scientists realize is unrealistic. What is challenging for Western museum personnel about the concept of cultural use is that this use takes place outside the museum, with no museum personnel present. The museum has to relinquish control.

After about an hour of discussion, the CM selected several items from the storage tray, and the registrar entered their catalog numbers on a loan form made out in the name of the leader in charge of the upcoming ceremony. She carefully packed the items for transport, and the CM picked them up the next morning to take home. The artifacts took part in their first ceremony in about forty years and came back to the museum a few weeks later. Will MNA loan these artifacts and others again? Yes.

A BOLD PROPOSAL

This story brings together many ideas that have been discussed as the museum has pursued collaborative programs with the Hopi Tribe. We will examine two conclusions:

1. Artifacts are members of communities and can continue functioning in a meshwork of relationships with humans in the home community, as well as in the museum. Museum personnel therefore should rethink the concept of "objects" and animacy.

2. Everything has a natural life cycle analogous to the human life cycle of birth, growth, useful life, rest/repose/retirement, and death. Museum personnel therefore should rethink the concept of "preservation."

We will point to evidence for each of these assertions and provide examples from MNA discussions and from limited comparative material in archaeological, anthropological, and museum literature. We will then discuss implications for museum curation.

MUSEUM ARTIFACTS ARE ANIMATE

Museum science typically views objects as inanimate its. For Hopi people and many other Native Americans, objects, whether shaped by humans or natural processes, are animate in the sense that they are part of the flow of life in a meshwork of relationships. In order to properly care for collections, museum personnel should respect a source community's assertion that all items in the museum are Thou's rather than its. Most of the artifacts in museums have been removed from their cultural and ecological locations and webs of relationships and, we argue, are now in new cultural contexts, new and unnatural environments.

Though the concept of animacy is rarely unpacked in museum literature (but for anthropology, see Harvey 2005; Ingold 2006), Hopi people clearly are not the only Native Americans to express a concern with animacy and museum collections. In a discussion about the National Museum of the American Indian, "one consistent belief among the museum's Native constituent base [was] that objects are 'living' entities or retain a 'living spirit.' These spirits are believed to be conscious beings with human-like emotions that, in some instances, require feeding and human interaction to remain 'healthy'" (Henry 2004:108).

What can be done to help reconnect persons and artifacts? The "answer" for many museums is to have a Native person offer a prayer or a blessing and to schedule individual or group consultations about the kind and frequency of such visits. We suggest that more should be done. Curators and collections managers should seek and accept recommendations for care (including loans for cultural use) on a case-by-case basis and seek deeper understanding of each community's values, needs, and concerns. For museum personnel to understand the descendant community's ontology in greater depth, apply comparative methods, and explore the possibility of general transformations in museum practice to accommodate a wider range of practices, descendant communities must be willing to share at least some knowledge with outsiders. For the chance to transform existing hierarchies of authority, they must risk exposure and the possibility of being misunderstood. Discomfort on the part of everyone involved in the discussion is probably inevitable and not necessarily to be avoided.

It is important to Hopi people that non-Hopi people recognize and respect their I–Thou relationships with artifacts in museum collections, but it is also important to urge non-Hopi people not to overemphasize animacy. For Hopi people, artifacts are not considered to be persons, though they have some person-like relationships. The ways in which artifacts are person-like include experiencing social relationships with persons, evoking/experiencing emotion, and having a life cycle. Many Hopi people (and others) consider baskets, pots, carvings, tools, and other artifacts to be what Westerners may understand as "like people," because of how Western thought constructs and values humans, not because they are actually persons. These artifacts have their own individual identities and jobs to do. Some are given names, but naming them does not equate them with humans any more than naming a dog or a car means we think our dog or car is human. For Hopi people, artifacts are not really like people; they simply are what they are, but they are *not* inanimate its. Naming is about relating in more than an I–it relationship; that is, naming can be evidence of an I–Thou relationship. It is not about making something a person or even person-like, although for some other Native American communities, this may well be the case, as in Plains medicine bundles, which become persons in their own right (Zedeño 2008).

Museums are curating the artifacts and must pay attention to and facilitate human relationships with them, but in this and similar cases, we would suggest that the museum is not curating relationships in the sense of taking responsibility for or reenacting cultural practices associated with artifacts. So, for example, it is not the proper role of non-Native museum personnel to make offerings or prayers, and when artifacts are given names prior to taking part in a ceremony, these names should not go into the database that describes the artifact and its loan history. New Age adherents' appropriation of Hopi spirituality is just as damaging as missionaries' efforts to destroy it, and museums should endeavor to partner with Hopi people to promote respect for Hopi spirituality without encouraging non-Hopi people to emulate Hopi practices. Hopi people want curators to know that community members have emotional connections with artifacts and to respect that; they are not asking them to share those emotions. Hopi people are not foisting their experiences on others, and they do not appreciate their practices being appropriated by others.

If museums generally wish to explore the possibility of accepting relationships as being just as important as artifacts, we must ask whether artifacts are animate in the same ways to all indigenous source communities. Clearly not. Perusal of ethnographic, museum, and archaeological literature suggests a range of orientations and emphases. Artifacts can be animate because of their materiality and common source in materials that come from a living earth. They can be animate because of their relationships and interactions with the humans who made and used them. They can accumulate power with repeated use, from contact with other powerful artifacts, substances, places, and persons or as recipients of songs, prayers, and offerings. In the end, the social relationships between artifacts and humans are important, not the question of whether animacy is a fact or a metaphor. In trying to untangle internalist and externalist views of animacy and agency, Alfred Gell wrote:

> "Social agents" can be drawn from categories which are as
> different as chalk and cheese (in fact, rather more different)

because "social agency" is not defined in terms of "basic" bio-logical attributes (such as inanimate thing vs. incarnate person) but is relational—it does not matter, in ascribing "social agent" status, what a thing (or a person) "is" in itself; what matters is where it stands in a network of social relations. All that may be necessary for stocks and stones to become "social agents" in the sense that we require, is that there should be actual human persons/agents "in the neighbourhood" of these inert objects, not that they should be biologically human persons themselves. (Gell 1998:123)

For example, a Basketmaker era atlatl on display at MNA has bluejay feathers wound into the wrapping near its handle. The artifact is two thou-sand years old, and this type of throwing stick was replaced by the bow and arrow about fifteen hundred years ago, so there is no equivalent in Hopi life today. To interpret this artifact for exhibition, archaeologists fall back on what they can observe and infer from their point of view as scientists. They infer that these feathers do not function to enhance the speed or accuracy of a thrown dart, nor are these visible enough to signal the own-er's social identity to all but the closest observers. Archaeologists there-fore call the feathers "decorative" and might venture a guess that they had ritual or symbolic meaning. In contrast, Hopi and Navajo exhibit planning consultants called them significant evidence of the maker's spirituality. One suggested that the word "spirituality" has been misappropriated and overused and that it would be more correct to say that the feathers are evidence of important connections, of correct relationships of reciprocity, among birds, prey animals, and the human makers and users of this arti-fact. None said outright that the feathers imparted breath or clothing or other "human" characteristics to the atlatl, but they did agree that "tool" and "technology" are not adequate words to describe an item like this or its role in human lives, past and present. All consultants objected to the 1980s era exhibit's organization, which separated artifacts and texts into anthropological categories of "technology," "subsistence," "trade," and so forth. These traditional categories are still important for research and for some narratives that a museum might present in exhibitions; we are not advocating replacement of them, but an expansion of categorizations and contextualizations.

Meanwhile, in the ethnology gallery consultations, MNA interviews about how to exhibit Hopi-made artifacts to outsiders made it clear that in Hopi practice, making something is like gestation and birth—carving, weaving, and shaping and firing pottery vessels are acts of transformation, giving life to something or, more precisely, transforming the life that is already there in the materials into something perceptible, with which humans can interact, and giving it a job to do. Hopi potters refer to vessels as being like children, who emerge from the give-and-take with the clay; their life and breath are given tangible form when they are fired. Hopi pots emerge from the fire with blush-like orange mottling that shows they have emotion. When fired well, they ring out when tapped, showing they have a voice in the world (Charley and McChesney 2007). As humans, we need to see and hear their emotion and voice to interact with them.

Attributing human-like characteristics to artifacts makes them more perceptible. By this, we mean something more than "making tangible," perhaps "making more accessible for person-like relationships." For example, katsina dolls (*tithu*) are carved as gifts for girls who are learning about play, learning about role modeling, learning about their relationships with these beings, who embody clouds, ancestors, and all good things in life and with whom humans engage in reciprocity. The dolls themselves are not katsinas, but playing with the dolls shapes and focuses a Hopi girl's relationship with the real katsinas. Significantly, girls receive dolls that mimic their own growth and development. Infants receive simple, flat "cradle dolls," and as girls grow, the dolls they receive have more defined limbs, faces, and postures. This brings us to life cycles.

ARTIFACTS HAVE LIFE CYCLES

For Hopi people, the Western animate/inanimate, inside essence/outward shell dichotomies are oversimplified. To them, there are *three* sides to this coin. It is all integrated, not separated. We can all recognize whether a person is alive or dead, but the Western view is that when a person dies, that's it; life is over, and now the body is inanimate. For Hopi people, it is true that the person is not breathing, communicating, or moving and there are no person-to-person relations going on, but there is still molecular movement in the corpse. It is not a living entity, but it is still undergoing change. It is festering and decomposing at a cellular level—but more than that, it is transforming into something else. Burial is more than putting a body in a hole in the ground; it is returning it to the womb (Ferguson, Dongoske, and Kuwanwisiwma 2001:15). That is why Hopi people use no coffin. The death process does not just happen for the moment but continues beyond that. The body decomposes naturally and becomes part of the earth again; flowers bloom from that area; bees get pollen from the flowers and make honey; and humans consume the honey. Life keeps on going.

FIGURE 10.1

Pottery Mound: Germination *by Michael Kabotie and Delbridge Honanie, 2002. Acrylic on canvas, three panels, 6 feet x 15 feet (MNA C2417A-C). Photograph by Gene Balzer, courtesy of the Museum of Northern Arizona.*

Linguist Benjamin Whorf (1975:123–124) described the Hopi language as imposing on the universe "two grand cosmic forms, which as a first approximation in terminology we may call manifested and manifesting" (see also Whorf 1956). One can say that the birth of a person or the manufacture of an artifact is when it becomes manifest, but the person or the artifact is still undergoing change; it is manifesting until it completes its own life cycle. From our human point of view, we might say that everything has a human-like life cycle, but it may be more appropriate to say that all things have similar life cycles, which oscillate between this earthly world and the underworld, order and disorder, work and repose, life and death. Expressing this as a continuous process of change, not as dichotomies, is more accurate.

Many American Indians consider museums' emphasis on preservation to be unnatural and inappropriate. Relationships among people and artifacts involve affection, responsibilities, and reciprocity. Disruption of the intended roles and natural life cycles of persons or artifacts can cause emotional and psychological distress; likewise, the participation of artifacts and humans in beneficial activities can be the source of positive emotions and relationships.

Hopi artist Michael Kabotie described what is going on in the large triptych called *Pottery Mound: Germination* that he and Delbridge Honanie painted for MNA (figure 10.1). The abstract, swirling elements in the lower register represent the chaos and creativity of the underworld, which is necessary for life to continue. The butterfly man, corn and squash maidens, birds, and butterflies emerging out of the earth-altar base band represent growth and life in this world. These young, growing beings reach maturity, bear offspring, and ultimately return to the earth, where they disintegrate into the disorder from which a new array of living things will germinate and grow. In this narrative, Kabotie did not distinguish between body and soul, substance and spirit, nor does Laguna poet Leslie Marmon Silko in the following quote:

> You see that after a thing is dead, it dries up. It might take weeks or years, but eventually, if you touch the thing, it crumbles under your fingers. It goes back to dust. The soul of the thing has long since departed. With the plants and wild game the soul may have already been born back into bones and blood or thick green stalks and leaves. Nothing is wasted. What cannot be eaten by people or in some way used must then be left where other living creatures may benefit. What domestic animals or wild scavengers can't eat will be fed to the plants. The plants feed on the dust of these few remains.
>
> The ancient Pueblo people buried the dead in vacant rooms or in partially collapsed rooms adjacent to the main living quarters.... Corncobs and husks, the rinds and stalks and animal bones were not regarded by the ancient people as filth or garbage. The remains were merely resting at a midpoint in their journey back to dust. Human remains are not so different. They should rest with the bones and rinds where they all may benefit living creatures—small rodents and insects—until their return is completed. (Silko 1996:25–26)

Both Silko and Kabotie express the idea that all things and persons have an inevitable, natural life cycle. Although museum professionals are charged with interfering in this cycle by working to prevent disintegration to dust, rot, or becoming food, Pueblo people and perhaps other indigenous people find this interference to be problematic. For example, the purpose of the wooden figures called Ahayu:da, or Zuni war gods, is to serve a term guarding shrines surrounding Zuni Pueblo and then to retire and "go back to the earth" by means of natural weathering processes (Ferguson, Anyon, and Ladd 1996; Merrill, Ladd, and Ferguson 1993). Since the 1990s, Zuni Pueblo has made the repatriation of Ahayu:da its top priority in dealing with outside museums. More than eighty Ahayu:da have returned to Zuni to continue their intended life cycles in a secluded, fenced outdoor area that is patrolled against looters. Zuni leaders have had to adjust their ritual practices to accommodate the return of these "persons" whose forced departure via museum collecting and looting disrupted their intended life cycles.

Zuni leaders have reached a solution to the problem of war gods in museums, but they are still trying to address the problem of masks and other religious items in museum collections. Anthropologist Edmund Ladd wrote of a visit with some Zuni leaders to the Smithsonian: "The Zuni religious leaders know that in the long run the objects in the museum will 'eat themselves up' no matter what the museum does to preserve them. Prolonging that process of disintegration, however, is still wrong" (qtd. in Merrill, Ladd, and Ferguson 1993:547).

For museums, the issue of insect infestation of organic artifacts is particularly telling. Museum professionals invest a good deal of time, training, and effort in preventing such infestations. But past treatment of Hopi katsina friends[4] with pesticides, such as arsenic, has prevented the reuse of many katsina friends, because the health effects of wearing a tainted item are unknown but likely dangerous (Odegaard and Saydongei 2000). Today, when an insect infestation is discovered, items are typically frozen, put in a low-oxygen tent, or fumigated with lethal chemicals to kill insects and their eggs. This continues to be problematic for some source communities because pesticide contamination makes it difficult or impossible to use repatriated objects for their original purposes and, as Henry (2004:108) puts it, "the museum is artificially extending the normal life cycle of certain items that, in their original cultural contexts and under normal use, would have worn down over time through use or been claimed by the elements." At the National Museum of the American Indian (NMAI), he notes, some Native consultants have advised that "pest infestations are part of an object's 'normal' life cycle and should not be prevented" because killing pests is "harmful to the living spirit of the object" (Henry 2004:108). Insects have jobs to do, including helping take apart used-up items so that they can return to the earth, but consultants have not yet suggested that the museum end its integrated pest management program. NMAI acknowledges the difference between accepted museum practices and Native viewpoints about the life cycles of artifacts and accepts that there are trade-offs between preservation for future generations and allowing nature to take its course.

This raises questions about what museums are, what they can be, and who decides. For the most part, indigenous communities have not had much say in curation and exhibition. Many museums display old things but have difficulty communicating what present-day cultures and communities are like. Lomatewama once recommended that a certain East Coast museum put a beer can in the model cornfield of a new Hopi exhibit, to give an accurate picture, to be fair to the living culture and to reality. The point of the beer can would have been to illustrate that Hopi communities encompass a variety of lifeways, are faced with the same issues as other communities, and are responding to those issues right now. They need to be—and are—modern people, too. Tribal museums offer communities more choices, but they still have to grapple with museums as modern cultural places where natural cycles are not allowed to unfold, at least not in the same way. Some tribal museums have made a conscious decision not to collect and curate artifacts at all or to do so minimally (Isaac 2007).

This situation is more urgent in the case of human remains and grave goods in museums. Most archaeologists now understand that when they encounter human remains that clearly were deliberately buried, we can infer that this individual's relatives intended to commit him or her to the earth. Mummy bundles in caves can be viewed differently. We do not know whether they were intended to disintegrate or to be preserved for a time so that descendants could visit them or for some other reason. This was the practice in many Mesoamerican and a few Southwestern cases, at least for certain kinds of individuals, such as the Hidden House mummy bundle from central Arizona (Dixon 1956). We can be sure, however, that their relatives did not intend for their loved one's remains to be placed in a cabinet for perpetual scientific study. We can also assume that any items buried with that individual were intended to accompany him or her on the journey to the next phase of a natural life cycle and that they were not intended to be displayed in a glass case or sold to the highest bidder on the antiquities market. The reburial of human remains and associated funerary objects is well accepted by museums today, but we caution that even here, opinions vary among communities. Jemez Pueblo, for example, reburied human remains from Pecos Pueblo but asked the National Park Service to continue curating associated pottery vessels in its museum so that future generations of Pecos descendants at Jemez could learn from them about their ancestors.

IMPLICATIONS FOR MUSEUM PRACTICE

We intend in this section to present suggestions for exploration and discussion. This is not a list of things museums should definitely do to accommodate more culturally appropriate use and curation of collections from Hopi, Pueblo, and other American Indian communities.

First, we suggest that museum curators not be afraid to document "this is how other people feel about what we are doing," to explore what we can do differently, and then to try out new practices with periodic evaluations of what is working, or not, and for whom. Museums should discuss what can be done with representatives of source communities, keeping in mind that a range of opinions should be solicited. Most people will have conflicted feelings about preservation versus cultural use versus allowing or even encouraging the natural deterioration of objects. Scientists, too, have mixed feelings.

Repatriation

Most Hopi consultants to MNA clearly and consistently set priorities and speak openly about their emotional connection to the remains of ancestors and their personal conflicts about taking responsibility for laying them to rest. The director of the Hopi Cultural Preservation Office has co-authored with two archaeologists an article to explain Hopi views of death, mortuary treatment, repatriation, and reburial; the authors advocate dialogue and negotiation (Ferguson, Dongoske, and Kuwanwisiwma 2001).

First, human remains, artifacts, and ancient structures should not be disturbed at all. But once they are disturbed (as a result of development projects, natural erosion, or research), it is most important to return human remains and funerary artifacts to the earth to complete their intended life cycles; religious paraphernalia should be returned to religious leaders for continued use or proper retirement; some artifacts should be returned for use in the community; and some should simply be made more available to descendants (which can be defined as the kin group, village, clan, or whole community, depending on the culture), who can learn about their history by viewing and handling these artifacts. Federal laws, such as the American Indian Religious Freedom Act of 1978 and the Native American Graves Protection and Repatriation Act of 1990, have forced the first two issues, but the rest must be handled on a case-by-case basis until clear patterns and precedents emerge. When osteological research might yield information of interest to the Hopi Tribe, the tribal government is open to discussion (Ferguson, Dongoske, and Kuwanwisiwma 2001:16).

At the very least, museum professionals must insist on the careful handling of human remains and funerary objects and respect for their descendants. Hays-Gilpin remembers when one could walk into a lab or classroom at an American university and see Indian skulls on display. Sometimes they sported hats, sunglasses, silly nametags, and other accoutrements that served to belittle them, deny their connections to present-day Indian people, and construct instead subordinate relationships to anthropology students. In other words, they were made into its and denied their Thouness. Native students, especially parents who inadvertently exposed their children to such museum or classroom displays of ancestral remains, will never forget and cannot be blamed for not forgiving (Cooper 2008).

R-E-S-P-E-C-T

Hopi, Navajo, and Zuni consultants to MNA agree that they would like to see museums pay more attention to the respectful treatment of artifacts from their communities, not just human remains. It is up to museums to find out what the consultants mean by "respect." The following is merely a preliminary probe (but see guidelines from the National Museum of the American Indian and other museums in Sullivan and Edwards 2004:pts. 2 and 3). MNA's Native consultants recognize security, cataloging, climate control, and control of access and handling to be evidence of respect. In turn, most of the consultants respect the scientific values of education and knowledge, but they would like to see scientists' values opened up for discussion in the same way that museum personnel ask them about source community values. They are willing to discuss compromise and want scientists to be open as well.

In particular, consultants would like to see respect for relationships, not just objects; this can be phrased as "care of the artifacts' life force, not just their physical parts." For MNA's new Easton Collections Center, this meant blessing the foundation at the groundbreaking ceremony and blessing the building again at its opening, just before collections were moved in. It meant designing the building with as many natural materials as possible, with a living roof in which native plants, grasses, and wildflowers grow and bloom, moving water features, and points of entry for natural light, including a door oriented to the east. This last was important because the artifacts inside need to know what time of year it is. The door is opened on equinoxes so that the rising sun can shine into the storage area. The building itself is alive: it breathes, responds to the movement of the sun, interacts with visitors, and forms relationships with humans and others. All tribal representatives, not just Hopi people, agreed about this.

Jim Enote, director of the A:shiwi A:wan Museum and Heritage Center at Zuni Pueblo, spoke on behalf of the consultants at the building's public dedication ceremony. He remarked that "concerned tribal peoples have said cultural artifacts in museums do not receive the respect they deserve" but now "the Center stands as testimony that there are people willing and able to make accommodations and open the door to changing the way museums do business with source communities" (Enote 2009:3). He added that the center is a place "for tribes to visit objects that could be considered old friends and family." A pan-American group of indigenous consultants had expressed the same concerns to the design team for the National Museum of the American Indian.

Emotion and Kinship

Emotional and kin relationships are more important in the Hopi world than in the museum world. For example, a Hopi museum employee described to one of us her reaction at seeing Hopi wedding garments and a wedding basket in the museum's collection. Her description of the roles of these items in Hopi weddings and burials clearly shows that the baskets and textiles made for exchange between the families of the bride and groom partake of kin relationships, with specific jobs to do in the wedding ceremony, in subsequent married life, and finally at burial as vehicles for the bride and groom's journey to the afterlife. They are active participants in a kin network and in the life cycles of humans. When removed from this cycle to a museum, they not only cease doing those jobs but also are visible reminders that particular marriages have ended in divorce, that life cycles have been broken, and that particular members of the community might be unable to reach the underworld after death (and therefore might be unable to return as clouds).

Zuni anthropologist Edmund Ladd expressed similar thoughts in his account of serving as a bridge for his community between Zuni religious leaders and Smithsonian personnel: "Emotions were strong during the visits to the Smithsonian Institution to view religious artifacts that had been removed from Zuni" (qtd. in Merrill, Ladd, and Ferguson 1993:547). "They said, 'We are very sad. Why have these things been put here? Who sold these things?'" They "felt a sadness that their children, the artifacts in the museum, were being held in ways that for the Zunis were insensitive." Ladd noted that when a mask is artificially preserved in a museum, rather than buried with its owner and maker, "the person who originally owned the mask is thus left without a passport to enter the afterworld or to come back to Zuni for spring rains and winter storms. As a result, the spirit [that inheres in the mask] is not doing his job" (Merrill, Ladd, and Ferguson 1993:547).

That said, American Indians today are modern people and adapt as they always have and in new ways. Lomatewama was once commissioned to craft a certain Hopi garment for display in a museum. Because such an item would not be used in its cultural context, it would have different relationships in the museum than in a Hopi village. Therefore, he did not put certain things on it that would usually be added by family members in the course of dedicating it to a particular task in a particular family. Museums can adapt, too, by becoming more flexible in their definitions of what is authentic, accurate, and appropriate. They must attend not only to things but also to relationships, not only between indigenous and museum communities but also within communities, where nested identities, such as gender, kinship, ethnicity, residence, and age, intersect in complicated ways.

Clan identity is the primary social identity for most Hopi people and for most other western Pueblos, including Zuni, Acoma, and Laguna people. Clan identity links one to some members of one's own community, and it also cross-cuts villages, language groups, and, today, state lines. There are Corn Clans in all the western Pueblos, for example, and the members see themselves as related. Leslie Marmon Silko (Laguna; 1986:1005) explains that clan identities also cross-cut the human and nonhuman worlds: "Human identity is linked with all the elements of Creation through the clan: you might belong to the Sun Clan or the Lizard Clan or the Corn Clan or the Clay Clan." Pueblo clans have ritual and social responsibilities linked to their clan identities. For example, Hopi Katsina Clan members are charged with taking care of katsinas. This responsibility extends to advising the museum on the respectful depiction of katsinas in publications and advising law enforcement agents about the repatriation of katsina friends. Clan leaders from all pueblos are also called on to advise the National Park Service and other land-managing agencies about archaeological sites along their ancestral migration routes.

Knowledge and Access

Respect means finding out which artifacts are culturally sensitive and should be handled only by certain people (e.g., men, women, nonmenstruating women, initiates, and clan members). Museum personnel are aware that some restrictions may go against existing nondiscrimination policies (a Western response to a problem of discrimination by many white males against women and members of ethnic minorities, a problem that does not exist in nonwhite communities in the forms that prompted the formulation of these policies), but a voluntary compliance policy is a good first step and is an example of compromise. In Hays-Gilpin's experience, for example, most young Euro American anthropology students are eager to learn about the varied cultural meanings of menstrual taboos. In Native America, many groups (including Hopi people) do not have menstrual taboos, but where restrictions on encounters between menstruating women and certain kinds of artifacts do exist (for example, in some Plains tribes), they are not about pollution or dirt. Rather, they are about power and the protection of women's creative abilities (e.g., Henry 2004:107), and most feminists can respect that.

More important to Hopi people is the restriction of access to some artifacts and knowledge to the individuals who have been properly initiated into the katsina society or into specific men's and women's ceremonial societies (sodalities). In some cases, what an uninitiated Hopi does not know *can* hurt him in ways that would not affect an uninitiated non-Hopi. At a consultation about one of the museum's archaeological field projects, an older Hopi man confided that one of his relatives had stayed home for fear that artifacts might be displayed that he should not see due to his lack of know-ledge (and the responsibility that goes with knowledge). He then informed the curator that nothing in fact was present that would present a danger, and he provided general guidelines about the kinds of items that might be problematic. The curator promised to consult an initiate about such items in the future before displaying them, so that all Hopi people could feel welcome at future events.

Breaking Down Disciplinary Barriers

A suggestion for science museums is that they work on the accommodation and encouragement of emotional experiences. Mike Kabotie said that life is about balancing the rational and the intuitive, the head and the heart (personal communication 2008). We must have both to be healthy as individuals or as communities. How? One way is to break down disciplinary boundaries, as well as ethnic/racial boundaries. MNA has a natural advantage over most museums in the United States in that it embraces both art and science. MNA's co-founders were a scientist, Harold S. Colton, and an artist, Mary-Russell Ferrell Colton. Like the marriage of its founders, the museum has always been striving for the balance of rational and intuitive approaches. We see a continuum of sorts among its departments, from geology to biology to ecology to anthropology to fine arts, each bleeding into the next—though not yet coming full circle. (MNA's geologists insist that geology, art, and anthropology must be presented in separate galleries.) The MNA ecology program, for example, embraces traditional ecological knowledge, does service projects that assist Native communities in water resources planning (including protection of the religious value of springs), and includes a wide range of artworks and indigenous oral traditions in its exhibits, for example, in its vision statement for a planned exhibit on dragonflies.

A suggestion for art museums is that they provide more cultural and historical context to help visitors stretch their imaginations beyond their own experiences. All artists, including contemporary American Indian artists, are not just commenting on themselves; they are today, here, the mythmakers, making our shared world meaningful, perceptible, and approachable in all its complexities. Joseph Campbell (2010[1988]) said, "A ritual is the enactment of a myth. By participating in a ritual, you are participating in the myth." Likewise, the creative process of shaping a pot, weaving a sash, or making a painting parallels the process of roasting corn, raising children, or telling the story of Hopi emergence and migration. Art museums, already places meant to evoke emotion, also can be places for experiencing how the world works, by emphasizing more the process of making, becoming, and participating and by exploring how we know what we know.

Context

One way to reunite artifacts and contexts is to display objects in more natural groupings and settings. For example, Hopi, Zuni, and Navajo consultants helping MNA plan a new archaeology exhibit all made critical remarks about objects being glued to boards; the artificial separation of technology, trade, and subsistence; and the lack of discussion of connections between past and present. But they liked murals that showed landscape settings, and they liked groupings of artifacts that mimicked the way the items would have been used together in the past. They suggested including sound (birdsong, running water, wind, grinding corn, songs) and video (movement through a landscape, weather, seasonal and daily changes) to bring the exhibit alive. Things like this have been done elsewhere. For example, at the history museum in Stockholm, one stoops to enter a dark Neolithic passage tomb where caches of ritual artifacts are tucked into small cases in the walls, as if they are in situ in side chambers. At the rear of a reconstructed house, video and sound imply people moving around in the background.

Reuniting landscape and objects is one way to honor the life in the artifacts, life that comes from the earth and from association with humans and their activities. Connecting past and present is vitally important for all audiences, indigenous and otherwise, to understand the context and meaning of artifacts. Without those connections, everything in the museum is merely a distant it.

MORE THAN A HOPI CONCERN?

Are our propositions about museum collections, which are based on Hopi views, applicable beyond Hopi? Yes. The notion of an animate world may well be generalizable to all humans, with the possible exception of some scientists and those well steeped in Western industrial culture (see Harvey 2005). For thoughtful discussions of landscapes, animacy, and agency, see Bender 1993, Ingold 2000, 2006, 2007a, and Tilley 1997[1994];

see Harrison and Rose 2010 for heritage practices and Alberti and Bray 2009 for archaeology. Clearly, many of the characteristics of Hopi ontology as explored in this chapter are shared rather widely. We need to bring these insights into museums, where the concept of respectful behavior toward human remains is understood as universal, though what it means to act respectfully toward them differs. (The public display of "relics" that include human bones is common in Mexican churches, for example, but on the US side of the border, this type of display is virtually outlawed.) Museums also need to attend to artifacts and their roles in the flow of life. Harrison and Rose (2010:264) suggest that for heritage practice, "a dialogical concept of heritage suggests that heritage making is interactive—meaningfulness arises out of encounter and dialogue among multiple objects, some of whom are human."

The understanding that all things have a natural life cycle is nearly universal, but values vary in different communities. Conservators, collections specialists, other museum personnel, and many scientists strive to prolong the lives of artifacts, whereas many indigenous people think interfering in natural life-cycle processes is wrong. But many Native people also see some benefit in having artifacts made by their ancestors available for future generations to experience firsthand. We might also ask, cynically, whether members of Western industrial culture really support prolonging the lives of old things—reluctance to finance collection repositories is perhaps evidence of apathy and, in some cases, outright hostility. Who has not heard one legislator or another say, "Why are we spending tax dollars to save old buildings when live citizens need...[fill in the blank: food, health care, lower taxes, more government services, smaller government]?" Certainly, a great many non-indigenous people value the construction of new businesses, housing, roads, and mines over the preservation of archaeological sites. Unfortunately, we seldom make opportunities to discuss our priorities and values within our communities, much less cross-culturally.

In conclusion, this is a good time for museum professionals to broaden their thinking about the relationships between humans and artifacts in museum collections, starting with outreach to source communities and responsive discussion and action. Concerns about the classification of museum collections as inanimate objects (its) versus artifacts that have reciprocal relationships with humans (and perhaps one another) in terms of life force, personhood, emotion, kin, life cycle, and jobs to do (Thou's) appear to be widespread among American Indians and indigenous communities in many parts of the world. Responding to these concerns need not threaten the continued existence of collections but would place more emphasis on living people and reciprocal relationships between museum staff and representatives from source communities. Pursuing such relationships would be time-consuming and could be emotionally risky for all concerned, but we suggest that the benefits, not to mention duty and ethics, outweigh the risks. At the very least, we would do well to join forces against the common threats of cultural fragmentation and the absorption of regional traditions into a materialistic culture of consumerism and instant gratification, pushed by profit-oriented multinational corporations, xenophobia, and intolerance, which increasingly characterizes mainstream American culture (and other regions where the effects of global industrial capitalism are similar).

Lomatewama gets the last word in this chapter:

> Cultures interpret their "reality" in a variety of ways. Some rely heavily on empirical data or evidence. Others employ paths of least resistance. In other words, the means by which they comprehend themselves and their environment vary.
>
> Empiricism normally requires following a series of steps, one of which may include dismantling a given subject or object. In this way, things can be categorized. The advantage to this is that one can see all the parts. But not all minds work this way. The Hopi language (as I see it) recognizes those who have a close affinity to the Hopi reality. Unlike the Western mindset, the Hopi mindset focuses on relationships with the world (I–Thou) rather than breaking down and categorizing things (I–it). For example, the word *tsiro* refers to any number of bird species. Then there are specific words for certain birds (*kwaahu* = eagle, *paakiw* = duck, *kowaako* = chicken, and so on). These and other birds have a definite place within the Hopi reality, and the Hopi people have an affinity to them. A variety of birds is acknowledged, but the "idea" of birds is an inherent part of the grand design. If you regard a bird as *just* a bird, you are changing a Thou to an it. Furthermore, there is no continual affirmation of the significance of its place in "reality."
>
> By establishing an I–Thou relationship with the world and all that occupies it, one begins to understand that all the parts work together to keep the universal cycle in motion. Although the Hopi people have had little experience with laboratory science or museum science, they have gained valuable knowledge through maintaining relationships with the world around them.

Acknowledgments

Heartfelt thanks to Doreen Elizabeth Martinez (Department of Ethnic Studies, University of Colorado), Robert Breunig (director, Museum of Northern Arizona), the MNA collections staff, Rodney Harrison, Sarah Byrne, an anonymous reviewer (for helpful comments on drafts of this chapter), Jim Enote (director, A:shiwi A:wan Museum, Zuni Pueblo), and many Hopi, Zuni, and Navajo consultants, too numerous to name here, for sharing their thoughts and feelings with museum staff about exhibits, collections care, research, educational programs, ethics, and many other topics.

Notes

1. To many Hopi people, writing things down seems to render them nonnegotiable. The information or idea becomes a thing, becomes trapped in time. It cannot be edited or amplified or adjusted according to the level of understanding already held by a particular audience. When you write, you cannot know how your audience will understand or use the information. Some might need a very basic explanation, and some might be ready for the responsibility that comes with a detailed explanation.

2. Recent literature (e.g., Gosden 2004; Wingfield, chapter 3, this volume) discusses "thingness" and useful distinctions between "things" ("artifacts"), which are embedded in the flow of life, and "objects," which are not, and the roles of perceivers as to which term applies in which context. We make the distinction in a simpler way because we have been unable to find an English word that adequately captures the way Hopi people relate to "things."

3. Editor's note (S. Byrne): There is an interesting irony here. Many objects were specifically collected by museums *because* they had been used; this use gave them legitimacy, but then the museum effectively froze them in time. Perhaps we need to reorient curatorial practice so that we not only keep the value of an object alive by preserving it but also add value to it by releasing it to be used once again?

4. "Friends" is the English translation of the Hopi word and is preferred to "mask." Note that a friend is a Thou, and a mask is an it.

References

Abt, Jeffrey

2011   The Origins of the Public Museum. *In* A Companion to Museum Studies. Sharon Macdonald, ed. Pp. 115–134. Malden, MA: Wiley-Blackwell.

Adams, Monni

2009   Both Sides of the Collecting Encounter: The George W. Harley Collection at the Peabody Museum of Archaeology and Ethnology, Harvard University. Museum Anthropology 32(1):17–32.

Alberti, Benjamin, and Tamara L. Bray

2009   Introduction to Special Section: Animating Archaeology: Of Subjects, Objects, and Alternative Ontologies. Cambridge Archaeological Journal 19(3):337–343.

Alberti, Benjamin, and Yvonne Marshall

2009   Animating Archaeology: Local Theories and Conceptually Open-Ended Methodologies. Cambridge Archaeological Journal 19(3):344–356.

Alivizatou, Marilena

2006   Museums and Intangible Heritage: The Dynamics of an Unconventional Relationship. Papers from the Institute of Archaeology 17:47–57.

Allen, Jim

1977   Sea Traffic, Trade and Expanding Horizons. *In* Sunda and Sahul: Prehistoric Studies in Southeast Asia, Melanesia and Australia. Jim Allen, Jack Golson, and Rhys Jones, eds. Pp. 387–417. London: Academic Press.

Allen, Lindy, and Louise Hamby

2011   Pathways to Knowledge: Research, Agency and Power Relations in the Context of Collaborations between Museums and Source Communities. *In* Unpacking the Collection: Networks of Material and Social Agency in the Museum. Sarah Byrne, Anne Clarke, Rodney Harrison, and Robin Torrence, eds. Pp. 209–230. New York: Springer.

REFERENCES

Allen, N. J.
2000   The Division of Labour and the Notion of Primitive Society. *In* Categories and Classifications: Maussian Reflections on the Social. N. J. Allen, ed. Pp. 61–74. Oxford: Berghahn.

Ames, Michael M.
1992   Cannibal Tours and Glass Boxes: The Anthropology of Museums. Vancouver: University of British Columbia Press.
1999   How to Decorate a House: The Re-negotiation of Cultural Representations at the University of British Columbia Museum of Anthropology. Museum Anthropology 22(3):41–51.

Anderson, Christopher
1990   Australian Aborigines and Museums—A New Relationship. Curator: The Museum Journal 33(3):165–179.

Appadurai, Arjun
1986   Introduction: Commodities and the Politics of Value. *In* The Social Life of Things: Commodities in Cultural Perspective. Arjun Appadurai, ed. Pp. 3–63. Cambridge: Cambridge University Press.
1996   Modernity at Large. Minneapolis: University of Minnesota Press.

Ardener, Edwin
1985   Social Anthropology and the Decline of Modernism. *In* Reason and Morality. J. Overing, ed. Pp. 47–70. London: Tavistock.

Artifact
2009   http://www.artifact.com/auction-lot/nineteenth-century-nickel-telescope -with-leather-1-c-8, accessed 15 April 2009.

Askew, Marc
2010   The Magic List of Global Status: UNESCO, World Heritage and the Agendas of States. *In* Heritage and Globalisation. Sophia Labadi and Colin Long, eds. Pp. 19–44. New York: Routledge.

Australian National Parks and Wildlife Service
1986   Nomination of Uluru (Ayers Rock–Mount Olga) National Park for Inclusion on the World Heritage List. Canberra: Australian National Parks and Wildlife Service.

Babcock, Barbara
1986   Modeled Selves: Helen Codere's "Little People." *In* The Anthropology of Experience. Victor W. Turner and Edward M. Bruner, eds. Pp. 316–343. Champaign: University of Illinois Press.

Babcock, Barbara, and Nancy Parezo
1988   Daughters of the Desert: Women Anthropologists and the Native American Southwest, 1880–1980. Albuquerque: University of New Mexico Press.

Bakker, Karel, and Liana Müller
2010   Intangible Heritage and Community Identity in Post-apartheid South Africa. Museum International 62(1–2):48–54.

Bandarin, Francois, ed.
2007   World Heritage—Challenges for the Millennium. Paris: UNESCO World
         Heritage Centre.

Barad, Karen
2007   Meeting the Universe Halfway: Quantum Physics and the Entanglement of
         Matter and Meaning. Durham, NC: Duke University Press.

Bardof, C. F.
1924   The Story of Sugar. Easton, PA: Chemical Publishing.

Barker, John
2001   Dangerous Objects: Changing Indigenous Perceptions of Material Culture in
         a Papua New Guinea Society. Pacific Science 55(4):359–375.

Barnard, Alan
2006   Kalahari Revisionism, Vienna and the "Indigenous Peoples" Debate. Social
         Anthropology 14:1–16.

Barrett, John
1994   Fragments of Antiquity: An Archaeology of Social Life in Britain 2900–1200
         BC. Oxford: Blackwell.

Barringer, Tim J., and Tom Flynn, eds.
1998   Colonialism and the Object: Empire, Material Culture, and the Museum.
         London: Routledge.

Barton, Francis Rickman
1902–1903 Addendum to Report, C.D. Annual Report on British New Guinea. Pp.
         18–20. London: British Government.
1910   The Annual Trading Expedition to the Papuan Gulf. In The Melanesians of
         British New Guinea. Charles Gabriel Seligmann, ed. Pp. 96–120. Cambridge:
         Cambridge University Press.

Basu, Paul
2011   Object Diasporas, Resourcing Communities: Sierra Leonean Collections in
         the Global Museumscape. Museum Anthropology 34(1):28–42.

Bateson, Gregory
1973[1935] Culture Contact and Schismogenesis. In Steps to an Ecology of Mind:
         Collected Essays in Anthropology, Psychiatry, Evolution, and Epistemology.
         G. Bateson, ed. Pp. 35–46. St. Albans, England: Chandler.

Battaglia, Debbora
1990   On the Bones of the Serpent: Person, Memory, and Mortality in Sabarl
         Island Society. Chicago: University of Chicago Press.

Batty, Philip, Lindy Allen, and John Morton, eds.
2005   The Photographs of Baldwin Spencer. Melbourne: Museum Victoria.

Baudrillard, Jean
1994   The System of Collecting. In Cultures of Collecting. John Elsner and Roger
         Cardinal, eds. Pp. 7–24. London: Reaktion.
2005[1968] The System of Objects. London: Verso.

REFERENCES

BBC

2011   London Museums Urged to Show More "Hidden" Artefacts. http://www.bbc
.co.uk/news/uk-england-london-12214145, accessed 19 January 2011.

Beck, Ulrich

1992   Risk Society: Towards a New Modernity. London: Sage.

Belk, Russell W.

1995   Collecting in a Consumer Society. London: Routledge.

Bell, Joshua

2006   Intersecting Histories: Materiality and Social Transformation in the Purari
Delta of Papua New Guinea. PhD dissertation, Oxford University.

2010a   Out of the Mouths of Crocodiles: Eliciting Histories in Photographs and
String-Figures. History and Anthropology 21(4):351–373.

2010b   Sugar Plant Hunting by Airplane in New Guinea: A Cinematic Narrative of
Scientific Triumph and Discovery in the "Remote Jungles." Journal of Pacific
History 45(1):37–56.

In press   Mistaken Gods and Other Misnomers of First Contact of the U.S.
Department of Agriculture's 1928 Sugarcane Expedition to New Guinea. In
Expeditions, Anthropology and Popular Culture: Reinventing First Contact
(1914–1939). J. A. Bell, A. Brown, and R. J. Gordon, eds. Lanham, MD:
Rowman and Littlefield.

Bell, Joshua A., and Haidy Geismar

2009   Materializing Oceania: New Ethnographies of Things in Melanesia and
Polynesia. Australian Journal of Anthropology 20(1):3–27.

Benavides, O. Hugo

2009   Translating Ecuadorian Modernities: Pre-Hispanic Archaeology and the
Reproduction of Global Difference. In Cosmopolitan Archaeologies. Lynn
Meskell, ed. Pp. 228–248. Durham, NC: Duke University Press.

Bender, Barbara, ed.

1993   Landscape: Politics and Perspectives. Oxford: Berg.

Benedict, Ruth

1934   Patterns of Culture. New York: Houghton Mifflin.

Bennett, Jane

2010   Vibrant Matter: A Political Ecology of Things. Durham, NC: Duke University
Press.

Bennett, Tony

1995   The Birth of the Museum: History, Theory, Politics. London: Routledge.

1998   Culture: A Reformer's Science. London: Sage.

2004   Pasts beyond Memory: Evolution, Museums, Colonisation. London:
Routledge.

2005   Museums as Civic Laboratories. Cultural Studies 19(5):521–547.

2006   Exhibition, Difference and the Logic of Culture. In Museum Frictions:

Public Cultures/Global Transformations. Ivan Karp, Corinne A. Kratz, Lynn Szwaja, and Tomás Ybarra-Frausto, eds. Pp. 46–69. Durham, NC: Duke University Press.

2009   Museum, Field, Colony: Colonial Governmentality and the Circulation of Reference. Journal of Cultural Economy 2(1–2):99–116.

2010   Making and Mobilising Worlds: Assembling and Governing the Other. *In* Material Powers: Cultural Studies, History and the Material Turn. Tony Bennett and Patrick Joyce, eds. Pp. 188–208. London: Routledge.

2011a   Civic Seeing: Museums and the Organization of Vision. *In* A Companion to Museum Studies. Sharon Macdonald, ed. Pp. 261–281. Malden, MA: Wiley-Blackwell.

2011b   Habit, Instinct, Survivals: Repetition, History, Biopolitics. *In* The Peculiarities of Liberal Modernity in Imperial Britain. Simon Gunn and James Vernon, eds. Pp. 102–118. Berkeley: University of California Press.

Berger, John, and Jean Mohr
1982   Another Way of Telling. New York: Pantheon.

Best, Elsdon
2005[1925] The Maori Canoe. Wellington, New Zealand: Te Papa Press.

Béteille, André
1998   The Idea of Indigenous People. Current Anthropology 39(2):187–191.

Bianchi, Fred A.
1977   Cyril Eugene Pemberton, 1886–1975: A Biographical Sketch. Proceedings of Hawaii Entomological Society 22(3):417–441.

Binford, Lewis
1962   Archaeology as Anthropology. American Antiquity 28(2):217–225.

1973   Interassemblage Variability: The Mousterian and the "Functional" Argument. *In* The Explanation of Culture Change: Models in Prehistory. Colin Renfrew, ed. Pp. 227–254. London: Duckworth.

1982   The Archaeology of Place. Journal of Anthropological Archaeology 1(1):5–31.

Boas, Franz
1887   Museums of Ethnology and Their Classification. Science 9:587–589.

1940   Race, Language and Culture. New York: Macmillan.

Boast, Robin
2011   Neocolonial Collaboration: Museum as Contact Zone Revisited. Museum Anthropology 34(1):56–70.

Bolton, Lissant
2001   Classifying the Material: Food, Textiles and Status in North Vanuatu. Journal of Material Culture 6(3):251–268.

2003   The Object in View: Aborigines, Melanesians and Museums. *In* Museums and Source Communities: A Routledge Reader. Laura Peers and Alison K. Brown, eds. Pp. 42–54. London: Routledge.

REFERENCES

Bonshek, Elizabeth
2009   A Personal Narrative of Particular Things: Tevau (Feather Money)
        from Santa Cruz, Solomon Islands. Australian Journal of Anthropology
        20(1):74–92.

Bouquet, Mary
2001   Introduction. *In* Academic Anthropology and the Museum: Back to the
        Future. Mary Bouquet, ed. Pp. 1–17. Oxford: Berghahn.

Bowker, Geoffrey C.
2005   Memory Practices in the Sciences. Cambridge, MA: MIT Press.

Bradley, Phillip
2010   To Salamaua. Cambridge: Cambridge University Press.

Bragge, Lawrence, Ulrike Claas, and Paul Roscoe
2006   On the Edge of Empire: Military Brokers in the Sepik "Tribal Zone."
        American Ethnologist 33(1):100–113.

Brandes, E. W.
1929   Into Primeval Papua by Seaplane: Seeking Disease-Resisting Sugar
        Cane, Scientists Find Neolithic Man in Unmapped Nooks of Sorcery and
        Cannibalism. National Geographic 56(3):253–332.

Brandes, E. W., and G. B. Sartoris
1936   Sugar Cane: Its Origin and Improvement. *In* United States Department of
        Agriculture Yearbook. Pp. 561–623. Washington, DC: Government Printing
        Office.

Brown, Alison, Jeremy Coote, and Chris Gosden
2000   Tylor's Tongue: Material Culture, Evidence, and Social Networks. Journal of
        the Anthropological Society of Oxford 31(3):257–276.

Brown, Alison, and Laura Peers, eds.
2003   Museums and Source Communities: A Routledge Reader. London:
        Routledge.

Buber, Martin
1958   I and Thou. New York: Scribner.

Buchli, Victor
2002   Introduction. *In* The Material Culture Reader. Victor Buchli, ed. Pp. 1–22.
        Oxford: Berg.

Burston, Roy
1913   Records of the Anthropometric Measurements of One Hundred and Two
        Australian Aborigines. Bulletin of the Northern Territory, no. 7:2–15.

Burton, John
1985   Axe Makers of the Wahgi: Pre-colonial Industrialists of the Papua New
        Guinea Highlands. PhD dissertation, Australian National University.

Buschmann, Rainer F.
2009   Anthropology's Global Histories: The Ethnographic Frontier in German

New Guinea, 1870–1935. Honolulu: University of Hawaii Press.

Busse, Mark W.

1987   Sister Exchange among the Wamek of the Middle Fly. PhD thesis, University of California, San Diego.

Butts, David

2002   Maori and Museums: The Politics of Indigenous Recognition. *In* Museums, Society, Inequality. Richard Sandell, ed. Pp. 225–243. London: Routledge.

Byrne, Denis

1991   Western Hegemony in Archaeological Heritage Management. History and Anthropology 5:269–276.

1995   Buddhist Stupa and Thai Social Practice. World Archaeology 27(2):266–281.

1996   Deep Nation: Australia's Acquisition of an Indigenous Past. Aboriginal History 20:82–107.

2003   The Ethos of Return: Erasure and Reinstatement of Aboriginal Visibility in the Australian Historical Landscape. Historical Archaeology 37(1):73–86.

2008   Heritage as Social Action. *In* The Heritage Reader. Graham Fairclough, Rodney Harrison, John H. Jameson Jr., and John Schofield, eds. Pp. 149–173. New York: Routledge.

2009   Archaeology and the Fortress of Rationality. *In* Cosmopolitan Archaeologies. Lynn Meskell, ed. Pp. 68–88. Durham, NC: Duke University Press.

Byrne, Sarah

2011   Trials and Traces: A. C. Haddon's Agency as Museum Curator. *In* Unpacking the Collection: Networks of Material and Social Agency in the Museum. Sarah Byrne, Anne Clarke, Rodney Harrison, and Robin Torrence, eds. Pp. 306–325. New York: Springer.

Byrne, Sarah, Anne Clarke, Rodney Harrison, and Robin Torrence

2011a   Networks, Agents and Objects: Frameworks for Unpacking Museum Collections. *In* Unpacking the Collection: Networks of Material and Social Agency in the Museum. Sarah Byrne, Anne Clarke, Rodney Harrison, and Robin Torrence, eds. Pp. 3–26. New York: Springer.

Byrne, Sarah, Anne Clarke, Rodney Harrison, and Robin Torrence, eds.

2011b   Unpacking the Collection: Networks of Material and Social Agency in the Museum. New York: Springer.

Callon, Michel

2005   Why Virtualism Paves the Way to Political Impotence: A Reply to Daniel Miller's Critique of "The Laws of the Markets." Economic Sociology: European Electronic Newsletter 6(2):3–20.

Calma, Graeme, and Lynette Liddle

2003   Uluru-Kata Tjuta National Park: Sustainable Management and Development. *In* Cultural Landscapes: The Challenges of Conservation. UNESCO World Heritage Centre, ed. Pp. 104–119. Paris: UNESCO World Heritage Centre.

REFERENCES

Cameron, Duncan F.
1971   The Museum: A Temple or the Forum. Curator 16(1):11–24.

Cameron, Fiona
2010   Liquid Governmentalities, Liquid Museums and the Climate Crisis. *In* Hot Topics, Public Culture, Museums. Fiona Cameron and Lynda Kelly, eds. Pp. 112–128. Newcastle: Cambridge Scholars.
2011a   From Mitigation to Creativity: The Agency of Museums and Science Centres and the Means to Govern Climate Change. Museum and Society 9(2):84–89.
2011b   Guest Editorial: Climate Change as a Complex Phenomenon and the Problem of Cultural Governance. Museum and Society 9(2):90–106.

Campbell, Joseph
2010[1988] Joseph Campbell and the Powers of Myth, with Bill Moyers. Part 3: The First Storytellers. Mystic Fire Video.

Chaat Smith, Paul
2008   Critical Perspectives on the Our Peoples Exhibit: A Curator's Perspective. *In* The National Museum of the American Indian: Critical Conversations. Amy Lonetree and Amanda J. Cobb, eds. Pp. 131–143. Lincoln: University of Nebraska Press.

Chakrabarty, Dipesh
2000   Provincializing Europe: Postcolonial Thought and Historical Difference. Princeton, NJ: Princeton University Press.

Chalmers, James
1886   Adventures in New Guinea. London: London Religious Tract Society.

Champion, Ivan
1932   Across New Guinea from the Fly to the Sepik. London: Constable.

Chapman, William
1985   Arranging Ethnology. *In* Objects and Others: Essays on Museums and Material Culture. George Stocking, ed. Pp. 15–49. Madison: University of Wisconsin Press.

Charley, Karen Kahe, and Lea S. McChesney
2007   Form and Meaning in Indigenous Aesthetics: A Hopi Pottery Perspective. American Indian Art 32(4):84–91.

Chavez Lamar, Cynthia
2008   Collaborative Exhibit Development at the Smithsonian's National Museum of the American Indian. *In* The National Museum of the American Indian: Critical Conversations. Amy Lonetree and Amanda J. Cobb, eds. Pp. 144–164. Lincoln: University of Nebraska Press.

Clarke, Anne, and Robin Torrence
2011   Archaeology and the Collection: Tracing Material Relationships in Colonial Papua from 1875 to 1925. Journal of Australian Studies 35(4):433–448.

2012   "Decorated in Red, Black and White": Papuan "Curiosities" and the
        Identification of Cross-Cultural Interaction in Sale and Auction Catalogues.
        Paper presented at the Art/Artifact/Commodity Symposium, Buffalo
        Science Museum, 7–8 January.

Clavir, Miriam
2002   Preserving What Is Valued: Museums, Conservation, and First Nations.
        Vancouver: University of British Columbia Press.

Cleere, Henry
2001   The Uneasy Bedfellows: Universality and Cultural Heritage. *In* Destruction
        and Conservation of Cultural Property. Robert Layton, Julian Thomas, and
        Peter G. Stone, eds. Pp. 22–29. London: Routledge.

Clifford, James
1988   The Predicament of Culture: Twentieth-Century Ethnography, Literature,
        and Art. Cambridge, MA: Harvard University Press.
1995   Paradise. Visual Anthropology Review 11(1):97–117.
1997   Routes: Travel and Translation in the Late Twentieth Century. Cambridge,
        MA: Harvard University Press.
2001   Indigenous Articulations. Contemporary Pacific 13(2):468–490.
2004   Looking Several Ways: Anthropology and Native Heritage in Alaska. Current
        Anthropology 45(1):5–30.

Collingwood, R. G.
1946   The Idea of History. Oxford: Clarendon.

Colwell-Chanthaphonh, Chip
2010   The Problem of Collaboration? Reflections on Engagements of Inclusivity,
        Reciprocity, and Democracy in Museum Anthropology. Western Humanities
        Review 64(3):49–63.

Colwell-Chanthaphonh, Chip, and T. J. Ferguson
2006   Memory Pieces and Footprints: Multivocality and the Meanings of
        Ancient Times and Ancestral Places among the Zuni and Hopi. American
        Anthropologist 108(1):148–162.

Conklin, Alice C.
2002a   Civil Society, Science, and Empire in Late Republican France: The
        Foundation of Paris's Museum of Man. Osiris 17:255–290.
2002b   The New "Ethnology" and "la Situation Coloniale" in Interwar France.
        French Politics, Culture and Society 20(2):29–46.
2008   Skulls on Display: The Science of Race in Paris's Musée de l'Homme,
        1928–1950. *In* Museums and Difference. Daniel J. Sherman, ed. Pp. 250–288.
        Bloomington: Indiana University Press.

Conn, Steven
1998   Museums and American Intellectual Life, 1876–1926. Chicago: University of
        Chicago Press.

REFERENCES

Coombes, Annie E.

1994   Reinventing Africa: Museums, Material Culture and Popular Imagination in Late Victorian and Edwardian England. New Haven, CT: Yale University Press.

Coombes, Annie E., ed.

2006   Rethinking Settler Colonialism: History and Memory in Australia, Canada, Aotearoa New Zealand and South Africa. Manchester, England: Manchester University Press.

Cooper, Karen

2008   Spirited Encounters: American Indians Protest Museum Policies and Practices. Lanham, MD: AltaMira.

Cooper, Wiremu

1989   Taonga Maori: Treasures of the New Zealand Maori People. Canberra: Australian Museum.

Cramer, P. J. S.

1952   Sugar-Cane Breeding in Java. Economic Botany 6(2):143–150.

Cranstone, Brian A. L.

1961   Melanesia: A Short Ethnography. London: British Museum.

Crooke, Elizabeth M.

2007   Museums and Community: Ideas, Issues and Challenges. London: Routledge.

Cruikshank, Julie

1995   Imperfect Translations: Rethinking Objects of Ethnographic Collection. Museum Anthropology 19(1):25–38.

Cuno, James

2008   Who Owns Antiquity?: Museums and the Battle over Our Ancient Heritage. Princeton, NJ: Princeton University Press.

Cushing, Frank Hamilton

1892   Manual Concepts: A Study of the Influence of Hand-Usage on Culture-Growth. American Anthropologist 5(4):289–318.

Danto, Arthur C.

1988   Artifact and Art. *In* ART/ARTIFACT: African Art in Anthropology Collections. Susan Vogel, ed. Pp. 8–32. New York: Center for African Art.

Daru

1927a   Patrol Report 3. A.R.M. Wm. J. Lambden. 17 August—22 September.

1927b   Patrol Report 4. A.R.M. Wm. J. Lambden. 22 September—17 October.

Darvill, Timothy, ed.

2008   Concise Oxford Dictionary of Archaeology. Oxford: Oxford University Press.

Dauncey, Harry M.

1913   Papuan Pictures. London: London Missionary Society.

Davies, Susan
2011   A Passing Trade: Papuans Trading Indigenous Artifacts with Europeans in South-West Papua New Guinea during the 1800s. *In* Unpacking the Collection: Networks of Material and Social Agency in the Museum. Sarah Byrne, Anne Clarke, Rodney Harrison, and Robin Torrence, eds. Pp. 83–115. New York: Springer.

Davis, Peter
1999   Ecomuseums: A Sense of Place. Leicester, England: Leicester University Press.

Davison, Patricia
2005   Museums and the Re-shaping of Memory. *In* Heritage, Museums and Galleries: An Introductory Reader. Gerard Corsane, ed. Pp. 184–194. London: Routledge.

Deacon, Harriet, with Luvuyo Dondolo, Mbulelo Mrubata, and Sandra Prosalendis
2004   The Subtle Power of Intangible Heritage: Legal and Financial Instruments for Safeguarding Intangible Heritage. Capetown: HSRC Press.

Debaene, Vincent
2010   L'adieu au voyage: L'ethnologie française entre science et littérature. Paris: Gallimard.

Defert, Daniel
1982   A Collection of the World: Accounts of Voyages from the Sixteenth to the Eighteenth Centuries. Dialectical Anthropology 7(1):11–20.

de la Cadena, Marisol, and Orin Starn, eds.
2007   Indigenous Experience Today. Oxford: Berg.

De Landa, Manuel
1997   A Thousand Years of Nonlinear History. New York: Zone / Swerve.
1998   Meshworks, Hierarchies and Interfaces. *In* The Virtual Dimension: Architecture, Representation, and Crash Culture. John Beckman, ed. Pp. 274–285. Princeton, NJ: Princeton Architectural Press.
2006a   A New Philosophy of Society: Assemblage Theory and Social Complexity. London: Continuum.
2006b   Real Virtuality: Meshworks and Hierarchies in the Digital Domain. Rotterdam: Netherlands Architecture Institute.

Deleuze, Gilles
2006[1988] Foucault. London: Continuum.

Deleuze, Gilles, and Félix Guattari
2004[1987] A Thousand Plateaus: Capitalism and Schizophrenia. London: Continuum.

Deloria, Vine, Jr.
1969   Custer Died for Your Sins: An Indian Manifesto. New York: Macmillan.

REFERENCES

Delugan, Robin Maria

2010   Indigeneity across Borders: Hemispheric Migrations and Cosmopolitan Encounters. American Ethnologist 37(1):83–97.

Dening, Greg

1996   Performances. Chicago: University of Chicago Press.

Dias, Nélia

1991   Le Musée d'Ethnographie du Trocadéro (1878–1908): Anthropologie et muséologie en France. Paris: Éditions du Centre National de la Recherche Scientifique.

1998   The Visibility of Difference: Nineteenth-Century French Anthropological Collections. In The Politics of Display: Museums, Science, Culture. Sharon Macdonald, ed. Pp. 36–52. London: Routledge.

2004   La mesure des sens: Les anthropologues et le corps humain au XIXe siècle. Paris: Aubier.

2008   Cultural Difference and Cultural Diversity: The Case of the Musée du Quai Branly. In Museums and Difference. Daniel Sherman, ed. Pp. 124–154. Bloomington: Indiana University Press.

Dibley, Ben

2005   The Museum's Redemption: Contact Zones, Government and the Limits of Reform. International Journal of Cultural Studies 8(1):5–27.

2011   Museums and a Common World: Climate Change, Cosmopolitics, Museum Practice. Museum and Society 9(2):154–165.

Dixon, Keith A.

1956   Hidden House: A Cliff Ruin in Sycamore Canyon, Central Arizona. Museum of Northern Arizona Bulletin 29.

Dobres, Marcia-Anne, and John Robb, eds.

2000   Agency in Archaeology. London: Routledge.

Douglas, Bronwen

1998   Across the Great Divide: Journeys in History and Anthropology. Amsterdam: Harwood Academic.

Douglas, Mary

1992   Risk and Blame: Essays in Cultural Theory. London: Routledge.

2010[1966] Purity and Danger: An Analysis of Concepts of Pollution and Taboo. London: Routledge and Kegan Paul.

Duclos, Rebecca

2004   The Cartographies of Collecting. In Museums and the Future of Collecting. 2nd edition. Simon J. Knell, ed. Pp. 84–101. Aldershot, England: Ashgate.

Dudley, Sandra

2010   Museum Materialities: Objects, Sense and Feeling. In Museum Materialities: Objects, Engagements, Interpretations. Sandra Dudley, ed. Pp. 1–18. London: Routledge.

Duncan, Carol
1995   Civilizing Rituals: Inside Public Art Museums. London: Routledge.

Dutton, Thomas, ed.
1982   The Hiri in History. Canberra: Australian National University.

Edelfeld, E. G.
1887   Travels in the Neighbourhood of Mount Yule. *In* Picturesque New Guinea. J. W. Lindt, ed. Pp. 125–134. London: Longmans, Green.

Edge-Partington, James
1915   Fishing Appliance from Ysabel Island (Bugotu). Man 84–85:145.
1996[1890–1898]   An Album of the Weapons, Tools, Ornaments, Articles of Dress of the Natives of the Pacific Islands. 2nd edition. Bangkok: SDI.

Edgeworth, Matt, ed.
2006   Ethnographies of Archaeological Practice: Cultural Encounters, Material Transformations. Lanham, MD: AltaMira.

Edinburgh Evening News
2008   Museum Set to Welcome a Masterpiece of Ancient War, 5 September.
2009   Edinburgh Art Centre Hosts Maori Artist, 24 October.

Edwards, Elizabeth
2001   Raw Histories: Photographs, Anthropology and Museums. Oxford: Berg.
2005   Photographs and the Sounds of History. Visual Anthropology Review 21(1–2):27–46.

Edwards, Elizabeth, Chris Gosden, and Ruth B. Phillips, eds.
2006   Sensible Objects: Colonialism, Museums and Material Culture. Oxford: Berg.

Elsner, Jas, and Roger Cardinal
1994   Introduction. *In* The Cultures of Collecting. Jas Elsner and Roger Cardinal, eds. Pp. 1–6. London: Reaktion.

English, Anthony
2003   The Sea and the Rock Give Us a Feed: Mapping and Managing Gumbaingirr Wild Resource Places. Hurstville: New South Wales National Parks and Wildlife Service.

Enote, Jim
2009   Easton Collection Center Dedication: Remarks. Museum of Northern Arizona Notes (Summer):3.

Ewers, John C.
1959   A Century of American Indian Exhibits in the Smithsonian Institution. Annual Report of the Board of Regents of the Smithsonian Institution 1958. Pp. 520–522. Washington, DC: Government Printing Office.

Fabian, Johannes
1983   Time and the Other: How Anthropology Makes Its Object. New York: Columbia University Press.

REFERENCES

2000   Out of Our Minds: Reason and Madness in the Exploration of Central Africa. Berkeley: University of California Press.

Fardon, Richard

2005   Tiger in an Africa Palace. *In* The Qualities of Time: Anthropological Approaches. W. James and D. Mills, eds. Pp. 73–93. Oxford: Berg.

Feldman, Alice

2002   Making Space at the Nations' Table: Mapping the Transformative Geographies of the International Indigenous Peoples' Movement. Social Movement Studies 1(1):147–178.

Ferguson, T. J., Roger Anyon, and Edmund J. Ladd

1996   Repatriation at the Pueblo of Zuni: Diverse Solutions to Complex Problems. American Indian Quarterly 20(2):251–273.

Ferguson, T. J., Kurt E. Dongoske, and Leigh J. Kuwanwisiwma

2001   Hopi Perspectives on Southwestern Mortuary Studies. *In* Ancient Burial Practices in the American Southwest: Archaeology, Physical Anthropology, and Native American Perspectives. Douglas R. Mitchell and Judy L. Brunson-Hadley, eds. Pp. 9–26. Albuquerque: University of New Mexico Press.

Fforde, Cressida, Jane Hubert, and Paul Turnbull, eds.

2002   The Dead and Their Possessions: Repatriation in Principle, Policy and Practice. London: Routledge.

Finley, Carol

1999   The Art of African Masks: Exploring Cultural Traditions. Minneapolis, MN: Lerner.

Flood, Milton J.

1902   Letter sent to Robert Etheridge Jr., Curator, 15 January 1902. Australian Museum Archives F24/1902.

Flynn, Gillian A., and Lynn Snyder

2002   Research Files, Exhibit Halls, Museum Support Center. Washington, DC: National Museum of Natural History.

Foucault, Michel

1986   Of Other Spaces. Diacritics 16(1):22–27.

2002[1972] The Archaeology of Knowledge. London: Routledge.

2007   Security, Territory, Population: Lectures at the Collège de France, 1977–1978. New York: Picador.

2011   The Government of Self and Others: Lectures at the Collège de France, 1982–1983. New York: Picador.

Fournier, Marcel

2006   Marcel Mauss: A Biography. Princeton, NJ: Princeton University Press.

Fouseki, Kalliopi

2010   "Community Voices, Curatorial Choices": Community Consultation for the 1807 Exhibitions. Museum and Society 8(3):180–192.

Fowler, Peter

2003   World Heritage Cultural Landscapes 1992–2002. Paris: UNESCO World Heritage Centre.

2004   Landscapes for the World: Conserving a Global Heritage. Bollington, England: Windgather Press.

Francioni, Francesco, ed.

2008   The 1972 World Heritage Convention: A Commentary. Oxford: Oxford University Press.

Frey, Bruno S., and Stephan Meier

2011   Cultural Economics. In A Companion to Museum Studies. Sharon Macdonald, ed. Pp. 398–414. Malden, MA: Wiley-Blackwell.

Galloway, J. H.

2005   The Modernization of Sugar Production in Southeast Asia, 1880–1940. Geographic Review 95(1):1–23.

Gammage, Bill

1998   The Sky Travellers: Journeys in New Guinea 1938–1939. Melbourne: Miegunyah Press / Melbourne University Press.

Gascoigne, John

1996   The Ordering of Nature and the Ordering of Empire: A Commentary. In Visions of Empire: Voyages, Botany, and the Representations of Nature. David Philip Miller and Peter Hans Reill, eds. Pp. 107–116. Cambridge: Cambridge University Press.

Gell, Alfred

1992   The Technology of Enchantment and the Enchantment of Technology. In Anthropology, Art and Aesthetics. J. Coote and A. Shelton, eds. Pp. 40–66. Oxford: Oxford University Press.

1998   Art and Agency: An Anthropological Theory. Oxford: Clarendon.

Gewertz, Deborah B.

1983   Sepik River Societies: A Historical Ethnography of the Chambri and Their Neighbors. New Haven, CT: Yale University Press.

Giddens, Anthony

1990   The Consequences of Modernity. Cambridge: Polity.

Ginzburg, Carlo

1980   Morelli, Freud and Sherlock Holmes: Clues and the Scientific Method. History Workshop 9:5–36.

Glass, Aaron

2009   Frozen Poses: Hamat'sa Dioramas, Recursive Representation, and the Making of a Kwakwaka'wakw Icon. In Photography, Anthropology and History. Christopher Morton and Elizabeth Edwards, eds. Pp. 89–118. London: Ashgate.

REFERENCES

Godwin, Mike

1994 Meme, Counter-Meme. Wired 2(10)(October). http://www.wired.com
/wired/archive/2.10/godwin.if.html, accessed 1 June 2011.

Gonzalez-Ruibal, Alfredo

2009 Vernacular Cosmopolitanism: An Archaeological Critique of Universalistic
Reason. *In* Cosmopolitan Archaeologies. Lynn Meskell, ed. Pp. 113–139.
Durham, NC: Duke University Press.

Gorgus, Nina

2003 Le magician des vitrines: Le muséologue Georges Henri Rivière. Paris:
Éditions de la Maison des Sciences de l'Homme.

Gosden, Chris

1999 Anthropology and Archaeology: A Changing Relationship. London:
Routledge.

2004 Making and Display: Our Aesthetic Appreciation of Things and Objects. *In*
Substance, Memory, Display: Archaeology and Art. C. Renfrew, C. Gosden,
and E. DeMarrais, eds. Pp. 35–45. Cambridge: McDonald Institute for
Archaeological Research.

2005 What Do Objects Want? Journal of Archaeological Method and Theory
12:193–211.

Gosden, Chris, and Chantal Knowles

2001 Collecting Colonialism: Material Culture and Colonial Change. Oxford: Berg.

Gosden, Chris, and Frances Larson, with Alison Petch

2007 Knowing Things: Exploring the Collections at the Pitt Rivers Museum
1884–1945. Oxford: Oxford University Press.

Graburn, Nelson H. H.

1976 Introduction. *In* Ethnic and Tourist Arts: Cultural Expressions from the
Fourth World. Nelson H. Graburn, ed. Pp. 1–32. Berkeley: University of
California Press.

1999 Epilogue: Ethnic and Tourist Arts Revisited. *In* Unpacking Culture: Art
and Commodity in Colonial and Postcolonial Worlds. Ruth B. Phillips and
Christopher B. Steiner, eds. Pp. 335–354. Berkeley: University of California
Press.

Gray, Geoffrey

2007 A Cautious Silence: The Politics of Australian Anthropology. Canberra:
Aboriginal Studies Press.

Greenfield, Jeannette

1996 The Return of Cultural Treasures. 2nd edition. Cambridge: Cambridge
University Press.

Greenhalgh, Paul

1988 Ephemeral Vistas: The Expositions Universelles, Great Exhibitions and
World's Fairs, 1851–1939. Manchester, England: Manchester University Press.

Gressitt, Linsley J.
1971   Chrysomelid Beetles from the Papuan Subregion, 7 (Donaciinae). Pacific Insects 13(3–4):607–609.

Griffiths, Tom
1996   Hunters and Collectors: The Antiquarian Imagination in Australia. Melbourne: Cambridge University Press.

Groves, Murray
2011   The Motu of Papua: Tradition in a Time of Change. Vancouver: Webzines.

Haber, Alejandro F.
2009   Animism, Relatedness, Life: Post-Western Perspectives. Cambridge Archaeological Journal 19(3):418–430.

Haddon, Alfred Cort
1901   Head-Hunters: Black, White, and Brown. London: Methuen.
1937   The Canoes of Melanesia, Queensland, and New Guinea. Honolulu: Bernice P. Bishop Museum.
1946   Smoking and Tobacco Pipes in New Guinea. Philosophical Transactions of the Royal Society of London, series B. Biological Sciences 232(586).

Hall, Stuart
1986   On Postmodernism and Articulation: An Interview with Stuart Hall. Journal of Communication Inquiry 10(2):45–60.

Hall, Stuart, ed.
1997   Representation: Cultural Representations and Signifying Practices. London: Sage.

Hamilton, Augustus
1896   The Art Workmanship of the Maori Race in New Zealand. Dunedin: Fergusson and Mitchell.

Handler, Richard
1992   On the Valuing of Museum Objects. Museum Anthropology 16(1):21–28.

Haraway, Donna
2008   When Species Meet. Minneapolis: University of Minnesota Press.

Harrison, David, and Michael Hitchcock
2005   The Politics of World Heritage: Negotiating Heritage and Conservation. Clevedon, England: Channel View.

Harrison, Rodney
2002   Archaeology and the Colonial Encounter: Kimberley Spearpoints, Cultural Identity and Masculinity in the North of Australia. Journal of Social Archaeology 2(3):352–377.
2004a   Kimberley Points and Colonial Preference: New Insights into the Chronology of Pressure Flaked Point Forms from the Southeast Kimberley, Western Australia. Archaeology in Oceania 39(1):1–11.
2004b   Shared Landscapes: Archaeologies of Attachment and the Pastoral Industry in New South Wales. Sydney: University of New South Wales Press.

REFERENCES

2006   An Artefact of Colonial Desire?: Kimberley Points and the Technologies of Enchantment. Current Anthropology 47(1):63–88.

2010a   Stone Artefacts. *In* The Oxford Handbook of Material Culture Studies. Dan Hicks and Mary Beaudry, eds. Pp. 515–536. Oxford: Oxford University Press.

2010b   What Is Heritage? *In* Understanding the Politics of Heritage. Rodney Harrison, ed. Pp. 5–42. Manchester, England: Manchester University Press; Milton Keynes, England: Open University.

2011a   Consuming Colonialism: Curio-Seller's Catalogues, Souvenir Objects and Indigenous Agency in Oceania. *In* Unpacking the Collection: Networks of Material and Social Agency in the Museum. Sarah Byrne, Anne Clarke, Rodney Harrison, and Robin Torrence, eds. Pp. 55–82. New York: Springer.

2011b   Surface Assemblages: Towards an Archaeology *in* and *of* the Present. Archaeological Dialogues 18(2):141–161.

2012   Heritage: Critical Approaches. New York: Routledge.

Harrison, Rodney, and Deborah Bird Rose

2010   Intangible Heritage. *In* Understanding Heritage and Memory. Tim Benton, ed. Pp. 238–276. Manchester, England: Manchester University Press; Milton Keynes, England: Open University.

Harrison, Simon

1989   Magical and Material Polities in Melanesia. Man, n.s., 24(1):1–20.

Harvey, Graham

2005   Animism: Respecting the Living World. London: Hurst.

Hays-Gilpin, Kelley

2011   Crafting Hopi Identities at the Museum of Northern Arizona. *In* Unpacking the Collection: Networks of Material and Social Agency in the Museum. Sarah Byrne, Anne Clark, Rodney Harrison, and Robin Torrence, eds. Pp. 185–208. New York: Springer.

Healy, Chris

2008   Forgetting Aborigines. Sydney: University of New South Wales Press.

Healy, Chris, and Andrea Witcomb, eds.

2006   South Pacific Museums: Experiments in Culture. Clayton, Victoria: Monash University ePress.

Heidegger, Martin

1962   Being and Time. Oxford: Blackwell.

Henare, Amiria

2005   Museums, Anthropology and Imperial Exchange. Cambridge: Cambridge University Press.

Henare, Amiria, Martin Holbraad, and Sarah Wastell

2007   Introduction: Thinking through Things. *In* Thinking through Things: Theorising Artefacts Ethnographically. Amiria Henare, Martin Holbraad, and Sarah Wastell, eds. Pp. 1–31. London: Routledge.

Henry, James Pepper

2004   Challenges in Managing Culturally Sensitive Collections at the National Museum of the American Indian. *In* Stewards of the Sacred. Lawrence E. Sullivan and Alison Edwards, eds. Pp. 105–112. Washington, DC: American Association of Museums.

Herle, Anita

1998   The Life Histories of Objects: Collections of the Cambridge Anthropological Expedition to the Torres Strait. *In* Cambridge and the Torres Strait: Centenary Essays on the 1898 Anthropological Expedition. Anita Herle and Sandra Rouse, eds. Pp. 77–105. Cambridge: Cambridge University Press.

2002   Objects, Agency and Museums: Continuing Dialogues between the Torres Straits and Cambridge. *In* Pacific Art: Persistence, Change and Meaning. Anita Herle, Nick Stanley, Karen Stevenson, and Robert L. Welsch, eds. Pp. 231–250. Honolulu: University of Hawaii Press.

Herle, Anita, and Sandra Rouse, eds.

1998   Cambridge and the Torres Strait: Centenary Essays on the 1898 Anthropological Expedition. Cambridge: Cambridge University Press.

Herzog, Iris Hahner, Maria Kecskesi, and Laszlo Vajda

1998   African Masks from the Barbier-Mueller Collection, Geneva. New York: Prestel.

Hetherington, Kevin

2002   The Unsightly: Touching the Parthenon Frieze. Theory, Culture and Society 19(5–6):187–205.

2008   The Time of the Entrepreneurial City: Museum, Heritage and Kairos. *In* Consuming the Entrepreneurial City: Image, Memory, Spectacle. Anne M. Cronin and Kevin Hetherington, eds. Pp. 273–294. New York: Routledge.

Hicks, Dan

2010   The Material-Cultural Turn: Event and Effect. *In* The Oxford Handbook of Material Culture Studies. Dan Hicks and Mary C. Beaudry, eds. Pp. 25–98. Oxford: Oxford University Press.

Hicks, Dan, and Mary C. Beaudry, eds.

2010   The Oxford Handbook of Material Culture Studies. Oxford: Oxford University Press.

Hill, Jude

2006   Travelling Objects: The Wellcome Collection in Los Angeles, London and Beyond. Cultural Geographies 13:340–366.

2007   The Story of the Amulet. Journal of Material Culture 12(1):65–87.

Hinsley, Curtis M., Jr.

1981a   Savages and Scientists: The Smithsonian Institution and the Development of American Anthropology, 1846–1910. Washington, DC: Smithsonian Institution Press.

1981b   The Smithsonian and the American Indian: Making a Moral Anthropology in Victorian America. Washington, DC: Smithsonian Institution Press.

REFERENCES

Hinsley, Curtis, and Bill Holm

1976   A Cannibal in the National Museum: The Early Career of Franz Boas in America. American Anthropologist 78:306–316.

Hodder, Ian

1979   Economic and Social Stress and Material Culture Patterning. American Antiquity 44(3):446–454.

Hoerig, Karl A.

2010   From Third Person to First: A Call for Reciprocity among Non-Native and Native Museums. Museum Anthropology 33(1):62–74.

Hoffenberg, Peter

2001   An Empire on Display: English, Indian, and Australian Exhibitions from the Crystal Palace to the Great War. Berkeley: University of California Press.

Hooper, Steven

2007   Embodying Divinity: The Life of A'a. Journal of the Polynesia Society 116(2):131–179.

Hooper-Greenhill, Eileen

2000   Museums and the Interpretation of Visual Culture. London: Routledge.

Hope, Penelope

1979   Long Ago Is Far Away: Accounts of the Early Exploration and Settlement of the Papuan Gulf Area. Canberra: Australian National University Press.

Hopwood, Nick, Simon Schaffer, and Jim Secord, eds.

2010   Seriality and Scientific Objects in the Nineteenth Century. History of Science 46(3–4).

Hoskins, Janet

2006[1998] Biographical Objects: How Things Tell the Stories of People's Lives. London: Routledge.

Howe, Kerry, ed.

2007   VakaMoana, Voyages of the Ancestors: The Discovery and Settlement of the Pacific. Honolulu: University of Hawaii Press.

Hughes, Ian

1977   New Guinea Stone Age Trade: The Geography and Ecology of Traffic in the Interior. Canberra: Research School of Pacific Studies, Australian National University.

1978   Good Money and Bad: Inflation and Devaluation in the Colonial Process. Mankind 11(3):308–318.

Humphrey, Carolyn, and Stephen Hugh-Jones

1992   Introduction: Barter, Exchange and Value. In Barter, Exchange and Value: An Anthropological Approach. Carolyn Humphrey and Stephen Hugh-Jones, eds. Pp. 1–20. Cambridge: Cambridge University Press.

Hutchins, Edwin

1995   Cognition in the Wild. Cambridge, MA: MIT Press.

Ingold, Tim
1992   Editorial. Man 27(4):693–696.
2000   The Perception of the Environment: Essays in Livelihood, Dwelling, and Skill. London: Routledge.
2006   Rethinking the Animate, Re-animating Thought. Ethnos 71(1):9–20.
2007a   Lines: A Brief History. London: Routledge.
2007b   Materials against Materiality. Archaeological Dialogues 14(1):1–16.
2008a   Anthropology Is *Not* Ethnography. British Academy Review 11:21–23.
2008b   When ANT Meets SPIDER: Social Theory for Arthropods. *In* Material Agency: Towards a Non-anthropocentric Approach. Carl Knappett and Lambros Malafouris, eds. Pp. 209–216. New York: Springer.
2011   Being Alive: Essays on Movement, Knowledge and Description. London: Routledge.

Irwin, Geoffrey
1985   The Emergence of Mailu. Canberra: Research School of Pacific Studies, Australian National University.

Isaac, Gwyneira
2005   Re-observation and the Recognition of Change: The Photographs of Matilda Coxe Stevenson (1879–1915). Journal of the Southwest 47(3):411–455.
2007   Mediating Knowledges: Origins of a Zuni Tribal Museum. Tucson: University of Arizona Press.
2009   Responsibilities towards Knowledge: The Zuni Museum and the Reconciling of Different Knowledge Systems. *In* Contesting Knowledge: Museums and Indigenous Perspectives. Susan Sleeper-Smith, ed. Pp. 303–321. Lincoln: University of Nebraska Press.
2010   Whose Idea Was This?: Museums, Replicas and the Reproduction of Knowledge. Current Anthropology 52(2):211–233.

Ivison, Duncan
2006   Emergent Cosmopolitanism: Indigenous Peoples and International Law. *In* Between Cosmopolitan Ideals and State Sovereignty. Ronald Tinnevelt and Gert Verschraegen, eds. Pp. 120–134. New York: Palgrave.

Jacknis, Ira
1985   Franz Boas and Exhibits: On the Limitations of the Museum Method of Anthropology. *In* Objects and Others: Essays on Museums and Material Culture. George W. Stocking, ed. Pp. 75–111. Madison: University of Wisconsin Press.
2002   The Storage Box of Tradition: Kwakuitl Art, Anthropologists, and Museums, 1881–1981. Washington, DC: Smithsonian Institution Press.

Jacobs, Nancy N.
2006   The Intimate Politics of Ornithology in Colonial Africa. Comparative Studies in Society and History 48(3):564–603.

REFERENCES

James, George W.
1920   New Mexico: The Land of the Delight Makers. Boston: Page.

Jenkins, David
1994   Object Lessons and Ethnographic Displays: Museum Exhibitions and the
        Making of American Anthropology. Comparative Studies in Society and
        History 36(2):242–270.

Jessup, Lynda, and Shannon Bagg
2002   On Aboriginal Representation in the Gallery. Quebec: Canadian Ethnology
        Service, Canadian Museum of Civilization.

Jeswiet, Jacob
1938   Met de vliegmachine opzoeknaardenstam-vorm vanhet suikerriet op Nieuw
        Guinea. Tijdschrift Nieuw Guinea 3:425–427.

Johannesson, Sissel, and Christine A. Hastorf, eds.
1994   Corn and Culture in the Prehistoric New World. Boulder, CO: Westview.

Johnson, Matthew
2006   The Tide Reversed: Prospects and Potentials for a Postcolonial Archaeology
        of Europe. In Historical Archaeology. M. Hall and S. W. Silliman, eds. Pp.
        313–331. Oxford: Blackwell.

Jones, Anna Laura
1993   Exploding Canons: The Anthropology of Museums. Annual Review of
        Anthropology 22:201–220.

Jones, Jonathan
2009   The British Museum Brings the Dead to Life. Guardian, 2 November, http://
        www.guardian.co.uk/artanddesign/jonathanjonesblog/2009/nov/02
        /british-museum-day-of-dead, accessed 1 August 2010.

Jones, Owain, and Paul Cloke
2008   Non-human Agencies: Trees, Relationality, Time and Place. In Material
        Agency: Towards a Non-anthropocentric Approach. Carl Knappett and
        Lambros Malafouris, eds. Pp. 79–96. New York: Springer.

Jones, Philip
1987   South Australian Anthropological History: The Board for Anthropological
        Research and Its Early Expeditions. Records of the South Australian
        Museum.

2007   Ochre and Rust: Artefacts and Encounters on Australian Frontiers. Kent
        Town, South Australia: Wakefield.

Joyce, Patrick, and Tony Bennett
2010   Material Powers: Introduction. In Material Powers: Cultural Studies, History
        and the Material Turn. Tony Bennett and Patrick Joyce, eds. Pp. 1–21. New
        York: Routledge.

Joyce, R. A.
2000   Heirlooms and Houses: Materiality and Social Memory. In Beyond Kinship:

Social and Material Reproduction in House Societies. R. A. Joyce and
S. D. Gillespie, eds. Pp. 189–212. Philadelphia: University of Pennsylvania Press.

Kahn, Miriam
2000   Not Really Pacific Voices: Politics of Representation in Collaborative
        Museum Exhibits. Museum Anthropology 24(1):57–74.

Karp, Ivan, Corinne A Kratz, Lynn Szwaja, and Tomás Ybarra-Frausto, eds.
2006   Museum Frictions: Public Cultures/Global Transformations. Durham, NC:
        Duke University Press.

Karp, Ivan, and Steven D. Lavine, eds.
1991   Exhibiting Cultures: The Poetics and Politics of Museum Display.
        Washington, DC: Smithsonian Institution Press.

Katzenberg, Anne, and Shelley Rae Saunders
2008   Biological Anthropology of the Human Skeleton. London: Wiley-Liss.

Kelly, Lynda, and Phil Gordon
2002   Developing a Community of Practice: Museums and Reconciliation in
        Australia. *In* Museums, Society, Inequality. Richard Sandell, ed. Pp. 153–174.
        London: Routledge.

Kilborn, Nicole
2009   Producing Partnerships, Misperceptions, and Native American-ness: The
        Museum of Northern Arizona's Heritage Program Festivals. Master's
        internship paper, Northern Arizona University.

Kingston, Sean
2007   Dangerous Heritage: Southern New Ireland, the Museum and the Display
        of the Past. *In* The Future of Indigenous Museums: Perspectives from the
        Southwest Pacific. Nick Stanley, ed. Pp. 47–69. Oxford: Berghahn.

Kirsch, Stuart
2001   Lost Worlds: Environmental Disaster, "Culture Loss" and the Law. Current
        Anthropology 42(2):167–198.

2006   Reverse Anthropology: Indigenous Analysis of Social and Environmental
        Relations in New Guinea. Stanford, CA: Stanford University Press.

Kirshenblatt-Gimblett, Barbara
1991   Objects of Ethnography. *In* Exhibiting Cultures: The Poetics and Politics
        of Museum Display. Ivan Karp and Steven D. Lavine, eds. Pp. 386–443.
        Washington, DC: Smithsonian Institution Press.

1998   Destination Culture: Tourism, Museums, and Heritage. Berkeley: University
        of California Press.

2004   Intangible Heritage as Metacultural Production. Museum International
        56(1–2):52–65.

2006   World Heritage and Cultural Economics. *In* Museum Frictions: Public
        Cultures/Global Transformations. Ivan Karp, Corinne A. Kratz, Lynn Szwaja,
        and Tomás Ybarra-Frausto, eds. Pp. 161–202. Durham, NC: Duke University
        Press.

References

Knappett, Carl

2007   Materials with Materiality. Archaeological Dialogues 14(1):20–23.

Knappett, Carl, and Lambros Malafouris, eds.

2008   Material Agency: Towards a Non-anthropocentric Approach. New York: Springer.

Knowles, Chantal

2011   "Objects as Ambassadors": Representing Nation through Museum Exhibitions. *In* Unpacking the Collection: Networks of Material and Social Agency in the Museum. Sarah Byrne, Anne Clarke, Rodney Harrison, and Robin Torrence, eds. Pp. 231–248. New York: Springer.

Kononenko, Nina, Robin Torrence, Huw Barton, and Ariane Hennell

2010   Cross-Cultural Interaction on Wuvulu Island, Papua New Guinea: The Perspective from Use-Wear and Residue Analyses of Turtle Bone Artifacts. Journal of Archaeological Science 37:2911–2919.

Kopytoff, Igor

1986   The Cultural Biography of Things: Commoditization as Process. *In* The Social Life of Things: Commodities in Cultural Perspective. Arjun Appadurai, ed. Pp. 64–91. Cambridge: Cambridge University Press.

Kramer, Jennifer

2006   Switchbacks: Art, Ownership, and Nuxalk National Identity. Vancouver: University of British Columbia Press.

Kratz, Corinne A., and Ivan Karp

2006   Introduction: Museum Frictions: Public Cultures/Global Transformations. *In* Museum Frictions: Public Cultures/Global Transformations. Ivan Karp, Corinne A. Kratz, Lynn Szwaja, and Tomás Ybarra-Frausto, eds. Pp. 1–31. Durham, NC: Duke University Press.

Kreps, Christina

2003   Liberating Culture: Cross-Cultural Perspectives on Museums, Curation, and Heritage Preservation. London: Routledge.

2009   Indigenous Curation, Museums, and Intangible Cultural Heritage. *In* Intangible Heritage. Laurajane Smith and Natsuko Akagawa, eds. Pp. 193–208. London: Taylor and Francis.

2011   Non-Western Models of Museums and Curation in Cross-Cultural Perspective. *In* A Companion to Museum Studies. Sharon Macdonald, ed. Pp. 457–472. Malden, MA: Wiley-Blackwell.

Küchler, Susanne

1988   Malangan: Objects, Sacrifice and the Production of Memory. American Ethnologist 15(4):625–637.

1997   Sacrificial Economy and Its Objects: Rethinking Colonial Collecting in Oceania. Journal of Material Culture 2(1):39–60.

Kuhlmann, Annette
1992 Collaborative Research among the Kickapoo Tribe of Oklahoma. Human
Organization 51(3):274–283.

Kuklick, Henrika
1991 The Savage Within: The Social History of British Anthropology, 1885–1945.
Cambridge: Cambridge University Press.
2006 "Humanity in the Chrysalis Stage": Indigenous Australians in the
Anthropological Imagination, 1899–1926. British Journal for the History of
Science 39(4):535–568.
2011 Personal Equations: Reflections on the History of Fieldwork, with Special
Reference to Sociocultural Anthropology. Isis 102:1–33.

Kuper, Adam
2003 The Return of the Native. Current Anthropology 44(3):389–402.

Kurin, Richard
2004 Museums and Intangible Heritage: Culture Dead or Alive? ICOM News
4:1–9.

Lanmon, Dwight P.
2006 We'wha: A Zuni Man-Woman and His Pottery. *In* Walpole Society Notebook,
2003–2004. Pp. 84–103. Walpole, MA: Walpole Society.

Larson, Frances, Alison Petch, and David Zeitlyn
2007 Social Networks and the Creation of the Pitt Rivers Museum. Journal of
Material Culture 12(3):211–239.

Latour, Bruno
1987 Science in Action: How to Follow Scientists and Engineers through Society.
Cambridge, MA: Harvard University Press.
1993 We Have Never Been Modern. Cambridge, MA: Harvard University Press.
1999 Pandora's Hope: Essays on the Reality of Science Studies. Cambridge, MA:
Harvard University Press.
2004a Politics of Nature: How to Bring the Sciences into Democracy. Cambridge,
MA: Harvard University Press.
2004b Why Has Critique Run out of Steam? From Matters of Fact to Matters of
Concern. Critical Inquiry 30(2):225–248.
2005 Reassembling the Social: An Introduction to Actor-Network Theory. Oxford:
Oxford University Press.
2010 On the Modern Cult of the Factish Gods. Durham, NC: Duke University
Press.

Laurière, Christine
2008 Paul Rivet, le savant et le politique. Paris: Musée National d'Histoire
Naturelle.

Law, John
1994 Organising Modernity. Oxford: Blackwell.

REFERENCES

Lawes, Reverend William George
1876–1884 Journals. Mitchell Library, Sydney.

Layton, Robert, and Sarah Titchen
1995   Uluru: An Outstanding Australian Aboriginal Cultural Landscape. *In*
        Cultural Landscapes of Universal Value. Bernd von Droste, Harald Plachter,
        and Mechtild Rossler, eds. Pp. 174–181. Stuttgart: Gustav Fischer Verlag Jena
        / UNESCO.

Leach, James
2002   Drum and Voice: Aesthetics and Social Process on the Rai Coast of Papua
        New Guinea. Journal of the Royal Anthropological Institute, n.s., 8:713–734.

Leask, Anna, and Alan Fyall, eds.
2006   Managing World Heritage Sites. Oxford: Butterworth-Heinemann.

Lebovics, Herman
2004   Bringing the Empire Back Home: France in the Global Age. Durham, NC:
        Duke University Press.

L'Estoile, Benoît de
2007   Le goût des autres: De l'exposition coloniale aux arts premiers. Paris:
        Flammarion.

Lévi-Strauss, Claude
1966   The Savage Mind. John Weightman and Doreen Weightman, trans. Chicago:
        University of Chicago Press.
1969[1949] The Elementary Structures of Kinship. London: Eyre and Spottiswoode.

Lidchi, Henrietta
1997   The Poetics and Politics of Exhibiting Other Cultures. *In* Representation:
        Cultural Representations and Signifying Practices. Stuart Hall, ed. Pp.
        151–222. London: Sage; Milton Keynes, England: Open University.

Liljeblad, Aune, and Ethel Lillieblade, comps.
1993   The Family of Liljeblad in Finland and Sweden and Australia. Miriam
        Nauenburg, ed. Weston Creek, Australia: Genie.

LMS
1826   Catalogue of the Missionary Museum, Austin Friars. London: London
        Missionary Society.
1860   Catalogue of the Missionary Museum, Blomfield Street, Finsbury. London:
        London Missionary Society.

Lonetree, Amy
2006   Missed Opportunities: Reflections on the NMAI. American Indian Quarterly
        30(3–4):632–645.

Lonetree, Amy, and Amanda J. Cobb, eds.
2008   The National Museum of the American Indian: Critical Conversations.
        Lincoln: University of Nebraska Press.

Lucas, Gavin
2010   Time and the Archaeological Archive. Rethinking History: The Journal of Theory and Practice 14(3):343–359.

Lupton, Deborah
1999   Risk. London: Routledge.

Lurie, Nancy
1966   Women in Early American Anthropology. *In* Pioneers of American Anthropology: The Uses of Biography. June Helm, ed. Pp. 29–81. Seattle: University of Washington Press.

Lydon, Jane
2005   Eye Contact: Photographing Indigenous Australians. Durham, NC: Duke University Press.

2009   Young and Free: The Australian Past in a Global Future. *In* Cosmopolitan Archaeologies. Lynn Meskell, ed. Pp. 28–47. Durham, NC: Duke University Press.

Lydon, Jane, and Uzma Z. Rizvi
2010   Introduction: Poscolonialism and Archaeology. *In* Handbook of Postcolonial Archaeology. Jane Lydon and Uzma Z. Rizvi, eds. Pp. 17–33. Walnut Creek, CA: Left Coast Press.

Macdonald, Sharon
2002   On "Old Things": The Fetishization of Past Everyday Life. *In* An Anthropology of Britain. Nigel Rapport, ed. Pp. 89–106. Oxford: Berg.

2011   Expanding Museum Studies: An Introduction. *In* A Companion to Museum Studies. Sharon Macdonald, ed. Pp. 1–12. Malden, MA: Wiley-Blackwell.

Macdonald, Sharon, and Roger Silverstone
1990   Rewriting the Museums: Fictions, Taxonomies, Stories and Readers. Cultural Studies 4(2):176–191.

Mack, John
2000   Africa: Arts and Cultures. London: British Museum Press.

MacKenzie, John M.
2010   Museums and Empire: Natural History, Human Cultures and Colonial Identities. Manchester, England: Manchester University Press.

Marcus, George E.
1995   Ethnography in/of the World System: The Emergence of Multi-sited Ethnography. Annual Review of Anthropology 24:95–117.

Marcus, George E., and Fred R. Myers, eds.
1995   The Traffic in Culture: Reconfiguring Art and Anthropology. Berkeley: University of California Press.

Martinez Cobo, Jose R.
1986   Study of the Problem of Discrimination against Indigenous Populations. New York: United Nations.

References

Mason, Otis

1886   The Planting and Exhuming of a Prayer. Science 8(179):24–25.

Mauss, Marcel

1990   The Gift: The Form and Reason for Exchange in Archaic Societies. W. D. Halls, trans. London: Routledge.

May, Robert

1977   The Artifact Industry: Maximising Returns to Producers. Boroko, Papua New Guinea: Institute of Applied Social and Economic Research.

May, Sally

2010   Collecting Cultures: Myth, Politics and Collaboration in the 1948 Arnhem Land Expedition. Lanham, MD: AltaMira.

Maybin, Neil

2011   Rupert Brooke on Skyros. http://www.rupertbrookeonskyros.com, accessed 24 March 2011.

McArthur, Margaret

2000   The Curbing of Anarchy in Kunimaipa Society. Sydney: Oceania.

McBryde, Isobel

1990   "Those Truly Outstanding Examples…": Kakadu in the Context of Australia's World Heritage Properties—A Response. *In* A Sense of Place: A Conversation in Three Cultures. J. Domicelj and S. Domicelj, eds. Pp.15–19, 46–52. Canberra: Australian Heritage Commission.

2000   "Barter Immediately Commenced to the Satisfaction of Both Parties": Cross-Cultural Exchange at Port Jackson 1788–1828. *In* The Archaeology of Difference: Negotiating Cross-Cultural Engagements in Oceania. Robin Torrence and Anne Clarke, eds. Pp. 238–277. London: Routledge.

McCarthy, Conal

2007   Exhibiting Māori: A History of Colonial Cultures of Display. Oxford: Berg.

2011   Museums and Māori: Heritage Professionals, Indigenous Collections, Current Practice. Wellington, New Zealand: Te Papa Press.

McGee, W. J., William H. Holmes, J.N. Powell, Alice C. Fletcher, Washington Mathews, Stewart Culin, and Joseph D. McGuire

1900   In Memoriam: Frank Hamilton Cushing. American Anthropologist 2(2):354–380.

McGregor, Russell

1997   Imagined Destinies: Aboriginal Australians and the Doomed Race Theory, 1880–1939. Melbourne: Melbourne University Press.

McKinnon, Malcolm

2009   Bay of Plenty Region—Māori Traditions. TeAra: The Encyclopedia of New Zealand. http://www.TeAra.govt.nz/en/bay-of-plenty-region/4, accessed 13 April 2011.

McLean, Fiona

2008   Museums and the Representation of Identity. *In* The Ashgate Research

Companion to Heritage and Identity. Brian J. Graham and Peter Howard, eds. Pp. 283–298. Aldershot, England: Ashgate.

Melanesia Project
2005   Melanesia Project leaflet. In possession of author (Sarah Byrne).

Meleisea, Malama, and Penelope Schoeffel
1997   Discovering Outsiders. In The Cambridge History of Pacific Islanders. Donald Denoon, ed. Pp. 119–151. Cambridge: Cambridge University Press.

Merlan, Francesa
2008   Indigeneity: Global and Local. Current Anthropology 50(3):303–333.

Merrill, William J., Edmund J. Ladd, and T. J. Ferguson
1993   Return of the Ahayu:da: Lessons for Repatriation from Zuni Pueblo and the Smithsonian Institution. Current Anthropology 34(5):523–567.

Meskell, Lynn
2009   The Nature of Culture in Kruger National Park. In Cosmopolitan Archaeologies. Lynn Meskell, ed. Pp. 89–112. Durham, NC: Duke University Press.
2010   Human Rights and Heritage Ethics. Anthropological Quarterly 83(4):839–860.

Message, Kylie
2006   New Museums and the Making of Culture. Oxford: Berg.

Miller, Daniel
1987   Material Culture and Mass Consumption. Oxford: Blackwell.
2010   Stuff. Cambridge: Polity.

Miller, Daniel, ed.
2005   Materiality. Durham, NC: Duke University Press.

Miller, Darlis A.
2007   Matilda Coxe Stevenson: Pioneering Anthropologist. Norman: University of Oklahoma Press.

Mills, Barbara, and T. J. Ferguson
2008   Animate Objects: Shell Trumpets and Ritual Networks in the Greater Southwest. Journal of Archaeological Method and Theory 15:338–361.

Morphy, Howard
1996   More Than Mere Facts: Repositioning Spencer and Gillen in the History of Anthropology. In Exploring Central Australia: Society, Environment and the 1894 Expedition. S. R. Morton and D. J. Mulvaney, eds. Pp. 135–149. Chipping Nortin, New South Wales: Surrey Beatty.

Morrison-Low, Alison
2004   The Soldier-Astronomer in Scotland: Thomas Makdougall Brisbane's Scientific Work in the Northern Hemisphere. Historical Records of Australian Science 15(2):151–176.

References

Morton, S. R., and D. J. Mulvaney, eds.

1996   Exploring Central Australia: Society, Environment and the 1894 Expedition. Chipping Norton, New South Wales: Surrey Beatty.

Moutu, Andrew

2007   Collection as a Way of Being. *In* Thinking through Things: Theorising Artefacts Ethnographically. Amiria Henare, Martin Holbraad, and Sari Wastell, eds. Pp. 93–112. London: Routledge.

2009   The Dialectic of Creativity and Ownership in Intellectual Property Discourse. International Journal of Cultural Property 16:309–324.

Mpumlwana, Khwezi, Gerard Corsane, Juanita Pastor-Makhurane, and Ciraj Rassool

2002   Inclusion and the Power of Representation: South African Museums and the Cultural Politics of Social Transformation. *In* Museums, Society, Inequality. Richard Sandell, ed. Pp. 244–261. London: Routledge.

Mueggler, Erik

2005   The Lapponicum Sea: Matter, Sense, and Affect in the Botanical Exploration of Southwest China. Comparative Studies in Society and History 47(3):442–479.

Mulvaney, D. J., and J. H. Calaby

1985   "So Much That Is New": Baldwin Spencer, 1860–1929: A Biography. Melbourne: Melbourne University Press.

Mulvaney, John, Howard Morphy, and Alison Petch, eds.

1997   "My Dear Spencer": The Letters of F. J. Gillen to Baldwin Spencer. Melbourne: Hyland House.

Murray, John Hubert Plunkett

1912   Papua or British New Guinea. London: Fisher Unwin.

Museum of Northern Arizona

2005   Memorandum of Understanding between MNA and the Hopi Tribe. http://www.musnaz.org/trustees/hopimnamou.shtml, accessed 2 February 2012.

Myers, Fred R.

2001   Introduction: The Empire of Things. *In* The Empire of Things: Regimes of Value and Material Culture. Fred R. Myers, ed. Pp. 3–61. Santa Fe, NM: SAR Press.

Mytinger, Caroline

1946   New Guinea Headhunt. New York: Macmillan.

Nakata, Martin

2007   Disciplining the Savages, Savaging the Disciplines. Canberra: Aboriginal Studies Press.

National Museum

1893   Annual Report for the United States National Museum. Washington, DC: Government Printing Office.

1901   Annual Report for the United States National Museum. Washington, DC: Government Printing Office.

National Museum of Natural History
N.d.   Accession files 106509, 106585, and 137754. Smithsonian Institution, Washington, DC.

National Museums Scotland Archive
1827a   University of Edinburgh Natural History Museum, Daily Report Book 4, entry for 29 November.
1827b   University of Edinburgh Natural History Museum, Daily Report Book 4, entry for 22 December.

Neich, Roger
2008[2001]   Carved Histories: Rotorua Ngati Tarawhai Woodcarving. Auckland: Auckland University Press.

Newell, Jennifer
2006   Collecting from the Collectors: Pacific Islanders and the Spoils of Europe. *In* Cook's Pacific Encounters. Pp. 29–48. Canberra: National Museum of Australia.

Niezen, Ronald
2003   The Origins of Indigenism: Human Rights and the Politics of Identity. Berkeley: University of California Press.

Nunley, John Wallace, Cara McCarty, John Emigh, and Lesley K. Ferris
1999   Masks: Faces of Culture. St. Louis, MO: Abrams / St. Louis Art Museum.

Odegaard, Nancy, and Alice Saydongei
2000   Contaminated Cultural Materials in Museum Collections: Reflections and Recommendations for a NAGPRA Issue. WAAC Newsletter 22:2. http://cool .conservation-us.org/waac/wn/wn22/wn22-2/wn22-207.html, accessed 25 August 2010.

Odell, George H.
2004   Lithic Analysis. New York: Springer.

Ogden, Sherelyn
2004   Caring for American Indian Objects: A Practical and Cultural Guide. St. Paul: Minnesota Historical Society Press.

O'Hanlon, Michael
1992   Unstable Images and Second Skins: Artefacts, Exegesis and Assessments in the New Guinea Highlands. Man 27(3):587–608.
1993   Paradise: Portraying the New Guinea Highlands. London: British Museum Press.
1999   "Mostly Harmless"?: Missionaries, Administrators and Material Culture on the Coast of British New Guinea. Journal of the Royal Anthropological Institute 5(3):377–397.

REFERENCES

2000   Introduction. The Ethnography of Collecting: From Obscurity to Obloquy. *In* Hunting the Gatherers: Ethnographic Collectors, Agents and Agency in Melanesia, 1870s–1930s. Michael O'Hanlon and Robert L. Welsch, eds. Pp. 1–34. Oxford: Berghahn.

O'Hanlon, Michael, and Robert L. Welsch, eds.
2000   Hunting the Gatherers: Ethnographic Collectors, Agents and Agency in Melanesia, 1870s–1930s. Oxford: Berghahn.

Oldham, Eric R.
1929   Western Division. *In* Territory of Papua Annual Report for the Year 1927–1928. Pp. 19–20. Canberra: Australian Commonwealth.

Oldman, William Ockelford
1976   Illustrated Catalogue of Ethnographical Specimens from the W. O. Oldman Catalogues (1903–1914). London: Hales, Wilberg.

Olsen, Bjørnar
2003   Material Culture after Text: Re-membering Things. Norwegian Archaeological Review 36(2):87–104.
2007   Keeping Things at Arm's Length: A Genealogy of Asymmetry. World Archaeology 39(4):579–588.
2010   In Defense of Things: Archaeology and the Ontology of Objects. Lanham, MD: AltaMira.

Oram, Nigel
1976   Colonial Town to Melanesian City. Canberra: Australian National University Press.

O'Regan, Stephen
1994   Maori Control of Maori Heritage. *In* The Politics of the Past. Peter Gathercole and David Lowenthal, eds. Pp. 95–106. London: Routledge.

Ouzman, Sven
2006   The Beauty of Letting Go: Fragmentary Museums and Archaeologies of Archive. *In* Sensible Objects: Colonialism, Museums and Material Culture. Elizabeth Edwards, Chris Gosden, and Ruth B. Phillips, eds. Pp. 269–301. Oxford: Berg.

Parezo, Nancy
1988   Matilda Coxe Stevenson. *In* Women Anthropologists: A Biographical Dictionary. Ute Gacs, Aisha Khan, Jerrie McIntyre, and Ruth Weinberg, eds. Pp. 337–343. New York: Greenwood.
1993   Matilda Coxe Stevenson: Pioneer Ethnologist. *In* Hidden Scholars and the Native American Southwest. Nancy Parezo, ed. Pp. 38–62. Albuquerque: University of New Mexico Press.

Parezo, Nancy J., and Don Fowler
2007   Anthropology Goes to the Fair: The 1904 Louisiana Purchase Exposition Lincoln: University of Nebraska Press.

Parks Australia

2009 Uluru-Kata Tjuta National Park Note—Please Don't Climb. http://www
.environment.gov.au/parks/publications/uluru/pn-please-dont-climb.html,
accessed 4 October 2011.

Parsons, Elsie Clews

1916 The Zuni La'mana. American Anthropologist 18(4):521–528.

Pearce, Susan M.

1995 On Collecting: An Investigation into Collecting in the European Tradition.
London: Routledge.

Pearson, Mike, and Michael Shanks

2001 Theatre/Archaeology. London: Routledge.

Peer, Shanny

1998 France on Display: Peasants, Provincials, and Folklore in the 1937 Paris
World's Fair. Albany: State University of New York Press.

Peers, Laura, and Alison K. Brown, eds.

2003 Museums and Source Communities: A Routledge Reader. London:
Routledge.

Pels, Peter

1997 The Anthropology of Colonialism: Culture, History, and the Emergence of
Western Governmentality. Annual Review of Anthropology 26:163–183.

Pemberton, C. E.

N.d. Report of Explorations in New Guinea and New Britain, May 26, 1928—July
21, 1929. Archives of the Hawaii Agriculture Research Center, Kunia Village,
Oahu.

1930 Looking for Sugar in Papua. Mid-Pacific Magazine 39(1):25–30.

Penny, H. Glenn

2003 Objects of Culture: Ethnology and Ethnographic Museums in Imperial
Germany. Chapel Hill: University of North Carolina Press.

Petch, Alison

2007 Notes and Queries and the Pitt Rivers Museum. Museum Anthropology
30(1):1348–1379.

Peterson, Nicolas, Lindy Allen, and Louise Hamby, eds.

2008 The Makers and Making of Indigenous Australian Museum Collections.
Melbourne: Melbourne University Press.

Phillips, Ruth B.

1999 Nuns, Ladies and the "Queens of the Human": Appropriating the Savage
in Nineteenth-Century Huron Tourist Art. In Unpacking Culture: Art and
Commodity in Colonial and Postcolonial Worlds. Ruth B. Phillips and
Christopher B. Steiner, eds. Pp. 33–50. Berkeley: University of California Press.

Phillips, Ruth B., and Christopher B. Steiner, eds.

1999 Unpacking Culture: Art and Commodity in Colonial and Postcolonial
Worlds. Berkeley: University of California Press.

REFERENCES

Philp, Judith

2009   Days of Desolation on the New Guinea Coast. *In* The Wake of the Beagle: Science in the Southern Oceans from the Age of Darwin. Ian McCalman and Nigel Erskine, eds. Pp. 125–137. Sydney: University of New South Wales Press.

2011   Exchanging Culture for Science: Hedley in New Caledonia. *In* Unpacking the Collection: Networks of Material and Social Agency in the Museum. Sarah Byrne, Anne Clarke, Rodney Harrison, and Robin Torrence, eds. Pp. 269–288. New York: Springer.

Pinney, Christopher

2004   Photos of the Gods: The Printed Image and Political Struggle in India. London: Reaktion.

2005   Things Happen; or, From Which Moment Does That Object Come? *In* Materiality. D. Miller, ed. Pp. 256–272. Durham, NC: Duke University Press.

Popular Science Monthly

1929   Airplane Explorers Find a New Sugar. June 114(6):52.

Port Moresby

1928   Patrol Report 5. A.R.M. Ivan Champion, 22 August—6 September.

Povinelli, Elizabeth A.

2002   The Cunning of Recognition: Indigenous Alterities and the Making of Australian Multiculturalism. Durham, NC: Duke University Press.

Prasad, Pushkala

2003   The Return of the Native: Organizational Discourses and the Legacy of the Ethnographic Imagination. *In* Postcolonial Theory and Organizational Analysis. A. Prasad, ed. Pp. 149–170. New York: Palgrave Macmillan / St. Martin's.

Pratt, Mary Louise

1992   Imperial Eyes: Travel Writing and Transculturation. London: Routledge.

Prior, Nick

2011   Postmodern Restructurings. *In* A Companion to Museum Studies. Sharon Macdonald, ed. Pp. 509–524. Malden, MA: Wiley-Blackwell.

Putnam, James

1991   Art and Artefact: The Museum as Medium. London: Thames and Hudson.

Quanchi, Max, and Susan Cochrane, eds.

2007   Hunting the Collectors: Pacific Collections in Australian Museums, Art Galleries and Archives. Newcastle: Cambridge Scholars.

Rabinow, Paul

1989   French Modern: Norms and Forms of the Social Environment. Cambridge, MA: MIT Press.

2003   Anthropos Today: Reflections on Modern Equipment. Princeton, NJ: Princeton University Press.

Raffles, Hugh

2002   In Amazonia: A Natural History. Princeton, NJ: Princeton University Press.

Reimer, Francis J.

2008   Addressing Ethnographic Inquiry. *In* Research Essentials: An Introduction to Designs and Practices. Stephen Lapan and Marylynn Quartaroli, eds. Pp. 203–221. San Francisco: Jossey-Bass.

Rivière, Georges H.

1931   Rapport sur la réorganisation général du Musée. Musée de l'Homme Archives, file 2, AM 1 G2b.

Roscoe, Paul

1988   The Far Side of Hurun: The Management of Melanesian Millenarian Movements. American Ethnologist 15(3):515–529.

Roscoe, Will

1988   We'wha and Klah: The American Indian Berdache as Artist and Priest. American Indian Quarterly 12(2):127–150.

1991   The Zuni Man-Woman. Albuquerque: University of New Mexico Press.

Rose, Deborah Bird

1996   Nourishing Terrains: Australian Aboriginal Views of Landscape and Wilderness. Canberra: Australian Heritage Commission.

2004   Reports from a Wild Country: Ethics for Decolonisation. Sydney: University of New South Wales Press.

2008   On History, Trees and Ethical Proximity. Postcolonial Studies 11(2):157–167.

2011   Wild Dog Dreaming: Love and Extinction. Charlottesville: University of Virginia Press.

Rose, Deborah, Diana James, and Christine Watson

2003   Indigenous Kinship with the Natural World in New South Wales. Hurstville: New South Wales National Parks and Wildlife Service.

Rose, Deborah Bird, and Libby Robin

2004   The Ecological Humanities in Action: An Invitation. Australian Humanities Review 31–32. http://www.australianhumanitiesreview.org/archive /Issue-April-2004/rose.html, accessed 28 October 2011.

Rössler, Mechtild

1995   UNESCO and Cultural Landscape Protection. *In* Cultural Landscapes of Universal Value. Bernd von Droste, Harald Plachter, and Mechtild Rössler, eds. Pp. 42–49. Stuttgart: Gustav Fischer Verlag Jena / UNESCO.

Rowlands, Michael

2008   Relating Anthropology and Archaeology. *In* A Companion to Archaeology. John L. Bintliff, ed. Pp. 473–489. Oxford: Blackwell.

Rowse, Tim

1998   White Flour, White Power: From Rations to Citizenship in Central Australia. Cambridge: Cambridge University Press.

REFERENCES

2008   Indigenous Culture: The Politics of Vulnerability and Survival. *In* The Sage Handbook of Cultural Analysis. Tony Bennett and John Frow, eds. Pp. 406–426. London: Sage.

2009   The Ontological Politics of "Closing the Gaps." Journal of Cultural Economy 2(1–2):33–48.

Ruppert, Evelyn

2009   Becoming Peoples: "Counting Heads in Northern Wilds." Journal of Cultural Economy 2(1):11–31.

Russell, Lynette

2001   Savage Imaginings: Historical and Contemporary Constructions of Australian Aboriginalities. Melbourne: Australian Scholarly Publishing.

Russell, Margo, and Martin Russell

1979   Afrikaners of the Kalahari. Cambridge: Cambridge University Press.

Ryan, Peter, ed.

1972   Encyclopedia of Papua and New Guinea. Melbourne: Melbourne University Press / University of Papua New Guinea.

Sackett, James

1986   Style, Function, and Assemblage Variability: A Reply to Binford. American Antiquity 51(3):628–634.

Sahlins, Marshall

1972   Stone Age Economics. Chicago: Aldine-Atherton.

Salmond, Anne

1997   Between Worlds: Early Exchanges between Maori and Europeans 1773–1815. Auckland: Viking.

Samuel, Raphael

1996   Theatres of Memory, vol. 1: Past and Present in Contemporary Culture. London: Verso.

Sanders, Douglas

1989   The United Nations Working Group on Indigenous Populations. Human Rights Quarterly 11(3):406–433.

Saunders, Shirley

2004   Sir Thomas Brisbane's Legacy to Colonial Science: Colonial Astronomy at the Parramatta Observatory, 1822–1848. Historical Records of Australian Science 15(2):177–209.

Scarre, Chris, ed.

2005   The Human Past: World Prehistory and the Development of Human Societies. London: Thames and Hudson.

Schiffer, Michael B.

1972   Archaeological Context and Systemic Context. American Antiquity 37(2):156–165.

1976   Behavioral Archeology. New York: Academic Press.

1987   Formation Processes of the Archaeological Record. Albuquerque: University of New Mexico Press.

1999   The Material Life of Human Beings: Artefacts, Behavior, and Communication. London: Routledge.

2010   Behavorial Archaeology: Principles and Practices. London: Equinox.

Schildkrout, Enid, and Curtis A. Keim

1998   Objects and Agendas: Re-collecting the Congo. *In* The Scramble for Art in Central Africa. Enid Schildkrout and Curtis A. Keim, eds. Pp. 1–36. Cambridge: Cambridge University Press.

Schindlebeck, Markus

1993   The Art of Collecting: Interactions between Collectors and the People They Visit. Zeitschrift für Ethnologie 118:57–67.

Schlanger, Nathan

2010   Series in Progress: Antiquities of Nature, Numismatics and Stone Implements in the Emergence of Prehistoric Archaeology. History of Science 48(3–4):343–369.

Schoorl, Johan W.

1993   Culture and Change among the Muyu. Leiden: KITLV Press.

Schultz, Lainie

2011   Collaborative Museology and the Visitor. Museum Anthropology 34(1):1–12.

Schumaker, Lynette

1996   A Tent with a View: Colonial Officers, Anthropologists, and the Making of the Field in Northern Rhodesia. Osiris, 2nd series, 11:237–258.

Scott, David

1995   Colonial Governmentality. Social Text 43:191–220.

Scott, James C.

1998   Seeing like a State: How Certain Schemes to Improve the Human Condition Have Failed. New Haven, CT: Yale University Press.

Scott, Michael

2007   The Severed Snake: Matrilineages, Making Place and a Melanesian Christianity in Southeast Solomon Islands. Durham, NC: Carolina Academic Press.

Seligmann, Charles Gabriel, ed.

1910   The Melanesians of British New Guinea. Cambridge: Cambridge University Press.

Serres, Michel

2008   The Five Senses: A Philosophy of Mingled Bodies. London: Continuum.

Shanks, Michael

1992   Experiencing the Past: On the Character of Archaeology. London: Routledge.

REFERENCES

2007   Symmetrical Archaeology. World Archaeology 39(4):589–596.

2008   The Archaeological Imagination. http://documents.stanford.edu
/michaelshanks/57, accessed 3 March 2011.

2009   A Theory of Assemblage. http://documents.stanford.edu/michaelshanks
/390?view=print, accessed 23 May 2012.

2012   The Archaeological Imagination. Lanham, MD: Left Coast Press.

Shanks, Michael, and Randall H. McGuire
1996   The Craft of Archaeology. American Antiquity 61(1):75–88.

Shanks, Michael, and Chris Witmore
2010   Memory Practices and the Archaeological Imagination in Risk Society:
Design and Long-Term Community. *In* Unquiet Pasts: Theoretical
Perspectives on Archaeology and Cultural Heritage. Ian Russell and
Stephanie Koerner, eds. Pp. 269–290. Aldershot, England: Ashgate.

Shelton, Anthony Alan
2000   Museum Ethnography: An Imperial Science. *In* Cultural Encounters:
Representing "Otherness." Elizabeth Hallam and Brian V. Street, eds. Pp.
155–193. London: Routledge.

2011   Museums and Anthropologies: Practices and Narratives. *In* A Companion
to Museum Studies. Sharon Macdonald, ed. Pp. 64–80. Malden, MA:
Wiley-Blackwell.

Sherman, Daniel
2004   "Peoples Ethnographic": Objects, Museums, and the Colonial Inheritance of
French Ethnology. French Historical Studies 27(3):669–703.

2011   French Primitivism and the Ends of Empire, 1945–1975. Chicago: University
of Chicago Press.

Sherman, Daniel, ed.
2008   Museums and Difference. Bloomington: Indiana University Press.

Sherratt, A.
1993   The Relativity of Theory. *In* Archaeological Theory: Who Sets the Agenda?
N. Yoffee and A. Sherratt, eds. Pp. 119–130. Cambridge: Cambridge
University Press.

Shott, Michael
1998   Status and Role of Formation Theory in Contemporary Archaeological
Practice. Journal of Archaeological Research 6(4):299–329.

Shurcliff, Sidney N.
1930   Jungle Islands: The "Illyria" in the South Seas. New York: Putnam's Sons.

Siebeud, Emmanuelle
2004   Marcel Mauss: "Projet de présentation d'un bureau d'ethnologie." Revue
d'Histoire des Sciences Humaines 10:105–115.

2007   The Metamorphosis of Ethnology in France, 1839–1930. *In* A New History of
Anthropology. Henricka Kuklick, ed. Pp. 96–110. Malden, MA: Blackwell.

Silko, Leslie Marmon

1986   Landscape, History, and the Pueblo Imagination. Antaeus 57:1003–1014.

1996   Yellow Woman and a Beauty of the Spirit: Essays on Native American Life Today. New York: Touchstone.

Silverman, Eric Kline

1999   Tourist Art as the Crafting of Identity in the Sepik River (Papua New Guinea). *In* Unpacking Culture: Art and Commodity in Colonial and Postcolonial Worlds. Ruth B. Phillips and Christopher B. Steiner, eds. Pp. 51–66. Berkeley: University of California Press.

Simpson, Moira

1996   Making Representations: Museums in the Post-colonial Era. London: Routledge.

2008   Revealing and Concealing: Museums, Objects, and the Transmission of Knowledge in Aboriginal Australia. *In* New Museum Theory and Practice: An Introduction. Janet Marstine, ed. Pp. 153–174. Oxford: Blackwell.

Singer, Beverly R.

2008   The Making of "Who We Are": Now Showing at the National Museum of the American Indian Lelawi Theater. *In* The National Museum of the American Indian: Critical Conversations. Amy Lonetree and Amanda J. Cobb, eds. Pp. 165–180. Lincoln: University of Nebraska Press.

Sleeper-Smith, Susan, ed.

2009   Contesting Knowledge: Museums and Indigenous Perspectives. Lincoln: University of Nebraska Press.

Smith, Laurajane

2006   Uses of Heritage. New York: Routledge.

Southwest Museum

1879   Letter from Cushing to Col. James Stevenson, 15 October. Hodge Cushing Collection, envelope 69.

Spencer, Baldwin

1914   The Aboriginals of Australia. *In* Federal Handbook Prepared in Connection with the Eighty-Fourth Meeting of the British Association for the Advancement of Science Held in Australia, August 1914. G. H. Knibbs, ed. Melbourne: Commonwealth of Australia.

1921   Blood and Shade Divisions of Australian Tribes. Proceedings of the Royal Society of Victoria, n.s., 34(1):2–6.

1922   Guide to the Ethnological Collection Exhibited in the National Gallery of Victoria. 3rd edition. Melbourne: Government Printers.

Spencer, Baldwin, and Frank Gillen

1899   The Native Tribes of Central Australia. London: Macmillan.

Spivak, Gayatri Chakravorty

1996   Subaltern Studies: Deconstructing Historiography. *In* The Spivak Reader. Donna Landry and Gerald MacLean, eds. Pp. 203–236. London: Routledge.

REFERENCES

Stable, Charles
2012   Maximum Intervention: Renewal of a Maori *Waka* by George Nuku and National Museums Scotland. Journal of Conservation and Museum Studies 10. http://www.jcms-journal.com/article/view/37/36, accessed 23 May 2012.

Stahl, Ann Brower
2010   Material Histories. *In* The Oxford Handbook of Material Culture Studies. D. Hicks and M. C. Beaudry, eds. Pp. 148–170. Oxford: Oxford University Press.

Stanley, Nick, ed.
2007   The Future of Indigenous Museums: Perspectives from the Southwest Pacific. Oxford: Berghahn.

State Records Authority of New South Wales
N.d.   Mariners and Ships in Australian Waters: Ellengowan. http://mariners .records.nsw.gov.au/1885/019ell.htm, accessed 15 April 2009.

Steinmetz, George
2007   The Devil's Handwriting: Precoloniality and the German Colonial State in Qingdao, Samoa, and Southwest Africa. Chicago: University of Chicago Press.

Stevenson, Matilda Coxe
1904   The Zuni Indians: Their Mythology, Esoteric Fraternities and Ceremonies. *In* Twenty-Third Annual Report of the Bureau of American Ethnology, 1901–1902. Pp. 1–608. Washington, DC: Government Printing Office.

Stewart, Susan
1993   On Longing: Narratives of the Miniature, the Gigantic, the Souvenir, the Collection. Durham, NC: Duke University Press.

Stocking, George W., Jr.
1987   Victorian Anthropology. New York: Free Press.
1991   Colonial Situations: Essays on the Contextualization of Ethnographic Knowledge. Madison: University of Wisconsin Press.

Stocking, George W., ed.
1985   Objects and Others: Essays on Museums and Material Culture. Madison: University of Wisconsin Press.

Stoler, Ann Laura
2009   Along the Archival Grain: Epistemic Anxieties and Colonial Common Sense. Princeton, NJ: Princeton University Press.

Stone, Octavius C.
1880   A Few Months in New Guinea. London: Sampson Low.

Stone, Peter, and Brian Molyneaux
1994   The Presented Past: Heritage, Museums, and Education. London: Routledge.

Strathern, Marilyn
1988   The Gender of the Gift. Berkeley: University of California Press.

1990   Artefacts of History: Events and the Interpretation of Images. *In* Culture and History in the Pacific. J. Siikala, ed. Pp. 25–44. Helsinki: Finnish Anthropological Society.

1992   The Decomposition of an Event. Cultural Anthropology 7(2):244–254.

1993   Entangled Objects: Detached Metaphors. Social Analysis 34:88–98.

1996   Cutting the Network. Journal of the Royal Anthropological Institute 2(3):517–535.

1999   Property, Substance and Effect: Anthropological Essays on Persons and Things. London: Athlone.

Sturtevant, William C.
1969   Does Anthropology Need Museums? Proceedings of the Biological Society of Washington 82:619–650.

Sullivan, Lawrence E., and Alison Edwards, eds.
2004   Stewards of the Sacred. Washington, DC: American Association of Museums.

Sully, Dean, ed.
2007   Decolonizing Conservation: Caring for Maori Meeting Houses outside New Zealand. Walnut Creek, CA: Left Coast Press.

Swadling, Pamela
1996   Plumes from Paradise: Trade Cycles in Outer Southeast Asia and Their Impact on New Guinea and Nearby Islands until 1920. Boroko: Papua New Guinea National Museum / Robert Brown.

Sydney Gazette
1830   In New Zealand. 30 December.

Sydney Mail
1879   Native of New Guinea. 8 February.

Tapsell, Paul
2000   Pukaki: A Comet Returns. Auckland: Reed.

Taylor, Luke
1988   The Aesthetics of Toas: A Cross-Cultural Conundrum. Canberra Anthropology 11(1):86–99.

Taylor, Paul Michael
2006   Introduction: Revisiting the Dutch and American New Guinea Expedition of 1926. *In* By Aeroplane to Pygmyland: Revisiting the 1926 Dutch and American Expedition to New Guinea. http://www.sil.si.edu/expeditions /1926, accessed 20 February 2012.

Texier, Pierre-Jean, Guillaume Porraz, John Parkington, Jean-Philippe Rigaud, Cedric Poggenpoel, Christopher Miller, Chantal Tribolo, Caroline Cartwright, Aude Coudenneau, Richard Klein, Teresa Steele, and Christine Verna
2010   A Howiesons Poort Tradition of Engraving Ostrich Eggshell Containers Dated to 60,000 Years Ago at Diepkloof Rock Shelter, South Africa. Proceedings of the National Academy of Sciences 104(14):6180–6185.

REFERENCES

Thomas, Nicholas

1989　Out of Time: History and Evolution in Anthropological Discourse. Cambridge: Cambridge University Press.

1991　Entangled Objects: Exchange, Material Culture, and Colonialism in the Pacific. Cambridge, MA: Harvard University Press.

1994　Colonialism's Culture: Anthropology, Travel and Government. Cambridge: Polity.

1999a　The Case of the Misplaced Ponchos. Journal of Material Culture 4(1):5–20.

1999b　Possessions: Indigenous Art/Colonial Culture. London: Thames and Hudson.

2000　Epilogue. *In* Hunting the Gatherers: Ethnographic Collectors, Agents and Agency in Melanesia, 1870s–1930s. Michael O'Hanlon and Robert L. Welsch, eds. Pp. 273–277. Oxford: Berghahn.

2010　The Museum as Method. Museum Anthropology 33(1):6–10.

Thomas, Nicholas, and Diane Losche, eds.

1999　Double Vision: Art Histories and Colonial Histories in the Pacific. Cambridge: Cambridge University Press.

Thompson, Christina

1997　A Dangerous People Whose Only Occupation Is War: Maori and Pakeha in 19th-Century New Zealand. Journal of Pacific History 32(1):109–119.

Tilley, Christopher

1997[1994]　A Phenomenology of Landscape: Places, Paths and Monuments. Oxford: Berg.

Tilley, Christopher, Webb Keane, Susan Kuechler, Mike Rowlands, and Patricia Spyer, eds.

2006　Handbook of Material Culture. London: Sage.

Torrence, Robin

1993　Ethnoarchaeology, Museum Collections, and Prehistoric Exchange: Obsidian-Tipped Artifacts from the Admiralty Islands. World Archaeology 24(3):467–481.

2000　Just Another Trader?: An Archaeological Perspective on European Barter with Admiralty Islanders, Papua New Guinea. *In* The Archaeology of Difference: Negotiating Cross-Cultural Engagements in Oceania. Robin Torrence and Anne Clarke, eds. Pp. 104–141. London: Routledge.

2002　Obsidian-Tipped Spears and Daggers: What We Can Learn from 130 Years of Museum Collecting. *In* Admiralty Islands: Art from the South Seas. Christian Kaufmann and Sylvia Ohnemus, eds. Pp. 73–80. Zurich: Museum Rietberg.

Torrence, Robin, and Anne Clarke

2011　"Suitable for Decoration of Halls and Billiard Rooms": Finding Indigenous Agency in Historic Auction and Sale Catalogues. *In* Unpacking the Collection: Networks of Material and Social Agency in the Museum. Sarah Byrne, Anne Clarke, Rodney Harrison, and Robin Torrence, eds. Pp. 29–54. New York: Springer.

Toyne, Phillip, and Daniel Vachon
1984   Growing Up the Country: The Pitjantjatjara Struggle for Their Land. Fitzroy, Australia: Penguin.

Trouillot, Michel-Rolph
1995   Silencing the Past: Power and the Production of History. Boston: Beacon.

Tsing, Anna L.
2005   Friction: An Ethnography of Global Connection. Princeton, NJ: Princeton University Press.

Tuhiwai Smith, Linda
2006[1999] Decolonizing Methodologies: Research and Indigenous Peoples. London: Routledge.

Turkle, Sherry
2007   Introduction: The Things That Matter. *In* Evocative Objects: Things We Think With. Sherry Turkle, ed. Pp. 3–11. Cambridge, MA: MIT Press.

Turner, William Y.
1878   The Ethnology of the Motu. Journal of the Anthropological Institute of Great Britain and Ireland 7:470–499.

Tylor, Edward B.
1885   How the Problems of American Anthropology Present Themselves to the English Mind. Anthropological Society of Washington Transactions 3:81–95.
1920[1871] Primitive Culture. New York: Putnam's Sons.

Ulrich, Laurel Thatcher
2001   The Age of Homespun: Objects and Stories in the Creation of an American Myth. New York: Knopf.

UNESCO
1987   World Heritage Nomination: IUCN Summary 447: Uluru (Ayers Rock–Mount Olga) National Park Australia. http://whc.unesco.org/archive/advisory_body_evaluation/447rev.pdf, accessed 20 May 2010.
1992   Item 14 of Provisional Agenda: Revision of the Operational Guidelines for the Implementation of the World Heritage Convention. http://whc.unesco.org/archive/1992/whc-92-conf002-10adde.pdf, accessed 4 October 2011.
2003   Convention for the Safeguarding of the Intangible Cultural Heritage. http://unesdoc.unesco.org/images/0013/001325/132540e.pdf, accessed 4 June 2009.
2010[1972] Convention Concerning the Protection of the World Cultural and Natural Heritage. http://whc.unesco.org/en/conventiontext, accessed 22 July 2010.
2011   Proclamation 2003: Oral and Graphic Expressions of the Wajapi. http://www.unesco.org/culture/ich/index.php?topic=mp&cp=BR#TOC1, accessed 17 February 2011.

Van Gennep, Arnold
1909   Les rites de passage. Paris: Nourry.

REFERENCES

Vaquero, Manuel
2008   The History of Stones: Behavioural Inferences and Temporal Resolution
        of an Archaeological Assemblage from the Middle Palaeolithic. Journal of
        Archaeological Science 35:3178–3185.

Vergo, Peter, ed.
1989   The New Museology. London: Reaktion.

Vernes, Théodore
1867   Exposition universelle de 1867 à Paris: Section des missions protestantes
        évangéliques: Catalogue et notices. Paris: Dentu.

Viola, Herman
1981   Diplomats in Buckskins: A History of Indian Delegations in Washington City.
        Washington, DC: Smithsonian Institution Press.

Viveiros de Castro, Eduardo
2004   Exchanging Perspectives: The Transformation of Objects into Subjects in
        Amerindian Ontologies. Common Knowledge 10(3):463–484.

Walsh, Kevin
1992   The Representation of the Past: Museums and Heritage in the Post-modern
        World. London: Routledge.

Webb, Virginia-Lee
1995   Photographs of Papua New Guinea: American Expeditions 1928–29. Pacific
        Arts 11–12(July):72–81.

1996   Framing Time: Photographs of New Guinea from the Crane Pacific
        Expedition, 1928–29. PhD dissertation, Columbia University.

Webmoor, Timothy
2007   What about "One More Turn after the Social" in Archaeological Reasoning?
        Taking Things Seriously. World Archaeology 39(4):563–578.

2012   An Archaeological Metaphysics of Care: On Epistemography, Heritage
        Ecologies, and the Isotopy of the Past(s). In Modern Materials: The
        Proceedings of CHAT Oxford, 2009. Brent R. Fortenberry and Laura
        McAtackney, eds. Pp. 13–23. Oxford: Archaeopress.

Webster, William Downing
1895   Catalogue of Ethnological Specimens: European and Eastern Arms and
        Armour, Prehistoric and Other Curiosities on Sale by W. D. Webster. Oxford
        House, Bicester: privately published.

1897   Illustrated Catalogue of Ethnographic Specimens: European and
        Eastern Arms and Armour, Prehistoric and Other Curiosities on Sale by
        W. D. Webster. No. 12. Oxford House, Bicester: privately published.

Weiner, James F.
2003   Tree Leaf Talk: A Heideggerian Anthropology. Oxford: Berg.

Welsch, Robert L.

1998   An American Anthropologist in Melanesia: A. B. Lewis and the Joseph N. Field South Pacific Expedition, 1909–1913, vol. 2. Honolulu: University of Hawaii Press.

Wengrow, David

2008   Prehistories of Commodity Branding. Current Anthropology 49(1):7–34.

West, Harry

2007   Ethnographic Sorcery. Chicago: University of Chicago Press.

West, W. Richard, Jr.

2004a   The Changing Presentation of the American Indian: Museums and Native Cultures. Seattle: University of Washington Press.

2004b   Keynote Address: The National Museum of the American Indian. *In* Stewards of the Sacred. Lawrence E. Sullivan and Alison Edwards, eds. Pp. 7–17. Washington, DC: American Association of Museums.

White, Richard

1991   The Middle Ground: Indians, Empires, and Republics in the Great Lakes Region, 1650–1815. Cambridge: Cambridge University Press.

White Deer, Gary

1997   Return to the Sacred. *In* Native Americans and Archaeologists: Stepping Stones to Common Ground. Nina Swidler, Kurt Dongoske, Roger Anyon, and Alan Downer, eds. Pp. 37–43. Walnut Creek, CA: AltaMira.

Whorf, Benjamin Lee

1956   Language, Thought, and Reality: Selected Writings of Benjamin Lee Whorf. John M. Carroll, ed. Cambridge, MA: MIT Press.

1975   An American Indian Model of the Universe. *In* Teachings from the American Earth: Indian Religion and Philosophy. Dennis Tedlock and Barbara Tedlock, eds. Pp. 121–129. New York: Liveright.

Wijesuriya, Gamini

2007   Conserving Living Taonga: The Concept of Continuity. *In* Decolonizing Conservation: Caring for Maori Meeting Houses outside New Zealand. Dean Sully, ed. Pp. 59–70. Walnut Creek, CA: Left Coast Press.

Wilder, Gary

2005   The French Imperial Nation-State: Negritude and Colonial Humanism between the Two World Wars. Chicago: University of Chicago Press.

Wingfield, Chris

2005   Historical Time versus the Imagination of Antiquity. *In* The Qualities of Time: Anthropological Approaches. W. James and D. Mills, eds. Pp. 119–135. Oxford: Berg.

2010   Touching the Buddha: Encounters with a Charismatic Object. *In* Museum Materialities: Objects, Engagements, Interpretations. Sandra Dudley, ed. Pp. 53–70. London: Routledge.

REFERENCES

2011 Donors, Loaners, Dealers and Swappers: The Relationships behind the English Collections at the Pitt Rivers Museum. *In* Unpacking the Collection: Networks of Material and Social Agency in the Museum. Sarah Byrne, Anne Clarke, Rodney Harrison, and Robin Torrence, eds. Pp. 119–140. New York: Springer.

2012 The Moving Objects of the London Missionary Society: An Experiment in Symmetrical Anthropology. PhD thesis, University of Birmingham.

Witmore, Christopher

2007 Symmetrical Archaeology: Excerpts of a Manifesto. World Archaeology 39(4):546–562.

Witz, Leslie

2006 Transforming Museums on Post-apartheid Tourist Routes. *In* Museum Frictions: Public Cultures/Global Transformations. Ivan Karp, Corinne A. Kratz, Lynn Szwaja, and Tomás Ybarra-Frausto, eds. Pp. 107–134. Durham, NC: Duke University Press.

Wolfe, Patrick

1999 Settler Colonialism and the Transformation of Anthropology: The Politics and Poetics of an Ethnographic Event. London: Cassell.

Yate, William

1835 An Account of New Zealand, and of the Formation and Progress of the Church Missionary Society's Mission in the Northern Island. London: Seeley and Burnside.

Young, David E., and Jean-Guy Goulet, eds.

1998 Being Changed by Cross-Cultural Encounters: The Anthropology of Extraordinary Experience. Ontario: Broadview.

Zedeño, Maria Nieves

2008 Bundled Worlds: The Roles and Interactions of Complex Objects from the North American Plains. Journal of Archaeological Method and Theory 15:362–378.

Index

1912 Geneva agreement, 43

A'a (Polynesian "god"), 85–86
Aboriginal Land Rights Act, 114n5
Aboriginality, 49, 53, 56, 59n26
Aborigines, 9, 57n10, 58n12; in Australia, 41–43, 45–49, 53–55, 59n23, 107, 109; in Canada, 40–41; and exhibit displays, 101; and land ownership, 55–56; as "Other," 46–48; performances of, 45–49; and whites, 47, 55
accessioning, of objects, 62, 71–72, 74, 143–144, 155–156, 164–165, 173, 177, 182, 212, 236
Acoma Pueblo, 278
actor-network theory (ANT), 4–5, 15, 23–24, 65, 77, 85, 210, 221
Admiralty Islands/Islanders, 129, 175, 183
Africa, 53, 61–63, 65, 68, 81–84, 93
Africa: Arts and Cultures, 85
African Americans, 202
agency, 29, 40, 106, 118–119, 138, 280; and animacy, 268–269; definition of, 24; distribution of, 15–17, 21–24, 40, 44, 48–49, 120; forms of, 7, 27,

35, 40, 44–48, 118–121; and forms of encounter, 43; of heritage lists, 99; human, 16, 67, 201, 221, 249, 252–253, 255; indigenous, 3–8, 13–14, 21, 27, 31–32, 34, 43–44, 49, 55, 92, 99–101, 108, 110–111, 124–125, 165, 168, 173; mediation of, 24, 30; and museums, 20, 30–32, 34, 91–92, 165; networks of, 22–23, 117; of objects, 4–5, 14–17, 28, 32–33, 35, 66–67, 111, 117, 120, 249–253; social, 145, 268–269
Ahayu:da (Zuni war gods), 272–273
Aitutaki carved figure, 74
Alaska-Yukon-Pacific Exposition, 163
Amazon, 90
Ambunti, 128
American civil rights movement, 202
American Indian Religious Freedom Act, 275
American Indians, 262, 271–275, 277–279, 281. *See also* Native Americans
American Museum of Natural History, 56n1
American Southwest, 146, 149, 156, 261, 274. *See also* Bureau of American Ethnology (BAE) expedition; specific pueblos; specific tribes

Americas, 261

Anangu people, 101–105, 114n5

animacy, of artifacts, 24, 33, 266–270, 273, 275–276, 280–281

anthropology, 57n4; and archaeology, 201–202; biological focus of, 66–67; development of, 8, 92, 94; first husband-and-wife team of, 149–150; formative years of, 143, 146; functionalist approaches to, 93; materiality of, 201–201; museum, 92–94; and notions of culture, 94–95; object-centered approach of, 5, 18; physical, 42, 50; practices of, 145, 166; social, 42, 50, 58n20, 66, 208–209; socio-cultural, 114n3; symmetrical, 63–69, 72, 82, 84

Anthropology Committee of the Australian National Research Council, 53

Anthropology Society of Washington, 149

antiquities market, 274

antiracist programs (France), 52

Apaches, 161

Arapahos, 149

archaeological: assemblage, 19–20, 32, 77, 80, 173–174, 204–205, 209; contexts, 19, 205, 209; sites, 19–20, 32, 39, 109, 173, 205, 214, 278, 281

archaeological sensibility, 4, 7, 18, 20, 22, 27, 34, 66–69, 71, 79, 81, 83, 85, 200–201, 203, 226

archaeology, 114n3; and anthropology, 201–202; and assemblage, 203–204; and daily life, 66–67; and ethnographic collections, 173–176; focuses of, 201; object-centered approach of, 22, 173–174, 202; and objects/space relationship, 207; and reassembling fragments, 76–77; site-based, 204; techniques of, 71

Archaeology of Knowledge, The (Foucault), 18

architecture, 85, 99, 276, 281

archival records, 18, 67, 74–75, 77, 119, 176, 207, 230, 232, 234–237, 239, 241–242, 250. *See also* documentation, of artifacts/objects

Arizona, 259, 274. *See also* Hopi people

armbands, 188, 190–191, 227

Arrernte peoples, 49

arrows, 121, 133–136, 181, 269

art/artist, definition of, 264

art-culture market, 17, 259

articulation theory, 11

artifacts, 50, 84, 117, 121, 164; of ancestral importance, 233–234, 246–248, 257n10, 274, 281; archaeological context of, 209; associated sets of, 203; biographies of, 67–69; collecting of, 94; culturally sensitive, 278; definition of, 3, 72–73, 260–261, 264, 283n2; deposition of, 205; "detachment of," 80; as embodiment of ancestors, 109; and everyday life, 253; examination of, 161–162; found at the same site, 203–204; and intangible heritage, 224; made for trade with Westerners, 17, 179–187, 194; of marginalized social groups, 100; material properties of, 173, 176, 177, 242, 250–253, 265, 268; meaning/significance of, 227, 249, 280; as "members of communities," 266; museum staffs' relationships with, 263–264; and normative notions of culture, 93–94; "objectification of," 72; origin of, 264; power/significance of, 268; production of, 174, 253; and relations with humans, 33, 263–264, 268, 270–271, 276, 280–281; relationships with each other, 33; respectful treatment of, 6, 34, 276–279; restricted access to, 279; social "place" of, 228. *See also* objects; specific collections; specific types

Arts and Humanities Research Council, 211

A:shiwi A:wan Museum and Heritage Center, 276

Asia, 93, 100, 131

assemblages, 11, 15, 27, 206, 209; definition of, 203–205, 210; historical relationships in, 208; of household objects, 227–228; of materials, 4, 81, 93; of missionary collections, 76–81, 85, 87; museum collections as, 18–20, 30–34, 200, 210, 220, 226; and museum objects, 210–211; in museum storerooms, 20, 204–209, 213–214, 218, 257n10; museums as, 4, 15, 21–22, 30, 203–204, 221; notions of, 18–22; of objects, 172; and social practice, 221–226

Auckland Museum, 231, 241, 256n3, 256n4

auction catalogs, 173, 179, 182, 186, 190

auction houses, 210

Australia, 9, 56n1, 57n4, 59n23, 97, 101–109, 121, 174–177, 202–203. *See also* Aborigines

Australian Association for the Advancement of Science, 58n19
Australian Museum (Sydney), 176–187, 191–193
Australian National Parks and Wildlife Service, 114n5
authenticity, 11, 19, 93, 229, 241, 248, 278
authority, 12–14, 21, 27, 31, 33–34, 42
authorizing heritage discourse (AHD), 100

Bacon, Francis, 39
Balfour, Henry, 94
bamboo, 134, 136, 183–185, 187–188, 215–216
Bannon, Roy, 125, 141n6
barkcloth, 213
Barker, John, 178
bartering, 17, 171, 175, 179–184, 188, 194–195. *See also* trade/trade goods
Basketmaker-era atlatl, 269
basketry, 136, 161–162, 259, 267, 277
Bateson, Gregory, 82–83
Bay of Plenty (Te Moana a Toi) region, 233, 248
beads, 179, 191–192
Beasley, Harry, 78–79, 81
Beck, Ulrich, 98
behavior, 5, 16, 19, 22, 28, 42, 174, 201, 204, 253
Bell, Joshua, 31, 254
"belt-maker" mannequin, 163–165
Bender, Barbara, 280
Bennet, George, 70
Bennett, Jane, 21
Bennett, Tony, 17, 30, 92–93, 100–101
berdache. See *lhamana* ("man/woman")
Berger, John, 165
Béteille, André, 10
betel-nut chewing, 213, 215–216, 218–219
Binford, Lewis, 201, 205
biodiversity, 106
biographies: of humans, 67, 71–72, 75; and material exchanges, 174; of objects, 67–69, 71–76, 86, 201, 239, 248
biological sciences, 93
birds of paradise, 131, 133–135, 137, 176
Birmingham Museum (England), 80, 87n1
Birth of the Museum, The (Bennett), 93, 100–101

Bishop Museum, 118, 122, 141n3
blessings, 267, 276
Bloomsbury (London, England), 65
Boas, Franz, 56n1, 94–95, 224
boat models, 188–193
Boazi-speaking peoples, 131–132
body decoration, 90, 182, 227
Borneo, 89
botanical specimens, 117–118, 120–122, 125, 128–130
Brandes, E. W., 118, 121–129, 131, 133–139, 140n3
Brenchley, Julius, 215–216
Brisbane, Sir Thomas Makdougall, 232–233, 235, 238, 248–249
British Association for the Advancement of Science, 59n23
British Association's Anthropometric Committee, 43
British colonists, 175, 235
British Māori community, 236
British Museum (BM) (London): African Galleries in, 61–63, 82, 85; and Evelyn Tetehu, 226–228; London Missionary Society objects in, 62–63, 77–78, 80–82, 85–86; Māori exhibition of, 256n6; Melanesian collections of, 32, 200, 211–216, 218–221; and object labels, 74; and Papua New Guinea, 176, 183–184, 186–187; staged events at, 225; storeroom of, 200, 212–216. *See also* ostrich eggshell
British New Guinea, 172, 176–177, 179–180, 191
Broca, Paul, 50
Brooke, Rupert, 63–65, 68, 85
Buber, Martin, 263
Bureau of American Ethnology (BAE) expedition, 148–151, 155–156, 158, 160, 162
burials, 19, 68, 85, 270, 272, 274–275, 277
Burston, Roy, 42–43
Burt, Ben, 213
Busse, Mark, 132–133
Byrne, Denis, 99
Byrne, Sarah, 22, 32, 213

Cabinets of curiosity, 39
California Pacific Exposition (San Diego), 163

Callon, Michel, 16, 40

Cambridge Anthropological Expedition, 89

Cambridge Museum of Archaeology and Anthropology, 184, 187, 211, 213

Campbell, Joseph, 280

Canada, 9, 40, 54, 202

Canberra, 124, 241

canoes, 234, 240–241, 251–252. See also *waka* (canoe)

Canterbury Museum, 231, 256n2

capitalism, 171, 282

card catalogs, 155–157, 165, 231–232

Caribbean, 62

Carlisle Indian School, 160

carvings, 128, 178, 260, 267, 269, 272–273. See also *waka* (canoe)

catalogs/cataloging, 12, 31, 62, 70–71, 75, 173, 178, 231, 276

categories, 110; of archaeologists, 260; "assemblages," 204–205; ethnic, 167; of heritage, 108; of museum objects, 206, 229–230, 235–237, 247–248, 269, 282; of museums, 10–13, 25, 32

Celotex Company (Chicago), 140n2

censuses, 40–41, 54–55, 177

Central Province (New Guinea), 172, 174–176; museum collections of, 176–177, 193–195; and objects made for trade, 179–183; strategic gifting in, 177–179; traditional pipes of, 182–188; valuable objects of, 188–193; and Western contact, 177, 194. See also Australian Museum (Sydney)

ceremonies, 43, 73, 83, 279; Hopi artifacts for, 264–266, 268; objects for, 155, 179, 189, 218–220; and pottery making, 150–151; regalia for, 167; of the Zunis, 150–151, 153, 155–158, 161. See also prayer feathers

Champion, Ivan, 125–126, 128, 132, 141n6

Chicago, 77, 160

Chicago World's Fair, 144, 160–163

Christianity, 85, 87, 177. See also missionaries

civilization, 45, 54, 86–87, 92, 94, 112

clans/tribal groups, 54, 167, 187, 194, 227, 259–260, 275, 278

Clarke, Anne, 31–32

classification, of objects, 11, 13, 28, 31, 40, 98, 146, 171, 195, 229–236, 248, 252, 281

Cleere, Henry, 99

Cleveland, Grover, 152

Clifford, James, 11, 28–29, 43, 93, 166

cloth, 123, 179, 191–192, 213

Cobo, Martinez, 9

Colin, M. Achille, 160

collecting, 17, 27, 30, 44, 57n9, 89, 91, 118, 121, 140n1, 207, 210, 215–216, 227; in Central Province (New Guinea), 177; collecting of, 94; criteria of, 206; of culture, 93–94; demise of, 93–94; "encounter," 173; forms of, 43; guides for, 178; and identity formation, 55; indigenous materials, 55–56, 56n1, 57n6, 110; indigenous peoples' influence on, 110; of materials, 39–40, 49, 52, 55; and museums, 8, 32, 68–69, 85, 92–93, 95–96, 232; in nineteenth century, 215; by non-Natives, 259; and objects in storerooms, 204; objects made for, 182–183, 188; as ongoing process, 79–81; practices of, 44, 94, 171; as process of "detachment," 72–73; sites of, 39–40, 48–49, 52; of sugarcane expedition, 121–124; and threat of risk/loss, 31, 96–98; via airplanes, 130–131; by Westerners, 8, 195; and World Heritage Lists, 110. See also museum collections; specific collections; specific expeditions

Collecting Colonialism: Material Culture and Colonial Change (Gosden and Knowles), 193

collections care, 6, 259–261, 265–267

collections management, 12, 32, 203, 260, 263, 265, 267, 281

collectors, 30, 40, 121, 155, 174, 213, 215, 219, 221, 252. See also private collectors; specific names

colonial: administration, 40–41, 44, 48–49, 52–54; art-culture market, 110; contexts, 5, 16, 31, 57n3, 193, 202; culture, 84, 193–194, 246, 253; encounters, 28, 68, 82, 180, 187, 194, 249; humanism, 52–54; labor system, 128; museums, 44, 47; narrative, 93; period, 32, 190, 194; policy, 50; power relations, 3, 17; practices, 50; press, 235; rule, 17, 193; settings, 171–176; social relations, 123; society, 53, 172, 176, 186–187, 193; state, 9, 48, 126

Colonial Sugar Refining Company, 125, 140n2

colonialism, 8, 10, 44, 54, 92, 125, 193–195, 203
colonized peoples, 50–54, 171–177, 186–187, 193–195. *See also* decolonization; specific people
colonizer and colonized, 30, 40, 46, 48, 83–84, 184, 193, 195
commercial commodity, 171, 187
commodification, 109
commodity brands, 73–75
communities of engagement, 252–254
conservation, 27, 81, 203; global projects of, 29; of heritage, 97, 99, 101, 108–111; of Māori *waka* (canoe), 32, 229–231, 235–255
conservators, 229, 235–236, 239–241, 252, 260, 281. *See also* specific names
"contact zone," 5, 28–29, 43, 82, 84, 199
Convention Concerning the Protection of the World Cultural and Natural Heritage, 95
Convention for the Safeguarding of the Intangible Cultural Heritage, 224
Cook, Captain, 234
copies, of artifacts, 179–181, 194
Coranderrk, 45, 47, 57n10
Covenant of the League of Nations, 9
Crane Pacific Expedition, 128
Crombie, Linda, 43
cross-cultural: arenas, 165–166; contact, 29, 214; encounters, 254; engagement, 44; interactions, 29, 110, 180, 195; networks, 49; relationships, 193; settings, 174; translations, 166
Cruikshank, Julie, 167
cultural: adaptation, 153; assemblages, 99; behaviors, 173; capital, 44; contexts, 231, 249, 267, 273, 277, 279; continuity, 11; development, 94; differences, 262; diversity, 51, 94, 225; expression, 106–107; fragmentation, 282; geography, 206–207; identity, 184, 187; inscriptive practices, 166; "invention," 11; knowledge, 146, 151–152, 161, 164; landscapes, 101–106, 108, 112–114, 114n5; loss, 97–98; ownership, 5; practices, 84, 96, 109, 171–172, 213, 218, 221, 224, 268; processes, 19; relativism, 94–95, 111; rights, 107; spaces, 224; translation, 164, 166; use, 266–267, 275
culture: brokers of, 262; commodification of, 109; indigenous, 93–94, 106–107, 167; non-monumental, 105; notions of, 9, 29, 93–95; and risk/loss threat, 106, 108, 110–112
curators, 22, 203, 206, 212; collaborative efforts of, 158, 200, 202; influence of, 229; and mannequins, 160–162; and Native American art, 32–33, 261–263, 267–268, 274–275, 279; non-Western models of, 202; object-centered approach of, 221; practices of, 4, 6–7, 12–13, 215, 260, 283n3; research efforts of, 237, 265; role/responsibilities of, 4–6, 13–15, 20, 32, 35, 110, 210, 235–236, 241–242, 249–252; and source communities, 32, 210–211, 226, 273; and storerooms, 207–208, 210–211, 215, 223; and *waka* (canoe) restoration, 235–239, 241–242, 249–252. *See also* specific names
curios/souvenirs, 8, 45, 124, 187–189, 193, 232, 235, 247, 249, 259
Cushing, Frank Hamilton, 147–148, 152, 160–162, 169n8

D'Albertis, Luigi, 132–133
dance, 155, 206, 220–221, 223–225
Daru, 132
Darwin, 47, 58n12
databases, 12, 62, 74, 77, 155–156, 207–208, 212–213, 223, 231, 268
Dauncey, H. M., 189–192
Daviumbu, 131
de la Cadena, Marisol, 165
De Landa, Manuel, 20–21, 24, 209–210, 218, 222
Deacon, Harriet, 224
dealers, 210
death, 75, 270–272, 275–277
decolonization, 93, 95
decoration, of artifacts, 173–174, 178, 180, 182, 184, 187–188, 194–195, 215–216
Delana (Hall Sound, New Guinea), 189
Deleuze, Gilles, 16, 18, 20, 24, 85, 209–210
Dening, Greg, 119, 165
descendant communities, 14, 267
detachment, process of, 72–73
deterritorialization, 222, 225
Devam, 131, 133
display, 10, 20, 22, 35, 210, 215; cases for, 61–62, 64–65, 68, 75, 199, 240; of

ceremonial regalia, 167; dioramas for, 224; evolutionary, 47, 224; of Hopi art/artifacts, 261, 277, 279; of human remains, 274–276, 281; indigenous influence on, 14, 225; and intangible heritage, 224–225; modes of, 9, 203; of museum objects, 73–76, 81–83, 171, 199, 206, 215; of Native American artifacts, 280; new modes of, 224, 226; and relationship between objects, 204; of *waka* (canoe), 229–230, 232, 236, 238–240, 246–247, 250–252, 254

documentary sources, 69, 71, 79, 155

documentation, of artifacts/objects, 62, 76, 155–158, 160, 165, 173, 182, 228, 231–233, 235, 239, 241–242, 248, 250, 260

donations, 44, 46–47, 72, 179, 186, 215–216, 219

Douglas, Mary, 11, 97–98

drums, 120, 123, 128, 180

Duclos, Rebecca, 206–207

Duff, Roger, 231, 236, 256n2, 256n4

Dunbar, U. S. J., 160

Durkheim, Emile, 48, 58n20

Dutch-American Expedition (1926), 124

Dutch New Guinea, 124, 131, 141n3

Earth, 264, 268, 270, 272–275, 280

ecology, 129, 279

"ecomuseum" philosophy, 95, 224–226

economy, 42, 50, 54, 96, 129–130, 158, 172, 177

Edge-Partington, James, 178, 217, 219

Edge-Partington, Thomas, 219

Edinburgh, Scotland, 78, 241, 246

Edinburgh University Museum, 231–232, 256n1

education, 17, 51–52, 95, 210, 259, 261, 265, 276

educators, 260

Edwards, Alison, 276

Edwards, Elizabeth, 254

Egypt, 95

emotions, 33, 261–264, 267–270, 279–281

England, 64–65, 68, 78, 80, 89, 183. *See also* Great Britain

Enote, Jim, 276

environmental conditions, 52, 54, 109

ethics, 5, 10, 254, 282

ethnographers, 66–67

ethnography, 40, 46, 48, 51, 72–73, 76, 93

Euro Americans, 28, 147–149, 152–153, 167–168, 262, 278

Europe, 8, 85, 93, 99, 177

Europeans: and civilization, 45; collectors, 32, 123, 128–129; and demand for ethnographic objects, 178–180, 235; and the Māori, 232–233, 235, 247–249, 254; and Papua New Guinea, 131–133, 138, 175, 192–193; traders, 188–189, 233, 235

Everill Junction, 125, 128, 130–132

Evocative Objects: Things We Think With (Turkle), 34

evolutionism, 9, 50, 53–54, 203

excavations, 65, 71, 76–77, 81, 173, 209, 211

exchange, 120, 123, 133, 138, 184–185; acts of, 72, 82, 174–175; artifacts made for, 277; ceremonial, 192; and European culture, 84; forms of, 43, 68, 175, 193; *hiri* system of, 176, 190; of information, 228; of locally valuable objects, 191–193; of material culture, 174–175, 194; and museum collections, 80, 191; regional networks of, 79–80; relations mediated through, 129; and social relations, 175–177, 187–188, 192–195; symbolic, 44

exhibitionary complex, 26–28

exhibitions, 9–10, 17, 20, 33, 94, 215, 265; of Aboriginal culture, 41, 44–48, 53, 57n6; arranged by cultural regions, 160; changing practices of, 44, 51–52; and curatorial narrative, 208; of Grenfell collection, 79–80; of Hopi art/artifacts, 260–261; and ICOM, 95; and indigenous peoples, 14, 44–45, 273; of London Missionary Society, 70–71; mannequins for, 159–165, 169n6; and the Māori, 44, 256n6; of Melanesian collections, 211; and the *museographie claire*, 51–52; and museum storerooms, 199; of Native American art/lifeways, 269, 279, 280; objects restored for, 229; reassembling objects in, 210–211; and staged events, 225; Western forms of, 55; of Zuni artifacts, 157. *See also* display; labels; museums

expeditions, 41, 56n1, 57n9, 58n15, 89, 93, 96, 118–119, 146–151, 158. *See also* specific names

explorers, 31, 174–175, 177, 179, 194–195
export, 44, 46
Exposition Universelle (Paris), 70–71
expositions, 160, 163. *See also* specific expos

Fabian, Johannes, 62, 93
fauna collections, 122, 126, 158
faunal collections, 204
feathers, 178, 181, 183, 232, 234, 244–246, 269. *See also* prayer feathers
fetishization, 221
field: notes, 89, 91, 162, 164; sites, 19, 200, 203–207; skills, 208–209
Field Museum (Chicago), 77, 79
fields of relations, 22, 25–29
fieldwork, 54, 76, 91; in Australia, 41–43, 46, 48–49; under Bureau of American Ethnology, 146–151; expeditions for, 56n1, 93; first woman in, 149; and laboratory, 44, 52–53, 94; and museums, 30–31, 40–41, 43, 45–47, 48, 52, 55, 57n9, 68–69, 96, 279; objects collected in, 31–32; sites of collection, 44, 48–49, 52–53, 69, 71, 77, 79
fighting (or mouth) ornaments, 178–181, 194
filming/films, 42–43, 45–49, 89, 117–118, 121, 124–128, 130–131, 133–139, 250, 254, 280
findspots, 79
flasks (lime), 215–216
flint knapping, 77, 79, 161
Flood, Milton, 191–193
Fly River (New Guinea), 128, 141n6
Flynn, Gillian, 160, 163–164, 169n6
Foucault, Michel, 18, 51
Fowler, Don, 160
France, 95; anthropology of, 50; colonies of, 51–54; ethnology of, 50, 54, 57n1
Frazer, James, 48
friction/conflict, 29–30, 82, 105, 129
Fuller, A. W. F., 77–79, 81
funerary objects. *See* grave goods

Gammage, Bill, 175
Gell, Alfred, 15, 66–67, 268–269
gender, 166, 168, 168n1, 221, 260, 278
geology, 279
German New Guinea, 180, 183
Gerrish, Sarah, 237, 243, 250, 252

gifting, 17, 42, 44, 123, 171, 175, 177–179, 226–227, 253, 270
Gill, William Wyatt, 179
Gillen, Frank, 46, 48–49, 53, 55, 56n1, 57n9, 58n12, 58n15, 58n19
Glass, Vicky, 212
globalization, 10–11, 29, 84, 91, 95, 97, 99, 109, 171
Godwin's Law, 74
Goldie, Andrew, 185–186
Goldsmiths College, 211
Goode, George Brown, 160
Gosden, Chris, 72, 161, 172, 177, 188, 192–194, 201
gourds, 181, 187
governance, 18, 51; colonial/imperial forms of, 6, 28, 41, 53, 91, 177; and cultural heritage lists, 102; and culture, 93; and heritage lists, 99; indigenous, 27; and indigenous agency, 7; of indigenous forms of knowledge, 28; museological forms of, 7, 92
Grant, Lyonel, 256n6, 257n10
grave goods, 274–276
Gray, Geoffrey, 46
Great Britain, 8, 66, 69, 71, 82, 84–85, 179, 201. *See also* England
Greenhalgh, Paul, 100
Grenfell, George, 79–80, 87n1
Guardian, 225
Guattari, Félix, 16, 20, 24, 85, 210

Haddon, Alfred Cort, 56n1, 57n9, 89–90, 184, 187
Hagen peoples/region (New Guinea), 175–176
Hall, Stuart, 11
Handler, Richard, 166
Hargrave, Lawrence, 186
Harrington, John P., 164
Harrison, Rodney, 30–31, 109, 209–210, 281
Harvard University, 92–93
Hawaii, 76
Hawaii Agriculture Research Center, 118
Hawaiian Sugar Planters Association (HSPA), 118, 124, 140n2, 141n3
Hawke, Bob, 114n5
Hayden Geological Survey, 149
Hays-Gilpin, Kelley, 33, 260, 275, 278
Head-Hunters: Black, White, and Brown (Haddon), 89–90

Head, Mazula, 212

headhunting, 132–133

heads, 235. *See also* trophy heads

Heidegger, Martin, 72

Henare, Amiria, 55, 232

Henry, James, 273

heritage, 34; collecting of, 110; cultural, 101–106, 108, 224; definition of, 96–97, 100, 104–106, 108–109; and identity politics/representation, 101; indigenous management of, 102–106, 108; indigenous perception of, 111; industry of, 96; management of, 102–106; "natural," 101–106, 109; nonmonumental, 108; objects, 98–99; organizations, 99; places, 98–99; practices, 13, 98–101, 109–112, 226, 281; production, 92, 110; and risk/loss threat, 96–97, 106, 108–109, 112; safeguarding of, 95; tangible vs. intangible, 233; universal, 99–101, 106; Western traditions/views of, 100, 105. *See also* conservation; intangible heritage; lists/registers; World Heritage: lists

hermaphrodite. See *lhamana* ("man/woman")

Hidden House mummy bundle, 274

Hill, Judy, 206–207

Hillers, John K., 146–147

Hinsley, Curtis, 161–162

hiri exchange system, 176, 190

historical: accounts, 176, 228; contexts, 249, 279; continuity, 10; events, 76; inscription, 145–146, 164–166; narratives, 211; processes, 66, 83, 172, 174, 176–177, 202–203; record, 180; science, 202; site formation processes, 20

Hodder, Ian, 205

Hoffenberg, Peter, 45

Hoffman, Walter, 161

Holmes, W. H., 160–162

Honanie, Delbridge, 271–272

Hooper, Steven, 85

Hopi art and artifacts: animacy of, 33, 266–270; curation of, 261–262; exhibition of, 274; life cycles of, 33, 270–275, 277; and makers' social identities, 260; in museum collections, 259–262, 273, 274, 277, 280; naming of, 267–268; respectful treatment of, 276–279. *See also* specific types

Hopi Cultural Preservation Office, 275

Hopi Festival of Art and Culture, 261, 263

Hopi Katsina Clan, 278

Hopi people, 282, 283n1, 283n2; and clan identity, 278; culture of, 262–263; and emotional/spiritual connection to art/artifacts, 261–264, 267–270; and "feeding" of ceremonial artifacts, 264; identities of, 259–260; lifeways of, 274; and museum collections, 260–261, 269–270, 275–276, 280; ontology of, 32–33, 260, 281; and proper care of collections, 265; request museum loan, 263, 265–268; and restriction of artifacts/knowledge, 279; views on death, 270–272, 275–277, 281

Horniman Museum (Forest Hill, England), 77–78, 81, 203

Hough, Walter, 160

Hugh-Jones, Stephen, 175

Hula women, 187

human: remains, 50, 272, 274–276, 281; rights, 95, 107; sociality, 46, 120, 130

human-nonhuman (object) relations, 4, 13–16, 19–24, 29–30, 34, 65, 82–83, 92, 99, 108–109, 111, 120, 126, 201, 204, 208, 254, 268, 270, 278

Human Past, The (Scarre), 18

humanism, 49–54

humanities, 4–5, 13

Humphrey, Carolyn, 175

Hutchins, Edwin, 15

Identity, 10, 31, 55, 62, 203, 227, 259–260, 269, 278; indigenous, 173, 176, 184, 187–189, 193–194, 224; and Native Americans, 167

imperialism, 5, 8, 16, 28, 92

India, 62

indigeneity, 4, 6, 8–11, 82–84, 106–108, 165

Indigenous and Tribal Peoples Convention, 9

indigenous peoples: as category, 25; and collaborative programs, 32; customs of, 42, 48, 53; definition of, 9–10; economic/technological systems of, 53; and exhibitions, 45; influence on collections, 110, 119; influence on heritage lists, 111; and loss of culture, 96–97; made artifacts for trade, 179–183, 194; mixed heritage of, 83–84; and museum collections, 119, 121, 171; and museums, 5–8, 12–14, 26, 32, 92,

100, 108, 111, 158, 195, 202, 211, 224, 273, 281–282; subjectification of, 6; and Westerners, 173–177, 184–185, 187, 190–191, 192, 195; withhold valuable objects, 188–193, 221
indigenous rights movements, 9–10, 92, 107, 111
Indochina, 51–52
Ingold, Tim, 23–24, 26, 280
inscription, 63–65, 74–76, 80, 145–146, 164–166, 166–168
insect collection, 118, 122
insect infestation, 273
Institut d'Ethnologie, 50, 52
intangible heritage, 31, 92, 98, 101, 106–108, 114n2, 224–225, 233
International Council of Museums (ICOM), 95
International Council on Monuments and Sites (ICOMOS), 102–105
International Federation of Landscape Architects, 103
International Union for Conservation of Nature (IUCN), 101–103
interpretation: of artifacts, 269; of material culture, 201; of materials, 49; of museum objects, 91, 164–165, 224–225, 230, 236, 248, 250
Inuits, 160
Isaac, Gwyneira, 31
Ivison, Duncan, 107

James, George Wharton, 148–149
Java, 118, 140n2, 140n3
Jemez Pueblo, 274
Jessop, Maia, 250
Jeswiet, Jacob, 118, 121–125, 128, 140n3
Jones, Jonathan, 225
Jones, Philip, 43

Kabotie, Michael, 271–272, 279
Kahn, Miriam, 207
Kakadu region, 107, 114n5
Kalahari, 83
Kane, Elisha Kent, 160
kastom (customs), 212, 221
katsina, 154; ceremonies, 263; dolls (tithu), 259–260, 270, 278; friends, 273, 278, 283n4; society, 279
Kaundoma, 131, 133–139

Kenbi land claim, 56
Khoisan language, 83
Kikori, 128
kin: groups, 175, 233, 260, 275, 277; objects as, 13–17, 33, 109; relationships, 130, 277. See also kinship
Kingap, Peter Solo, 212, 220–221
Kingston, Sean, 207
kinship, 51, 278, 281. See also kin
Kirschbaum, Franz Joseph, 128–129, 141n7
Kirshenblatt-Gimblett, Barbara, 72, 98
Kleinoscheg, Mrs. C. A., 124
knowledge: conjectural, 119; embodied/embedded, 242; esoteric, 155; global, 30; indigenous, 28, 145–146; new forms of, 14, 27; new frameworks of, 209; practices, 12; production, 6; repatriation of, 222; sets of, 126; sharing of, 267; Western practices of, 43, 259, 265
Knowles, Chantal, 14, 32, 172, 177, 188, 192–194
koiyu. See shells/shell ornaments
Kopytoff, Igor, 72, 75
Kuklick, Henrika, 47, 56n1, 58n16
Kunimaipa region, 191
Kurin, Richard, 225
kusiwa graphic art, 90–91
Kwa'ioloa, Michael, 212–213

La Petite-Pierre, France, 103, 112–114
labels: attached to objects, 69–71, 73–75; for exhibited objects, 61–63, 68, 70–71, 166, 254; explanatory, 73–74, 81, 254; important role of, 76; institutional, 73–75; on objects in storerooms, 208; technology of, 74–75, 81
labor, 9, 129
laboratories, 44, 52–53, 94
Ladd, Edmund, 273, 277
Laguna Pueblo, 272, 278
Lake District National Park (England), 103
Lake Murray-Middle Fly region (New Guinea), 119, 125, 128–130, 131–138
Lake Murray (New Guinea), 133–134, 137, 141n5
land issues, 49, 54–56, 102–106, 114n5, 194, 233, 245, 278
landscape, 65, 68, 79, 85, 106, 109, 200–201, 204, 280. See also cultural: landscapes
Lanmon, Dwight, 156, 168n4

Larson, Frances, 161

Latin America, 99–100

Latour, Bruno, 4–5, 21–22, 30, 39–40, 52–53, 57n3, 65–66, 76–77, 81, 84, 89, 91, 94, 97, 210, 221

Law, John, 98

Lawes, William George, 179, 192

Layton, Robert, 101

Lévi-Strauss, Claude, 34

lhamana ("man/woman"), 31, 143, 147–149, 151, 168

liberalism, 47, 58n12

life cycles, 33, 75, 264–267, 267, 270–275, 277, 281–282

Liljeblad, Hillel Fredrick, 178, 180–185, 195

List of Intangible Cultural Heritage in Need of Urgent Safeguarding, 91, 114n2, 114n4

List of World Heritage in Danger, 107

Lister, J. K. B., 215

lists/registers, 27, 91–92, 96–99, 101–106, 111, 114n2. *See also* World Heritage: lists; World Heritage: sites

lithic assemblages, 204

loan requests, 263, 265–268

Lomatewama, Ramson, 33, 260, 273–274, 277, 282

London, England, 31, 48, 62–63, 65, 77, 78, 80–81, 212. *See also* British Museum (BM) (London)

London Missionary Society (LMS), 31, 62–63, 179–180; catalogues of, 70–71; collections of, 67–69, 74–76, 81, 84–87; dispersal of collections, 79–81, 85, 87; headquarters of, 78; and object biographies, 67–69, 71–76; and object labels, 69–71, 74–76

looms, 143–145, 154–156, 158, 164

looting, 17, 171, 273

Louisiana sugarcane industry, 118

Lucas, Gavin, 205

Lurie, Nancy, 149

Lydon, Jane, 107

Macleay Museum (University of Sydney), 176

Madagascar, 62

magic/sorcery, 138–140, 178–179, 191, 194, 216, 218

mairi. See shells/shell ornaments

"man-catchers," 181–182

mannequins, 159–165, 169n6

Māori Antiquities Act (1901), 44–45

Māori people/culture, 14, 32, 44–45, 55, 103–104, 229–255, 256n6, 256n7, 257n10. *See also waka* (canoe)

Marienburg Mission Station, 127–129

Marx, Karl, 73

masks, 155, 206, 215, 273, 277, 283n4. *See also* katsina: friends

Mason, Otis, 153, 157–158, 160, 162

Masterpieces of the Oral and Intangible Heritage of Humanity, 90–91, 96, 114n2, 114n4

material culture, discipline of, 201–202

Mauss, Marcel, 50, 52–53, 58n20

McArthur, Annie, 212, 215–216

McArthur, Margaret, 191

McBryde, Isobel, 174–175

McCarthy, Conal, 44, 47, 246

measuring/measurements, 42–43, 48–50

Melanesia, 120, 140, 203

Melanesia Project, 32, 200, 211–221, 226–228

Melbourne, Australia, 45, 47–48, 57n3, 59n23

menstrual taboos, 278

Merlan, Francesa, 9

meshworks, 22–28, 33, 35, 119, 260

Mesoamerican cultures, 264, 274

metal objects, 162, 179, 181

Middle Sepik (New Guinea), 129

Mill, John Stuart, 47

minorities, 10, 13, 92, 99–101, 106–108, 111, 278. *See also* indigenous peoples

Mirrar people, 107

missionaries, 31, 42, 45, 80, 85, 87, 141n7, 174, 179, 189, 210, 268. *See also* London Missionary Society (LMS); specific individuals

Möbius strip, 25–26, 83

modernity, 9, 65, 86, 93, 97–98

monuments, 64–65, 68, 99

Mooney, James, 161

Moore, Henry, 85–86

Morphy, Howard, 58n12

mosaic virus, 118, 120, 140n3

Mother Earth, 151

mother-of-pearl spoon, 218–219

Motu peoples, 176, 187, 192

mouth ornaments. *See* fighting (or mouth) ornaments

Moutu, Andrew, 81

movio/mobio. *See* shells/shell ornaments

Mulvaney, John, 58n12

mummy bundles, 274

Musée de l'Homme (MH), 49–53, 57n1, 57n9, 95

Musée d'Ethnographie du Trocadéro, 50

museological practices, 27, 32, 94–95, 109–112, 202, 215, 224

museum collections, 107–109; absences in, 220–221, 224; access to, 12; agencies within, 20, 117, 120; and archaeological excavations, 173–174; and colonial rule, 193; composition of, 121; as contemporary "ambassadors," 110; debate about, 95–96; engagement with, 254–255; formation of, 4, 6–7, 18–19, 30–31, 89, 91, 93, 173, 226; historical development of, 16; and indigenous communities, 119, 165, 173, 179–180, 195; indigenous peoples' influence on, 17; intellectural care of, 265; meaning/significance of, 167, 212; multiple histories within, 123; power/significance of, 111; reconceptualizing of, 14; reconfiguring of, 210; and risk/loss threat, 89–92, 96–99, 111–112; spatial aspects of, 206–207; structure of, 32, 219–220, 224

museum objects: acquisition of, 61–64, 68–69, 72, 77, 85, 229; animacy of, 266–270; becoming "Other," 75; cultural importance of, 230, 238–239, 242, 247, 254; deposition of, 207; "detachment of," 9, 72–73, 75–76, 80, 85, 166, 208; human relationships with, 268, 278; impact of, 85; important role of, 177; as "inanimate," 266; and indigenous peoples, 224; making of, 71–76, 81; and use, 283n3. *See also* labels

Museum of Northern Arizona (MNA), 261; collection studies, 260; and curation/exhibition, 260, 262, 269, 279; Easton Collections Center of, 276; exhibitions of, 280; Hopi art collection of, 259–261, 277; and Hopi loan request, 263, 265–266; and Native American consultants, 259–262, 265, 269–270, 275–276, 280; rational/intuitive

approach of, 279; triptych painted for, 271–272. *See also* Hopi Festival of Art and Culture

museum professionals, 14, 40, 95, 260, 263. *See also* curators

museum storerooms, 5, 12, 39, 68, 73–75, 173; collaborative research in, 32, 199–200, 208, 212, 214, 218, 221–226; as field site, 205–207; of Museum of Northern Arizona, 263, 276; objects languish in, 229–230, 238, 247–249, 251; opened up to visitors, 207–208, 214–215, 223; power of, 214–215; and relationship between objects, 204, 206, 209; restricted access to, 20, 199; as "site of translation," 199, 207, 212, 214–215, 226

museums, 6, 51, 56, 265–268; as "archaeological site," 18–20, 32; as centers of calculation, 30, 57n3, 91–92; as centers of collection, 30, 91–92, 111; collaboration in, 29–30, 33; and community, 207; dominant cultures in, 100–101; encounters in, 22, 82–83, 251–255, 281; history/development of, 92–93, 121; as modern cultural places, 274; non-Western models of, 202; nondiscrimination policies of, 278; object-centered approach of, 221; practices of, 33, 95, 221–222, 226, 254, 260, 273; and risk/loss threat, 111; role of, 3, 9, 29, 48, 55, 93–96, 172, 229, 265, 273; as "sites of deposition," 79–80; social responsibility/accountability of, 207; as space for reconciliation, 12; study rooms of, 214–215; transformation of, 14–15; "weight" of things in, 5, 13–14, 35; "wider landscapes of," 68. *See also* specific museums

music, 45, 224–225, 225

musikaka. *See* fighting (or mouth) ornaments

myths/mythmaking, 87, 98, 130, 228, 279–280

Mytinger, Caroline, 127, 132–133, 140, 141n9

Nalangu, Walter, 212

narratives, 10, 21, 31, 45–46, 118, 202, 211, 218–219, 222–224, 226–228, 233, 240, 269

nation states, 9, 28, 41, 45, 56, 107

National Anthropological Archives (NAA), 118, 124, 144, 156, 162, 169n8

National Archives of the United States, 118, 124

National Geographic Society Archives (NGSA), 118, 124, 127, 130, 137, 139

National Herbarium, Wageningen (Netherlands), 118, 121–122, 141n4

National Mall (Washington, DC), 144–145, 164

National Museum of Natural History (NMNH), 118, 123–124, 129, 141n4, 143–145, 148, 153–167, 169n6

National Museum of the American Indian (NMAI), 167–168, 267, 273, 276–277

National Museum of Victoria (NMV), 46–48, 53, 58n11, 58n15

National Museums Scotland (NMS), 14, 32, 229–232, 235, 241, 246, 248–250, 256n1, 256n6, 256n7, 257n10. *See also* Pacific Gallery; *waka* (canoe)

National Park Service, 274, 278

Native American Graves Protection and Repatriation Act, 275

Native Americans, 160, 167–168, 202, 259, 261, 266–268, 278–279. *See also* American Indians; Pueblo people; specific peoples

natural history: habitat groups, 160; museums, 39, 40, 93, 101, 256n1; specimens, 117–118

natural sciences, 27, 44, 46–47, 56n1

nature vs. culture, 19–20, 109, 120

Navajos, 269, 276, 280

necklaces, 133–134, 136–137

Neich, Roger, 231–233, 256n4

networks, 21–29, 31, 39–40, 43–44, 72, 91, 193, 202, 209, 253, 260, 269, 277. *See also* actor-network theory (ANT)

New Britain, 188, 192–193

New Guinea, 57n9, 62, 89, 124, 141n7, 141n9, 185–186, 220. *See also* Papua/Papuans

New Guinea Highlands, 175

New Ireland *malangan* figures, 248

New South Wales, 124, 232

New Zealand, 9, 44–47, 103–104, 202, 231–235, 239–240, 246, 249, 256n3

newspaper accounts, 152–155, 168n3

NMNH Annual Report, 161–162

North America, 8, 84, 162, 167, 261

North Island, New Zealand, 233–235

Nuku, George, 236–246, 248–249, 251, 253–254

Object-focused approach, 5, 18, 22, 27

objects, 98; commodification of, 72–73; culturally sensitive, 260; definition of, 3, 72–73, 96–97, 260, 264; deposition of, 205; "detachment of," 206, 210; dissemination of, 208; enchanting qualities of, 5; hybridity of, 81–82, 84; indigenous viewpoints about, 12; made specifically for trade, 17, 179–188, 194, 235; manufacture of, 31, 119, 121; material properties of, 24, 119, 173–174, 177, 219, 242; meaning/significance of, 201, 209, 234; organized by place/type, 215; origin of, 19, 222, 228; physical engagement with, 208; and place, 200; politicized, 55, 110; power/significance of, 111, 173, 248; relationships between, 204, 206, 221, 223, 228; as "sites of intersecting histories," 254; social function of, 223; tangible vs. intangible, 224–225; as "things" that mediate an encounter, 76; withholding of, 17, 176, 188–193. *See also* artifacts; specific collections; specific types

obsidian, 129, 183

Oceania, 100

offerings, 176, 268

Ogamobu Plantation (Papuan Gulf), 123

O'Hanlon, Michael, 69, 181

Oldham, E. R., 132

Oldman, W. O., 78–79, 81, 186

online databases, 212–213, 223

ontologies, 12–13, 32–33, 55, 108–112, 117, 119–120, 125, 209, 260, 267, 281

"Oral and Graphic Expressions of the Wajapi," 90, 96

oral tradition, 167, 224, 279

Organising Modernity (Law), 98

Oro Province, 178

ostrich eggshell, 61–63, 65–66, 68, 74, 81–83, 85

Other/Otherness, 8, 10, 46–48, 51, 54, 56n1, 75, 140

Pacific, 62, 84, 173, 178, 219, 229, 232, 240, 256n7

Pacific Gallery (National Museums of Scotland), 229–231, 248, 253–255

Pakeha people, 44–45

Pan-American Exposition (Buffalo, NY), 163

Papua/Papuans, 141n6, 172; and arrival of Westerners, 176, 192; collecting of artifacts by, 123, 138, 140n1; and exchanges of material culture, 174–178, 183–184, 187–190, 193; and USDA expedition, 31, 118, 122, 125–128, 131, 138, 140n2

Papuan Constabulary, 125–126, 128

Papuan Gulf, 128, 176, 192

Parezo, Nancy, 160

Pariente, Tahiarii, 244–245

Paris Exposition, 160

Paris, France, 48, 52–53, 57n3, 70–71, 90

Parks Australia, 105

Peabody Museum (Harvard University), 92–93

Pearson, Mike, 226

Peck, Richard K., 118, 123–125, 128–129, 131, 133–134, 141n3

Pecos Pueblo, 274

Pemberton, C. E., 118, 122–125, 128, 133, 141n3, 141n5

performances, 45, 83, 145, 165, 167, 194, 225–226. See also staged events

personhood, 33, 55, 120, 281

photographs, 42–43, 45–48, 89, 185, 207, 254; of artifacts, 228, 256n7; for documentation, 232, 236, 239, 241, 250; for making mannequins, 161, 165; of Papua New Guinea valuables, 189–191; of Solomon Islands objects, 213; taken by USDA sugarcane expedition, 117–118, 121, 124, 126–128, 130, 133, 138–140; of We'wha (Zuni Indian), 143–147, 154–160, 162, 165–166

Picasso Gold Medal, 105

Picasso, Pablo, 85–86

Pickering, Felicia, 157

Piney Branch site, 162

Pinney, Christopher, 119

pipes, 134, 136, 182–188, 194

Pitt Rivers, Augustus Henry Lane Fox, 94, 161

Pitt Rivers Museum (Oxford, England), 77–78, 81, 203, 214

Plains medicine bundles, 268

Police Motu (pidgin language), 177

politics, 10; of agency, 168; contexts of, 7; of culture and identity, 52–53; of land claims, 55; and museum collections, 17; of museums, 7; of objects, 5; post-colonial, 202; of power, 167–168; of representation, 3–6, 11, 17, 111, 201–203

Popular Front, 52

Port Jackson (Australia), 174–175

Port Moresby (New Guinea), 125, 128–129, 172, 176–177, 180, 188, 191, 193

Portland Museum of Art, 166

post-colonial: critique, 100; literatures, 7; politics, 202; power relations, 121; studies, 18; world, 3–5, 203

post-processual archaeology, 201, 204

pottery, 76, 143, 148, 150–151, 156, 161–162, 164–166, 168n4, 259–260, 267, 270, 274, 280

Pottery Mound: Germination (Kabotie and Honanie), 271–272

Povinelli, Elizabeth, 49, 55–56

power, 16, 18, 21, 27, 44

power relations, 3, 17, 28–29, 174–175

Powhatans, 161

Pratt, Mary Louise, 28, 82

prayer feathers, 143–144, 156–158, 164, 166

prayers, 267–268

Presbyterian school (Zuni Pueblo), 146–147

preservation, 92, 259; American Indians' view of, 271–275, 281; and insect infestation, 273; of museum objects, 241–242, 247, 249, 251, 254, 265–266, 283n3; of Native American artifacts, 277, 281

prestige, 44, 233

primitiveness, 8, 10, 25, 31, 48, 54, 203

private collectors, 71, 79, 81, 171, 174, 177, 192, 226–228, 232. See also specific names

processual archaeology, 201, 203–205

prospectors, 177

public sphere, 14, 33, 40, 44, 47–53, 68, 92, 171, 207, 226, 238, 240, 248, 250, 253

Pueblo people, 264, 272, 274, 278. See also specific pueblos

Pukaki sculpture, 253

purification, 65–67, 75, 81–85, 98, 118

Purity and Danger (Douglas), 97–98

Queensland Museum (Brisbane), 176, 186

Race, 10–11, 41, 45–46, 48, 50–51, 53, 106, 279

racism, 58n12, 203

Raffles, Hugh, 126

Rasmussen Collection, 166

rattan cuirasses, 129

Raymond, Rosanna, 246

reassembling, 11, 209; of missionary collections, 76–81, 85, 87; of museum collections, 20, 31, 34, 210–211, 215–216, 218–228; of objects in storerooms, 210–212, 215, 218–221, 223–224, 226; of USDA expedition collections, 118, 121–124, 138, 140

Reassembling the Social (Latour), 4–5, 21

reciprocity, 33, 43, 47, 175, 269–271, 281

reenactment, practice of, 161–162

registers. *See* lists/registers

registrar, 263, 265. *See also* collections management

Reimer, Francis, 209

religious: artifacts, 273, 277; cultural landscapes, 113; importance, 101; knowledge, 152; leaders, 273, 275, 277; paraphernalia, 158, 275; practices, 158; programs, 54; societies, 151; springs, 279

repatriation, 12, 222; of Hopi art/artifacts, 261, 278; of human remains, 95, 275–276; of objects, 95, 273; of Zuni war gods, 272–273

Representative List of the Intangible Cultural Heritage of Humanity, 114n2, 114n4

research, 214–215; archaeological, 265; collaborative, 6, 13–14, 199–201, 221–226, 239, 241, 245–246, 254; on collections, 221, 225, 229, 235, 249–250, 255, 265; and Hopi art/artifacts, 263; material approach of, 236–239, 241–242, 250–252; and museum categories, 269; at Museum of Northern Arizona, 259; and preservation of objects, 265–266; social process of, 22

researchers, 5, 14, 199–200, 202, 206, 208–210, 210

restoration, 229, 236, 246, 248, 252, 254

rhizomes, 85

Rigo district (Papua), 128, 130, 141n5

rites of passage, 72–73, 75

rituals: associations of, 260; forms of, 72; and mythmaking, 280; objects for, 49; practices of, 273; responsibilities of, 278; spaces for, 83; staging of, 43

River Murray (Australia), 53

Rivers, W. H., 59n23

Rivet, Paul, 49–50, 52, 54, 95

Rivière, Georges Henri, 51

Robinson, Percy, 123–124

Rockefeller Foundation, 57n4

Roga, Kenneth, 212–213

Roro-speaking people, 192

Roscoe, Will, 147, 152, 154

Rose, Deborah, 109, 281

Rowlands, Michael, 203

Rowse, Tim, 9, 55

Rubin vase, 22–23

Ruppert, Evelyn, 40–41, 54

Rurutu deity figure, 85–86

Sago, 128, 133–134

Sahlins, Marshall, 174–175

Sainsbury African Galleries (British Museum), 61–63, 82, 85

sale catalogs, 173, 179, 182–183, 186

Samou, Salome, 212

San people (Botswana), 61

Santa Fe, New Mexico, 104

Santa Isabel, 215–216, 219, 227–228

Santa Isabel Cultural Heritage Programme, 228

"savages," 8, 10, 45–46, 180

Scarre, Chris, 18

Schiffer, Michael, 19, 209

Schultz, Lainie, 14, 33

science, 27, 31, 34, 47, 58n12, 121, 202, 262, 279, 282

Science, 153, 157

scientific: analysis, 151, 250; expeditions, 39; knowledge, 91; manipulation, 52; models for fieldwork, 56n1; networks, 48; practices, 11; prestige, 44; publications, 46, 48; rationalism, 92; study of materials, 52–53, 274; value, 229

scientists, 30, 40, 50, 174, 177, 260, 262–266, 269, 275–276, 280–281

Seligmann, Charles, 192

Sepik River (New Guinea), 123, 127–129

settlers, 9–10, 54, 83–84, 153, 202

Shanks, Michael, 200, 204, 208, 226
shells/shell ornaments, 137, 175, 178, 190–192, 218–219, 227, 245
Sherratt, Andrew, 66–67
Shindler, A. Z., 156, 160
Silko, Leslie Marmon, 272
silver overlay jewelry, 259
Simmons, David, 231, 236, 256n3, 256n4
Sioux, 160–161
skin color tests, 42–43
skulls, 129, 132–133, 275
Skyros, Greece, 63–65, 85
Smithsonian Institution, 31, 118, 124, 143–146, 148, 152, 155, 160, 163–164, 166, 273, 277
Smoking and Tobacco Pipes in New Guinea, 184
Snyder, Lynn, 160, 163–164, 169n6
social: assemblages, 4, 22, 221–222; categories, 75, 97; change, 12; collectives, 16–17; contexts, 175, 223; definition of, 210, 221; development, 53–54, 225; evolutionary frameworks, 215; identity, 269, 278; interactions, 4–5, 32, 176, 195; networks, 4–5, 98, 106, 166, 202, 253; practices, 164, 206, 208, 218–219, 221–226, 228; progress, 9, 93–94; responsibility, 175, 207, 278; structure, 20, 201, 204, 221
social relations, 4–5, 14–15, 17, 26, 66, 82–83, 171–179, 183–188, 190, 192–195, 267–268
social sciences, 4–5, 13, 15, 210
Soldier, The (Brooke), 64
Solomon Islands/Islanders, 32, 212–219, 226–228
Solomon Islands National Museum, 228
songs, 164, 166, 268. *See also* music
sorcery. *See* magic/sorcery
sound recordings, 42–43, 46–49, 89, 280
source communities, 14, 32–33, 119, 199–200, 202, 204, 208, 210–211, 214–215, 219–221, 225–226, 248, 265–266, 268, 273, 275–276, 281–282. *See also* indigenous peoples
South Africa, 83, 202
South Australia Museum, 53, 57n6
South Australian Board for Anthropological Research, 43
South Island, New Zealand, 235
souvenirs. *See* curios/souvenirs

spatial: boundaries, 222; contexts, 209; dimensions, 67; relationships, 206–207
spears, 175, 181, 183, 227
Spencer, Baldwin, 42–43, 46–50, 53–56, 56n1, 57n9, 58n11–12, 58n15–16, 58n18–19, 59n23
spiritual: connections, 261–262; lives of the Hopi, 268; resources, 49; significance, 34, 102, 104–105, 130, 179, 233–234, 245, 277
spirituality, 268–269
Stable, Charles, 237, 242–243, 250, 252
staged events, 224–226
Starn, Orin, 165
status, 11, 71–72, 178–179, 227
Steinmetz, George, 48
Stevenson, James, 31, 143, 146, 148–150, 152–153, 155, 158
Stevenson, Matilda Coxe, 31, 143, 146, 148–156, 158, 162–164, 166, 168n2, 169n8
Stockholm, 280
Stocking, George, 92
Stone, Octavius, 178
stone tools. *See* tools
storage. *See* museum storerooms
stories/storytellers, 119, 164–166, 168
Strathern, Marilyn, 15, 175
Strickland River (New Guinea), 125, 131, 133
sub-Saharan Africa, 100
Sugar Plant Hunting by Airplane in New Guinea (Brandes), 118, 124
sugarcane, 118, 120–122, 126, 128–131, 133, 138–139, 141n3–4
Sugarcane Expedition to the Territories of Papua and New Guinea, 118–120
Sullivan, Lawrence, 276
Sydney, 124, 129, 140n2, 180, 185, 232, 249. *See also* Australian Museum (Sydney)

Taonga (Māori artifacts), 233, 247–248
taphonomic process, 18–19, 79–80, 204–205
Tapsell, Paul, 253
tattoos, 187–188
Tauparaupi, 132
tautau. *See* shells/shell ornaments
taxes, 177
taxonomy, 39, 162, 247–248
Te Ara (Māori leader), 232

Te Toki-a-Tāpiri canoe, 241

Te Tūhono (Māori canoe), 14, 239, 242–243, 245–246, 248–250, 252–255. See also *waka* (canoe)

technology, 4, 9, 16, 28, 64–65, 69, 74–75, 83, 85, 93–94, 132, 153, 161, 225, 264, 269, 280

territorialization, 222

Tetehu, Evelyn, 32, 212–213, 215–219, 226–228

textiles, 143, 148, 154–156, 165, 213, 260, 277

texts, 48, 98, 106, 117, 199; biases inherent in, 173; collecting of, 30, 39–40, 44, 49–50, 57n9; historical inscription, 145–146, 164–166; material culture as, 69; newspaper accounts, 143, 145, 152–155; tomb inscriptions, 63–65. See *also* labels; inscription

things. See artifacts; objects

Thomas, Nicholas, 120, 172–173

Thompson, Ambong, 212

Tilley, Christopher, 280

Titchen, Sarah, 101

Tjukurpa, 105

Tlingit elders, 166

toas (Aboriginal way-markers), 43, 57n6

tobacco, 128, 132–133, 136, 182–184, 187, 194. See *also* pipes

toea. See armbands

tombs, 63–65, 68

Tongariro National Park, 103–104, 106

tools, 67, 120, 123, 162, 175, 203, 213, 220–221, 267, 269

Topinard, Paul, 50

Torrence, Robin, 31–32

Torres Strait Islands, 56n1, 89–90

tourists, 45, 102, 105, 109, 182, 188, 259

trade/trade goods, 17, 123, 128, 130–138, 173–191, 195, 232–233, 235, 248, 269, 280. See *also* bartering

traders, 173–175, 179, 185–186, 188–189, 192–195, 210, 232, 249

transvestites, 149

tribal museums, 274

trophy heads, 129, 132–133

True, Clara, 149

Tsing, Anna, 29

Turkle, Sherry, 34

Turner, William, 178

turtles, 178–179, 191–192

Tylor, Edward Burnett, 24, 47, 94, 149–150, 161

typology, 24

Uluṟu-Kata Tjuṯa National Park World Heritage Site, 101–106, 114n5

UNESCO, 90–92, 95–97, 101–102, 104, 106–108, 111, 224. See *also* World Heritage: lists; World Heritage: sites

United Kingdom, 78, 103, 212, 256n6

United Nations, 9–10, 95

United Nations Commission on Human Rights, 95

United Nations' International Labour Organization (ILO), 9

United States, 9, 97, 121, 146, 201–202, 281

Universal Copyright Convention, 95

Universal Declaration of Human Rights, 95

universality, principle of, 99–101, 106–107

universities, 44, 57n9, 92–93, 176. See *also* specific names

University of Adelaide's Board of Anthropological Research, 53

University of Cambridge's Museum of Archaeology and Anthropology (England), 78, 89

University of Sydney, 57n4

Unpacking the Collection (Byrne), 22

US Congress, 152

US Department of Agriculture (USDA) expedition, 140n1; agencies involved in, 138–140; botanical specimens collected by, 117–118, 120–122, 125, 128–130; and engagements in Lake Murray-Middly Fly region, 131–138; objects collected by, 31, 118–119, 133–138, 140n1; and the search for sugarcane, 124–131. See *also* filming/ films; photographs

US National Herbarium, 141n4

US National Museum. See National Museum of Natural History (NMNH)

USDA Bureau of Plant Industry's Office of Sugar Plants, 118

Utes, 149

Value, 3, 145, 175, 247; and aesthetics, 168; of ancestral objects, 233–234;

categories of, 11–13; cultural, 102, 158, 230, 264; of everyday objects, 187–188; of important Melanesian objects, 227; of important Papuan objects, 188–192; and indigenous culture, 103, 168; intangible, 224–225; monetary, 171; notions of, 94; scientific, 229; and trade objects, 181; universal, 100, 108, 111

Van Gennep, Arnold, 71–73

Vanapa, 125, 128, 132

Vanuatu Cultural Centre, 212

Victorian period, 203

Viola, Herman, 167

violence, 129, 131, 138

visitors, 22, 33, 44, 207–208, 213–215, 223, 236, 238, 279–280

Wajapi peoples, 90–91

waka (canoe), 14, 32, 229–255, 256n7

warfare, 178, 234–235, 248

Warner, Margaret, 132, 141n9

Washington, DC, 31, 143–146, 148–149, 151–155, 157–158, 160, 164–165, 167

Washington Evening Star, 155–156, 168n3

Washington National Tribune, 153, 168n3

wax cylinder recordings, 89

weapons, 182, 213, 235, 240

weaving, 143–145, 148, 153–156, 158–159, 162, 233, 270, 280

websites, 241. *See also* online databases

Webster, William, 183, 186

Wellcome, Henry, 206

Weredai massacre, 132

West Africa, 51–52

West, W. Richard, Jr., 259

Western Highlands, Papua New Guinea, 220

Westerners, 8, 83, 262; animate/inanimate dichotomy of, 270; European empires of, 93; heritage traditions of, 92, 99–100, 105; industrial culture of, 280–281; museum practices of, 206, 266; ontology of, 260; sociality of, 120; thoughts/views of, 267, 282; trade goods made for, 179–186; traders, 173

We'wha (Zuni Indian), 31, 167, 168n1, 168n3; prayer feathers; artifacts by, 143–144, 155, 164–165; ceremonial role of, 148, 150–151, 157–158; as *lhamana* ("man/woman"), 143, 147–149, 151, 168; and mannequin, 144–145, 158–161, 164–165; and Matilda Stevenson, 146, 148–152, 164, 166; pottery of, 148, 150–151, 156, 160, 168n4; weaving of, 144–145, 148, 153–156, 158–159, 162, 164. *See also* photographs: of We'wha

whaling expeditions, 184

White House, 152

Whorf, Benjamin, 271

Williams, John, 74

Wingfield, Chris, 31

women, 278; first to conduct fieldwork in US, 149; and Māori war canoes, 234; marginalization of, 100; and tattoos, 187–188

Wonga, Simon, 45

Wood, Charles F., 216

Woodman, H. E., 123

World Conservation Union, 101. *See also* International Union for Conservation of Nature (IUCN)

World Heritage: Committee, 99, 101, 103–104, 106–107; Convention, 96–97, 99–103, 105, 109, 112–114; lists, 91–92, 95–99, 101–104, 106–108, 110–113, 114n1, 114n2; sites, 97, 99–106. *See also* specific lists; specific sites

World War II, 84, 93, 96

World's Columbian Exposition, 160

world's fairs, 44, 160. *See also* specific titles

Wurundjeri people, 45

Yate, William, 234–235

Zabana, 217–219

Zimakani-speaking peoples, 131–132

zoological investigations, 90

Zuni Pueblo, 31, 143, 146–158, 161–162, 164–168, 272–273, 276–278, 280. See also *lhamana* ("man/woman"); We'wha (Zuni Indian)

School for Advanced Research Advanced Seminar Series

PUBLISHED BY SAR PRESS

CHACO & HOHOKAM: PREHISTORIC REGIONAL SYSTEMS IN THE AMERICAN SOUTHWEST
Patricia L. Crown & W. James Judge, eds.

RECAPTURING ANTHROPOLOGY: WORKING IN THE PRESENT
Richard G. Fox, ed.

WAR IN THE TRIBAL ZONE: EXPANDING STATES AND INDIGENOUS WARFARE
R. Brian Ferguson &
Neil L. Whitehead, eds.

IDEOLOGY AND PRE-COLUMBIAN CIVILIZATIONS
Arthur A. Demarest &
Geoffrey W. Conrad, eds.

DREAMING: ANTHROPOLOGICAL AND PSYCHOLOGICAL INTERPRETATIONS
Barbara Tedlock, ed.

HISTORICAL ECOLOGY: CULTURAL KNOWLEDGE AND CHANGING LANDSCAPES
Carole L. Crumley, ed.

THEMES IN SOUTHWEST PREHISTORY
George J. Gumerman, ed.

MEMORY, HISTORY, AND OPPOSITION UNDER STATE SOCIALISM
Rubie S. Watson, ed.

OTHER INTENTIONS: CULTURAL CONTEXTS AND THE ATTRIBUTION OF INNER STATES
Lawrence Rosen, ed.

LAST HUNTERS–FIRST FARMERS: NEW PERSPECTIVES ON THE PREHISTORIC TRANSITION TO AGRICULTURE
T. Douglas Price &
Anne Birgitte Gebauer, eds.

MAKING ALTERNATIVE HISTORIES: THE PRACTICE OF ARCHAEOLOGY AND HISTORY IN NON-WESTERN SETTINGS
Peter R. Schmidt & Thomas C. Patterson, eds.

CYBORGS & CITADELS: ANTHROPOLOGICAL INTERVENTIONS IN EMERGING SCIENCES AND TECHNOLOGIES
Gary Lee Downey & Joseph Dumit, eds.

SENSES OF PLACE
Steven Feld & Keith H. Basso, eds.

THE ORIGINS OF LANGUAGE: WHAT NONHUMAN PRIMATES CAN TELL US
Barbara J. King, ed.

CRITICAL ANTHROPOLOGY NOW: UNEXPECTED CONTEXTS, SHIFTING CONSTITUENCIES, CHANGING AGENDAS
George E. Marcus, ed.

ARCHAIC STATES
Gary M. Feinman & Joyce Marcus, eds.

REGIMES OF LANGUAGE: IDEOLOGIES, POLITIES, AND IDENTITIES
Paul V. Kroskrity, ed.

BIOLOGY, BRAINS, AND BEHAVIOR: THE EVOLUTION OF HUMAN DEVELOPMENT
Sue Taylor Parker, Jonas Langer, &
Michael L. McKinney, eds.

WOMEN & MEN IN THE PREHISPANIC SOUTHWEST: LABOR, POWER, & PRESTIGE
Patricia L. Crown, ed.

HISTORY IN PERSON: ENDURING STRUGGLES, CONTENTIOUS PRACTICE, INTIMATE IDENTITIES
Dorothy Holland & Jean Lave, eds.

THE EMPIRE OF THINGS: REGIMES OF VALUE AND MATERIAL CULTURE
Fred R. Myers, ed.

CATASTROPHE & CULTURE: THE ANTHROPOLOGY OF DISASTER
Susanna M. Hoffman &
Anthony Oliver-Smith, eds.

URUK MESOPOTAMIA & ITS NEIGHBORS: CROSS-CULTURAL INTERACTIONS IN THE ERA OF STATE FORMATION
Mitchell S. Rothman, ed.

REMAKING LIFE & DEATH: TOWARD AN ANTHROPOLOGY OF THE BIOSCIENCES
Sarah Franklin & Margaret Lock, eds.

TIKAL: DYNASTIES, FOREIGNERS, & AFFAIRS OF STATE: ADVANCING MAYA ARCHAEOLOGY
Jeremy A. Sabloff, ed.

GRAY AREAS: ETHNOGRAPHIC
ENCOUNTERS WITH NURSING HOME
CULTURE
  Philip B. Stafford, ed.

PLURALIZING ETHNOGRAPHY: COMPARISON
AND REPRESENTATION IN MAYA CULTURES,
HISTORIES, AND IDENTITIES
  John M. Watanabe & Edward F. Fischer, eds.

AMERICAN ARRIVALS: ANTHROPOLOGY
ENGAGES THE NEW IMMIGRATION
  Nancy Foner, ed.

VIOLENCE
  Neil L. Whitehead, ed.

LAW & EMPIRE IN THE PACIFIC:
FIJI AND HAWAI'I
  Sally Engle Merry & Donald Brenneis, eds.

ANTHROPOLOGY IN THE MARGINS
OF THE STATE
  Veena Das & Deborah Poole, eds.

THE ARCHAEOLOGY OF COLONIAL
ENCOUNTERS: COMPARATIVE
PERSPECTIVES
  Gil J. Stein, ed.

GLOBALIZATION, WATER, & HEALTH:
RESOURCE MANAGEMENT IN TIMES OF
SCARCITY
  Linda Whiteford & Scott Whiteford, eds.

A CATALYST FOR IDEAS: ANTHROPOLOGICAL
ARCHAEOLOGY AND THE LEGACY OF
DOUGLAS W. SCHWARTZ
  Vernon L. Scarborough, ed.

THE ARCHAEOLOGY OF CHACO CANYON:
AN ELEVENTH-CENTURY PUEBLO
REGIONAL CENTER
  Stephen H. Lekson, ed.

COMMUNITY BUILDING IN THE TWENTY-
FIRST CENTURY
  Stanley E. Hyland, ed.

AFRO-ATLANTIC DIALOGUES:
ANTHROPOLOGY IN THE DIASPORA
  Kevin A. Yelvington, ed.

COPÁN: THE HISTORY OF AN ANCIENT
MAYA KINGDOM
  E. Wyllys Andrews & William L. Fash, eds.

THE EVOLUTION OF HUMAN LIFE HISTORY
  Kristen Hawkes & Richard R. Paine, eds.

THE SEDUCTIONS OF COMMUNITY:
EMANCIPATIONS, OPPRESSIONS,
QUANDARIES
  Gerald W. Creed, ed.

THE GENDER OF GLOBALIZATION: WOMEN
NAVIGATING CULTURAL AND ECONOMIC
MARGINALITIES
  Nandini Gunewardena &
  Ann Kingsolver, eds.

NEW LANDSCAPES OF INEQUALITY:
NEOLIBERALISM AND THE EROSION OF
DEMOCRACY IN AMERICA
  Jane L. Collins, Micaela di Leonardo,
  & Brett Williams, eds.

IMPERIAL FORMATIONS
  Ann Laura Stoler, Carole McGranahan,
  & Peter C. Perdue, eds.

OPENING ARCHAEOLOGY: REPATRIATION'S
IMPACT ON CONTEMPORARY RESEARCH
AND PRACTICE
  Thomas W. Killion, ed.

SMALL WORLDS: METHOD, MEANING,
& NARRATIVE IN MICROHISTORY
  James F. Brooks, Christopher R. N. DeCorse,
  & John Walton, eds.

MEMORY WORK: ARCHAEOLOGIES OF
MATERIAL PRACTICES
  Barbara J. Mills & William H. Walker, eds.

FIGURING THE FUTURE: GLOBALIZATION
AND THE TEMPORALITIES OF CHILDREN
AND YOUTH
  Jennifer Cole & Deborah Durham, eds.

TIMELY ASSETS: THE POLITICS OF
RESOURCES AND THEIR TEMPORALITIES
  Elizabeth Emma Ferry &
  Mandana E. Limbert, eds.

DEMOCRACY: ANTHROPOLOGICAL
APPROACHES
  Julia Paley, ed.

CONFRONTING CANCER: METAPHORS,
INEQUALITY, AND ADVOCACY
  Juliet McMullin & Diane Weiner, eds.

DEVELOPMENT & DISPOSSESSION: THE
CRISIS OF FORCED DISPLACEMENT AND
RESETTLEMENT
Anthony Oliver-Smith, ed.

GLOBAL HEALTH IN TIMES OF VIOLENCE
*Barbara Rylko-Bauer, Linda Whiteford,
& Paul Farmer, eds.*

THE EVOLUTION OF LEADERSHIP:
TRANSITIONS IN DECISION MAKING FROM
SMALL-SCALE TO MIDDLE-RANGE SOCIETIES
*Kevin J. Vaughn, Jelmer W. Eerkins, &
John Kantner, eds.*

ARCHAEOLOGY & CULTURAL RESOURCE
MANAGEMENT: VISIONS FOR THE FUTURE
Lynne Sebastian & William D. Lipe, eds.

ARCHAIC STATE INTERACTION: THE
EASTERN MEDITERRANEAN IN THE BRONZE
AGE
*William A. Parkinson &
Michael L. Galaty, eds.*

INDIANS & ENERGY: EXPLOITATION
AND OPPORTUNITY IN THE AMERICAN
SOUTHWEST
Sherry L. Smith & Brian Frehner, eds.

ROOTS OF CONFLICT: SOILS, AGRICULTURE,
AND SOCIOPOLITICAL COMPLEXITY IN
ANCIENT HAWAI'I
Patrick V. Kirch, ed.

PHARMACEUTICAL SELF: THE GLOBAL
SHAPING OF EXPERIENCE IN AN AGE OF
PSYCHOPHARMACOLOGY
Janis Jenkins, ed.

FORCES OF COMPASSION: HUMANITARI-
ANISM BETWEEN ETHICS AND POLITICS
Erica Bornstein & Peter Redfield, eds.

ENDURING CONQUESTS: RETHINKING THE
ARCHAEOLOGY OF RESISTANCE TO SPANISH
COLONIALISM IN THE AMERICAS
*Matthew Liebmann &
Melissa S. Murphy, eds.*

DANGEROUS LIAISONS: ANTHROPOLOGISTS
AND THE NATIONAL SECURITY STATE
*Laura A. McNamara &
Robert A. Rubinstein, eds.*

BREATHING NEW LIFE INTO THE EVIDENCE
OF DEATH: CONTEMPORARY APPROACHES
TO BIOARCHAEOLOGY
*Aubrey Baadsgaard, Alexis T. Boutin, &
Jane E. Buikstra, eds.*

THE SHAPE OF SCRIPT: HOW AND WHY
WRITING SYSTEMS CHANGE
Stephen D. Houston, ed.

NATURE, SCIENCE, AND RELIGION:
INTERSECTIONS SHAPING SOCIETY AND
THE ENVIRONMENT
Catherine M. Tucker, ed.

THE GLOBAL MIDDLE CLASSES:
THEORIZING THROUGH ETHNOGRAPHY
*Rachel Heiman, Carla Freeman, &
Mark Liechty, eds.*

KEYSTONE NATIONS: INDIGENOUS PEOPLES
AND SALMON ACROSS THE NORTH PACIFIC
Benedict J. Colombi & James F. Brooks, eds.

BIG HISTORIES, HUMAN LIVES: TACKLING
PROBLEMS OF SCALE IN ARCHAEOLOGY
John Robb & Timothy R. Pauketat, eds.

Timeless Classics from SAR Press

The Archaeology of Lower Central America
Frederick W. Lange & Doris Z. Stone, eds.

Chan Chan: Andean Desert City
Michael E. Moseley & Kent C. Day, eds.

Demographic Anthropology: Quantitative Approaches
Ezra B. W. Zubrow, ed.

The Dying Community
Art Gallaher, Jr. & Harlan Padfield, eds.

Elites: Ethnographic Issues
George E. Marcus, ed.

Entrepreneurs in Cultural Context
Sidney M. Greenfield, Arnold Strickon, & Robert T. Aubey, eds.

Explorations in Ethnoarchaeology
Richard A. Gould, ed.

Late Lowland Maya Civilization: Classic to Postclassic
Jeremy A. Sabloff & E. Wyllys Andrews V, eds.

Lowland Maya Settlement Patterns
Wendy Ashmore, ed.

Methods and Theories of Anthropological Genetics
M. H. Crawford & P. L. Workman, eds.

The Origins of Maya Civilization
Richard E. W. Adams, ed.

Photography in Archaeological Research
Elmer Harp, Jr., ed.

Reconstructing Prehistoric Pueblo Societies
William A. Longacre, ed.

Simulations in Archaeology
Jeremy A. Sabloff, ed.

Structure and Process in Latin America
Arnold Strickon & Sidney M. Greenfield, eds.

The Valley of Mexico: Studies in Pre-Hispanic Ecology and Society
Eric R. Wolf, ed.

PUBLISHED BY CAMBRIDGE UNIVERSITY PRESS

THE ANASAZI IN A CHANGING ENVIRONMENT
George J. Gumerman, ed.

REGIONAL PERSPECTIVES ON THE OLMEC
Robert J. Sharer & David C. Grove, eds.

THE CHEMISTRY OF PREHISTORIC HUMAN
BONE
T. Douglas Price, ed.

THE EMERGENCE OF MODERN HUMANS:
BIOCULTURAL ADAPTATIONS IN THE LATER
PLEISTOCENE
Erik Trinkaus, ed.

THE ANTHROPOLOGY OF WAR
Jonathan Haas, ed.

THE EVOLUTION OF POLITICAL SYSTEMS
Steadman Upham, ed.

CLASSIC MAYA POLITICAL HISTORY:
HIEROGLYPHIC AND ARCHAEOLOGICAL
EVIDENCE
T. Patrick Culbert, ed.

TURKO-PERSIA IN HISTORICAL PERSPECTIVE
Robert L. Canfield, ed.

CHIEFDOMS: POWER, ECONOMY, AND
IDEOLOGY
Timothy Earle, ed.

**PUBLISHED BY UNIVERSITY OF
CALIFORNIA PRESS**

WRITING CULTURE: THE POETICS
AND POLITICS OF ETHNOGRAPHY
James Clifford & George E. Marcus, eds.

**PUBLISHED BY UNIVERSITY OF
ARIZONA PRESS**

THE COLLAPSE OF ANCIENT STATES AND
CIVILIZATIONS
Norman Yoffee & George L. Cowgill, eds.

PUBLISHED BY UNIVERSITY OF NEW MEXICO PRESS

NEW PERSPECTIVES ON THE PUEBLOS
Alfonso Ortiz, ed.

THE CLASSIC MAYA COLLAPSE
T. Patrick Culbert, ed.

SIXTEENTH-CENTURY MEXICO:
THE WORK OF SAHAGUN
Munro S. Edmonson, ed.

ANCIENT CIVILIZATION AND TRADE
*Jeremy A. Sabloff &
C. C. Lamberg-Karlovsky, eds.*

EXPLANATION OF PREHISTORIC CHANGE
James N. Hill, ed.

MEANING IN ANTHROPOLOGY
Keith H. Basso & Henry A. Selby, eds.

SOUTHWESTERN INDIAN RITUAL DRAMA
Charlotte J. Frisbie, ed.

SHIPWRECK ANTHROPOLOGY
Richard A. Gould, ed.

Participants in the School for Advanced Research advanced seminar "Reassembling the Collection: Indigenous Agency and Ethnographic Collections," co-chaired by Sarah Byrne, Anne Clarke, Rodney Harrison, and Robin Torrence, September 26–30, 2010. *Standing, from left:* Robin Torrence, Tony Bennett, Chantal Knowles, Rodney Harrison, Anne Clarke, Kelley Hays-Gilpin, and Chris Wingfield; *seated, from left:* Joshua A. Bell, Gwyneira Isaac, and Sarah Byrne. Photograph by Jason S. Ordaz.

www.ingramcontent.com/pod-product-compliance
Lightning Source LLC
Chambersburg PA
CBHW020454270326
41926CB00008B/591